iMovie HD *& iDVD 5*

THE MISSING MANUAL

*The book that
should have been
in the box*

Reviews of Previous Editions

If you use iMovie, you need this book.

Those who read it will save huge amounts of trial-and-error learning. The book offers instant access to tricks like continuing the sound track from one clip as voiceover to a second one as it fades in, a favorite of the pros but nearly impossible to accomplish without Pogue's hand-holding.

—James Coates, The Chicago Tribune

Years ago, Apple figured out it doesn't need to write manuals for its products because David Pogue will, and he'll do it much better. Attempting to make an actual movie on iMovie was near impossible without the aid of the Missing Manual, but an amazing joy once this book was in hand... The Missing Manual series is simply the most intelligent and useable series of guidebooks on any subject.

—Kevin Kelly, cofounder of Wired

With characteristic humility, author/publisher David Pogue describes this as "the book that should have been in the box"—and, well, yeah, he's right. To quote Dizzy Dean, it ain't braggin' if you done it.

If you're an iMovie novice, you need this book. If you're an iMovie intermediate, you'll want this book. If you're an iMovie expert—hey, you already have this book, and that's one of the reasons you're an expert.

—Jamie McCornack, About This Particular Macintosh (atpm.com)

An absolute must-have for getting the most out of iMovie & iDVD software. Highly recommended for amateur and professional moviemakers and movie editors working on the Macintosh.

—Library Bookwatch

iMovie: The Missing Manual is actually not so much a manual as a junior college degree in television production—and all for $24.95. This Pogue Press volume has packed every page with useful information...All in all, a wonderful book and highly recommended.

—The Review Zone

Most iMovie manuals stop after teaching you how to use the program. David Pogue stops there, too, but he *begins* by teaching you how to make a good movie. This is very, *very* important.

iMovie 4 & iDVD: The Missing Manual is such a valuable resource for iMovie users that Apple should offer to ship it with every Macintosh purchased. More importantly, they should hand it out to every newly engaged couple, so their friends and relatives won't have to sit through another horribly dull wedding video.

Kirk Hiner, AppleLinks.com

Quite simply the best computer book I have ever purchased. It is a very straightforward, lucid, step-by-step explanation of how to get the most out of this program...Using this book is like having an iMovie guru sitting next to you, helping you along.

—Stephen E. Rosenblum, Ann Arbor, MI

iMovie HD *& iDVD 5*

THE MISSING MANUAL

David Pogue

POGUE PRESS™

O'REILLY®

Beijing • Cambridge • Farnham • Köln • Paris • Sebastopol • Taipei • Tokyo

iMovie HD & iDVD 5: The Missing Manual

by David Pogue

Published by O'Reilly Media, Inc., 1005 Gravenstein Highway North, Sebastopol, CA 95472.

O'Reilly Media books may be purchased for educational, business, or sales promotional use. Online editions are also available for most titles: *safari.oreilly. com*. For more information, contact our corporate/institutional sales department: (800) 998-9938 or *corporate@oreilly.com*.

April 2005:   First Printing

RepKover™ This book uses RepKover™, a durable and flexible lay-flat binding.

ISBN: 0-596-10033-7

Table of Contents

The Missing Credits

About the Authors

David Pogue is the weekly computer columnist for the *New York Times*, an Emmy award-winning correspondent for *CBS News Sunday Morning*, and the creator of the Missing Manual series. He's the author or co-author of 35 books, including thirteen in this series and six in the "For Dummies" line (including *Macs, Magic, Opera,* and *Classical Music*). In his other life, David is a former Broadway show conductor, a magician, and a pianist. News and photos await at *www.davidpogue.com*.

He welcomes feedback about his books by email at *david@pogueman.com*. (If you're seeking technical help, however, please refer to the sources in Appendix B.)

Erica Sadun (iDVD chapters) holds a PhD in Computer Science from the Georgia Institute of Technology. She has written, co-written and contributed to almost two dozen books about technology, particularly in the areas of programming, digital video, and digital photography. An unrepentant geek, Erica has never met a gadget she didn't need. Her checkered past includes run-ins with NeXT, Newton, and a vast myriad of both successful and unsuccessful technologies. When not writing, she and her geek husband parent three adorable geeks-in-training, who regard their parents with unrestrained bemusement. Email: *erica@mindspring.com*.

About the Creative Team

Rose Cassano (cover illustration) has worked as an independent designer and illustrator for 20 years. Assignments have spanned everything from the nonprofit sector to corporate clientele. She lives in beautiful southern Oregon, grateful for the miracles of modern technology that make living and working there a reality. Email: *cassano@cdsnet.net*. Web: *www.rosecassano.com*.

Dennis Cohen (technical reviewer, previous editions) has served as the technical reviewer for many bestselling Mac books, including several editions of *Macworld Mac Secrets* and most Missing Manual titles. He is the author or co-author of *FileMaker Pro 7 Bible, Mac Digital Photography, Teach Yourself Visually iLife '04*, and numerous other books. Email: *drcohen@mac.com*.

Tim Geaney (still photos) has shot editorial photos for *Self, GQ, Glamour,* and *Mademoiselle* magazines, among others. His commercial photography clients include Victoria's Secret, Nautica, J.Crew, Spiegel, Nordstrom, Neiman Marcus, and Saks Fifth Avenue. (The DV filmmaking bug has bit him. Check out his short films at *www.timgeaney.com*.)

Karl Petersen (technical reviewer, co-author Appendix B) lives with his wife, Joan, and a Collie on Bainbridge Island, Washington, a 30-minute ferry ride from Seattle. (It's the ferry Michael Douglas runs onto in *Disclosure*.) A break between jobs (including a stint in the Peace Corps and a career in insurance) gave Karl the chance to explore the first Macs, and he never looked back. He also writes software.

Phil Simpson (design and layout) works out of his office in Stamford, Connecticut, where he has had his graphic design business since 1982. He is experienced in many facets of graphic design, including corporate identity, publication design, and corporate and medical communications. Email: *pmsimpson@earthlink.net.*

Acknowledgments

The Missing Manual series is a joint venture between Pogue Press (the dream team introduced on these pages) and O'Reilly & Associates (a dream publishing partner).

A special group did great favors for this project: Jim Kanter and Irene Lusztig were my video gurus and technical editors for the book's first edition, whose hearts beat on in this one. (Jim also wrote some terrific sidebars about video equipment.) Arwen O'Reilly, Doug Graham, Charles Petzold, Phil Lefebvre, Michael Krein, Charles Wiltgen, and the members of the Mac DV discussion list (*www.themacintoshguy. com*) all pitched in with small favors and info-bits. Tim Franklin expertly drafted Chapter 13.

Glenn Reid, iMovie's lead programmer, agreed to serve as technical editor for the second and third editions of this book. For this edition, iMovie product manager Paul Towner and his team shared their expert advice, answers, and—most importantly—their enthusiasm for the project. I'm also grateful to Sohaila Abdulali, John Cacciatore, Kate Chase, Linley Dolby, and Dawn Mann for their copy editing and proofreading smarts; to the indispensable Lesa Snyder for her brilliant help in reshooting the book's color graphics; and to David Rogelberg.

Finally, thanks to Kelly, Tia, and Jeffrey, my favorite iMovie stars, and my wife, Jennifer, who made this book—and everything else—possible.

The Missing Manual Series

Missing Manuals are witty, superbly written guides to computer products that don't come with printed manuals (which is just about all of them). Each book features a handcrafted index; cross-references to specific page numbers (not just "see Chapter 14"); and RepKover, a detached-spine binding that lets the book lie perfectly flat without the assistance of weights or cinder blocks.

Recent and upcoming titles include:

- *Mac OS X: The Missing Manual,* Tiger Edition by David Pogue

- *iPhoto 5: The Missing Manual* by David Pogue

- *GarageBand 2: The Missing Manual* by David Pogue

- *iPod & iTunes: The Missing Manual,* 3rd Edition by J.D. Biersdorfer

- *iLife '05: The Missing Manual* by David Pogue et al.

- *AppleScript: The Missing Manual* by Adam Goldstein

- *Office 2004 for Macintosh: The Missing Manual* by Mark H. Walker, Franklin Tessler, and Paul Berkowitz

- *FileMaker Pro 7: The Missing Manual* by Geoff Coffey

- *Switching to the Mac: The Missing Manual,* Tiger Edition by David Pogue and Adam Goldstein

- *Excel: The Missing Manual* by Matthew MacDonald

- *Photoshop Elements 3: The Missing Manual* by Barbara Brundage

- *Google: The Missing Manual* by Sarah Milstein and Rael Dornfest

- *Mac OS X Power Hound,* Panther Edition by Rob Griffiths

- *Dreamweaver MX 2004: The Missing Manual* by David Sawyer McFarland

- *AppleWorks 6: The Missing Manual* by Jim Elferdink and David Reynolds

- *Windows XP Home Edition: The Missing Manual,* 2nd Edition by David Pogue

- *Windows XP Pro: The Missing Manual,* 2nd Edition by David Pogue, Craig Zacker, and Linda Zacker

THE MISSING CREDITS

Introduction

O ver the years, home movies have developed a bad name, one that's not entirely undeserved. After all, you know what it's like watching other people's camcorder footage. You're held prisoner on some neighbor's couch after dessert to witness 60 excruciating, unedited minutes of their trip to Mexico, or maybe 25 too many minutes of the baby wearing the overturned spaghetti bowl.

Deep down, most camcorder owners are aware that the viewing experience could be improved if the video were edited down to just the good parts. They just had no idea how to accomplish that. Until iMovie came along, editing camcorder footage on the computer required several thousand dollars' worth of digitizing cards, extremely complicated editing software, and the highest-horsepower computer equipment available.

Some clever souls tried to edit their videos by buying two VCRs, wiring them together, and copying parts of one tape onto another. That worked great—if you didn't mind the bursts of distortion and static at each splice point and the massive generational quality loss.

You know what? Unless there was a paycheck involved, editing footage under those circumstances just wasn't worth it. The fast-forward button on the remote was a lot easier.

All of that changed when iMovie came along. It certainly wasn't the first digital video (DV) editing software. But it was the first DV-editing software for *nonprofessionals,* people who have a life outside of video editing. Within six months of its release in October 1999, iMovie had become, in words of beaming iMovie papa (and Apple CEO) Steve Jobs, "the most popular video-editing software in the world."

Apple only fanned the flames when it released iMovie 2 in July 2000 (for $50), iMovie 3 in January 2003 (for free), and iMovie 4 in January 2004 (part of the $50 iLife package).

Meet iMovie HD

iMovie is video-editing software. Over a special wire (a FireWire cable), iMovie grabs a copy of the raw footage from your digital camcorder. Then it lets you edit this video easily, quickly, and creatively.

iMovie is the world's least expensive version of what the Hollywood pros call *nonlinear editing* software for video, just like its much more powerful (and much more complex) rivals, like Final Cut Express ($300), Final Cut Pro ($1,000), and Avid editing suites ($100,000). The "nonlinear" part is that no tape is involved while you're editing. There's no rewinding or fast-forwarding; you jump instantly to any piece of footage as you put your movie together.

Your interest in video may be inspired by any number of ambitions. Maybe you want to create professional looking shows for your local cable station's public-access channel. Or you aspire to create the next *Blair Witch Project* (which was created by nonprofessionals using a camcorder and nonlinear editing software) or the next *Tarnation,* an iMovie project that was a hit at the Sundance and Cannes Film Festivals.

On the other hand, maybe all you want to do is make better home movies—much, *much* better home movies. Either way, iMovie can accommodate you.

The world of video is exploding. People are giving each other tapes and DVDs instead of greeting cards. People are watching each other via video on their Web sites. People are quitting their daily-grind jobs to become videographers for hire, making money filming weddings and creating living video scrapbooks. Video, in other words, is fast becoming a new standard document format for the new century.

If you have iMovie and a camcorder, you'll be ready.

What's New in iMovie HD

iMovie HD (called iMovie 5 in certain dialog boxes and other spots) represents a deep overhaul of the program, one that will challenge the iMovie veteran with a good deal of unlearning and relearning.

Big-Ticket Features

Here's a summary of the really big improvements in iMovie HD, the ones that Apple either advertises or should:

- **HD video.** iMovie can now edit high-definition (HDTV) footage, as captured by so-called HDV camcorders. These are semi-professional cameras that record high-definition video onto an ordinary MiniDV tape, with spectacular widescreen results. Now, high-def video consumes three or four times the amount of disk space as regular video, so if you're lucky enough to have access to an HDV camcorder ($2,200 to $3,100), come prepared with lots of empty disk space and some understanding of the real-time conversion tricks described on page 103.

- **More formats.** That's not the only new kind of video that iMovie HD welcomes. It can also work with MPEG-4 video, which is what you get with those super-mini "palmcorders" from Fisher and Panasonic that record onto memory cards instead of tape. iMovie is also compatible with widescreen (16:9) footage that many recent digital camcorders can capture—video that's not high-definition, but still looks fantastic on a widescreen TV set.

- **Automatic dumping.** iMovie offers Magic iMovie: an extremely simple, automated method of importing an entire tape, slapping up an opening title, backing it up with music from your iTunes collection, and adding crossfades between scenes—all without any intervention from you.

  iDVD offers something similar called OneStep DVD, which slurps all of a tape's footage directly onto a blank DVD. Again, your editing options are very limited here, but the whole idea is to get your footage from tape to DVD without any effort on your part. After all, DVDs last longer than tape, cost less, are easier to show on TV, and are easier to send around to other interested parties.

- **More draggability.** You can now drag individual video clips around in iMovie's timeline view—even back up to the Clips pane. In fact, you can drag clips clear out of the iMovie window and to the Finder (where they show up as individual clip icons) or into other programs, like iDVD or QuickTime Player.

- **Overhauled Trash.** The Trash mechanism in iMovie HD is utterly unlike the Trash in any previous version. You can now open it to view, rescue, or delete individual trashed items, just as you can in the Finder. Emptying the Trash no longer means that you can't restore chopped-up clips to their pre-chop conditions. And emptying the Trash in mid-project is no longer an invitation to corrupting your entire movie project.

- **Overhauled safety nets.** iMovie HD is far more forgiving than previous versions. Its Undo command lets you take back an unlimited number of steps, all the way back to the last saved version of your project, if you like. The new Save As command lets you spin out half-finished variations of a movie, and the Revert to Saved command does what it does in other programs: undoes all work you've done since the last Save command. Finally, you can trim clips, split clips, chop them up, delete pieces of them—and recover them at any time, months or years later.

  There is, alas, a dark side to the new Trash, Undo, and Save features. To provide these generous safety nets, iMovie hangs onto a lot more of the footage you've imported from the camera. iMovie doesn't care that you've deleted 19 out of 20 minutes of a clip and then emptied the Trash; if you've incorporated even a single frame of that clip into your movie, behind the scenes, iMovie holds onto all of those gigabytes. Emptying the Trash, in other words, doesn't restore free space to your hard drive except when you're deleting an entire, untouched clip that you haven't used in the project.

Note, furthermore, that you lose your entire Undo trail every time you use the Save command. As a result, hitting ⌘-S is both a step forward and a step backward in project safety.

- **Self-contained project icons.** In the past, each iMovie movie you worked on took the form of a folder on your hard drive, not a document icon. But iMovie HD sews that folder up into a new, single, double-clickable "document" icon called a package.

Here again, the change is a blessing and a curse. The nice part is that having only one icon to deal with makes it so easy to name, copy, move, or back up. Unfortunately, the actual project document—the text file that records which pieces of footage come when—is now sealed away inside the package icon, where it's no longer recognized by (for example) iDVD.

You'll find many more details about this change on page 112.

Finer Points

Apple's most intriguing enhancements to iMovie HD, though, are the little nips and tucks that lie scattered throughout—features that go unmentioned on the iMovie Web site or on the "What's New" Help page, but taken together, will make a big difference in your moviemaking career.

- **Burn Project to Disc.** This new command preserves your entire project on a blank DVD (or a CD, if the project is tiny and short). This is strictly a backup feature, one that creates a safety copy of your entire project so that you can edit it later; the resulting disc doesn't play in a DVD player.

- **Copyable clips.** You can now copy or cut clips out of one project and paste them into another—a great way to re-use key scenes in other movies. (But note the important caveats on page 478.)

- **Playhead pasting.** Speaking of copying and pasting: When you paste copied footage, iMovie always deposits it at the location of the Playhead—even if that means splitting an existing clip in half to accommodate the pasted material.

- **Effect and transition improvements.** Transitions between video clips (like crossfades) can last ten seconds now, up from four. Reverse, slow motion, and fast motion are now listed in the Effects panel, just like all the other effects. (So don't keep scouring the bottom of the Timeline Viewer looking for these controls; they're not there anymore.) You have a few new effects, transitions, and sound effects to choose from. And you can be much more precise with your effects, transitions, and titles, because you can directly edit the timing numbers in the Preview window just by typing over them.

• **Quick access to audio features.** You know the audio waveforms—the visual representation of the loud and soft parts in an audio clip? You used to have to pay a visit to the iMovie Preferences dialog box to turn them on and off; now you have both a menu command and a keystroke that can hide or show them.

Hiding or showing the horizontal, draggable volume-graph lines on audio clips is easier now, too; this feature, too, has a menu command and a keystroke.

• **Search your photos.** A standard, iTunes-type Search box now appears underneath the Photos pane. You can pluck one of your photos out of thousands just by typing a few letters of its name.

• **Stills = videos.** Still photos you've incorporated into your movie now behave like video clips in one useful regard: You can drag their edges horizontally to make them "play" longer or shorter in the movie.

• **Speed.** iMovie HD processes just about everything faster: effects, transitions, and emptying the Trash.

iDVD Changes

As you'll see in Chapters 15 through 18, iDVD 5 is loaded with enhancements that help you make your DVD look even more like a commercial Hollywood DVD.

• **More blank-disc formats.** iDVD can record on both DVD-R and DVD+R blanks (see the difference in punctuation?), if you have a relatively recent Mac.

• **More themes.** Version 5 comes with 15 new themes (ready-to-use menu screen designs complete with attractive backgrounds and coordinating typeface, background music, and graphics). The key attraction is *moving* drop zones (design elements that you can fill with your own photos or movies).

• **Drop zone editor.** A new, special window lets you fill or rearrange the contents of all your drop zones at once. It's especially handy because in iDVD 5's new themes, all of the drop zones are rarely on the screen at once.

• **Editable Map view.** As your menu and button layouts grow more complex, you can use the Map screen to help you keep track of your menu structure. In iDVD 4, the Map was just a frozen image. But in iDVD 5, you can batch-change your transitions, themes, button settings, and music right in this schematic view.

• **Widescreen DVDs.** If you've filmed and edited widescreen video (with an HDTV camcorder or a regular one) in iMovie, iDVD can burn it onto a widescreen DVD for you. On standard, squarish TV sets, you'll get a letterboxed picture; on widescreen sets, you'll see video that fills your entire rectangular field of view.

About This Book

Don't let the rumors fool you. iMovie may be simple, but it isn't simplistic. It offers a wide range of special effects and flexible features for creating transitions between scenes, superimposing text on your video, layering multiple soundtracks together, and more. Unfortunately, many of the best techniques aren't covered in the only "manual" you get with iMovie—its electronic help screens.

This book was born to address three needs. First, it's designed to give you a grounding in professional filming and editing techniques. The camcorder and iMovie produce video of stunning visual and audio quality, giving you the *technical* tools to produce amazing videos. But most people don't have much experience with the *artistic* side of shooting—lighting, sound, and composition—or even how to use the dozens of buttons packed onto the modern camcorder. This book will tell you all you need to know.

Second, this book is designed to serve as the iMovie manual, as the book that should have been in the box. It explores each iMovie feature in depth, offers illustrated catalogs of the various title and transition effects, offers shortcuts and workarounds, and unearths features that the online help doesn't even mention.

Finally, this book comes with a free bonus book: *iDVD 5: The Missing Manual,* which constitutes Chapters 15, 16, 17, and 18. If your Mac has a DVD burner like Apple's SuperDrive, iDVD can preserve your movies on home-recorded DVDs that look and behave amazingly close to the commercial DVDs you rent from Netflix or Blockbuster.

About the Outline

iMovie HD & iDVD 5: The Missing Manual is divided into five parts, each containing several chapters:

- Part 1, **Capturing DV Footage,** covers what happens *before* you get to iMovie. It explains the DV format, helps you buy and learn to use a camcorder, and offers a crash course in professional film technique.

- Part 2, **Editing in iMovie,** is the heart of the book. It leads you through transferring your footage into iMovie, editing your clips, placing them into a timeline, adding crossfades and titles, working with your soundtracks, and more.

- Part 3, **Finding Your Audience,** helps you take the cinematic masterpiece on your screen to the world. Even if you don't have the necessary gear to burn your work onto DVD, iMovie excels at exporting your work in two different ways: back to your camcorder (from which you can play it on TV, transfer it to your VCR, and so on) or to a QuickTime movie file (which you can burn onto a CD, post on a Web page, or send to friends by email). This part of the book offers step-by-step instructions for each of these methods, and also shows you how you can use QuickTime Player Pro to supplement the editing tools in iMovie.

- Part 4, **iDVD 5: The Missing Manual,** is just what you'd expect: a bonus volume dedicated to the world's easiest-to-use DVD design and burning software, written by guest author (and bestselling digital-video goddess) Erica Sadun. It goes way, way beyond the basics, as you'll see.

At the end of the book, three appendixes provide a menu-by-menu explanation of the iMovie menu commands, a comprehensive troubleshooting handbook, and a new master cheat sheet of iMovie's keyboard shortcuts.

About→These→Arrows

Throughout this book, and throughout the Missing Manual series, you'll find sentences like this one: "Open your Home→Library→Preferences folder." That's shorthand for a much longer instruction that directs you to open three nested folders in sequence, like this: "In the Finder, choose Go→Home. In your Home folder, you'll find a folder called Library. Open that. Inside the Library window is a folder called Preferences. Double-click to open it, too."

Similarly, this kind of arrow shorthand helps to simplify the business of choosing commands in menus, as shown in Figure I-1.

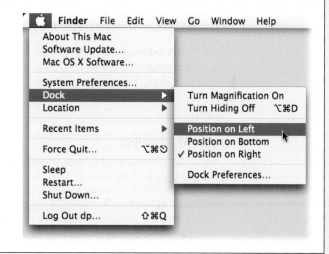

Figure I-1:
In this book, arrow notations help to simplify folder and menu instructions. For example, "Choose ⌘*→Dock→Position on Left" is a more compact way of saying, "From the* ⌘ *menu, choose Dock; from the submenu that then appears, choose Position on Left," as shown here.*

Technical Notes for PAL People

If you live in the Americas, Japan, or any of 30 other countries, your camcorder, VCR, and TV record and play back a video signal in a format that's known as *NTSC*. Even if you've never heard the term, every camcorder, VCR, TV, and TV station in your country uses this same signal. (The following discussion doesn't apply to high-definition video, which is the same across continents.)

What it stands for is National Television Standards Committee, the gang who designed this format. What it *means* is incompatibility with the second most popular format, which is called PAL (Phase Alternating Line, for the curious). In Europe, Africa, the Middle East, Australia, and China (among other places), everyone's equipment uses the PAL format. You can't play an American tape on a standard VCR in Sweden—unless you're happy with black-and-white, sometimes jittery playback.

Tip: France, the former Soviet Union countries, and a few others use a third format, known as SECAM. iMovie doesn't work with SECAM gear. To find out what kind of gear your country uses, visit a Web site like *www.vidpro.org/standards.htm*.

Fortunately, iMovie converses fluently with both NTSC and PAL camcorders. When you launch the program, it automatically studies the camcorder you've attached and determines its format. (And if it detects wrong, you can tell it what kind of gear you have by choosing iMovie→Preferences and clicking either NTSC or PAL.)

However, most of the discussions in this book use NTSC terminology. If you're a friend of PAL, use the following information to translate this book's discussions.

The Tech Specs of NTSC

Whether you're aware of it or not, using the NTSC standard-definition format means that the picture you see is characterized like this:

- **30 frames per second.** A *frame* is one individual picture. Flashed before your eyes at this speed, the still images blend into what you perceive as smooth motion.

- **575 scan lines.** The electron gun in a TV tube paints the screen with this number of fine horizontal lines.

- **The DV picture measures 720 x 480 pixels.** This figure refers to the number of screen dots, or *pixels,* that compose one frame of image in the *DV* (digital video) version of the NTSC format. (But don't count on these specs if your intention is to crop photos or graphics to just that size, thinking that they'll fit neatly. They won't, as described on page 249.)

The Tech Specs of PAL

When iMovie detects a PAL camcorder (or when you inform it that you're using one), it makes the necessary adjustments automatically, including:

- **25 frames per second.** Video fans claim that the lower frame rate creates more flicker than the NTSC standard. On the other hand, this frame rate is very close to the frame rate of Hollywood films (24 frames per second). As a result, many independent filmmakers find PAL a better choice when shooting movies they intend to convert to film.

- **625 scan lines.** That's 20 percent sharper and more detailed than NTSC. The difference is especially visible on large-screen TVs.

- **The DV picture measures 720 x 576 pixels.** This information may affect you as you read Chapter 9 and prepare still images for use with iMovie.

About MissingManuals.com

At *www.missingmanuals.com,* you'll find news, articles, and updates to the books in this series.

But if you click the name of this book and then the Errata link, you'll find a unique resource: a list of corrections and updates that have been made in successive printings of this book. You can mark important corrections right into your own copy of the book, if you like.

In fact, the same page offers an invitation for you to submit such corrections and updates yourself. In an effort to keep the book as up to date and accurate as possible, each time we print more copies of this book, we'll make any confirmed corrections you've suggested. Thanks in advance for reporting any glitches you find!

In the meantime, we'd love to hear your suggestions for new books in the Missing Manual line. There's a place for that on the Web site, too, as well as a place to sign up for free email notification of new titles in the series.

The Very Basics

You'll find very little jargon or nerd terminology in this book. You will, however, encounter a few terms and concepts that you'll see frequently in your Macintosh life. They include:

- **Clicking.** This book offers three kinds of instructions that require you to use the mouse or trackpad attached to your Mac. To *click* means to point the arrow cursor at something onscreen and then—without moving the cursor at all—press and release the clicker button on the mouse (or laptop trackpad). To *double-click*, of course, means to click twice in rapid succession, again without moving the cursor at all. And to *drag* means to move the cursor while keeping the button continuously pressed.

  When you're told to ⌘-*click* something, you click while pressing the ⌘ key (next to the Space bar). Such related procedures as *Shift-clicking, Option-clicking,* and *Control-clicking* work the same way—just click while pressing the corresponding key on the bottom row of your keyboard.

- **Menus.** The *menus* are the words in the lightly striped bar at the top of your screen. You can either click one of these words to open a pull-down menu of commands (and then click again on a command), or click and *hold* the button as you drag down the menu to the desired command (and release the button to activate the command). Either method works fine.

Note: Apple has officially changed what it calls the little menu that pops up when you Control-click something on the screen. It's still a contextual menu, in that the menu choices depend on the context of what you click—but it's now called a shortcut menu. That term not only matches what it's called in Windows, but it's slightly more descriptive about its function. Shortcut menu is the term you'll find in this book.

- **Keyboard shortcuts.** Every time you take your hand off the keyboard to move the mouse, you lose time and potentially disrupt your creative flow. That's why many experienced Mac fans use keystroke combinations instead of menu commands wherever possible. ⌘-P opens the Print dialog box, for example, and ⌘-M minimizes the current window to the Dock.

When you see a shortcut like ⌘-Q (which closes the current program), it's telling you to hold down the ⌘ key, and, while it's down, type the letter Q, and then release both keys.

If you've mastered this much information, you have all the technical background you need to enjoy *iMovie HD & iDVD 5: The Missing Manual.*

Part One: Capturing DV Footage

1

The DV Camcorder

T o edit video using iMovie, you must first *shoot* some video, which is why the first three chapters of this book have nothing to do with your iMovie software. Instead, this book begins with advice on buying and using a digital camcorder, getting to know the equipment, and adopting professional filming techniques. After all, teaching you to edit video without making sure you know how to shoot it is like giving a map to a 16-year-old without first teaching him how to drive.

Meet Digital Video

Technically speaking, you don't need a camcorder to use iMovie. You can work with QuickTime movies you find on the Web, or use it to turn still photos into slideshows.

But to shoot your own video—and that is the real fun of iMovie—you need a *digital* camcorder. This is a relatively new camcorder format, one that's utterly incompatible with the tapes you may have filled using earlier camcorder types as described on the following pages (and shown in Figure 1-1):

- **VHS.** These gigantic machines were the original camcorders, circa 1980. Because they were nearly a foot and a half long, you had to rest the butt of these cameras on your shoulder. VHS camcorders accepted full-size VHS cassettes that, after filming, you could insert directly into your VCR for playback. Convenient, sure, but the size, weight, and bulk of these camcorders condemned them to an early grave. These days, the only place you can find VHS camcorders is on eBay.

• **S-VHS.** This format, also known as Super VHS, accepts special, more expensive S-VHS tapes; requires a special, more expensive camcorder; and requires special, more expensive jacks on your TV or VCR. The advantage: sharper video quality.

The existence of the S-VHS format should be your first hint at a phenomenon you'll be reading, and hearing, a lot more about: For many home-video fans, the quality of the picture and sound is incredibly important. It's worth paying more for, buying add-on gear for, and reshooting scenes for. (Fortunately, you, a soon-to-be experienced *digital*-video [DV] producer, are ready to create videos that easily surpass the work of all of those long-suffering, pre-DV camcorder owners, no matter how much they spent on equipment.)

Figure 1-1:
The evolution–and the shrinking–of the modern camcorder. From top left: the full-size VHS camcorder; the 8mm/Hi-8 camcorder; and the modern DV camcorder–the one you need to work with iMovie.

• **VHS-C.** Here was Panasonic's attempt to solve the problems of the VHS camcorder's weight. This kind of camcorder is much smaller than full-size VHS units because it takes much smaller cassettes. After filming, you can pop one of these VHS-C (for "compact") cassettes into a VHS-sized *adapter* cassette, which you then insert into a standard VCR.

Clever, really, but still a nuisance. Now, when you want to play the video of the kids' birthday party, you have to find both the party cassette and the adapter cassette. Moreover, you can't send the tapes you make to friends or family without buying an adapter cassette for them, too.

• **8mm.** The 8-millimeter cassette is smaller even than VHS-C, which makes 8mm camcorders smaller still—now not much bigger than a six-inch sub sandwich. Makers of these camcorders make no apology for their tapes' inability to fit into a standard VCR. If you want to play back your footage, you run a cable from the camcorder to your TV or VCR, so that the camcorder itself becomes the VCR.

8mm camcorders are extremely inexpensive these days—under $300. Among non-digital camcorders, 8mm is the most popular format, but even these are rapidly being discontinued by camcorder makers.

- **Hi-8.** Hi-8 was the compact-camcorder equivalent of the S-VHS format described above: pricier camcorders, pricier tapes, better quality than regular 8mm. For several years, S-VHS and Hi-8 were popular *prosumer* camcorders—a cute way of saying that they bridged the gap between inexpensive *consumer* equipment and very expensive *professional* equipment. Because S-VHS and Hi-8 footage doesn't deteriorate as much from copy to copy as regular VHS and 8mm tape, it was a popular format for recording wedding videos, legal depositions, and even low-budget cable TV commercials.

Today, of course, DV camcorders dominate these functions.

iMovie works only with digital camcorders, but that doesn't mean you can't use all your older footage; Chapter 4 offers several ways to transfer your older tapes into iMovie. But from this day forward, shoot all of your new footage with a DV camcorder. At this writing, MiniDV camcorders cost about $400 for a basic model—and prices continue to sink, month by month. (See the end of this chapter for a DV buying guide.)

Tip: Selling your old camcorder eases much of the pain of buying a DV camcorder. Remember to transfer your old footage into DV format before you do so, however.

Why a DV Camcorder Is Worth It

A DV camcorder offers enormous advantages over previous formats.

It's smaller

The size of the camcorder is primarily determined by the size of the tapes inside it. A *MiniDV cassette* (tape cartridge) is tiny, as shown in Figure 1-2, so the camcorders are also tiny. The largest DV camcorder is about the size of the *smallest* 8mm camcorder, and the smallest DV camcorder is the size of a Sony Walkman.

Figure 1-2:
The various sizes of tapes that today's camcorders can accept differ in size, picture quality, and cost. For both home and prosumer filming, the standard-size VHS cassette (back) is nearly extinct. 8mm and Hi-8 cassettes (right) are extremely popular among people who don't have a computer to edit footage, and are very inexpensive. MiniDV tapes (left), like the ones required by most DV camcorders, are more expensive–but the enormous quality improvement makes them worth every penny.

The small size has lots of advantages. You can film surreptitiously when necessary. DV camcorders don't make kids or interview subjects nervous like bulkier equipment. The batteries last a long time, because they've got less equipment to power. And, of course, smaller means it's easier to take with you.

Still, DV cassettes aren't perfect. Most hold only 60 or 80 minutes of footage, and they're more expensive than analog tapes.

As you'll soon see, however, both of these limitations quickly become irrelevant in the world of iMovie. The whole idea is that iMovie lets you edit your footage and then, if you like, dump it back out to the camcorder. In other words, it's common iMovie practice to delete the boring footage from DV tape #1, preserve only the good stuff by dumping it onto DV tape #2, and then reuse DV cassette #1 for the next shooting session.

The quality is astounding

Video quality is measured in *lines of resolution:* the number of tiny horizontal stripes of color the playback uses to fill your TV screen. As you can see by this table, DV quality blows every previous tape format out of the water. (All camcorders, TVs, and VCRs have the same vertical resolution; this table measures *horizontal* resolution.)

Tape Format	Maximum Lines of Resolution
VHS, VHS-C	240
8mm	280
Live TV broadcast	300
S-VHS, Hi-8	400
Digital satellite broadcast	400
MiniDV	500
HDTV	720 or 1080

DV's 16-bit sound quality is dramatically better than previous formats, too. In fact, it's better than CD-quality sound, since DV camcorders record sound at 48 kHz instead of 44.1 kHz. (Higher means better.)

Tip: Most DV camcorders offer you a choice of sound-quality modes: 12-bit or 16-bit. The lower quality setting is designed to leave "room" on the tape for adding music after you've recorded your video. But avoid it like the plague! If you shoot your video in 12-bit video, your picture will gradually drift out of sync with your audio track—if you plan to save your movie to a DVD. Consult your manual to find out how to switch the camcorder into 16-bit audio mode. Do it *before* you shoot anything important.

You can make copies of copies

This is a big one. You probably know already that every time you make a copy of VHS footage (or other non-DV material), you lose quality. The copy loses sharpness, color fidelity, and smoothness of color tone. Once you've made a copy *of* a copy, the quality is terrible. Skin appears to have a combination of bad acne and radiation burns, the edges of the picture wobble as though leaking off the glass, and *video noise* (jiggling static dots) fills the screen. If you've ever seen, on the news or *America's Funniest Home*

Videos, a tape submitted by an amateur camcorder fan, you've seen this problem in action.

Digital video is stored on the tape as computer codes, not as pulses of magnetic energy. You can copy this video from DV camcorder to DV camcorder, or from DV camcorder to Mac, dozens of times, making copies of copies of copies. The last generation of digital video will be utterly indistinguishable from the original footage—which is to say, both will look fantastic.

Note: Technically speaking, you can't keep making copies of copies of a DV tape infinitely. After, say, 20 or 30 generations, you may start to see a few video *dropouts* (digital-looking specks), depending on the quality of your tapes and duplicating equipment. Still, few people have any reason to make that many copies of copies. (Furthermore, making infinite copies of a *single* original poses no such problem.)

A DV recording is forever

Depending on how much you read newspapers, you may have remembered the depressing story the *New York Times* broke in the late eighties: Because home video was such a recent phenomenon at the time, nobody had ever bothered to check out how long videotapes last.

The answer, as it turns out, was: not very long. Depending on storage conditions, the signal on traditional videotapes may begin to fade in as little as ten years! The precious footage of that birth, wedding, or tornado, which you had hoped to preserve forever, could in fact be more fleeting than the memory itself.

Your first instinct might be to rescue a fading video by copying it onto a fresh tape, but making a copy only further damages the footage. The bottom line, said the scientists: There is *no way* to preserve original video footage forever!

Fortunately, there is now. DV tapes may deteriorate over a decade or two, just as traditional tapes do. But you won't care. Long before the tape has crumbled, you'll have transferred the most important material to a new hard drive or a new DV tape or to a DVD. Because quality never degrades when you do so, you'll glow with the knowledge that your grandchildren and *their* grandchildren will be able to see your movies with every speck of clarity you see today—even if they have to dig up one of those antique "Macintosh" computers or gigantic, soap-sized "DV camcorders" in order to play it.

No fuzzy snow when rerecording

As on any camcorder, a DV unit lets you rerecord a scene on top of existing footage. But with DV, at the spot where the new footage begins or ends, you don't get five seconds of glitchy static, as you do with nondigital camcorders. Instead, you get a clean edit.

You can edit it

The fifth and best advantage of the DV format is, of course, iMovie itself. Once you've connected your DV camcorder up to your Mac (as described in Chapter 4), you can pour the footage from camcorder to computer—and then chop it up, rearrange scenes,

---

add special effects, cut out bad shots, and so on. For the first time in history, it's simple for anyone, even non-rich people, to edit home movies with professional results. (Doing so in 1990 required a $200,000 Avid editing suite; doing so in 1995 required a $4,000 computer with $4,000 worth of digitizing cards and editing software—and the quality wasn't great because it wasn't DV.)

Furthermore, for the first time in history, you won't have to press the fast-forward button when showing your footage to family, friends, co-workers, and clients. There won't *be* any dull footage worth skipping, because you'll have deleted it on the Mac.

Tip: Before you get nervous about the hours you'll have to spend editing your stuff in iMovie, remember that there's no particular law that every video must have crossfades, scrolling credits, and a throbbing music soundtrack. Yes, of course, you *can* make movies on iMovie that are as slickly produced as commercial films; much of this book is dedicated to helping you achieve that standard. But many people dump an entire DV cassette's worth of footage onto the Mac, chop out the boring bits, and dump it right back onto the camcorder—only about 20 minutes' worth of work after the transfer to the Mac.

What's It Good For?

If you're reading this book, you probably already have some ideas about what you could do if you could make professional-looking video. Here are a few possibilities that may not have occurred to you. All are natural projects for iMovie:

- **Home movies.** Plain old home movies—casual documentaries of your life, your kids' lives, your school life, your trips—are the single most popular creation of camcorder owners. Using the suggestions in the following chapters, you can improve the quality of your footage. Using a DV camcorder, you'll improve the quality of the picture and sound. And using iMovie, you can delete all but the best scenes

---

FREQUENTLY ASKED QUESTION

Three Camcorders Not to Buy

In their never-ending quest to come up with smaller and cooler camcorder designs, electronics manufacturers have already gone well beyond the MiniDV format. Unfortunately, some of these alternative formats are incompatible with iMovie.

Here, then, are two camcorders not to buy:

- **Sony MicroMV.** These camcorders are tiny, all right: they store their footage on a tape the size of a matchbox. Too bad they record in a format that popular editing programs like iMovie don't recognize.

- **DVD camcorders.** Sony, Panasonic, and Hitachi offer camcorders that use miniature DVD discs instead of tapes. Neat, but no FireWire jack.

iMovie HD can now edit video from two camera categories that iMovie 4 couldn't: high-definition footage and palm-sized, USB-connectable "camcorders" that record onto a memory card instead of tape.

Otherwise, though, stick to MiniDV camcorders. They're inexpensive, their quality is spectacular, and you won't be left behind when the next camcorder-format fad passes.

(and edit out those humiliating parts where you walked for 20 minutes with the camcorder accidentally filming the ground bouncing beneath it).

- **Actual films.** Don't scoff: iMovie is perfectly capable of creating professional video segments, or even plotted movies. If the three kids who made *The Blair Witch Project* could do it with *their* camcorder, you can certainly do it with yours. *They* didn't even have iMovie; they had to get $60,000 in loans to do the editing and processing that you can do right on your Mac.

  Moreover, new film festivals, Web sites, and magazines are springing up everywhere, all dedicated to independent makers of *short* movies. (More on this topic is coming up in Chapter 13.)

- **Business videos.** It's very easy to post video on the Internet or burn it onto a cheap, recordable CD-ROM, as described in Part 3. As a result, you should consider video a useful tool in whatever you do. If you're a realtor, blow away your rivals (and save your clients time) by showing movies, not still photos, of the properties you represent. If you're an executive, quit boring your comrades with stultifying PowerPoint slides and make your point with video instead.

- **Once-in-a-lifetime events.** Your kid's school play, your speech, someone's wedding, someone's birthday or anniversary party are all worth capturing, especially because now you know that your video can last forever.

- **Video photo albums.** A video photo album can be much more exciting, accessible, and engaging than a paper one. Start by filming or scanning your photos (you can read tips for doing this in Chapter 3). Assemble them into a sequence, add some crossfades, titles, and music. The result is a much more interesting display than a book of motionless images, thanks in part to iMovie's Ken Burns effect (page 251). This emerging video form is becoming very popular—videographers are charging a lot of money to create such "living photo albums" for their clients.

FREQUENTLY ASKED QUESTION

What's Digital About DV

I was a little surprised to find, when I bought my DV camcorder, that it requires tapes, just like my old nondigital one. If it still needs tapes, how can they call it digital?

Your confusion is understandable. After all, digital cameras don't require film, and digital TV recorders (such as the tapeless TiVo and ReplayTV "VCRs") don't use videotape.

Today's DV camcorders are really only half digital. They store their *signal* in digital form as a bunch of computer codes, but still record it on videotape just like the old camcorders. You still

have to rewind and fast-forward to find a particular spot in the footage. (Until you transfer the footage to iMovie, that is.)

Put another way, today's DV camcorders are a temporary technology, a halfway step toward the ultimate: a camcorder with a little iPod-like hard drive inside. (Already, JVC sells a camcorder that stores an hour of video on a removable 4-gigabyte hard drive; too bad it's not Mac-compatible.)

Until then, stick with old-fashioned tape that stores a modern digital signal.

- **Just-for-fun projects.** Never again can anyone over the age of eight complain that there's "nothing to do." Set them loose with a camcorder and the instruction to make a fake rock video, commercial, or documentary.

- **Training films.** If there's a better use for video than providing how-to instruction, you'd be hard-pressed to name it. Make a video for new employees to show them the ropes. Make a video that accompanies your product to give a humanizing touch to your company and help the customer make the most of her purchase. Make a tape that teaches newcomers how to play the banjo, grow a garden, kick a football, use a computer program—and market it.

- **Interviews.** You're lucky enough to live in an age where you can manipulate video just as easily as you do words in a word processor. Capitalize on this fact. Create family histories. Film relatives who still remember the War, the Birth, the Immigration. Or create a time-capsule, time-lapse film: Ask your kid or your parent the same four questions every year on his birthday (such as, "What's your greatest worry right now?" or "If you had one wish…?" or "Where do you want to be in five years?"). Then, after five or ten or twenty years, splice together the answers for an enlightening fast-forward through a human life.

- **Broadcast segments.** Want a taste of the real world? Call your cable TV company about its public-access channels. (As required by law, every cable company offers a channel or two for ordinary citizens to use for their own programming.) Find out the time and format restraints, and then make a documentary, short film, or other piece for actual broadcast. Advertise the airing to everyone you know. It's a small-time start, but it's real broadcasting.

- **Analyze performances.** There's no better way to improve your golf swing, tennis form, musical performance, or public speaking style than to study footage of yourself. If you're a teacher, camp counselor, or coach, film your students, campers, or players so that they can benefit from self-analysis, too.

- **Turn photos into video.** Technically, you don't need a camcorder at all to use iMovie; it's equally adept at importing and presenting still photos from a scanner or digital camera. In fact, iMovie's "Ken Burns" effect brings still photos to life, gently zooming into them, fading from shot to shot, panning across them, and so on, making this software the world's best slideshow creator.

Buying a DV Camcorder

If you already own a DV camcorder, you can safely skip to the next chapter—unless you've always wondered what this or that button on your camcorder does. In that case, surveying the following pages may enlighten you.

DV Camcorder Features: Which Are Worthwhile?

Like any hot new technology, DV camcorders started out expensive ($2,500 in 1996) and continue to plummet in price. At this writing, basic models start at $350; prosumer models hover around $2,000; many TV crews are adopting $3,500 models like the Canon XL1 or Sony's high-definition FX1; and the fanciest, professional, commercial-filmmaking models go for $10,000. All of these camcorders are *teeming* with features and require a thick brochure to list them all.

So how do you know which to buy? Here's a rundown of the most frequently advertised DV camcorder features, along with a frank assessment of their value to the quality-obsessed iMovie fan.

FireWire connector

FireWire is Apple's term for the tiny, compact connector on the side of most DV camcorders. When you attach a FireWire cable, this jack connects the camera to your FireWire-equipped Mac. Other companies have different names for this connector—you may see it called IEEE-1394, i.Link, DV In/Out, or DV Terminal.

If the camera you're considering doesn't have this feature, don't buy it; you can't use that camera with iMovie (or any other DV software).

Analog inputs

This single feature may be important enough to determine your camcorder choice by itself. *Analog inputs* are connectors on the camcorder (see Figure 1-3) into which you can connect older, pre-DV equipment, such as your VCR, your old 8mm camcorder, and so on. There's no easier, less expensive method of transferring older footage into your DV camcorder—or directly into iMovie.

This technique is described in more detail in Chapter 4. For now, note only that the alternative method of transferring pre-DV footage into DV format is to buy a $200 converter box—an unnecessary purchase if your DV camcorder has analog inputs.

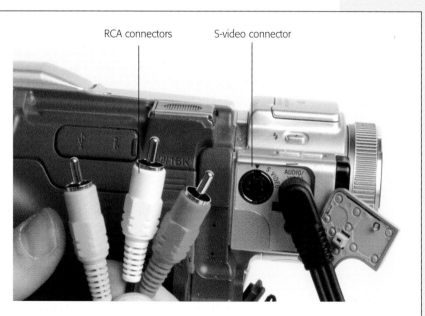

RCA connectors   S-video connector

Figure 1-3:
Most camcorders offer inputs known as RCA connectors. *Better models offer an* S-video *connector too, for much higher quality. (Most compact models require a special cable with RCA connectors on one end and a miniplug on the camcorder end, like the one shown here. Don't lose this cable! You also need it to play your camcorder footage on TV.)*

Tip: Using analog inputs, you can fill a couple of DV cassettes with, say, a movie you've rented. Then flip out the camcorder's LCD screen, plug in your headphones, and enjoy the movie on your cross-country flight—in economy class. Smile: The people up front in first class paid $1,000 more for the same privilege.

Three chips (three-CCDs)

Professional camcorders offer three individual image sensors, one for each color component of a video picture: red, green, and blue. These camcorders are advertised as having three chips or *CCDs* (*charge-coupled devices*—electronic plates, covered with thousands of individual light sensors, that convert light rays into a digital signal). The result is even more spectacular picture quality, resolution, and color rendition than the less-expensive, one-CCD cameras.

Unfortunately, you'll pay extra for this breathtaking video quality. Most three-chip camcorders are larger and more expensive than one-chip cams (see the photos in Figure 1-8)—but they deliver much better color.

Not all three-chip models are big and pricey. Panasonic sells one for $600 that's no larger than a standard MiniDV camcorder. Note, however, that it contains three very *small* CCDs, so the quality improvement is visible primarily in bright, outdoor scenes.

LCD viewfinder

In the olden days, you'd set up your shots and monitor your filming by looking through a tiny glass eyepiece, exactly like those on today's 35mm still cameras. Today, virtually all camcorders offer an alternative to the eyepiece: a small TV screen known as an *LCD*. (LCD stands for *liquid crystal display,* the technology used to produce the image. As you may have noticed, it's the same technology used in laptop screens.) In most cases, this LCD panel swings out from the side of the camera (see Figure 1-4).

Figure 1-4:
Your camcorder's LCD screen can rotate 180 degrees to face front; that's useful when you want to film yourself. Without an LCD screen, you'd have no idea whether or not you were centered in the frame.

You can usually flip the LCD so far around, in fact, that you can press it flat against the camcorder, screen side out. That's a nice way to play back your footage for a couple of onlookers.

The LCD means that when you're shooting, you can see what the camcorder sees without having to mash your face against the eyepiece. Better yet, after shooting, you can play back your footage. And thanks to the small, built-in speaker found on every sub-$1,500 camcorder, you can watch your work played back on the LCD screen while still "on location."

It's worth noting, by the way, that what you see isn't *exactly* what you get. For one thing, the LCD panel usually has its own brightness control, which, if not adjusted perfectly, may trick you into thinking a scene is better (or worse) lit than it actually is. The color and exposure revealed by the LCD screen may not exactly match what's going onto the tape, either.

When picture perfection counts, therefore, use your camcorder's eyepiece viewfinder instead of the LCD panel. You may also want to use the eyepiece when it's very bright and sunny out (the LCD display tends to wash out in bright light), when you don't want people around you to see what you're filming, and when you're trying to save battery juice. The LCD display depletes your battery about 50 percent faster than when the LCD is turned off.

Tip: The size of the LCD viewfinder is relative to two things: the size of the camcorder and its price. A camcorder with a 2.5-inch screen may cost hundreds of dollars less than one with a 4-inch screen.

Electronic image stabilizer (EIS)

As you'll read in Chapter 2, certain film techniques scream "Amateur!" to audiences. One of them is the instability of handheld filming. In a nutshell, professional video is shot using a camera on a tripod (Woody Allen's "handheld" period notwithstanding). Most home camcorder footage, in contrast, is shot from the palm of your hand.

A *digital* or *electronic* stabilizing feature (which may have a marketing name, such as Sony's SteadyShot) takes a half step toward solving that problem. As shown in Figure 1-5, this feature neatly eliminates the tiny, jittery moves present in handheld video. (It can't do anything about the bigger jerks and bumps, which are especially difficult to avoid when you're zoomed in.) It also uses up your battery faster.

Optical image stabilizer

On some camcorders, you get an *optical* image stabilizer instead. This mechanism involves two transparent plates separated by a special optical fluid. As the camera shakes, these plates create a prism effect that keeps handheld shots clearer and steadier than many electronic (digital) stabilizers. The images are clearer because optical stabilizers don't have to crop out part of the picture as a buffer, unlike the stabilizers illustrated in Figure 1-5.

Digital8 format

Here's another plan for getting your older footage into iMovie: Buy what Sony calls a *Digital8* camcorder. This fascinating hybrid doesn't use the MiniDV videotapes used by all other DV camcorders. Instead, it accepts the less expensive 8mm or, as Sony recommends, Hi-8 tapes.

Onto these cassettes, Digital8 camcorders record the identical DV signal found on MiniDV camcorders. But they can play back *either* digital video *or* traditional, analog video. (When recording digital video, however, the camera runs twice as fast—you still get only one hour of recording per tape, just as on MiniDV tapes.)

This kind of camcorder, in other words, is a good solution if you have a library of old 8mm tapes that you'd like to edit in iMovie. Your Mac can't tell which kind of tape the Digital8 camcorder is playing.

On the other hand, full-blown DV camcorders and tapes are no longer much more expensive than their 8mm predecessors, and Sony's Digital8 camcorder family has already begun to wind down.

Figure 1-5:
Digital stabilization features work by "taking in" more image than you actually see in the viewfinder. Because the camcorder has some buffer, its computer can compensate for small bumps and jitters by keeping an "eye" on prominent features of the image. On less expensive camcorders, unfortunately, this buffer zone means that your camcorder is absorbing less video information, to the detriment of picture quality.

Manual override

Better DV camcorders let you turn off the automatic focus, automatic exposure control, automatic white balance, and even automatic sound level. This feature can be useful in certain situations, as you'll find out in the next chapter. If you've decided to pay extra for this feature, look for a model that lets you focus manually by turning a ring around the lens, which is much easier than using sliders.

Optical zoom

When you read the specs for a DV camcorder—or read the logos painted on its body—you frequently encounter numbers like "12X/300X ZOOM!" The number before the slash tells you how many times the camera can magnify a distant image, much like a telescope. That number measures the *optical* zoom, which is the actual amount that the lenses themselves can zoom in. Such zooming, of course, is useful when you want to film something that's far away. (As for the number *after* the slash, see "Digital zoom," on the following page.)

You should know, however, that the more you've zoomed in, the shakier your footage is likely to be, since every microscopic wobble is magnified by, say, 12 times. You also have to be much more careful about focusing. When you're zoomed out all the way, everything is in focus—things near you, and things far away. But when you're zoomed in, very near and very far objects go out of focus. Put into photographic terms, the more you zoom in, the shorter the *depth of field* (the range of distance from the camera that can be kept in focus simultaneously).

Finally, remember that magnifying the picture doesn't magnify the sound. If you're relying on the built-in microphone of your camcorder, always get as close as you can to the subject, both for the sound and for the wobble.

Tip: As you'll discover in the next chapter, professional video and film work includes very little zooming, unlike most amateur video work. The best zooming is subtle zooming, such as when you very slowly "move toward" the face of somebody you're interviewing.

For this reason, when shopping for camcorders, test the zooming if at all possible. Find out if the camcorder has *variable-speed* zooming, where the zooming speed increases as you press the Zoom button harder. Some camcorders offer only two different speeds—fast and faster—but that's still better than having no control at all. (Variable-speed zooming isn't something mentioned in the standard camcorder literature; you generally have to try the camcorder in the store to find out how it does.)

Digital zoom

Much as computer owners mistakenly jockey for superiority by comparing the mega-hertz rating of their computers (higher megahertz ratings don't necessarily make faster computers), camcorder makers seem to think that what consumers want most in a camcorder is a powerful digital zoom. Your camcorder's packaging may "boast" zoom ratings of "50X," "100X," or "500X!"

When a camcorder uses its *digital* zoom—the number after the slash on the cam-corder box—it simply enlarges the individual dots that compose its image. Yes, the image gets bigger, but it doesn't get any *sharper*. As the dots get larger, the image gets chunkier, coarser, and less recognizable, until it ends up looking like the blocky areas you see superimposed over criminals' faces to conceal their identity on *Cops*. After your digital zoom feature has blown up the picture by 3X, the image falls to pieces. Greater digital zoom is not something worth paying extra for.

Minutes-remaining readout

Fortunately, the problems exhibited by camcorder batteries of old—such as the "mem-ory effect"—are a thing of the past. (When you halfway depleted a pre-DV camcorder battery's charge several times in a row, the battery would adopt that halfway-empty point as its new *completely* empty point, effectively halving its capacity.) Today's lithium-ion battery technology (used by DV camcorders) eliminates that problem.

Sony's InfoLithium batteries even contain circuitry that tells the camera how much juice it has remaining. A glance at the viewfinder or a small side-panel readout tells you how many minutes of recording or playback you've got left—a worthy feature.

Built-in light

As you can read in the next chapter, insufficient lighting is one of the leading causes of "amateuritis," a telltale form of poor video quality that lets viewers know that the footage is homemade. In the best—and most expensive—of all possible worlds, you'd get your scene correctly lit before filming, or you'd attach a light to the "shoe" (light connector) on top of the camera. Those few cameras that have such a shoe, or even have a built-in light, give you a distinct advantage in filming accurate colors.

Preprogrammed exposure options

Most DV camcorders come with a number of canned focus/shutter speed/aperture settings for different indoor and outdoor environments: Sports Lesson, Beach and Snow, Twilight, and so on. They're a useful compromise between the all-automatic operation of less expensive models and the all-manual operation of professional cameras.

Remote control

Some DV camcorders come with a pocket-sized remote control. It serves two purposes: First, its Record and Stop buttons give you a means of recording *yourself,* with or without other people in the shot. Second, when you're playing back footage with the camcorder connected to your TV or VCR, the remote lets you control the playback without needing to have the camcorder on your lap. You may be surprised at the remote's usefulness.

Backlight mode

As you can read in the next chapter, modern camcorders take much of the guesswork out of shooting video. For example, they can focus automatically.

Although few consumers appreciate it, today's camcorders also set their *aperture* automatically. The aperture is the hole inside the barrel of your camcorder's snout that gets bigger or smaller to admit more or less light, preventing you from under- or overexposing your footage. (Inside the camera is an *iris*—a circle of interlocking, sliding panels that move together to reduce or enlarge the opening, much like the one in a still camera.)

The automatic aperture circuitry works by analyzing the image. If it contains a lot of light—such as when you're filming against a snowy backdrop or aiming the camera toward the sun—the iris closes automatically, reducing the opening in the camera lens and thus reducing the amount of light admitted. The result: You avoid flooding the image with blinding white light.

Unfortunately, there may be times when you have no choice but to film somebody, or something, against a bright backdrop. In those cases, as you may have discovered through painful experience, the person you're trying to film shows up extremely dark, almost in silhouette (see Figure 1-6). Now the background is correctly exposed, but the *subject* winds up underexposed.

A Backlight button, then, is a valuable asset on a camcorder. Its purpose is to tell the camera, "OK, look, it's a bright scene; I can appreciate that. But I'm more interested in the subject that's coming out too dark at the moment. So do me a favor and open that aperture a couple of notches, will you?"

Figure 1-6:
Without the backlight mode, your camcorder is likely to turn your subject into a silhouette (left). The backlight button compensates by brightening everything up (right).

The camera obliges. Your subject no longer winds up too dark—in fact, modern camcorders do a great job at making sure the subject turns out just right. But overriding the automatic aperture control undoes the good the automatic iris originally did you—now everything *around* your subject is several shades too bright. Alas, there's no in between; *either* your subject or the background can be correctly exposed in very bright settings—but not both.

Tip: If your camcorder has a manual-exposure knob, you can similarly compensate for backlit scenes, but with much more control. Professionals and semi-pros, in fact, turn the auto-exposure feature off *completely.* True, they must now adjust the exposure knob for every single new shot, but their footage is then free from the bizarre and violent darkening or brightening that auto-exposure electronics can create as you pan across a scene.

FlexiZone or Push Focus

All camcorders offer automatic focus. Most work by focusing on the image in the center of your frame as you line up the shot.

That's fine if the subject of your shot *is* in the center of the frame. But if it's off-center, you have no choice but to turn off the autofocus feature and use the manual-focus ring. (Using the camcorder isn't like using a still camera, where you can point the camera directly at the subject for focusing purposes, and then—before taking the shot—shift the angle so that the subject is no longer in the center. Camcorders continually refocus, so pointing the camera slightly away from your subject makes you lose the off-center focus you've established.)

Some Canon, Sony, and Sharp camcorders let you point to a specific spot in the frame that you want to serve as the focus point, even if it's not the center of the picture. (This feature is called FlexiZone on the Canon models, or Push Focus on high-end Sony models. On Sony cams with touch-screen LCD panels, it's especially easy to indicate which spot in the frame should get the focus.) If the model you're eyeing has this feature, it's worth having.

Night-vision mode

Most Sony camcorders offer a mode called NightShot that works like night-vision goggles. In this mode, you can actually film (and see, as you watch the LCD screen) in total darkness. The infrared transmitter on the front of the camcorder measures the heat given off by various objects in its path, letting you capture an eerie, greenish night scene. Rent *The Silence of the Lambs* for an idea of how creepy night-vision filming can be. Or watch any episode of "Survivor."

The transmitter's range is only about 15 feet or so. Still, you may be surprised how often it comes in handy: on campouts, during sleepovers, on nighttime nature walks, and so on.

Still-camera mode

All DV camcorders offer a snapshot mode in which you can "snap" a still photo. The camcorder freezes one frame of what it's seeing, and records it either on the tape (for, say, a 7-second stretch) or on a memory card.

The still-image quality captured by most camcorders is pretty terrible. The resolution is OK on recent models (some camcorders offer two- or even three-megapixel resolution), but the quality isn't anywhere near what you'd get using a dedicated digital still camera. It turns out that the lenses and circuitry that best serve video are all wrong for stills.

If the camcorder you're considering offers this feature, fine. But it may be redundant for the iMovie owner. iMovie can grab one-megapixel still frames from *any* captured video, as described in Chapter 9.

Progressive-scan CCD

This special kind of image sensor is primarily useful for capturing still images. It ensures that the *entire* image is grabbed, not just one set of alternating, interlaced scan lines (the usual video signal). If you plan to catch still frames from your camcorder, a progressive-scan CCD will spare you some of the jagged lines that may appear. However, if your primary goal is to make movies, this expensive feature is not worth paying for, especially since you can buy a digital *still* camera, with much greater resolution, for about the same added cost.

Title generator

Some camcorders let you superimpose *titles* (that is, lettering) on your video as you film. In your case, dear iMovie owner, a title-generating feature is useless. Your Mac can add gorgeous, smooth-edged type, with a selection of sizes, fonts, colors, and even scrolling animations to your finished movies, with far more precision and power than the blocky text available to your camcorder. (Chapter 7 shows you how.)

Tip: A title generator on the camcorder is actually *worse* than useless, because it permanently stamps your original footage with something you may wish you could amend later.

In fact, as a general rule, you should avoid using (or paying for) *any* of the in-camera editing features described in this chapter—title generator, fader, special effects—because you can do this kind of editing much more effectively in iMovie. Not only are they redundant, but they commit you to an editing choice in advance, thus limiting how you can use your footage.

Fader

Most DV camcorders offer a Fade or Fader button. If you press it once before pressing the Record button, you record a smooth, professional-looking fade-in from black-ness. If you press it *as* you're recording, and then press the Record button again to stop recording, you get a smooth dimming of the picture (and, usually, a fading of the sound), all the way to black (and silence).

Even if your camcorder has a Fader button, don't use it, for several reasons:

- Pressing the Fade button in order to trigger a fade-out is very difficult to do. You're forced to look away from your subject to hunt for the button, and it's almost impossible to keep the camera steady in the process.

- iMovie offers much more graceful and controlled fade-ins and fade-outs. For example, you can specify exactly how many seconds long the fade should last, and you can even fade into a color other than black.

- When you use your camcorder's Fade button, you risk chopping off one last great wisecrack from your kid as she rides into the sunset, or one last backflip by the seal at Sea World. In other words, once you've started the fade, you can't stop it.

- If you need any more convincing, ask any camcorder owner about the embarrassment factor that comes from fading out on what he assumed would be the absolute perfect final shot, and then coming across another event that *had* to be included in the footage. When played back, the feeling of gentle, sighing finality created by the fade-out is jarringly shattered by the sudden appearance of that tacked-on scene.

Audio dubbing

In a few fancy camcorders, you can rerecord only the soundtrack on a piece of tape you've already shot. If you didn't have a Mac, you could conceivably use this feature to add, for example, an accompanying rock song to a montage of party scenes.

But iMovie offers far more flexibility in this department. For example, iMovie lets you add a piece of music to a scene *without* deleting the original voices, as your camcorder's audio-dub feature would. Don't pay extra for audio dubbing on your camcorder.

Special effects

Most DV camcorders offer a selection of six or seven cheesy-looking special effects. They can make your footage look solarized, or digitized, or otherwise processed (see Figure 1-7).

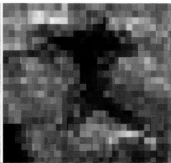

Figure 1-7:
Using the stock collection of special effects built into your camcorder, you can create special, hallucinogenic visuals. The question is: why?

Avoid using these built-in camcorder effects; iMovie comes with a number of such special effects—and gives you far greater control over when they start, when they end, and how intensely they affect the video (Chapter 6). And even then, unless you're shooting a documentary about nuclear explosions or bad drug episodes, consider avoiding these effects altogether.

Date/time stamp

Every camcorder offers the ability to stamp the date and time directly onto the footage. As you've no doubt seen (on *America's Funniest Home Videos* or *America's Scariest Cop Chases*), the result is a blocky, typographically hideous stamp that permanently mars the footage. Few things take the romance out of a wedding video, or are more distracting in spectacular weather footage, than a huge **20 SEP 05 12:34 PM** stamped in the corner.

Nor do you have to worry that you'll one day forget when you filmed some event. As it turns out, DV camcorders automatically and invisibly date- and time-stamp *all* footage. You'll be able to see this information when you connect the camcorder to your Mac; *then* you can choose whether or not to add it to the finished footage (and with much more control over the timing, location, and typography of the stamp).

Control-L or Lanc

You'll find this feature on some Canon and all Sony camcorders. It's a connector that hooks up to special editing consoles.

You, however, have a far superior editing console—iMovie—and a far superior connection method—FireWire. Control-L and Lanc are worthless to you.

Where and How to Buy

Virtually every camcorder manufacturer has adopted the DV format, including Sony, Panasonic, JVC, Sharp, RCA, Hitachi, and Canon. Each company releases a new line of models once or twice a year; the feature list always gets longer, the price always gets lower, and the model numbers always change.

Cameras come in all sizes, shapes, and price ranges (see Figure 1-8). In magazine reviews and Internet discussion groups, Sony and Canon get consistently high marks for high quality. JVC and Sony make the smallest, most pocketable models. Still, each manufacturer offers different exclusive goodies, and each camcorder generation improves on the previous one.

Figure 1-8:
The model lineup changes constantly, and new formats come and go. Here, for example, are three of Sony's digital camcorders.

Top left: The compact HC models are horizontally oriented cameras, some with widescreen (16:9) flip-out screens, as shown here.

Top right: The PC series represents some of the tiniest MiniDV camcorders you can buy.

Bottom: The awesome, three-chip, semi-pro HDTV camcorder known as the HDR-FX1 (not to scale)—a camcorder that Apple calls a perfect companion for iMovie HD.

Apple's "Supported Camcorders" list at *www.apple.com/compatibility/camcorder.html* identifies models that Apple has tested to confirm that they work with iMovie. They are certainly not the *only* models that do, however. They happen to be the ones whose manufacturers have given cameras to Apple for testing and endorsement.

To look over a company's latest camcorders, start by reading about them at the relevant Web site:

• **Sony.** Visit *www.sonystyle.com*, and then navigate your way to the Digital Camcorder page.

- **Canon.** Go to *www.canondv.com* to view the various models.

- **Panasonic.** Details are at *www.panasonic.com/consumer_electronics/camcorder*.

- **Sharp.** For more on Sharp's ViewCam series, hit *http://www.sharpusa.com/products/ TypeLanding/0,1056,70,00.html* (or just go to *sharpusa.com* and navigate your way to the camcorders).

- **JVC.** These camcorders have come a long way since the early days, when JVC's models were incompatible with iMovie. Now they work smoothly, and come in a wide variety of sizes and shapes. Details at *www.jvc.com/product.jsp*.

Camcorders, as it turns out, are famous for having hopelessly unrealistic list prices. The high-definition Sony HDR-FX1, for example, has an official price tag of $3,700, but you can find it for under $3,100 online.

Once you've narrowed down your interest, then, go straight to a Web site like *www. shopper.com* or *www.shopping.com* to see what the real-world price is. Such Web sites specialize in collecting the prices from mail-order companies all over the world. When you specify the camcorder model you're looking for, you're shown a list of online stores that carry it, complete with prices. (All of the prices in this chapter came from listings on those Web sites.)

As you'll quickly discover, prices for the same camcorder cover an *extremely* large range. Use the price-comparison Web sites if saving money is your priority.

Of course, you can also find DV camcorders at electronics and appliance superstores (Circuit City, Best Buy, and so on), mail-order catalogs, and even photo stores.

Turning Home Video into Pro Video

W hen you turn on the TV, how long does it take you to distinguish between an actual broadcast and somebody's home video? Probably about ten seconds.

The real question is: *How* can you tell? What are the visual differences between professionally produced shows and your own? Apple's advertising claims that a DV camcorder and iMovie let you create professional-quality video work. So why do even iMovie productions often have a homemade look to them?

Maybe Homemade Is What You Want

If you want to learn how to upgrade your filming techniques to make your finished videos look more professional, then this chapter is your ticket.

That's not to say, however, that "professional" *always* means "better." Not every video has to be, or should be, a finished-looking production. There are plenty of circumstances in which homemade-looking video is just fine. In fact, it's exactly what an audience of family members is probably expecting. When watching your footage of a one-of-a-kind scene for which preparation was obviously impossible, such as a baby's first steps or the eruption of a local volcano, rest assured that nobody will be critiquing your camera work.

Furthermore, sometimes amateur-looking video *is* the look your professional project calls for. In some movies, filmmakers go to enormous lengths to simulate the effect of amateur camcorder footage. (The color segment of *Raging Bull,* for example, is designed to look as though it's composed footage shot by a home movie camera.)

In other words, polished-looking video isn't necessarily superior video for every situation. Nonetheless, you should know how to get professional results when you want them; even Picasso mastered traditional, representational drawing before going abstract.

As it turns out, there are a number of discernible ways that home movies differ from professional ones. This chapter is dedicated to helping you accept the camcorder deficiencies you cannot change, overcome the limitations you can, and have the wisdom to know the difference.

Film vs. Videotape

There's only one crucial aspect of Hollywood movies that you can't duplicate with your DV camcorder and iMovie: Real movies are shot on *film,* not video. Film, of course, is a long strip of celluloid with sprocket holes on the edges. It comes on an enormous reel, loaded into an enormous camera. After you've shot it, a lab must develop it before you can see what you've got.

Videotape is a different ball game. As you know, it comes on a cartridge, pops into a compact camera, and doesn't have to be developed. Many TV shows, including sitcoms and all news shows, are shot on video.

Visually, the differences are dramatic. Film and videotape just look different, for several reasons:

- Film goes through many transfer processes (from original, to positive master, to negative master, to individual "prints," to movie screen), so it has a softer, warmer appearance. It also has microscopic specks, flecks, and scratches that tell you you're watching something filmed on film.

- Film has much greater resolution than video—*billions* of silver halide crystals coat each frame of the film. As a result, you see much more detail than video can offer. It has a subtle grain or texture that you can spot immediately. Furthermore, these specks of color are irregularly shaped, and different on every frame. A camcorder's sensors (CCDs), on the other hand, are all the same size and perfectly aligned, which also affects the look of the resulting image.

- Film is also far more sensitive to color, light, and contrast than the sensors in camcorders, and different kinds of film stock have different characteristics. Hollywood directors choose film stock according to the ambiance they want: One type of film might yield warmer colors, another type might offer sharper contrast, and so on.

- Film is composed of 24 individual frames (images) per second, but NTSC video (page 8) contains more flashes of picture per second (30 complete frames, shown as 60 alternating sets of interlocking horizontal lines per second). All of that extra visual information contributes to video's hard, sharp look and lends visual differences in the way motion is recorded. This discrepancy becomes particularly apparent to experts when film is *transferred* to video for broadcast on TV, for example. Doing so requires the transfer equipment to *duplicate* a frame of the original film here and there.

Of course, the *content* of the film or video is also a telltale sign of what you're watching. If it has a laugh track and a brightly lit set, it's usually videotape; if it's more carefully and dramatically lit, with carefully synchronized background music, it's usually film.

Film-Technique Crash Course

The bottom line is that two different issues separate film from video: the *technology* and the *technique*. What you can't change is the look of the basic medium: You're going to be recording onto tape, not film.

Tip: If the grain and softness associated with film are crucial to your project, you're not utterly out of luck. With the addition of a 320 video-processing program called Adobe After Effects and a $550 software add-on called CineLook (from DigiEffects), you can get very close to making video look like film. CineLook adds the grain, flecks, and scratches to taped footage, and plays with the color palette to make it look more like that of film. Another popular add-on called CineMotion (from the same company) adds subtle blur processing to make the *motion* of video look more like film, simulating 24-frames-per-second playback. (Needless to say, few iMovie fans go to that expensive extreme.)

What you can change with iMovie alone, however, is almost every remaining element of the picture. Some of the advice in this chapter requires additional equipment; some simply requires new awareness. Overall, however, the tips in this chapter should take you a long way into the world of professional cinematography.

The Very Basics

If you're using a camcorder for the first time, it's important to understand the difference between its two functions: as a camera and as a VCR.

The most obvious knob or switch on every camcorder lets you switch between these two modes (plus a third one known as Off). These two operating-switch positions may be labeled *Camera* and *VTR* (for Video Tape Recorder), *Camera* and *VCR,* or *Record* and *Play.*

But the point is always the same: When you're in Camera mode, you can record the world; the lens and the microphone are activated. When you're in VTR mode, the lens and the mike are shut down; now your camcorder is a VCR, complete with Play, Rewind, and Fast-Forward buttons (which often light up in VTR mode). When you want to *film* a movie, use Camera mode; to *watch* the movie you've recorded, put the camcorder into VTR mode. (You'll also have to put the camera in VTR mode when it comes time to record your finished iMovie creation, or when you want to copy video to or from another camcorder or VCR.)

Here, then, is the usual sequence for filming:

1. **Prepare the microphone, lighting, angle, and camera settings as described in this chapter.**

This is the moment, in other words, to play director and cinematographer, to set up the shot. You can read about all these important techniques in the rest of this chapter. They're extremely important techniques, at that: If the raw footage has bad sound, bad lighting, or the wrong camera settings, no amount of iMovie manipulation can make it better.

2. **Turn the main knob or switch to Camera (or Record) mode.**

   You've just turned the power on. The camera's now in standby mode—on, but not playing or recording anything. (See Figure 2-1.)

Figure 2-1:
The main button on every camcorder lets you turn the camera on by switching it into Camera or VTR mode (left). The red Record button is the trigger that makes the tape roll (right).

3. **Take off the lens cap.**

   The lens cap usually dangles from a short black string that you've looped around a corresponding hole on the front of the camera (or hooks onto the handstrap), unless you're lucky enough to have a camcorder with a built-in, auto-opening lens cap.

4. **Frame your shot (aim the camera).**

   Do so either by looking at the LCD screen or by looking through the eyepiece. Adjust the zoom controls until the subject nicely fills the frame. Get your performers ready (if they're even aware that they're being filmed, that is).

5. **Press the Record button.**

   It's usually bright red and located next to your right thumb. (The left-handers' lobby has gotten absolutely nowhere with camcorder manufacturers.)

   Some camcorders have an additional Record button on the top or side, plus another one on the remote control, for use when you're filming yourself or holding the camcorder down at belly level.

   In any case, now you're rolling.

6. Film the action as described in this chapter. When you've filmed enough of the scene—when you've *got the shot*—press the Record button a second time to stop rolling.

At this point, the camcorder is back in standby mode. It's using up its battery faster than when it's turned off. Therefore, if you don't expect to be filming anything else within the next few minutes, push the primary switch back to its Off position. (If you forget, no big deal; most camcorders turn off automatically after five minutes or so since your last activity.)

Now you, like thousands before you, know the basics. The rest of this chapter is designed to elevate your art from that of camera operator to cinematographer/director.

Get the Shot

Rule No. 1: Get the shot.

If you and the camcorder aren't ready when something great happens—whether you're trying to create a Hollywood-style movie with scripted actors or just trying to catch the dog's standoff with a squirrel—then everything else in this book, and in your new hobby, are for naught.

The Slate: Lights, Lens Cap, Action!

I'm getting tired of seeing that "clapper" board—it's the iMovie icon, it's the picture that shows up when you choose iMovie→About iMovie, it's the icon of every iMovie document. It's practically the world's most overused symbol. Everybody uses it to symbolize filmmaking. What the heck is that thing?

It's called the *slate* or *clapstick*, and they really do use it when they make commercial movies. Using a dry-erase marker, an assistant writes the movie's name, scene number, and date onto this plastic whiteboard (nobody uses chalk on slate anymore). As soon as the camera is rolling, the slate is held in front of the lens and the clapstick on top is slammed shut. The camera photographs the time-code readout (which is generated by the

sound-recording equipment) in the top part of the clapper. Only then does the director shout, "And, *action!*"

The purpose of this exercise is to make editing easier later. Although your camcorder records sound and video simultaneously, the soundtrack for *film* is actually recorded on a different machine. When editing, technicians can plug in the time-code number captured on film to cue up the audio track quickly and efficiently.

And if that sync-up circuitry fails for some reason, editors can synchronize the sound and picture manually, just as they did in the old days: by aligning the loud, crisp sound with the visual moment when the clapstick closes.

Both human and mechanical obstacles may conspire to prevent you from capturing the perfect footage. Here are some examples:

Is the Camera Ready?

Your camcorder is only ready when its battery is charged and it's got fresh tape inside. MiniDV cassettes these days cost about $4 apiece (from, for example, *www.bhphoto.com* or warehouse discount clubs like Costco), so you have no excuse not to have a stack of blanks, at least a couple of which should live in your camcorder carrying case for emergency purposes. If you bite the bullet and buy a box of ten or fifty, you'll save even more money, you won't have to buy any more for quite a while, and you'll be able to keep a couple of spares with the camera.

Tip: Professional broadcast journalists never go anywhere without fully charged batteries and blank tape in the camera. Even if you're not a pro, having enough tape and power at all times can pay off, since you can make good money selling your video to news shows because you caught something good on tape.

The same goes for battery power. The battery that comes with the camcorder is adequate as a starter battery, but buying a second one—especially if it's one of the fat, heavy, longer-capacity batteries—is further insurance that some precious shooting opportunity won't be shut down or lost by equipment failure.

Remember, too, that today's lithium-ion batteries are extraordinarily sophisticated. But even though they're rechargeable, they're not immortal; most can be recharged only a few hundred times before you start to notice a decrease in capacity. In other words, use the power cord whenever it's practical.

Tip: Camcorder batteries are far more fragile than they appear. Keep them dry at all costs. If one gets damp or wet, you may as well throw it away.

Are You Ready?

There's a human element to being ready, too. For example, remember that from the moment you switch on the power, your camcorder takes about eight seconds to warm up, load a little bit of tape, and prepare for filming. It's a good idea to flip the power on, therefore, even as you're running to the scene of the accident, earthquake, or amazing child behavior.

Is the Camera Actually Recording?

Every day, somewhere in the world, a family sits down in front of the TV, expecting to watch some exciting home movies, and instead watches 20 minutes of the ground bumping along beneath the camcorder owner's hand.

As you begin to shoot, *always* glance at the viewfinder to confirm that the Record indicator—usually a red dot, or the word REC or RECORD—has appeared. Make it a rigid and automatic habit. That's the only way you'll avoid the sickening realization later that you punched the Record button one too many times, thus turning the camera *on* when you thought it was *off,* and vice versa.

If your subject is a family member or friend, they may be able to confirm that you're getting the shot by checking the *tally light*—the small light on the lens end of the camcorder that lights up, or blinks, while you're recording. Most videographers, however, turn off the tally light (using the camcorder's built-in menu system) or put a piece of black tape over it. If you're trying to be surreptitious or to put your subject at ease, the light can be extremely distracting, especially when it starts *blinking* to indicate that you're running out of tape or power.

Similarly, make sure the indicator disappears when you punch the Record button a second time. Sometimes this button sticks and doesn't actually make the camera stop filming.

Tip: If the recording-the-ground syndrome has struck you even once, check your camcorder's feature list. Some models, including most Sony camcorders, offer a special feature that's designed to eliminate this syndrome. When you slide a switch into a mode Sony calls Anti-Ground Shooting, the camcorder records only *while* you're pressing the Record button. As soon as you remove your thumb, the camera stops recording. This scheme isn't ideal for long shots, of course, and it ties up your hands during shots when you might need to adjust the zoom or focus while filming. But it's extremely good insurance against missing important moments.

How Much to Shoot

For years, books and articles about camcorders have stressed the importance of keeping your shots *short*. In the pre-iMovie era, this was excellent advice. When you show your footage to other people, there's absolutely nothing worse than endless, monotonous, unedited scenes of babies/speeches/scenery. If you don't want your guests and family members to feel that they're being held hostage during your screenings, strive for short shots and very selective shooting. So goes the usual advice.

But the iMovie revolution turns that advice on its head. Yes, it's still agonizing and tedious to watch hours of somebody's unedited video, but thanks to iMovie, you won't be showing unedited video. By the time an audience sees it, your stuff won't be endless and boring. In fact, it will be far better than a bunch of short, selective shots on the average person's camcorder, because you'll have had a much greater selection of footage from which to choose the most interesting scenes.

In other words, it's safe to relax about how much you're shooting. It's much better, in the iMovie Age, to shoot too much footage than too little. After all, if your camcorder stops rolling too soon, you might miss a terrific moment. (Almost everyone who's used a camcorder has experienced such unfortunate timing.)

In Hollywood and professional TV production, in fact, shooting miles of footage is standard practice. When filming movies, Hollywood directors shoot every scene numerous times, even if nothing goes wrong in most of them, just so that they'll have a selection to choose from when it comes time to assemble the final film. (As an extreme example, legend has it that during the making of Stanley Kubrick's *Eyes Wide Shut*, the director asked the actors to repeat a scene 140 times, on the premise that eventually they'd no longer be acting—it would be *real*.) The more takes you get "in the can," especially if they're shot different ways (different angles, zoom levels, and so on), the more flexibility and choice you'll have when editing, and the better the finished product will be.

Don't go overboard, of course; there *is* still such a thing as shooting too much footage. You should still think in terms of capturing *shots* that you've thought about and framed in the viewfinder; don't just roll continuously, pointing the lens this way and that. And you should still remember all the extra time you'll have to spend transferring the footage into iMovie, reviewing it, and editing it. The more you shoot, the greater the editing time.

But it's certainly safe to say that in the age of iMovie, you'll improve your odds of catching memorable moments on tape if you keep the camera rolling as long as the kid/animal/tornado is performing.

Replace the Microphone

The built-in microphone on your camcorder can't be beat for convenience. It's always there, it's always on, and it's always pointing at what you're filming.

Unfortunately, camcorder microphones have several disadvantages. For example:

- They're usually mounted right on the camera body. In quiet scenes, they can pick up the sound of the camcorder itself—a quiet grinding of the electronic motor, or the sound of the lens zooming and focusing.

- If your subject is farther than a few feet away, the sound is much too faint. The powerful zoom lens on modern camcorders exaggerates this problem. If your subject is 50 yards away, the zoom may make it look as though you're right up close, but the sound still has to come from 50 yards away.

"Camcorder sound," that hollow, faraway sonic quality present on most home videos (including the ones shown on your cable station's public-access channel late at night), is one of the most obvious differences between amateur video and professional work. Even if viewers can't quite put their finger on *how* they know that something was shot with a camcorder, they'll know that it *was* shot with a camcorder just by listening.

Clip-on (Lavalier) Microphones

Few camcorder accessories, therefore, are more useful than an external microphone. And it doesn't have to cost a lot. For $20, Radio Shack will sell you a high-quality tie-clip microphone that resembles the one worn on the lapels of newscasters (see Figure 2-2).

Of course, if the problem of camcorder audio is that it gets worse when the subject is far away, an external microphone with a six-foot cord isn't of much use. Therefore, consider buying a couple of extension cords for your microphone; they come in lengths of 20 feet or more, and cost about $10. You can plug one into the next, using standard miniplug connectors (like the ones on the end of Walkman headphones).

Tip: In certain situations, plugging one cable into the next, as you do when connecting an external microphone to an extension cable, can introduce a hum on your soundtrack. To avoid ruining otherwise great footage, carry with you a pair of cheap Walkman headphones. Whenever you're using an external microphone, plug these headphones into the headphone jack on your camcorder and listen as you film. (In fact, you're wise to use headphones *anytime* you're filming.)

If a humming or buzzing does arise, try exchanging cables, eliminating extension cords, and running the camcorder on battery instead of AC power, until you've isolated the source of the problem.

Wireless Mikes

One of those inexpensive tie-clip microphones is ideal when you're filming interviews, speeches, or scripted dialog with actors. But in other situations, a cabled microphone like this is impractical, such as when you're shooting a jogger, somebody in a car, or an undercover agent.

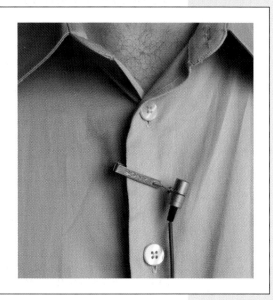

Figure 2-2:
A tie-clip microphone, known in the business as a Lavalier mike ("lava-LEER"), is a very inexpensive way to dramatically improve the audio on your footage, especially when accompanied by an extension cable or two. You plug it into the Mic In jack on the side of almost every DV camcorder. (This jack may be concealed by a protective plastic cap.)

For those circumstances, consider buying or renting a *wireless* microphone. These microphones come in two parts: the microphone held or worn by the actor or speaker, and a receiver that clips onto your camcorder and plugs into the Mic In jack. The receiver picks up the sound signal that's transmitted by radio waves. (Here again, be aware of interference. As you film, wear Walkman headphones to monitor the incoming sound. There's nothing worse than tender words of love being drowned out by a nearby trucker cursing on his overamplified CB radio that's picked up by your receiver.)

Other Microphones

If you're shooting documentary-style, it's impractical to attach *any* kind of microphone to the people you're filming. Depending on how serious you are about your filming, you have alternatives. A *shotgun mike* is elongated and thin; it's designed to pick up a distant sound source with pinpoint accuracy. (In Hollywood thrillers, shotgun mikes appear onscreen in the hands of the characters almost as often as they do behind the scenes.) Semi-pro camcorders like the Canon XL1 and the Sony VX2000 have shotgun mikes built right in. Clip-on shotgun mikes are available for less expensive Canon and Sony camcorders, too.

There's also the *boom mike,* which requires a helper to hold over the head of the actor on a long pole—another staple of professional film production. Unfortunately, this kind of mike, too, is likely to dampen your spontaneity.

Where to Buy Them

You won't find these fancier microphone types, which cost $100 or more, in the local Radio Shack. Online, however, they're everywhere. Video-supply companies like

BUYERS' GUIDE

How to Buy a Microphone

When you shop for an add-on mike for your camcorder, you'll have to choose between models based on three important microphone characteristics: its *technology* (dynamic vs. condenser), its *pickup pattern,* and its *connector.*

Dynamic microphones sense changes in air pressure caused by sound waves. They use relatively simple technology that's usually rugged, but not very sensitive to quiet sounds. These are the least expensive microphones.

A *condenser* mike (also called *electret condenser*), on the other hand, has a built-in amplifier, making it much more sensitive to both sound levels and frequency. These microphones require extra power; some use batteries; some can get their power from the cable that plugs into your camcorder using what's called "phantom power." The important thing to remember when using a condenser mike is to carry spare batteries, because the microphone may go dead at any time during shooting. These mikes are also more expensive and less rugged than dynamic models.

The *pickup pattern* refers to the area in space from which a particular microphone picks up sounds. For example, *omnidirectional* mikes pick up sound from every side—in front, to the side, from behind. They're great if you need to record groups of people or general environmental sounds, but they pick up too much ambient noise when you're trying to record dialog in a noisy environment.

Cardioid microphones block sound from behind, and dampen sound coming from the sides. In other words, they mostly capture sounds they're pointed at, but still pick up some general surrounding sound. This is the most common type used in Hollywood productions.

Supercardioid microphones, such as shotgun mikes, are extremely directional. They must point *straight* at the subject, or they may not pick up its sound at all. These specialized mikes are great in noisy environments, but they're expensive. They usually require an operator, someone who does nothing but point the mike at the sound's source.

Finally, consider the *connector* at the end of the microphone cable. *XLR* is the professional connection: a big, round, three-pin jack that doesn't fit any camcorder under $4,000. Instead, your camcorder probably accepts *eighth-inch, mini phono* plugs, which look like the end of a pair of Walkman headphones.

Several companies manufacture XLR to eighth-inch adapters, which let you use professional mikes on less expensive camcorders. These converters also have one or two *extra* jacks, so that you can plug in a second microphone, when necessary—a great feature for interviews. Such converters usually include signal-level control knobs, too, that let you manually adjust the sound volume as you're recording.

www.rentgear.com, *www.markertek.com*, and *www.bhphotovideo.com* are good starting points for your shopping quest. For good information about microphones in general, visit *www.audiotechnica.com/using/mphones/guide*.

Limit Zooming and Panning

In a way, camcorder manufacturers are asking for it. They put the zoom-in/zoom-out buttons right on top of the camcorder, where your fingers naturally rest. That tempting placement has led millions of camcorder owners to zoom in or out in almost every shot—and sometimes even several times *within* a shot. For the camcorder operator, zooming imparts a sense of control, power, and visual excitement. But for the viewer, zooming imparts a sense of nausea.

In other words, most home-movie makers zoom too much. In professional film and video, you almost never see zooming, unless it's to achieve a particular special effect. (Someday, rent a movie and note how many times the director zooms in or zooms out. Answer: almost never.)

Tips for Keeping Zooming Under Control

To separate yourself from the amateur-video pack, adopt these guidelines for using the zoom controls:

FREQUENTLY ASKED QUESTION

Automatic Gain Control

Where's the recording-volume knob on my camcorder?

There isn't one. Modern consumer camcorders use something called *automatic gain control* (AGC). They set the volume level automatically as you record.

That may sound like a neat feature, but it drives professionals nutty. AGC, in essence, strives to record all sound at exactly the same level. When something is very loud, the AGC circuit quiets it down to middle volume; when something is very soft, the AGC circuit boosts it to middle volume.

Over the years, automatic-gain circuitry has dramatically improved. The electronic boosting or quieting is smoother and less noticeable than it once was. Even some modern camcorders, however, sometimes exhibit the unpleasant side effects of AGC circuitry: Try filming something that's very quiet, and then suddenly clap right next to the microphone. On lesser camcorders, when you play the footage back, you'll

hear how the sudden, loud sound made the AGC back off, cutting the volume way down in anticipation of further loud noises. It takes the camcorder several seconds to realize that the surrounding sound is still quiet (and to boost the volume level back up where it had been).

Fortunately, that sudden-adjustment syndrome is a rare and usually harmless occurrence. For most purposes, camcorders do an excellent job of setting their own volume level (although it certainly evens out the dynamic highs and lows of, say, a symphony performance).

Besides, you don't have much of an alternative. Only a few, more expensive camcorders permit you to override the AGC circuit (and adjust the sound level manually). Even if you plug in an external microphone, most camcorders take it upon themselves to adjust the sound level automatically.

- The zoom button is ideal for adjusting the magnification level *between* shots, when the camcorder is paused—to *set up* a new shot. Be conscious of how many times you're using the zoom while the tape is rolling.

- Sometimes you may be tempted to zoom in order to create an *establishing shot*—to show the entire landscape, the big picture—before closing in on your main subject.

That's a worthy instinct, but zooming isn't the best way to go from an establishing shot to a closeup. Instead, consider an effect like the extremely effective, more interesting one that opens such movies as *Citizen Kane*: a series of successive shots that dissolve, one into the next, each closer to the subject than the previous. (See Figure 2-3.) Open with a wide shot that shows the entire airport; fade into a medium shot that shows the exiting masses of people; finally, dissolve to the worried face of the passenger whose luggage has vanished. Naturally, you can't create the fades and dissolves while you're shooting, but it's a piece of cake to add them in

Zooming   Cutting

Figure 2-3:
Zooming, as represented here by several sequential frames (left), is a dead giveaway that the movie is homemade.

Try a more professional sequence to set up your shot: Hold on a wider, scene-establishing shot, cut to a medium shot, and then cut to a closeup (right).

iMovie. Your job while filming is simply to capture the two or three different shots, each at a different zoom level.

- You don't have to avoid zooming altogether. As noted above, professional movie-makers rarely zoom. One of the exceptions, however, is when the director wants to pick one face out of a crowd, often just as some horrific realization is dawning. Furthermore, when you're filming somebody who's doing a lot of talking, a very slow, almost imperceptible zoom is extremely effective, especially if you do it when the speech is getting more personal, emotional, ominous, or important.

The point is to use zooming *meaningfully,* when there's a reason to do it.

- For the lowest motion-sickness quotient, use the *hold-zoom-hold* technique. In other words, begin your shot by filming without zooming for a moment; zoom slowly and smoothly; and end the shot by holding on the resulting closeup or wide shot. Don't begin or end the shot in mid-zoom.

***

Tip: Documentary makers frequently film with this pattern: Hold for five seconds; zoom in, and then hold for five seconds; zoom out again, and hold for five, then stop the shot. This technique gives the filmmaker a variety of shots, providing choice when editing the final movie.

All of this sheds light on another reason to hold at the end of a zoom, and another reason to avoid zooming in general: When editing, it's very difficult to make a smooth cut during a zoom. Cutting from one nonzooming shot to another is smoother and less noticeable than cutting in mid-zoom.

***

- Consider how much to zoom. There's no law that says that every zoom must use the entire 500X magnification range of your camcorder.

- Did you ever see *Wayne's World*—either the movie or the *Saturday Night Live* skit on which it was based? *Wayne's World,* of course, was a spoof of a hilariously amateurish public-access cable TV show that was supposedly shot with a camcorder in somebody's basement. The show's trademark camerawork: multiple zooms in a single shot. (Such annoying shots are always accompanied by Wayne and Garth shouting, "Unnecessary zoom!")

As rare as zooming is in professional TV and film, *multiple* zooms in a single shot are virtually unheard of. To avoid creating a *Wayne's World* of your own, consider zooming only once, in only one direction, and then *stop* to focus on the target. Don't zoom in, linger, and then continue zooming; and don't zoom in, linger, and then zoom back out (unless you intend to discard half of that shot during editing). Furthermore, on camcorders equipped with a variable-speed zoom, keep the zoom speed consistent. (The slowest zoom is usually the most effective.)

***

Note: There's an exception to the avoid-zooming-in-and-out-while-shooting rule. That's when you're filming a one-of-a-kind event and you're desperate to keep the camera rolling for fear of missing even a second of priceless footage. In that case, zoom all you want to get the shots you want. But do so with the understanding that the good stuff won't be the zooming footage—it will be the scenes *between* zooms.

Later, you can eliminate the unnecessary zooms during iMovie editing.

***

Panning and Tilting

Panning is rotating the camera while recording—either horizontally, to take in a scene that's too wide to fit in one lens-full, or vertically (called *tilting*), to take in a scene that's too tall.

In general, panning is justifiable more often than zooming is. Sometimes, as when you're filming a landscape, a skyscraper, or a moving object, you have no alternative. Standard camcorder lenses simply aren't wide-angle enough to capture grand panoramas in one shot, much to the frustration of anyone who's tried to film New Zealand landscapes, New York skyscrapers, or the Grand Canyon.

Even so, some of the guidelines listed above for zooming also apply to panning:

- Pan only when you have good reason to do so. One of the most common reasons to pan is to *track* a moving target as it moves through space. (Interestingly, professionals pan most of the time from left to right, the way people read, except when a shot is meant to be deliberately disturbing.)

  In fact, almost *any* pan looks better if there's something that "motivates" the camera movement. A car, train, bird flying, person walking, or anything else that draws the eye justifies the pan and gives a sense of scale to the image.

- Begin and end the pan by holding, motionless, on carefully chosen beginning and ending images.

- Make an effort to pan smoothly and *slowly*. This time, you can't rely on the camcorder's electronics to ensure smoothness of motion, as you can when

---

POWER USERS' CLINIC

Recording Entrances and Exits

When it's possible, record the "entrances and exits" of moving subjects in to, and out of, your camcorder's field of vision. For example, if you're filming two people walking, film the space where they're *about* to appear for a moment—and then, when they enter the frame, pan the camcorder to follow their movement. Finally, stop panning and let your subjects walk clear out of the frame.

Entrances and exits like this make more interesting footage than simple follow-them-all-the-way shots. By letting the motion occur within the frame, for example, you emphasize the motion. If a car zooms *across* the screen, and then exits the frame, your viewers can *see* how fast it was going. But if you track the car by panning all the way, you diminish the sense of motion. It's hard to tell how fast a car is moving if it's always centered in a panning shot.

More important, frame entrances and exits can help make your editing job easier, thanks to their ability to disguise discontinuous action. Suppose, for example, that you've got a medium shot of a schoolgirl starting to raise her hand. But the shot ends when her hand is only as high as her stomach. Now suppose that the next shot, a closeup of her face, begins with her hand *entering the frame* from below, whereupon it heads for, and finally scratches, her nose. You can safely cut from the stomach shot to the nose shot; because of the hand's entrance into the frame, your cut looks natural and motivated. The "entrance" disguises the fact that the hand was at stomach level in one frame and at face level in the next.

Without that entrance, you'd wind up with a *jump cut*—an irritating discontinuity in time from one shot to the next.

---

zooming. Bracing your elbows against your sides helps. (If you pan too fast, you may create what's known as a *swish pan*—a blurry shot that's *intended* to be disorienting, as when the main character, being chased through a crowd, is desperately turning his head this way and that in an effort to spot his pursuers.)

- Avoid panning more than once in a shot. Make an effort not to perform such classic amateur maneuvers as the Pan/Linger/Pan or the Pan-to-the-Right, Get-Distracted, Pan-Back-to-the-Left.

- If you're especially gifted with your camcorder, remember that you can also pan and zoom simultaneously. This, too, should be considered a special effect used rarely. But when you are, in fact, filming a closeup of somebody saying, "Look! The top of the building is exploding!" nothing is more effective than a smooth zoom out/pan up to the top of the building.

- *Practice* the pan, tilt, or zoom a couple of times before rolling tape. Each time, the result will be smoother and less noticeable.

- Be careful about panning when your camcorder's electronic image stabilizer (page 23) is turned on. If you're doing a slow pan when the camcorder is on a tripod (as it should be), the shot gets jittery and jumpy as the camera tries to hold onto (or "stabilize") one scene as you rotate a new one into view. If your camcorder is on a tripod, it's safe for you to turn off the electronic stabilization anyway. (*Optical* stabilization doesn't exhibit this problem.)

Tip: If you plan to save your finished iMovie work as a QuickTime movie—a file that plays on your computer screen, rather than a tape that will play on your TV (see Part 3)—panning and zooming slowly and smoothly is especially important. iMovie's compression software works by analyzing the subtle picture differences from one frame to another; if you zoom or pan too quickly, the QuickTime compressors won't understand the relationship between one frame and the next. Blotchiness or skipped frames (which cause jerky motion) may result in the finished QuickTime movie.

Keep the Camera Steady

Here's another difference between amateur and pro footage: Most camcorder movies are shot with a camera held in somebody's hand, which is extremely obvious to people who have to watch it later. Real TV shows, movies, and corporate videos are shot with a camera that's mounted on a massive rolling base, a hydraulic crane, or a *tripod*. (There are a few exceptions, such as a few annoying-to-watch Woody Allen movies. However, they were shot with handheld cameras for an artistic reason, not just because it was too much trouble to line up a tripod.)

It's impossible to overstate the positive effect a tripod can have on your footage. Nor is it a hassle to use such a tripod; if you get one that's equipped with a quick-release plate, the camcorder snaps instantly onto the corresponding tripod socket. Tripods

---

are cheap, too. You can buy one for as little as $20, although more expensive tripods have more features, last longer, and are less likely to nip your skin when you're collapsing them for transport.

Tip: If the camcorder on the tripod isn't perfectly level, the picture will start to tilt diagonally as you pan (the car will appear to be driving up or down a hill instead of across a flat plain). To prevent this phenomenon, make sure that the camera legs are carefully adjusted—slow and tedious work on most tripods. But on tripods with *ball-leveling heads* (an expensive feature, alas), achieving levelness takes just a few seconds: Just loosen a screw, adjust the head until it is level, and tighten the screw down again.

Of course, tripods aren't always practical. When you're trying to film without being noticed, when you don't have the luggage space, or when you must start filming *immediately*, you may have to do without. In those instances, consider one of these alternatives:

- **Turn on the image stabilization feature.** As noted on page 25, every modern DV camcorder includes an *image stabilization* feature, which magically irons out the minor jiggles and shakes associated with handheld filming. Using electronic/digital (as opposed to optical) image stabilization drains your battery faster, so feel free to turn it off when you're using a tripod. But at all other times, the improvement in footage is well worth the power sacrifice.

- **Make the camera as steady as possible.** If you can steady it on top of a wall, on top of your car, or even your own knee, you'll get better results. If there's absolutely nothing solid on which to perch the camcorder, keep your camcorder-hand elbow

---

BUYERS' GUIDE

How to Buy a Tripod

A tripod has two parts: the legs and the *pan head.* The camera attaches to the pan head, and the legs support the head.

You can buy a tripod with any of three pan head types. *Friction heads* are the simplest, least expensive, and most popular with still photographers. Unfortunately, they provide the bumpiest pans and tilts when used for videotaping. *Fluid heads* are the most desirable kind; they smooth out panning and tilting. They're more expensive than friction heads, but are well worth the money if you're after a professional look to your footage. Finally, *geared heads* are big, heavy, expensive, and difficult to use. These are what Hollywood productions use, because they can handle heavy film cameras.

The tripod's legs may be made of metal, wood, or composite. Metal is light and less expensive but easier to damage by accident (thin metal is easily bent). Wood and composite legs are much more expensive and are designed for heavier professional broadcast and film equipment. The bottoms of the legs have rubber feet, which is great for use indoors and on solid floors. Better tripods also have spikes, which work well outdoors on grass and dirt.

Good tripods also have *spreaders* that prevent the legs from spreading apart and causing the entire apparatus to crash to the ground. If your tripod doesn't have spreaders, you can put the tripod on a piece of carpet, which prevents the legs from slipping apart.

In general, you adjust a tripod's height by extending the legs' telescoping sections. Some tripods have a riser column, too, that lets you crank the pan head higher off the legs. Remember that the higher the camera is lifted up, the more unsteady it becomes, so sturdiness is an important characteristic.

pressed tightly against your side, use two hands, and breathe slowly and with control. When you pan, turn from the waist, keeping your upper body straight. Bend your legs slightly to serve as shock absorbers.

Tip: Regardless of your camcorder model, you'll get the best and steadiest results if you use your free hand to brace the *bottom* of the camera. Holding both *sides* of the camcorder isn't nearly as steady.

- **Zoom out.** When you're zoomed in to film something distant, magnifying the image by, say, 10 times, remember that a one-millimeter jiggle gets magnified many times. When you're zoomed in a lot, it's easy to produce extremely unsteady footage. Keep this in mind when deciding how much you want to zoom; the most stable picture results when you're zoomed out all the way. (Zooming also makes focus more critical, as described on page 58.)

- **Consider a monopod.** Despite the enormous boost in stability that a tripod gives your footage, you don't always have the time to unlatch, extend, and relatch each of the three legs. If the kind of shooting you do frequently requires such fast setup and takedown, consider a *monopod*. As much as it sounds like a creature from a sci-fi movie, a monopod is actually a closer relative to a walking stick. It's a collapsible metal post for your camcorder. When using a monopod, you still have to steady the camcorder with your hands (jiggles are still possible), but the monopod eliminates motion from one of the three dimensions (up and down), which is much better than nothing. And the monopod, of course, takes very little time to set up and take down.

- **Get a clamp.** You can also buy viselike clamps equipped with camera plates. You can clamp them to car windows, chair backs, tops of ladders, skateboards, and so on, for even more stable-shooting options. (Put a piece of cloth between the clamp and the surface to prevent scratching.)

Video Lighting: A Crash Course

Today's camera optics are good, but they're not human eyeballs. Every camera, from your camcorder to professional TV and film models, captures truer color, depth, and contrast if lighting conditions are good. The need for bright light grows more desperate if:

- **You record onto videotape instead of film.** Video picks up an even smaller range of light and shadow than film, so having enough light is especially important when using your camcorder. A movie whose acting, sound, and dialog are exceptional can be ruined by poor lighting.

- **You plan to turn your finished production into a QuickTime movie.** If the final product of your video project is to be a QuickTime movie (as described in Part 3), as opposed to something you'll view on TV, you need even *more* light.

  The compression software (*codecs*) that turn your video into QuickTime files do excellent work—*if* the original footage was well lit. When you turn a finished *dim*

---

iMovie production into a QuickTime movie, you'll notice severe drops in color fidelity and picture quality—and a severe increase in blotchiness.

This desperate need for light explains why some camcorders have a small built-in light on the front. Unfortunately, such lights are effective only when shooting subjects just a few feet away. Better still are clip-on video lights designed precisely for use with camcorders. Not every camcorder has a *shoe*—a flat connector on the top that secures, and provides power to, a video light. But if yours does, consider buying a light to fit it. The scenes you shoot indoors, or at close range outdoors, will benefit from much better picture quality.

If your camcorder doesn't have a light attachment, or if you want to get more serious yet, consider deliberately lighting the scene, just like TV and film cinematographers the world over.

Going to this extreme isn't always necessary, of course. If it's just you filming the New Year's Eve party, you're better off not asking the revelers to sit down and be quiet while you set up the lights. But when you're conducting interviews, shooting a dramatic film, making a video for broadcast, or making a QuickTime movie for distribution on a CD-ROM, lights will make your footage look much better.

The following discussion is dedicated to illuminating those more important filming situations. When you want the very best footage, lit the way the pros would light it, the following guidelines, theory, and equipment suggestions will serve you well indeed.

(If you're just shooting kids, relatives, or animals indoors, at least turn on every light in the room.)

Lighting Basics

Cinematographers spend entire careers studying the fantastically complex science of lighting. Here's what they worry about.

Exposure

Exposure refers to light—the amount of illumination the camera picks up. When the scene is too dark, you lose a lot of detail in dark shadows. Worse, your camcorder's AGC (Automatic Gain Circuit, the video equivalent of the audio-leveling circuitry described in the previous section) tries to amplify the available light. The result, which you can see for yourself by filming in dim light, is video *noise* (colored speckles) and unrealistic colors (black becomes a noisy, milky dark gray).

If the scene is too bright, on the other hand, details can wash out, disappearing in white areas.

Contrast

The *contrast ratio* is the ratio of the brightest highlights in a scene to the darkest shadows. Professional filmmakers often set up huge arrays of extra lights to *reduce* the contrast ratio, thus evening out the illumination so that the camera can record more detail accurately. (When watching a movie being filmed, you sometimes see huge lights set up, even in daylight: they're there to fill in the shadow areas, so that the camera can "see," for example, the actors' eyes.)

Film cameras can photograph details in a scene that has a 10:1 contrast ratio (highlights are 10 times brighter than the dark shadow areas). Video, on the other hand, can't capture details outside a contrast ratio of about 3:1 or 4:1. That's another reason lighting is much more important when using a camcorder, as noted above.

Hard light vs. soft light

Hard light comes from a small light source falling directly on an object. It creates hard edges between the highlight and shadow areas. For example, when someone's standing in direct sunlight, the shadows on his face are harsh and dark. This high contrast emphasizes wrinkles, skin blemishes, baggy eyes, and other facial features. In other words, hard light is unflattering light.

Soft light, on the other hand, is less direct, offering softer, smoother gradations of light from brightest to darkest areas. You get soft light from a large light source, usually reflected or diffused, like the outdoors light on an overcast day or the light reflected from the umbrellas used by photographers. The result: soft shadows or no shadows; everything is lit fairly evenly.

Soft light is much more flattering to human subjects, because it de-emphasizes wrinkles and other facial contours. Unfortunately, soft light can also make your subjects appear flat and lifeless. Harder light can reveal contours, shapes, and textures, making objects more interesting and three-dimensional.

The best video lighting, therefore, comes from direct light sources that are mechanically softened. That's why many video lights have milky translucent covers.

Key, fill, and backlight

In professional film and TV work, the most common lighting arrangement is called the *three-point lighting setup.* It requires that you set up at least three light sources, as shown in Figure 2-4:

- The *key* light is the primary source of illumination in a scene. This can be the light on the camera, the sun, the overhead light above a table, or the light from a window, for example.

- The *fill* light comes from a second light source. It's designed to fill in the shadows caused by the key light. By doing so, fill light reduces the *contrast ratio,* allowing the camcorder to pick up more details. If your camcorder has a built-in light, that's usually a fill light, too. It softens the shadows cast by the key light (such as the room lights).

- The *backlight* comes from behind the subject. It helps to separate the subject from the background. Backlight is especially helpful in distinguishing a dark subject (such as a person's hair) and a dark background, because it casts a glow around the rim of the subject's outline.

Be careful, of course: When the light behind the subject is *too* bright, camcorders respond by dimming the entire picture, as described on page 26.

• In professional film and video, technicians sometimes set up a fourth light: the *background* light, which is pointed at the background to make it easier to see (especially in very dark scenes).

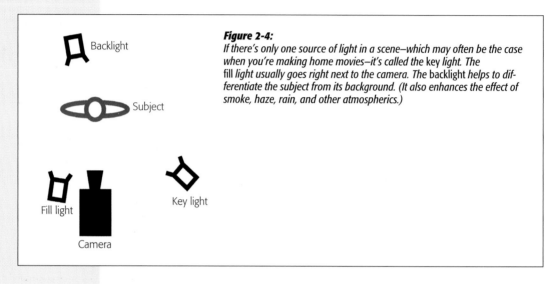

Figure 2-4:
If there's only one source of light in a scene—which may often be the case when you're making home movies—it's called the key light. *The* fill light *usually goes right next to the camera. The* backlight *helps to differentiate the subject from its background. (It also enhances the effect of smoke, haze, rain, and other atmospherics.)*

Labels in figure: Backlight, Subject, Fill light, Camera, Key light

Color temperature

Believe it or not, even ordinary daylight or room light also has a *color.* In general, daylight has a bluish cast, fluorescent light is greenish, and household bulbs give off a yellowish light.

Filmmakers call these color casts the *color temperature* of the light. We don't usually notice the color casts of these common light sources because our eyes and minds have adjusted to it. DV camcorders usually do an excellent job of compensating to avoid noticeable color casts, thanks to the *automatic white balance* in the circuitry of every modern model.

If, even so, you notice that certain shots are coming out too blue, green, or yellow, you can help the camcorder along by switching on one of its *programs* (as several manufacturers call them)—presets for Daylight, Indoor Light, Snow and Ski, and so on. Each is represented in your viewfinder by an icon (such as a sun or a light bulb). When you use these presets, the camcorder shifts its color perception accordingly.

And if even those adjustments don't fix a particular color-cast problem, your camcorder may offer a *manual* white-balance feature. White balancing means identifying to the camera some object that's supposed to look pure white (or colorless), so that it can adjust its circuitry accordingly. To use the manual white-balance feature, focus on something white that's illuminated by the key light—for example, a clean T-shirt or piece of paper. Zoom in until the white area fills the screen, then press the White

Balance button. The camcorder responds by compensating for the dominant color in the light.

The 45/45 Rule

This lighting guideline suggests that the key light be at a 45-degree angle to the camera-subject line and at a 45-degree angle above the ground (see Figure 2-5).

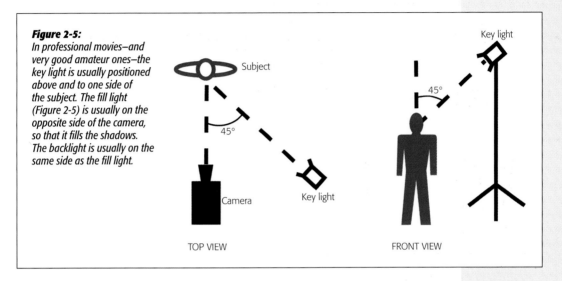

Figure 2-5:
In professional movies—and very good amateur ones—the key light is usually positioned above and to one side of the subject. The fill light (Figure 2-5) is usually on the opposite side of the camera, so that it fills the shadows. The backlight is usually on the same side as the fill light.

Subject

Camera

Key light

TOP VIEW

Key light

45°

FRONT VIEW

General Guidelines for Lighting

The preceding discussion gives you the theory of lighting design. Here's the executive summary—a distillation of that information down into just a few points to remember for the most professional-looking lighting.

- The subject should be brighter than the background. Don't shoot people with a bright window or doorway behind them, unless you want them to disappear into silhouette.

- If the background is bright, shine additional lights on the subject. If you can't do that, use your camcorder's Backlight button or its manual-exposure knob, if it has one, so that the subject is correctly exposed (even if that makes the background too bright).

- Stand so that the key light—the sun, for example—is behind you. Don't shoot a subject with the sun behind her (unless you want silhouettes).

- Avoid a key light that's *directly above* your subject. That arrangement causes ugly, heavy shadows under the eyes, nose, and chin. (The cinematographers for the *Godfather* movies set up lights this way on purpose, so that the mobsters' eyes would be hidden in shadows. That's not the effect you want when filming the mothers-in-law at a wedding ceremony. Usually.)

- If you decide to add lights to your setup, you don't need expensive movie lights. At the hardware store, buy some inexpensive photoreflector lights (those cheap, silver, bowl-shaped fixtures) and equip them with photoflood or tungsten work-light bulbs.

- If you're aiming for professional quality, create soft fill lights by bouncing light off a big square of white foam-core board (which you can get at Kmart, Home Depot, and so on), or a big piece of cardboard covered by foil or newspaper. This arrangement creates a beautiful soft light—great for closeups.

  Bouncing lights off a white ceiling makes for a pleasantly soft key light, too.

- Tracing paper, tissue paper, and translucent plastic (such as shower-door material) make great diffusers for soft light, too. (Just don't put the paper in *contact* with the bulb; this kind of paper, especially tissue paper, ignites easily if it gets too hot.)

- Be alert to the presence of shiny surfaces like windows, glass, chrome, and highly polished wood in your shots. They can reflect your lights into the camera, making it look as though someone is shining a light directly into the lens.

- If the backlight spills into the lens, you get *flares*—those oddly shaped patches of light that move across the frame as the camera pans. The sun behind the subject, or car headlights, often cause flares. If you can avoid this effect, do so.

Figure 2-6:
When you're filming the school play, somebody's head or hat may confuse the autofocus. When you're filming scenery, a nearby branch may similarly fool it (top). The front bars of zoo cages are also notorious for ruining otherwise great shots of the animals inside them. The only solution is to use manual focus (bottom).

Keep It in Focus

A camcorder is a camera, just like any other. If its lenses aren't focused on the subject, you wind up with a blurry picture.

In theory, the autofocus feature of every DV camcorder takes care of this delicate task for you. You point the camera, it analyzes the image and adjusts its own lens mechanisms, and the picture comes out in sharp focus. But in practice, the autofocus mechanism isn't foolproof. Camcorders assume that the subject of your filming is the *closest* object; most of the time, that's true. But now and then, your camcorder may focus on something in the foreground that *isn't* the intended subject. As a result, what you actually wanted to capture goes out of focus, as Figure 2-6 makes clear.

Another autofocus hazard is a solid or low-contrast background (such as a polar bear against a snowy background). The autofocus method relies on contrasting colors in the image. If you're aiming the camcorder at, say, a white wall, you may witness the alarming phenomenon known as autofocus *hunting,* in which the camcorder rapidly goes nearsighted, farsighted, and back again in a futile effort to find a focus level that works.

Other situations that freak out the autofocus include shooting when it's dark, shooting through glass, filming a subject that's not centered in the frame, and high-contrast backgrounds (such as prison or cage bars, French-window frames, and so on), which compete for the autofocus's attention.

Manual Focus

Fortunately, most DV camcorders offer a *manual focus* option: a switch that turns off the autofocus. Now you can (and must) set the focus by hand, turning a ring around the lens (or pushing + and – buttons) until the picture is sharp.

If neither you nor your subject has any intention of moving during the shot, that's all there is to manual focus. Moving shots are trickier, because as the distance between you and your subject changes, you may not have time to fiddle with the focus ring. The best approach is to keep the camera zoomed out all the way as you pan to track the action.

Another potential problem: zooming. When you zoom, your focus changes, too. Fortunately, there's an ancient and very clever trick that circumvents this problem: the zoom-out-and-focus trick. It goes like this:

1. **Zoom all the way in to your subject.**

   You haven't yet begun to record. You're just setting up the shot.

2. **Focus the camcorder manually.**

3. **Zoom back out again.**

As you zoom out, notice what happens: The camcorder remains in perfect focus all the way. (Figure 2-7 shows this sequence.) Now you can begin to film, confident that even when you zoom in, the picture will remain in sharp focus.

In other words, once you've focused at the maximum zoom level, you're free to set the zoom to any intermediate level without having to refocus (*if* you're zooming sparingly and with a purpose, of course).

Video Composition: A Crash Course

The tips in this chapter so far have been designed to turn you from an amateur into a more accomplished technician. Now it's time to train the artist in you.

Even when shooting casual home movie footage, consider the *composition* of the shot—the way the subject fills the frame, the way the parts of the picture relate to each other, and so on. Will the shot be clearer, better, or more interesting if you move closer? What about walking around to the other side of the action, or zooming in slightly, or letting tall grass fill the foreground? Would the shot be more interesting if it were framed by horizontal, vertical, or diagonal structures (such as branches, pillars, or a road stretching away)? All of this floats through a veteran director's head before the camera starts to roll.

Figure 2-7:
For freedom of zooming without worrying about going out of focus, begin by zooming in all the way (top). Then use the focus ring to focus (middle). Now you can zoom in or out to any level, before or during the shot (bottom), and your focus remains sharp all the way.

Be careful, though: Don't zoom in so far that you make the camcorder's digital zoom kick in. Most camcorders zoom in optically (true zoom) for several seconds, and then, as you continue to press the Zoom button, begin the artificial digital zoom that makes the image break up. You can detect the end of the optical zooming in two ways: First, a bar graph in the viewfinder usually identifies the ending point of the true zoom's range. Second, your camcorder may introduce a very short pause in the zooming as it switches gears into digital mode.

Either way, when using the manual focus trick described here, you want to zoom in all the way using your true, optical zoom only.

As an iMovie-maker, you, unlike millions of other camcorder owners, no longer need to be concerned with the sequence or length of the shots you capture, since you can rearrange or trim your footage all you want in iMovie. Your main concern when filming is to get the raw footage you'll need: you can't touch the composition of a shot once you're in iMovie.

Kinds of Shots

You'll hear film professionals talk about three kinds of camera shots: *wide, medium,* and *close* (see Figure 2-8):

- When you're zoomed out all the way, so that the camera captures as wide a picture as possible, you're using a *wide shot*. Wide shots establish context. They show the audience where we are and what's going on. Wide shots make great *establishing* shots, but they can also reveal a lot about the scale and scope of the action even after the scene has begun. (There's a famous crane shot in *Gone With the Wind* that starts on a medium shot of Scarlett O'Hara and then moves up and wide as she walks through a compound filled with hundreds of dying confederate soldiers to reveal a tattered Confederate flag. Thanks to the wide shot, you can see the people she's passing completely, from head to foot.

- *Medium shots* are useful because they eliminate many distractions from the background. By zooming in part way, you let your viewers concentrate more on individuals, and you establish a relationship between objects in the frame. People

Figure 2-8:
A wide shot captures the camcorder's biggest possible picture (top). It gives viewers a sense of place and direction. A medium shot (middle) begins to direct the audience's attention, but still captures some of the surroundings. And a closeup (bottom) is delightful for all concerned, especially if you plan to export your finished iMovie production as a QuickTime movie.

in medium shots are usually visible only from the waist up. Medium shots are by far the most common ones on TV.

- When you're zoomed in a lot, so that your subject fills the screen, you're using a *close shot, tight shot,* or *closeup.* These shots reveal detail, such as a character's reactions, which have a huge impact on how the audience reacts. Close shots are the best kind of shot if you plan to show your movie on a small screen, such as in a QuickTime movie or on a small TV.

Note: You'll hear professionals talk about lots of other kinds of shots, too: the extreme closeup, the extreme long shot, the medium closeup, and so on—but they're all variations on the Big Three.

Choosing your shots

After you're finished editing your video in iMovie, will it be viewed primarily on a computer screen or a TV screen? This important question may affect your choice of zoom level for each shot.

If you plan to make QuickTime movies (for playback on computer screens), use a lot of closeups. Remember that most QuickTime movies play in a small window on the computer screen. Beware the wide shot that looks great on the TV or in the viewfinder, but when shrunk to QuickTime-movie size, reduces faces to white specks on the screen.

Tip: If you're concerned about the *file size* of the finished QuickTime movies—if you intend to email them or post them on a Web site, for example—simpler and steadier shots work best. When iMovie creates the QuickTime movie, it reduces the file size by *discarding* information about parts of the frame that don't change from one frame to the next. Frames filled with clutter, and moving shots, therefore, result in larger QuickTime movie files that take longer to email and download from the Web.

If your iMovie productions are instead destined to be sent back to your camcorder for viewing on a TV, you don't need to be quite so worried about using mostly closeups (although they're still extremely effective on TV). Medium shots are fine, and so is *variety* in your shots, as described in the next section.

Combining shots

When editing footage, professional editors often use a wide shot to show where something is happening, then cut between medium and close shots. Example:

1. **A wide shot reveals the hustle and bustle of a city market.**

   No individual details stand out.

2. **Cut to a medium shot of two people standing next to each other, back to back.**

   Their hands are by their sides.

3. **Cut to a close-up showing the hand of one person passing a small envelope to the other.**

4. Cut back to a medium shot.

The exchange was barely noticeable.

5. Cut away to someone reading a newspaper.

6. Cut in to a closeup of the newspaper guy, showing that he's not actually reading, but is looking over the top of the paper.

7. Cut to a wide shot of the two people who made the hand-off, now starting to walk away from each other.

8. Cut to a medium shot of the person with the newspaper. As he stands up, someone sitting at the table behind him also gets up.

The audience didn't even notice the second person before, because the first shot of the newspaper guy was a closeup.

Of course, you'll do all of this fancy footwork in iMovie, during the editing phase. But you can't create such a dramatic sequence unless you capture the various close, medium, and wide shots to begin with—as you're filming.

As noted earlier, footage that you'll eventually save as a QuickTime movie file should consist mostly of closeups. But regardless of the final format, the best movies feature a variety of shots—a fact that doesn't occur to every camcorder operator.

Tip: It's an excellent idea to set a new scene with an establishing shot, but *when* you film that shot is unimportant. Ever watch a TV sitcom? Almost every segment that takes place in, for example, the Cosby family's apartment begins with an exterior establishing shot of the brownstone building's exterior. Needless to say, those interior and exterior apartment shots were filmed on different days, in different cities, by different film crews. The magic of video editing made it seem like the same time and place.

Figure 2-9:
The Rule of Thirds: Don't put the good stuff in the middle. When shooting someone's face, frame the shot so that the eyes fall on the upper imaginary line, a third of the way down the frame. When two people are in the frame, zoom in so that they're roughly superimposed on the two vertical "rule of thirds" lines. When shooting a panorama, put the horizon line at the bottom-third line to emphasize the sky or tall objects like mountains, trees, and buildings; put the horizon on the upper-third line to emphasize what's on the ground, such as the people in the shot.

The Rule of Thirds

Most people assume that the center of the frame should contain the most important element of your shot. As a result, 98 percent of all video footage features the subject of the shot in dead center. For the most visually *interesting* shots, however, dead center is actually the *least* compelling location for the subject. Artists and psychologists have found, instead, that the so-called Rule of Thirds makes better footage.

Imagine that the video frame is divided into thirds, both horizontally and vertically, as shown in Figure 2-9. The Rule of Thirds says that the intersections of these lines are the strongest parts of the frame. Putting the most interesting parts of the image at these four points, in other words, makes better composition.

Save the center square of the frame for tight closeups and "talking heads" (shots of people standing alone and talking to the camera, as in a newscast). Even then, try to position their eyes on the upper-third line.

Mind the Background

Most home videographers don't pay much attention to the background of the shot, and worry only about the subject. The result can be unfortunate juxtapositions of the background *with* the foreground image—tree branches growing out your boss's head, for example, or you and your camcorder accidentally reflected in a mirror or glass, or a couple of dogs in furious amorous passion 20 feet behind your uncle.

When possible, set up the shot so that the background is OK, and then place your subjects in front of it. If you have no such control—if you're shooting home-movie, reality-TV, or documentary style—move *yourself*. Find a spot where the subject looks better relative to the background, whether it's 6 inches away or 20 feet away.

Professional camera operators, in fact, train themselves to watch the *edges of the frame* while filming, rather than the actors' faces. Doing so ensures that they take in the background, spot such accidental intrusions as reflections of people standing behind the camera, and stand ready to pan or tilt if the subject should move into or out of the frame. If you pay some attention to the shapes rather than people in the frame, composing the shot well becomes much easier. (You can always watch the subject later when you play back your footage.)

Note: Even despite years of training, Hollywood film crews nonetheless occasionally catch unwanted reflections, equipment, and technicians on film. The Internet Movie Database (*www.imdb.com*), for example, maintains message boards where observant moviegoers can report gaffes, such as the scene in *Titanic* where both crew members and equipment are visible as a reflection in Rose's TV.

Framing the Shot

Another way to make a shot more interesting is to let something in the environment *frame* it, subtly altering the shape of the square image of the frame. You might, for example, shoot through a door or window, shoot down a hallway, and so on. Even a tree branch stretching across the top of the frame, emphasizing the horizontal component of the image, makes an interesting shot.

Camera Angle

The camera angle—that is, where you place the camcorder relative to your subject—is your greatest compositional tool. What position in the room or setting gives you the best framing, the best lighting, the least background distraction? Which position gives the shot the best composition?

You know the old stereotype of the movie director who walks slowly in a circle, squinting, peering through a square he frames with his thumbs and index fingers? It's a cliché, for sure, but old-time directors did it for a good reason: They were trying out different camera angles before committing the shot to film.

If you want to capture the best possible footage, do exactly the same thing (although you can just check the camcorder's LCD screen as you walk around instead of looking through your fingers like a weirdo). Before recording *any* shot, whether it's for a casual home movie or an independent film you plan to submit to the Sundance Film Festival, spend at least a moment cataloging your camera placement options.

Tip: When framing any shot, take a step to the left, then a step to the right, just to check things out. You may discover that even that slight a movement improves the shot substantially.

The *vertical* angle of the camera counts, too. Will you be shooting down on your subject, up at it, or straight on? In commercial movies, camera angle is a big deal. Shooting up at somebody makes him look large, important, or threatening; shooting down from above makes him look less imposing.

In home movies, you don't have as much flexibility as you might when shooting a Hollywood film. About all you can do is hold the camcorder while lying down, squatting, sitting up, standing, or standing on a chair. Still, that's a lot more flexibility than most camcorder owners ever exploit.

Tip: Choosing the angle is especially important when filming babies, toddlers, or other cuddly animals. Too many people film them exclusively from a parent's-eye view; you wind up with tapes filled with footage shot from five feet off the floor. As anyone who has ever watched a diaper commercial can tell you, baby footage is much more compelling when it's shot from baby height. Kneel or squat so that the camera puts the viewer in the baby's world, not the parent's.

Capturing Multiple Angles

When you make a movie, you're trying to represent a three-dimensional world on a two-dimensional screen. To give the audience the best possible feeling for the environment where the filming was done—and to create the most interesting possible videos—consider *varying* your shots.

When you're shooting longer scenes, such as performances, interviews, weddings, and scripted movies, consider changing the camera position during the same shooting session. Doing so gives you two benefits: First, it gives your audience a break; whenever the camera angle changes, your footage benefits from a small boost of energy and renewed interest.

In fact, whenever you're shooting something important, cover the same action from different angles and with different kinds of shots. Get wide shots, medium shots, *and* closeups. If you're shooting a scripted movie, have the actors repeat their actions for the different shots, when possible.

When shooting two people in conversation, get more than the standard "two shot" (a composition containing two people, equally prominent, in the same frame). Shoot the two people talking in a wide shot that establishes where they are and how their positions relate. Get a closeup of one person by shooting over the shoulder of the other subject (whose back is therefore to you). If you can shoot the scene a second time, shoot the conversation again, this time from over the other person's shoulder. Keep rolling even when that person's just listening, so that you'll have some *reaction shots* to edit into your finished iMovie.

The second advantage of capturing the same scene from different angles is that it gives you the luxury of *choice* when it comes time to assemble your movie in iMovie. You'll be able to conceal a flubbed line or a bad camera shot by cutting to a continuation of the action in a different piece of footage. Because the new footage will have been shot from a different angle or zoom level, the cut won't feel forced or artificial.

Capture Footage for Cutaways and Cut-Ins

Capturing a scene from more than one angle is a great precaution for another reason, too: You'll often find it extremely useful to be able to *cut away* to a shot of a secondary subject, such as an onlooker or the interviewer's face.

For example, when you're making a scripted movie, the first 30 seconds of dialog may have been terrific in the first take, but the next few lines may have been better in take

---

POWER USERS' CLINIC

The "180 Degree" Rule

When you're filming a scene from several different angles, don't cross "the Line." That's the invisible line that connects two people who are conversing, the two goalposts of the football field, and so on. Change camera angles and positions all you like, but stay on the same *side* of the action.

That's the "180 degree" rule they'll teach you about in film school. If you were to cross this 180-degree angle between the right and left objects in your shot, you'd confuse the audience. Imagine, for example, how difficult it would be to follow a football game if one shot showed the Browns rushing to the right side of the screen, and the next shot (of the same play) showed them running left. Similarly, the audience would become confused if an interviewer and interviewee shifted sides

of the frame from one shot to another. And if you're showing two people talking, you can imagine how disconcerting it would be if you cut from a closeup of one person to a closeup of the other, each facing the *same direction*.

As you watch TV and movies in the coming days and weeks, notice how rigidly directors and cinematographers obey the 180-degree rule. Once the right-to-left layout of the room, scene, or conversation has been established, it doesn't change for the duration of the scene.

The only exception: when the audience *sees* the camera cross the line, so that they get their new bearings as the camera moves. What you should avoid is *cutting* to a different shot on the other side of the 180-degree line.

---

number 4. You'd want to avoid simply editing the second take onto the end of the first; doing so would introduce a *jump cut,* an obvious and awkward splice between two shots of exactly the same image. But if you conceal the snip by briefly cutting away to, for example, the reaction of an onlooker, your viewers will never suspect that the dialog came from two different takes.

Another example, one that's especially pertinent when you're making training or how-to videos: Capture some footage that you can use for *cut-ins.* Cut-ins are like cutaways, in that they're brief interpolated shots that inject some variety into the movie. But instead of splicing in a wider shot, or a shot of somebody who's observing the scene, you splice in a *closer* shot.

When you're filming somebody for a cooking show, you can cut in to a closeup of the whisk stirring the sauce in the bowl. If it's a technology show, you can cut in to the computer screen, and so on. When you're filming a dramatic scene, you can cut to a closeup of the actor's hands twitching, a trickle of sweat behind the ear, or a hand reaching slowly for a weapon.

You'll do all of this cutting in and cutting away during the editing process, not while you're actually filming. Nonetheless, the point in all of these cases is to make sure you've captured the necessary footage to begin with, so that you'll have the flexibility and choice to use such techniques when it comes time to edit. Shoot cutaway candidates near and around your subject—clouds in the sky, traffic, someone sitting at a café table sipping cappuccino, a bird in a tree, and so on—*something* so that you'll have some shot variety when you assemble your final footage. (You can always film your cutaway material after the main shooting is over; when, or even *where,* this supplementary footage is shot makes no difference. In iMovie, you'll make it seem as though it all happened at once.)

Tip: Imagine the difficulty of shooting and editing a movie like *My Dinner With André* (1981)—a conversation between two men seated at the same restaurant table for the *entire* two-hour movie. If this movie had been shot with a single camcorder on a tripod, its audiences would have gone quietly insane. Only the variety of shot types, angles, shot length, and so on make the single setting tolerable. (That and the conversation itself, of course.)

Dolly Shots

One of Hollywood's most popular shot types is one that never even occurs to most camcorder owners: the *dolly shot* or *tracking shot.* That's when the camera moves while shooting.

To create a dolly shot, filmmakers mount the camera on a platform car that glides along what looks like baby train tracks. The purpose of this elaborate setup is, of course, to move the camera along with a moving subject—to follow Kevin Costner running with wolves, for example, or to show the axe-murderer-eye's view of a teenager running away in terror, or to circle the passionately embracing Joseph Fiennes and Gwyneth Paltrow at the end of *Shakespeare in Love.* As a film technique, this one works like gangbusters—not only is it a very exciting shot to watch, but it also puts the viewer directly into the action.

> **Note:** A dolly shot that moves forward isn't the same as simply zooming in. As a quick experiment will show you, the visual result is completely different.
>
> When you zoom, the camera enlarges everything in the picture equally, both foreground and background. When you move forward through space, on the other hand, the distant background remains the same size; only the subject in the foreground gets bigger, which is a much more realistic result. Your viewers are more likely to feel as though they're part of the action and actually in the scene if you dolly forward instead of just zooming.

As a camcorder owner hoping to film, for example, your daughter's field hockey championship, you may find that this business of laying down train tracks on the field isn't always well received by the other parents.

But don't let the expense and dirty looks stop you. When it counts, you can improvise. You can lean out of a car window or sunroof, holding the camcorder as steady as you can, as a relative drives slowly alongside the action. You can film while riding a bicycle. You can persuade a family member to drag you along in an actual Radio Flyer–style wagon in the name of getting more interesting, more professional footage.

The wheelchair solution

Or use a wheelchair. Wheelchairs are remarkably popular with low-budget filmmakers who want to create dolly shots inexpensively. Wheelchairs don't require tracks, are comfortable to sit in while shooting, and provide a stable moving platform.

Figure 2-10:
Both the GlideCam, shown here, and the Steadicam JR require lots of practice and a strong arm, but can create spectacular moving shots. Both Bonfire of the Vanities *and* Goodfellas *include very long shots where we follow the main character as he crosses the street, enters a building, goes down-stairs, through a hall-way, and so on—all in one continuous, very steady shot, thanks to the Steadicam.*

GlideCam and Steadicam JR

You might also consider buying or renting a special camera mount called GlideCam, a padded brace that keeps the camera steady (about $170, Figure 2-10), or even a Steadicam JR (about $550), a scaled-down version of the popular Hollywood tracking device. Both devices incorporate variations of a *gimbal* (a universal ball joint) that intercepts jerks and twists before they can reach the camera; they also distribute the camcorder's center of gravity to keep it even steadier. As a result, the camera stays level and stable even while you're running in a crowd, up and down stairs, and so on.

These ideas may sound extreme, but you'd be surprised at how effective they are. Suddenly you have access to one of Hollywood filmmakers' favorite tricks. Sure you'll feel silly riding through the neighborhood in your kid's Radio Flyer wagon—but how do you think professional camera operators feel riding along on their little choo-choos?

Special Event Filming

I f all you intend to do with your camcorder is to capture random events of child-hood charmingness around the house, you can skip this chapter. Just keep your camcorder lying handy, its battery charged and its tape compartment occupied, and you'll be all set.

Chances are, however, that once you've got the iMovie bug, you may become more inspired. It may occur to you to take your camcorder out of the house—to shoot the school play, your kid's sports game, your cousin's wedding, and so on. Maybe you'll decide to use the camcorder for more serious work, such as transferring your old photos to DV to preserve them forever, creating a family history by interviewing relatives, shooting a documentary, or even making a scripted movie.

Each of these situations can benefit from a little forethought, plus a few tips, tricks, and professional techniques. This chapter is designed as a handbook to help you make the most of these common camcorder-catchable events.

Interviews

What's great about an interview is that you know it's coming. You've got time to set up your tripod, arrange the lighting, and connect an external microphone, as described in Chapter 2. (Do all of this before your subject arrives, by the way, since nothing makes an interview subject more nervous than having to sit around beforehand, just growing apprehensive.) Because you've got this extra time to plan ahead, there's no reason your interview footage can't look almost identical in quality to the interviews you see on TV.

Chapter 2 describes the basics of good camcorder footage. Well, in an interview situation, the same tips apply. Lighting is important: avoid having the brightest light behind the subject's head. Sound is critical: fasten a tie-clip microphone to your subject's lapel or collar.

Above all, use a tripod. You'll be glad you did, not only because the picture will be stable, thus permitting the audience to get more "into" the subject's world, but also for your own sake. Even the lightest camcorder is a drag to hold absolutely motionless for more than five minutes.

But interviews offer some additional challenges. If you've ever studied interviews on TV, such as the *60 Minutes* interviews that have aired every Sunday night since 1968, you realize that the producers have always thought through these questions:

- **What's the purpose of the interview?** The answer affects how you shoot the scene. On *60 Minutes,* the purpose is often to demonstrate how guilty or shifty the subject is. Bright lights and a black background help to create this impression, as do the ultra-closeups favored by the *60 Minutes* crew, in which the camera is zoomed in so tight that the pores on the subject's nose look like the craters on Mars.

  In interviews that aren't designed to be especially incriminating, however, the purpose of the interview is often to get to know the subject better. The setting you choose can go a long way toward telling more of the subject's story. Set the interview somewhere that has some meaning for, or tells something about, your subject. If it's a CEO, shoot it in her office across her handsome mahogany desk; your wide establishing shot will telegraph to your viewers just how magnificent this office is. If it's your grandfather, shoot it in his study or living room, where the accumulated mementos on the end tables suggest his lifetime of experiences. (When possible, get these cutaway and establishing shots before or after the actual interview, so as not to overwhelm your interviewee or waste his time.)

- **Who's going to ask the questions?** In professional interviews, of course, the camera person doesn't ask the questions. One person operates the camera, while another conducts the interview. If you can arrange to have a buddy help with your interview, it'll go a *lot* better. She (or you) can chat with the subject while the lights and microphones are being adjusted, for example.

  If you, the camcorder operator, absolutely must double as the interviewer, take your microphone situation into account. If your subject is wearing a tie-clip microphone, then your questions will be recorded very softly, as though coming from far away. If you're not using an external microphone, you'll have the opposite problem. Since you're standing right next to the camera, the sound of your voice will be very loud on the finished tape, in unfortunate contrast to the much fainter sound of your subject's replies.

  You can usually find solutions to all of these problems. For example, you can use a single, *omnidirectional* mike (see page 42) that sits between you and your subject. Or you could connect *two* external mikes to your camcorder by way of a portable mixer, which accepts (and lets you adjust the volume of) several inputs simultaneously. (Radio Shack and video-equipment Web sites sell these items.)

Tip: If you are both the camera operator and the interviewer, and you decide that you want to be on-camera along with your interview subject, use the remote control that comes with most camcorder models. Open the LCD screen and rotate it so that it's facing you as you sit in front of the camera–that's the only way for you to frame the shot when you're not actually standing behind the camcorder.

- **Is the interviewer part of the interview?** In other words, will the audience see the person asking the questions? If so, you've got a challenge on your hands. You've got two people sitting across from each other, facing opposite directions, but only one camera to film them with.

  If you ever saw the 1987 movie *Broadcast News,* you know how TV professionals solve this problem. Before or after the interview, they capture some establishing-shot footage of the two people sitting there face to face. They also take some footage of the interviewer alone—nodding sagely in agreement, smiling in understanding, frowning in concern, and so on. They film him asking the questions again, even after the interview subject has left the scene. Later, when editing the finished product, they splice these reaction shots into the interview footage, as you can do in iMovie. The audience never suspects that the entire interview was shot with one camera.

  On the other hand, in many interviews, you don't see the interviewer at all. You hear her voice, but you don't see her on-camera. (A disembodied voice like this is called a *voice-over.* Voice-overs are extremely common in TV ads, movies with narration, and episodes of *The Wonder Years.*)

  Sometimes you don't see *or* hear the interviewer, such as when the producer just wants a comment or sound bite from the interview subject. In those situations, invite your subject to phrase his answers as complete sentences. Otherwise, after the questions have been edited out, you'll be left with an interview subject saying, "Yes…that's right…no, I don't think so," and other unhelpful utterances.

Tip: If you, the interviewer, will ultimately be edited out of the movie, you can greatly assist your own cause by framing your questions cleverly. Avoid yes-or-no questions. Don't ask, "Were you happy with your performance?" Instead, ask, "Tell us about how you felt," for example.

That's what professionals do. Now you know why, when asked "You just won the Olympics. Where are you going to go now?" nobody in the Disney World ads ever just says, "Disney World!"

- **How long will the interview be after editing?** If the finished product will be more than a couple of minutes long, think about keeping your viewers' interest up by introducing some variety into the camera work, as described in the previous chapter.

  Capture some wide shots, for example, for use as cutaways. That way, when you edit the interview in iMovie, you'll be able to offer a refreshing change of shot now and then.

Cutaways are also ideal for masking cuts in the interview footage. It's a convenient fact of life that you can't see somebody's lips moving when filming from behind them, or when the camera is far away. In other words, you can use a cutaway even while your interview subject is still talking. Your viewers won't be able to detect that the cutaway footage was actually shot at a different time. (TV news editors use this technique all the time—they briefly cut to a shot behind the subject's head in order to conceal an edit between two parts of the same interview.)

- **How conservative is the interview?** The answer to this question affects how you frame the subject in your lens. Some interviews are designed to be hip, like the ones on MTV, the *Bunting's Window* computer show shown on airplanes, or fight sequences in the old *Batman* series. These might feature a handheld camera, off-center framing, or even a camera mounted off-kilter on its tripod for that added wackiness.

If wackiness isn't exactly what you're going for, however, the framing shown in Figure 3-1 is about right.

Figure 3-1:
As in any footage, interviews should offer some variety of composition and zoom amount. But for maximum viewer comfort, most pro video interviews capture the speaker from shoulders up, with a little bit of space left above the head. (Here, you're seeing more of the subject's torso, just so you can see the tie-clip microphone.) If the subject is supposedly looking at something off-camera—the interviewer, for example—professionals leave some talk space in the shot. That is, a little extra room in front of the person's face, as shown here.

- **How is the shot set up?** In most interviews, the interview subject doesn't look directly into the camera—except when she's recording a Last Will and Testament. Usually she's looking just off-camera, at a spot a couple of feet to one side of the camcorder, or even directly across the camcorder's line of vision. That's where the interviewer should sit, so that the subject looks at the right spot naturally.

The camcorder should be level with the subject's face, which is yet another argument for using a tripod.

Tip: If you're the interviewer, here's one tip that has nothing to do with the technicalities of your camcorder and tripod: *Listen* to the answers. Many inexperienced interviewers are so busy thinking about the next question that they miss golden opportunities for further lines of questioning. Worse, the interview subject will detect that you're not really paying attention, so the interview won't go nearly as well as it could.

Music Videos

Few camcorder endeavors are as much fun as making a music video, whether it's a serious one or a fake one just for kicks.

Of course, your interest in this kind of video technique may depend on your age and taste. But music videos are worth studying, no matter who you are, because they frequently incorporate every conceivable camera trick, editing technique, and shooting style. The day you shoot a music video is the day you can try punching every button on your camcorder, unlocking those weird special effects you've never even tried, and using all the unnecessary zooms you want. Better yet, this is the day when you don't care a whit about microphones or sound. Eventually, you'll discard the camcorder's recorded sound anyway. As you splice your footage together in iMovie, you'll replace the camcorder's soundtrack with a high-quality original recording of the song.

Figure 3-2:
Because you have iMovie, you can pull off a fascinating visual stunt that's very common in rock videos: the jumping-flea-musician effect, in which, every few seconds, everybody in the scene blips into a new position (or appears and disappears), sometimes in time to the music. (You're actually creating jump cuts, *which you should avoid except when creating special effects like this.) Creating this effect is simple—if your camcorder has a tripod. Just shoot each segment, moving your musicians around when the camera isn't moving. In iMovie, the splices will be exactly as sharp and convincing as they are on MTV (or* Bewitched*).*

Some music videos are lip-synched—that is, the performers pretend that they're singing the words on the soundtrack. Other videos are voice-over, narrative, or experimental videos. In these videos, you don't actually see anybody singing, but instead you watch a story unfolding (or a bunch of random-looking footage). If you decide to create a lip-synched video, take a boom box with you in the field. Make sure it's playing as you film the singers, so that they're lip-synching with accurate timing.

When it comes time to edit the music video in iMovie, you'll be able to add the little lower-left-corner credits (the name of the song, the group name, and so on) with extremely convincing results. You'll also be able to add crossfades, transitions, graphics, and other common rock-video elements (see Figure 3-2).

Live Stage Performances

Filming a live stage performance, such as a play, musical, concert, or dance, is extremely challenging. It poses four enormous challenges: capturing the sound, getting power, capturing the picture, and getting permission in the first place.

Getting Permission

At most professional performances, the management doesn't permit camcorders. Whether union rules, copyright rules, house rules, or simple paranoia is at play, the bottom line is that using a camcorder (or any camera) is usually forbidden.

That leaves you two alternatives: Confine your footage to performances where camcorders are OK, such as the choir concert at the elementary school—or film surreptitiously. (As the size of DV camcorders shrinks year by year, the latter option is becoming ever more popular among people who don't mind flouting the rules.)

Capturing the Sound

When you're filming a performance from the audience, your camcorder gets hopelessly confused. It's programmed to record the closest sounds, which, in this case, are the little coughs, chuckles, and seat-creaks of the audience members around you. The people on stage, meanwhile, come through only faintly, with the hollow echo that comes from recording people who are far away from the microphone. As any camcorder buff who's filmed her kid's school play can tell you, the resulting video is often very unsatisfying.

You have alternatives, but they require some effort. One option is to equip your camcorder with an external microphone—a *unidirectional*-style one. Mount it on a pole that puts the microphone over the audience's heads.

If the show has its own sound system—that is, if it's miked and amplified—you may be able to snake an external microphone up to the speaker system, so that your camcorder is benefiting from the microphones worn by every actor. Better yet, you can sometimes persuade the management to let you hook up your camcorder to the sound system itself. Connect the cable to the *audio* input of your camcorder, if you have one. (Unfortunately, connecting it to the *microphone* input may overload your sound circuitry and produce distortion.)

Getting Power

Before worrying about the visual quality of your live-performance footage, worry about the power. Are the batteries charged? Do you have enough battery power to film the entire show? If so, have you thought about when you can swap batteries without missing something good?

If you're filming with permission, you may be able to plug your camcorder into a power outlet, which neatly solves this problem. Unfortunately, because of the extension cord tripping hazard, this solution presents itself fairly rarely. (If you do get permission to lay down extension cords, tape them to the floor using duct tape, like generations of professional film crews before you.)

Capturing the Picture

Now you've got to worry about where you're going to sit or stand. Sometimes you don't have a choice—you'll just have to sit in your seat and do the best you can. (Keep your LCD screen closed when shooting; keeping it open both distracts the other audience members and gets you in trouble with management.)

Thanks to the powerful zoom feature on today's camcorders, standing at the back of the theater is frequently a more attractive alternative. There you may even be able to use a tripod, much to the benefit of your footage and the relief of your muscles. Doing so means that the camcorder will be able to shoot over the heads of the audience members—another real advantage over shooting from your seat.

Technically speaking, filming a live performance on a fairly distant, brightly lit stage requires three special considerations:

- **Use the manual focus trick.** Nowhere is this secret (see page 59) more useful than when you're filming a live stage performance. Autofocus generally fails you in these circumstances, because the camera tries to focus on the nearest object—the head of the lady in row 34. This autofocus syndrome, which arbitrarily blurs the picture as you film, is the number-one destroyer of homemade performance videos.

  Use the manual focus to get the picture sharpened up in its fully zoomed-in state before you begin rolling tape. Then you'll be able to zoom in or out during the performance without ever worrying about the focus.

- **Adjust the exposure.** Stage lights and spotlights throw camcorders for a loop. These lights pour very bright light onto the performers' faces, but throw normal light on the rest of the set. The result is a broad spectrum of brightness—too broad for a camcorder's sensors. The auto-exposure feature of your camcorder does its best to figure out its mission, but it usually makes a mess of things in medium or wide shots, turning every actor's face into a radioactive white blur with no features at all (see Figure 3-3).

  Solving the problem requires you to *override* the auto-exposure feature. Consult the camcorder's manual for instructions. On Sony camcorders, for example, you press the Exposure button on the left side of the camera and then turn a thumb knob to adjust the exposure. Turn this knob downward to make the picture darker. After a moment, you'll see the features return to the actors' faces.

Be ready to turn that exposure knob the other way on short notice, however. You can expect the stage lights to be full up during the big, full-cast, song-and-dance numbers, but other scenes may be lit dimly for dramatic effect. Such scenes are equally troublesome for camcorders, since turning up the exposure knob can help a lot but may introduce graininess to the picture. There's not much you can do in this situation, because camcorders simply thrive on light.

Tip: Whenever you use your camcorder's manual exposure control, be very careful about trusting your LCD monitor for feedback. On most camcorders, this screen has its *own* brightness control, which, when set to a very bright or very dim setting, can lead you astray as you set your exposure knob. For best results, gauge the effect of your manual exposure fiddling by looking only through the eyepiece viewfinder.

Figure 3-3:
The solution to the bright-face syndrome in shows (left) is to turn down the exposure (right). Unfortunately, when the actors' faces look good, the set may wind up too dark.

- **Know the show.** The best performance videos are made by somebody who's familiar with the performance. Only they know in advance when to use a wide shot, when to use a closeup, and so on.

When you're zoomed out all the way, you can't see any faces—a distinct drawback in a dramatic performance. For this reason, you'll be tempted to use the zoom a lot when you're filming a theatrical performance. Unfortunately, actors have a habit of *moving* during the scene—from the camcorder operator's standpoint, a distinctly annoying behavior. No sooner have you found your kid and zoomed into his face when he *moves,* leaving you to film seven seconds of empty set as you try to hunt for a human being. (Professionals learn to keep both eyes open when shooting. One eye is on the eyepiece when framing, and the other eye occasionally looks around to see what else is happening in the scene and to prepare for subjects that might enter the frame.)

If it's possible to attend a dress rehearsal or a previous performance, therefore, your footage will be vastly improved. You'll know in advance when the big, full-stage moments come, and when to zoom in for closeups.

Tip: If the show is really important, consider shooting it *twice.* At the second performance, position the camera in a different place and shoot different kinds of shots. Later, you can use iMovie to combine the footage from the two performances. By splicing in one camera's shot, then the other—thereby changing camera angles and zoom amounts without missing a beat—you simulate the effect of having two cameras at the same performance.

You also have a backup in case you missed a key entrance, joke, or pratfall during the first performance.

Speeches

What to worry about when filming talks, presentations, and speeches: the sound. Exactly as when filming live stage performances, your camcorder's built-in microphone does a lousy job of picking up a speaker more than 10 feet away. To remedy the problem, use a tie-clip microphone on extension cords, get a wireless mike, or run an external microphone to the loudspeakers (if the talk is amplified) or even directly to the sound system's mixing board.

Otherwise, the only other problem you'll encounter is the question-and-answer session, if there is one. In an auditorium situation, not only will you have a terrible time (because there isn't *enough* time) trying to train the camera on the person asking the question, but you won't pick up the sound at all. You can only pray that the guest speaker will be smart enough to repeat the question before providing the answer.

Tip: Capturing audience reaction shots for use as cutaways is a great idea when you're recording a talk. Splicing these shots into the finished iMovie film can make any speech footage more interesting, and gives you the freedom to *edit* the speech if necessary.

If your goal is to capture the entire talk, and you've got only a single camcorder, you'll have to get the reaction shots *before or after* the talk. Don't just pan around to the audience while the speaker is speaking.

Sports

Filming sporting events is, in general, a breeze. Most take place outdoors, neatly solving all lighting problems, and the only sound that's important at a sporting event is usually the crowd's reaction, which your camcorder captures exquisitely. Most of the time, you'll be zoomed out all the way, because there's too much motion to worry about closeups. (And when you *do* want closeups, you'll know exactly when to zoom out again, thanks to the structured nature of most sports. Every baseball play begins the same way, for example.)

If your aim is to film a player for training purposes, or to study a golf swing or tennis stroke as it's played back in slow motion or frame by frame, consider using your camcorder's *high-speed shutter* feature. When you use this special recording mode, the camcorder records the action in a strange, frame-flashing sort of way. When you play this footage back, you can use the slow-motion or freeze-frame controls on your camcorder with sensational, crisp, clear results.

Caution: The high-speed shutter is effective only in *very* bright, sunny, outdoor light. If you try to use it indoors, outdoors when it's overcast, or in shadow, all kinds of unpleasant side effects result. You may get flickering and stuttering motion, the autofocus feature may stop working, colors may not look right, and the picture in general will seem too dim.

Photos and Old Movies

Most people associate video with *moving* images, but video "slideshows" can be extremely satisfying to watch, especially if you add commentary or music in iMovie, as described in Chapter 8. With a tripod, a music stand, and good lighting, your camcorder is all set to preserve your family photos forever.

If the photos were taken with a digital camera, there's nothing to it: Just import them as described in Chapter 9.

The challenge is what to do about photos that *aren't* digital—the old kind, the paper kind, the kind you'll confront if you put together a biographical video about anyone who's more than six years old.

Old Photos

Tactic one: Get the old pictures into the Mac using a scanner. As described in Chapter 9, you can then drop them into your iMovie storyboard electronically, without having to mess with lights, focus, tripod, and so on.

Tactic two: Film the photos with the camcorder. Take each photo out of its frame, prop it on a music stand or tape it to the wall, and slip a big black piece of cardboard behind it. Set up the camcorder so that it's directly aimed at the photo (otherwise, the photo may look skewed or distorted when filmed). Use the manual focus on your camcorder, zoom in an appropriate amount, position the tripod and lights so that there's no glare, and begin shooting. If you're getting glare from the photo, use two lights, one on each side of the photo, each at a 45-degree angle to it.

Scanning produces a more professional effect. Still, filming the photos gives you some interesting creative possibilities, like surrounding each photo with meaningful memorabilia, capitalizing on late-afternoon sun slanting in through a window, and so on.

Shooting Slides

You can transfer slides to your movie in either of two ways:

- Project the slides onto a slide screen or white wall, and then film them with your camcorder. To make the slide's image sharper, put the projector as close as possible to the screen. Position the camera right next to the projector, so that it doesn't wind up filming the projected slide at an angle.

- Have a Kodak shop or a local service bureau scan your slides, transferring them to a CD-ROM. (If your scanner has a slide attachment, you may even be able to do this yourself, although it can be a finicky procedure.) Then you can import the slides electronically into iMovie, as described in Chapter 9. This method ensures the highest possible quality and saves you a lot of setup hassle.

Transferring Old Movies to DV

Transferring old movies to the camcorder is another good idea. If these older movies are on videotape, such as VHS cassettes or 8mm videotapes from an older camcorder, you're in good shape. Transferring them onto your DV camcorder is fairly easy, if you have the right equipment (see Chapter 4).

Transferring old *film* to your camcorder is a more difficult proposition. Photographic catalogs sell mirror-based gadgets just for this purpose. In essence, this apparatus lets you run the film projector, which projects the old movie onto a tiny movie screen. Your camcorder simply films the film. Unfortunately, the camcorder can pick up quite a bit of grain and picture deterioration in the process.

You can also send your old reels out to a commercial transfer shop. Most local photo-developing outfits and camera shops will handle this transaction for you.

Weddings

Ah, weddings! Everybody loves weddings—especially camcorder manufacturers. Talk about once-in-a-lifetime (all right, very-*few*-times-in-a-lifetime) occasions! What bigger event could there be to drive somebody to buy a camcorder?

Where to Stand

If you're just a friend or family member in the audience, you've got no choice about where to position the camcorder. You'll have to shoot from your seat or stand in the back.

But suppose that you're a wedding videographer—or becoming one. (That's an excellent idea, by the way, if you've been thinking about going into business for yourself. You, with your *digital* camcorder and iMovie, can advertise your superior equipment, lower costs, and greater editing flexibility when compared with all the poor slobs still lugging around older, analog equipment.)

From the videographer's standpoint, weddings are tricky. If you've only got one camcorder, where do you stand during the vows? From the spectators' side, where you can't capture the faces of the bride and groom? Or from the opposite side, where you get the bride and groom, but can't see the scene the way the spectators see it? Here are a few solutions:

- **Film the rehearsal.** The idea is that later, in iMovie, you can splice in some of this footage as though it were captured with a second camera on the day of the wedding. The rehearsal isn't usually "in costume," of course, so you won't fool anyone with your footage of the bride and groom in their sweatshirts and blue jeans. But the presiding official (minister, rabbi, justice of the peace) may well be in official garb at rehearsal time. At the very least, you can grab some footage of him at the rehearsal. With his lines and reaction shots already in the can, you can spend your time during the actual ceremony standing and filming from behind him.

- **Really use a second camera.** Videographers make about $1,000 per wedding, so after one wedding, you'll have made enough money to buy a second camcorder. If you have an assistant who can operate it, you've solved your "where should I stand?" dilemma.

  But if you don't have an assistant, you can set this second camcorder up in the back of the hall, in the balcony, or behind the presiding official, and just let it run unattended. Once again, iMovie will be your salvation; you'll be able to incorporate footage from the second camcorder whenever your editing instincts tell you that it's time for a refreshing new angle.

- **Shoot from behind the official.** If none of these ideas work for you, film some of the wedding from the audience's point of view. But during the vows, get yourself up onto the dais and shoot over the official's shoulder. In the end, what everybody wants from your wedding video is to see the faces of the bride and groom as they pledge their love forever—something they *didn't* get to see during the actual wedding.

Getting the Sound

This is the big one. If there was ever an event where recording the words was important, this is it. If you're just a friend shooting from the audience, the sound will probably be weak unless you use one of the tricks described on page 72.

If you're the hired videographer, however, your responsibility to get clearly audible sound is even greater. Maybe you bought one of the pro camcorders with a shotgun mike described in Chapter 1. It will do splendidly if you film from behind the presiding official, only a few feet from the bride and groom.

Otherwise, equip the groom with a wireless mike, if he'll permit it. This usually entails slipping a little transmitter into his pocket and running a tiny wire up to his lapel.

If he objects, well, it's his wedding. But remind him that his one wireless mike will also pick up the words of the bride and the official, too, thanks to their close proximity during the vows.

And for goodness' sake, wear Walkman headphones to monitor the sound when you shoot the actual ceremony. Your videography career will come to a quick and miserable end if you play back the footage and discover that the wireless mike wasn't transmitting.

Tip: Many professional videographers these days invest in a Sony MiniDisc recorder, which looks like a Walkman but contains a half-size, recordable CD. It records extremely high-quality sound, and serves as a great backup sound-recording unit at weddings. When you return to your Mac, you can transfer the audio into the computer and then import it into iMovie (as described in Chapter 8). The sound won't perfectly match the video for more than a few minutes at a time, but your clips are probably short enough that such "sync drift" won't be a problem.

Being Unobtrusive

Anyone who hires a wedding videographer has already swallowed hard and accepted that there's going to be somebody running around the ceremony with a bunch of

22 Shots for Your Wedding Video

Take it from a wedding-video veteran, Doug Graham of Panda Video Productions: There's a certain set of shots you've *got* to include if you're the one who's been asked to film it. Here they are:

1. Bride and bridesmaids dressing. (Keep it G-rated!)

2. Exterior of the church.

3. Wedding party arriving at church.

4. Continuous roll of the ceremony, from prior to bride's entrance to the couple's walk down the aisle at the end. Use two cameras, if you can—place one in the back third of the church. Using the handheld, position yourself on the bridesmaids' side of the aisle at the altar steps. Shoot the procession. After the bride arrives, move to a tripod placed behind the officiant and on the groom's side. This gives the best shot of the bride during the vows. (Coordinate and clear this with the officiant beforehand.)

If you can, take a moment later to film a reenactment of the ring ceremony. Get a good closeup of rings being slipped onto fingers, which you can splice into iMovie later.

5. Any special touches in the ceremony, like a solo song, unity-candle lighting, and so on.

6. Reaction shots of bride's and groom's families.

7. The photographer's formal posed shots.

8. Wedding party leaving church.

9. Wedding party arriving at reception. (This'll take some good planning and fast driving on your part!)

10. Bride and groom entering reception.

11. First dance.

12. Mom's dance with the groom.

13. Dad's dance with the bride.

14. Best man's toast.

15. Cake cutting.

16. Garter toss.

17. Guestbook signings.

18. Special dances and ceremonies at the reception.

19. Interviews with guests.

20. Interview with the bride and groom.

21. Footage for use as cutaways: cake, presents, decorations, flower arrangements, the DJ or band. Get a copy of the wedding announcement, and souvenirs (such as specially printed napkins), so that you can film them for closeups later.

22. Guests saying goodbye.

Don't shoot: People eating. Backs of heads. People backlit by windows. Drunks.

Interviews at a wedding are a real art. I just have the guests pass around the mike and ask them to "say a few words to the happy couple." Some good leading questions might be:

- What can you tell me about how Bill and Sue met?

- What did you feel when you learned they were engaged?

- What do you think Bill should do to keep Sue happy?

- Where do you think Bill and Sue will be years from now?

- What do you think Sue loves most about Bill?

When interviewing the bride and groom, I do it individually, rather than together. I ask each of them the same questions: How did you meet? Tell me how the relationship grew. When did you first know Tim was the "one"? Tell me about how he proposed? What are your plans for the future?

Then I cut the responses together when editing. The juxtaposition of the two viewpoints can be funny, touching, or poignant.

I always remind my on-camera folks to answer questions in complete sentences. For example, if I ask "What's your name?", I don't want, "Joe." I want, "My name is Joe." That way, I can edit out my questions later, and the response will be complete in itself.

electronics. Fortunately, your equipment is much smaller than non-DV equipment—a great feature at weddings.

Still, you should use as much tact and foresight as possible. Scope out the hall before the ceremony, and speak to the presiding official to discuss your plans. Use video lights if you can, but accept that your clients may object to the clutter. And use only battery power, as duct-taping extension cords to the carpeting doesn't always go over well in houses of worship.

Tip: If it's your responsibility to film a wedding or some other important event, take an extra fully charged battery and extra blank tapes. You may think that this is obvious advice, but there's absolutely nothing worse than forgetting it and missing half of the most important day of your client/friend/sister's life.

Actual Scripted Films

For a steadily growing subset of camcorder owners, this is the Big Kahuna, the *raison d'être*, the Main Event: making a real movie, complete with dialog, actors, and a plot. Ever since *The Blair Witch Project* made $140 million—a movie made by recent film-school grads with a camcorder, no funding, and no Hollywood connections—independent films have become a *very* big deal.

You can post your homemade movies on the Web sites listed in Chapter 14, where 200 million Internet citizens can watch them. The most popular ones get Hollywood-studio attention. There are even a growing number of film festivals dedicated to showing homemade (usually DV) films. In the sixties, Americans used to say that anyone could grow up to be president. Today, we say that anyone can make a Hollywood movie.

The world, and the library, is filled with books on making traditional movies. However, the process is much more difficult than making the kinds of movies described so far in this chapter. In addition to all of the technique and technical considerations you've read about so far, you now have to worry about plot, scripts, continuity, marketing, actors, characters, costumes, props, sets, locations—and budget. You'll go through these phases of creation:

- **Writing the screenplay.** Most movies begin with a script—or at the very least, a *treatment* (a 5- to 30-page prose synopsis of the movie's story line that's usually designed to attract interest from backers).

  If you send your screenplay to Hollywood in hopes of getting it made into a movie, your competition is 250,000 other people every year who also send unsolicited scripts. Like them, you'll get yours back soon enough, too; to avoid being accused of stealing ideas, Hollywood studios don't even open unsolicited scripts. Even if you have a connection to someone who'll look at your screenplay, it won't be taken seriously unless it's prepared using extremely specific page formatting, which you can read about in any of dozens of screenwriting books.

Fortunately, if you're going to make your own movie, it doesn't make one bit of difference how your screenplay is formatted. Format it however you like, just so your actors can read it.

- **Location.** You'll have to figure out where you're going to shoot each scene—and get permission to shoot there. Does the restaurant owner know, for example, that you'll be bringing in lights and sound equipment?

Tip: Instead of traveling to a special location for shooting, you can often save money and hassle by turning your own backyard or living room into a set. Just a few key props and set dressings may be enough to suggest, for example, an office, jungle, or police station—especially if it's preceded, in your movie, by an establishing shot showing your characters going *into* such a building.

- **Preproduction.** Before shooting, make "shopping lists." Go through the script and make lists of which actors are in which scenes, what clothes and props they'll need for those scenes, and so on. *Preproduction,* the planning phase, is where a production is set up to succeed or fail.

  You should also make a written list of the shots that you want to get, so that when everyone arrives on the set and all hell breaks loose, you won't forget any critical shots. Lists prevent memory blocks.

- **Actors.** Who's going to star in your movie? You can get friends to do it, of course. You can recruit people from acting classes, colleges, or theaters in your area. They'll probably be delighted to participate, in exchange for nothing but the experience, good treatment, and *good food.* (You'd be surprised how important the food is.)

  Or you can get professional actors, with the help of a talent agency. You choose them by holding an audition, and you pay for their participation.

- **Editing.** After you've shot the various scenes of your movie—which, of course, you don't have to do in sequence—you'll assemble the film in iMovie. This is where you decide how long each shot should take, which camera angle to use, which *take* to use (which of several versions of the scene you've shot), and so on.

  In the real film world, this editing phase, called *postproduction,* often takes longer than the actual filming. Incredible magic takes place in the cutting room; the film editor alone can make or break the feeling, mood, and impact of the movie. You can read more about editing tricks in Chapter 10.

If you've never made an actual movie before, start small. Make a *short* (a brief movie), which, in the age of independent films, is becoming an increasingly popular format. (In March 2000, Woody Allen made a *six-minute* movie to protest the construction of a skyscraper in a beloved area of Manhattan.) Starting with a short film is a great idea not just because it prevents you from biting off more than you can chew, but also because the average Mac's hard drive can't hold more than about 60 minutes of raw footage at a time.

Making a short is also excellent practice for reducing a movie down to its absolutely essential elements, trimming out the superfluous shots and scenes—a highly prized talent that will pay off when you graduate to full-length movies. As they say in the biz: "If it doesn't move the story forward, it holds it back." (More editing advice in Chapter 10.)

Part Two:
Editing in iMovie

2

Camcorder Meets Mac

Phase 1 is over. You've captured the raw footage on your camcorder, you've now assembled the ingredients you need, and you're ready to enter the kitchen. Now it's time for Phase 2, the heart of this book: editing your footage on the Mac using iMovie. This chapter introduces you to both iMovie and FireWire, the high-speed cable system that transfers footage from the camcorder to the Mac, gives you a tour of the iMovie window, and walks you through your first transfer.

iMovie HD: The Application

So far in this book, you've read about nothing but *hardware*—the equipment. In the end, however, the iMovie story is about *software*, both the footage as it exists on your Mac and the iMovie program itself.

iMovie on a New Mac

If you bought a new Mac since the spring of 2005, iMovie HD is probably already on your hard drive. Open the Macintosh HD icon→Applications folder. Inside is the icon for iMovie itself.

If you plan to use iMovie a lot, consider adding its icon to your Dock, if it's not there already. (Just drag its icon there.)

iMovie for an Existing Mac

If your Mac didn't come with iMovie HD, you'll have to buy it as part of the $80 iLife '05 software suite, a DVD containing the latest versions of GarageBand, iMovie, iTunes, iPhoto, and iDVD. (It's available from Apple's Web site, or popular Mac mail-order sites like *www.macmall.com* and *www.macwarehouse.com*.)

Apple says that iMovie HD requires a Mac OS X machine (10.3.4 or later) with at least 256 MB of memory; QuickTime 6.5.2 or later; 2 GB of free hard drive space (for all of iLife, or 256 megabytes for just the i-programs), and a screen that can show at least 1024 x 768 pixels. In addition, more memory and a faster processor are always better. (For high-definition video, you need 512 megs of memory and a 1-gigahertz G4 chip or faster—and that's the *bare* minimum.)

Apple also says that iMovie requires a Mac with FireWire ports, but that part isn't quite true:

- You do need a Mac with FireWire ports if you want to transfer footage from your DV camcorder. Most add-on FireWire cards (for Power Macs and PowerBooks) qualify for this requirement.

- But if you simply want to *edit* your movies on your Mac, without involving the camcorder, then almost any Mac OS X–compatible will do. It doesn't have to have FireWire circuitry.

  This presumes, of course, that you've got some footage to work on. You can edit still pictures or QuickTime movies (Chapter 9) without even involving a camcorder or FireWire. Or you can work with DV clips that you've copied from a Mac that *does* have FireWire. Transferring this footage from the FireWire Mac to your non-FireWire Mac is fairly easy once you understand how iMovie organizes its files, as described on page 112.

If you've bought iLife, run its installer and choose which programs you want. When the installer is finished, you'll find an icon called iMovie (not iMovie HD) in your Applications folder.

Tip: If you've got some previous version of iMovie already on your Mac, the installer automatically upgrades it to the newer version. (iMovie HD can open and edit projects from the older iMovies, too.)

If you want to back up your older iMovie copy so that you can return to it if you don't care for the new version, rename your older copy. Call it "iMovie 4," for example. You'll wind up with both programs in your Applications folder: "iMovie 4" and "iMovie" (which is version 5).

".0.1" Updates

Like any software company, Apple occasionally releases new versions of iMovie: version 5.0.1, version 5.0.2, and so on. Each free upgrade adds better reliability to the program. In general, they're well worth installing.

You don't have to look far to find them. One day you'll be online, and the Mac's Software Update dialog box will appear, letting you know that a new version is available and offering to install it for you. (You can also download the updates from *www.apple.com/imovie.*)

When the updater is finished with its installation, your original copy of iMovie, wherever you've been keeping it, will have morphed into the newer version of the program. You'll find it in the same place it was before, but now it has enhancements of the updated version. (One way to find out what version of iMovie you have is to open the program and then choose →About iMovie HD.)

This book assumes that you have at least iMovie HD.0.1, which is far more reliable and stable than the 5.0 version was.

Connecting to FireWire

The FireWire jack on the front, side, or back of your computer is marked by a radio-active-looking Y symbol.

If you intend to edit your own camcorder footage, you'll also need a FireWire *cable*, like the one shown in Figure 4-1.

Figure 4-1:
Plug the larger end of the FireWire cable—the six-pin end, as Apple calls it—into the corresponding jack on the Mac. The tiny end may look almost square, but it fits only in one particular way, thanks to a little indentation on one side. Be gentle with it.

On the other end is a much smaller, squarish plug (the four-pin connector). Plug this tiny end into the FireWire connector on your camcorder, which, depending on the brand, may be labeled "FireWire," "i.Link," or "IEEE 1394."

This single FireWire cable communicates both sound and video, in both directions, between the Mac and the camcorder.

Now, if you plan to transfer video to your Mac from a tape in the camcorder, you should turn the camcorder to its *VCR* or *VTR* mode.

Tip: Occasionally, you may even want to capture *live* video into iMovie—to pass whatever your camcorder lens is seeing directly to the Mac, without ever recording it on tape. In that case, put the camcorder into *Camera* mode instead.

For best results, plug in your camcorder's power adapter instead of running it from battery power. At last, you're ready to begin editing video!

Getting into iMovie

After you've connected and turned on your camcorder, open iMovie by double-clicking its icon, or single-clicking it on the Dock. But before you're treated to the main iMovie screen (shown in Figure 4-4), iMovie may ask you to take care of a few housekeeping details.

Monitor Resolution

All modern Mac monitors let you adjust the resolution, which is a measurement of how much it can show as measured in *pixels* (the tiny dots that make up the screen picture). If you choose →System Preferences→Displays, you'll see the available choices.

Why is it important to understand monitor resolution when you're about to edit video? Because iMovie likes a very big screen—a *high*-resolution monitor. If your monitor is set to one of the lower resolution settings when you launch iMovie, you'll get an error message like the one shown in Figure 4-2.

To use iMovie, your screen size must be set to at least 1024 x 768.

Reset your screen size in the Displays pane of System Preferences, then open iMovie.

OK

Figure 4-2:
If your monitor is set to 800 x 600 or lower resolution, iMovie won't run.

UP TO SPEED

The iMovie Tutorial

iMovie no longer comes with a sample project that you're supposed to build as you learn the ropes; the kids-washing-a-dog movie is long gone.

In its place, Apple now offers a choice of two very helpful learning kits.

First, your copy of iMovie came with an 83-page PDF file (Acrobat Reader file) that can serve as a starting point for your iMovie education. To open it, choose Help→ iMovie HD Help from within iMovie, click Learn About iMovie HD, and then click the

Getting Started link. After a moment, the PDF document opens up on the screen, so that you can print it or read it electronically.

Second, Apple has provided a series of basic but helpfully narrated videos that walk you through the entire core of iMovie. They're online, but the quickest way to find them is to choose Help→ iMovie HD Support from within iMovie. You're taken to the main iMovie help page online, which contains links to the tutorials like the one shown here.

The bottom line: Choose a setting that's 1024 x 768 or larger. Poor iMovie can't even run at any lower setting.

Caution: If you switch your resolution to a resolution lower than 1024 x 768 **while** iMovie is open, the program has no choice but to quit. (At least it does you the courtesy of offering to save the changes to the project file you've been working on.)

The program is more graceful when you switch between two *higher* resolutions; it instantly adjusts its various windows and controls to fit the resized screen. In other words, whenever you switch resolutions while the program is open, be extra careful not to choose, for example, 800 x 600 by mistake.

The Create Project Dialog Box

If everything has gone well, and iMovie approves of your monitor setting, your next stop is the window (Figure 4-3).

Figure 4-3:
Click Create Project to begin working on a new movie, Open Existing Project to open an existing movie, Magic iMovie to let the program assemble a movie unattended, or Quit to back out of the whole thing. The little ? button opens up the iMovie HD Help system.

You've reached a decision point: You must now tell the program whether you want to begin a new movie (called a *project* in iMovie lingo), open one you've already started, use the new Magic iMovie feature (page 105), or quit the program.

After the first time you run iMovie, you may not see the dialog box shown in Figure 4-3 very often. After that, each time you launch iMovie, it automatically opens up the movie you were working on most recently. If you ever want to see the Project dialog box again, in fact, you'll have to do one of the following:

- Instead of *quitting* iMovie when you're finished working, just close its window, so that the Create Project screen reappears. If you quit iMovie *now*, it won't open any project the next time you fire up the program; it will show the Create Project dialog box instead.

- Discard the last movie you were working on (by trashing it from your hard drive), or move it to a different folder.

- Throw away the iMovie Preferences file (which is where iMovie records which movie you were editing most recently). It bears the uncatchy name com.apple.iMovie.plist, and it's inside your Home→Library→Preferences folder.

Saving a New Project File

If you click Create a New Project (Figure 4-3), you're now asked to select a name and location for the movie you're about to make—or, as iMovie would say, the *project* you're about to make (Figure 4-4).

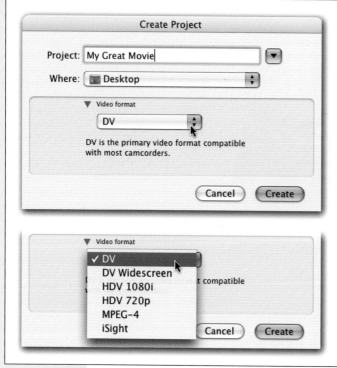

Figure 4-4:
Top: In the Create Project dialog box, you name your new movie and specify where you want to save it.

Bottom: You can also tell iMovie what format to expect for the incoming video. In most cases, though, you don't need to bother; iMovie will automatically accommodate whatever camera you attach.

This is a critical moment. Starting a new iMovie project isn't as casual an affair as starting a new word processing file. For one thing, iMovie requires that you save and name your file *before* you've actually done any work. For another, you can't bring in footage from your camcorder without first naming and saving a project file.

Where to save

Above all, the *location* of your saved project file—your choice of hard drive to save it on—is important. Digital video files are enormous. Standard DV footage consumes about 3.6 MB of your hard drive *per second*. Therefore:

This much video	Needs about this much disk space
1 minute	228 MB
15 minutes	3.5 GB
30 minutes	7 GB
60 minutes	13 GB
2 hours	28 GB
4 hours	53 GB

As you could probably guess, high-definition footage is even more massive; each minute of it takes between three and four times as much disk space as standard DV footage.

Note: That's "between three and four," because there are two primary HDTV standards, known as 720p and 1080i (see page 92). Video shot in 720p consumes slightly under three times the amount of disk space as standard DV (about 9 MB per second, or 34 gigabytes per hour), and 1080i takes up four times as much (14 MB per second, or 52 gigs per hour).

When you save and name your project, you're also telling iMovie *where* to put these enormous, disk-guzzling files. If, like most people, you have only one hard drive, the one built into your Mac, fine. Make as much empty room as you can, and proceed with your video-editing career.

But many iMovie fans have more than one hard drive. They may have decided to invest in a larger hard drive, as described in the box on page 95, so that they can make longer movies. If you're among them, save your new project *onto* the larger hard drive if you want to take advantage of its extra space.

Tip: People who have used other space-intensive software, such as Photoshop and Premiere, are frequently confused by iMovie. They expect the program to have a Scratch Disk command that lets them specify where (on which hard drive) they want their work files stored while they're working.

As you now know, iMovie has no such command. You choose your scratch disk (the hard drive onto which you save your project) on a movie-by-movie basis.

Note, by the way, that digital video requires a fast hard drive. Therefore, make no attempt to save your project file onto a floppy disk, Zip disk, Jaz disk, SuperDisk, iDisk, CD-R, DVD-R, or another disk on the network. It won't be fast enough, and you'll get nothing but error messages.

Video format

Unlike previous versions, iMovie HD offers a new pop-up menu in the Create Project dialog box called "Video format." The most important lesson to learn about this pop-up menu is that, in general, you should *ignore it*.

Here, you *can* specify what kind of incoming video iMovie should expect, but you don't have to. iMovie detects what kind of camcorder you've attached *automatically*, and it creates the right kind of project no matter what this pop-up menu says.

Note: iMovie can even change the project's format after you've created it, but only if the project is completely empty. Once you've created a clip—even an empty black clip or a Ken Burns photo clip—the format is locked down. Of course, even then, you can delete all the clips and empty the iMovie Trash; at that point, iMovie will once again resize its own window according to the kind of camcorder you plug into it.

So why did Apple provide this pop-up menu? Primarily for situations in which you're *not* going to use a video camera to provide the footage. For example, you might want to use iMovie HD to create a spectacular slideshow from your digital photos in high-definition, or at least in widescreen. (No, there's no such thing as a Mac that burns high-definition DVDs. But there will be one day soon. If you create your slideshows in high-def format today, you'll be ready.)

In such cases, you'll be happy to have this pop-up menu so that you can choose a format manually.

Your choices are:

- **DV** stands for digital video—the usual signal from standard MiniDV camcorders.

- **DV Widescreen** is also for MiniDV camcorders, but specifically the ones that offer a so-called 16:9 shooting mode. That is, these camcorders can film a widescreen, rectangular image, shaped like an HDTV picture but without the high resolution. You'd choose this option when importing footage filmed in 16:9 mode. (For your reference, the traditional, squarish video picture is known as 4:3. Both ratios refer to the width:height proportions of the picture.)

- **HDV 1080i, HDV 720p** refer to the new, high-definition camcorders that inspired the creation of iMovie HD. 1080i and 720p are two different flavors of high-def TV; Sony's HDR-FX1 camcorder uses 1080i, and JVC's GR-HD1 records in 720p. Both of them are HDV camcorders, a reference to the format they use to store a high-definition picture on ordinary MiniDV cassettes.

Note: If you're scoring at home: 1080i creates the picture on your screen by blasting 1,080 fine horizontal lines onto the screen in two alternating, interlaced sets of 540. A 720p picture is painted progressively down the screen in a single pass, but using "only" 720 lines of resolution.

Online, people argue about which format is superior until they're blue in the keyboard, but let's just put it this way: both pictures look absolutely spectacular compared with 480i (the interlaced picture of regular TV) or even 480p (what you get from standard DVDs).

- **MPEG-4** is the video format used by many "flash-based" video devices like the Fisher FVDC1 CameraCorder, which are extremely compact handheld camcorders that store video on a memory card instead of tape. (See page 102.)

- **iSight** is Apple's pocket-sized, $150 video-chat camera. For instructions on capturing video from an iSight, see page 101.

Once you've set up your Create Project dialog box, click the Create button.

Tip: Alternatively, you can press your Return or Enter key. A reminder: On the Mac, pressing Return or Enter is the same as clicking the blue button in the dialog box.

iMovie Controls

Once you've saved your file, you finally arrive at the main iMovie window. Figure 4-5 is a cheat sheet for what all of iMovie's various screen elements do. Spend no time memorizing their functions now; the rest of this book covers each of these tools in context and in depth.

Figure 4-5:
iMovie HD doesn't look much like any program you've used before—except perhaps earlier versions of iMovie.

iMovie appears in its own window, which you can resize, send to the background, drag to a second monitor, and otherwise manipulate like any other program's window.

Monitor   Clips pane

Scrubber bar   Playhead   Volume   Pane buttons

Clip Viewer/ Timeline Viewer switch   Camera/Edit Mode switch   Home, Play, Full Screen   Clip Viewer (Movie Track)   Free space   Project Trash

- **Monitor.** You watch your footage in this window.

- **Clips pane.** These little cubbyholes store the *clips*—pieces of footage, individual shots—that you'll rearrange into a masterpiece of modern storytelling.

  This pane won't always be the Clips pane, incidentally. It becomes the Photos pane, the Audio pane, and so on, when you click one of the buttons beneath it. The one thing all of these incarnations have in common is that they offer you lists of materials you can incorporate into your movie.

- **Pane buttons.** Each of these buttons—Clips, Photos, Audio, Titles, Trans (Transitions), Effects, iDVD—fills the Clips pane area with tools that add professional touches to your movie, like crossfade styles, credit sequences, footage effects (like brightness and color shifting), still photos, sound effects, and music. Chapters 6, 7, 8, and 16 cover these video flourishes in detail.

- **Clip Viewer/Timeline Viewer.** You'll spend most of your editing time down here. Each of these tools offers a master map that shows which scenes will play in which order, but there's a crucial difference in the way they do it.

   When you click the Clip Viewer button (marked by a piece of filmstrip), you see your movie represented as *slides*. Each clip appears to be the same size, even if some are long and some are short. The Clip Viewer offers no clue as to what's going on with the audio, but it's a supremely efficient overview of your clips' sequence.

   When you click the Timeline Viewer button (marked by the clock), on the other hand, you can see the relative lengths of your clips, because each shows up as a colored band of the appropriate length. Parallel bands (complete with visual "sound waves," if you like), underneath indicate blocks of sound that play simultaneously.

- **Camera Mode/Edit Mode switch.** In Camera Mode, the playback controls operate your camcorder, rather than the iMovie film you're editing. In Camera Mode, the Monitor window shows you what's on the tape, not what's in iMovie, so that you can choose which shots you want to transfer to iMovie for editing.

   In Edit Mode, however, iMovie ignores your camcorder. Now the playback controls govern your captured clips instead of the camcorder. Edit Mode is where you start piecing your movie together.

Tip: You can drag the blue dot between the Camera Mode and Edit Mode positions, if you like, but doing so requires sharp hand-eye coordination and an unnecessary mouse drag. It's much faster to click *on* one of the icons, ignoring the little switch entirely. Click directly on the little camera symbol for Camera Mode, for example, or on the scissors for Edit Mode.

- **Home.** Means "rewind to the beginning." *Keyboard equivalent:* the Home key on your keyboard. (On laptops, you must hold down both the Fn key and the left-arrow key to trigger the Home function.)

Note: In Camera Mode, the Home, Play/Stop, and Full Screen buttons described here are replaced by the Rewind, Stop, Play, Pause, and Fast Forward buttons, as described later in this chapter.

- **Play/Stop.** Plays the tape, movie, or clip. When the playback is going on, the button turns blue; that's your cue that clicking it again stops the playback.

- **Play Full Screen.** Clicking this button makes the movie you're editing fill the entire Mac screen as it plays back, instead of playing just in the small Monitor window. (It still doesn't look nearly as good as it will on your TV, however, as described on page 97. Unless, of course, you have an Apple 23-inch Cinema HD Display, in which case you see every juicy drop of the full, spectacular resolution.)

Tip: The Full Screen button doesn't play your movie back from the beginning. Instead, it plays back from the location of the Playhead.

If you *do* want to play in full-screen mode from the beginning, press the Home key (or click the Home button just to the left of the Play button) before clicking the Play Full Screen button.

- **Scrubber bar.** This special scroll bar lets you jump anywhere in one piece of footage, or the entire movie.

- **Playhead.** The Playhead is like the little box handle, or *thumb,* of a normal scroll bar. It shows exactly where you are in the footage.

- **Volume slider.** To adjust your speaker volume as you work, click anywhere in the slider's "track" to make the knob jump there. (Keep in mind that you can also boost the Mac's *overall* speaker volume by pressing the volume keys on the keyboard, using the volume slider in your menu bar, or using the Sound panel in System Preferences.)

- **Project Trash.** You can drag any clip onto this icon to get rid of it. (Or just highlight a clip and press the Delete key.)

- **Free space.** This indicator lets you know how full your hard drive is. In the world of video editing, that's a very important statistic, as described on page 101.

Importing Camcorder Footage

Suppose you've opened iMovie and clicked the Create a New Project button. At this moment, then, you're looking at an empty version of the screen shown in Figure 4-5. Connect your camcorder to the FireWire cable and turn it on. This is where the fun begins.

Click the little movie-camera symbol on the iMovie screen, if necessary, to switch into Camera Mode, as shown in Figure 4-6.

FREQUENTLY ASKED QUESTION

Saving to External FireWire Drives

I need more hard drive space. What should I do? Can I save a project onto an external FireWire drive?

It's a natural question; most Macs have two FireWire jacks. What better way to capitalize on them than by hooking up the camcorder and an external FireWire hard drive simultaneously?

For example, at the time of this writing, you can get an 80 GB FireWire hard drive for under $160 (from *www.promax.*

com, for example), which is enough to hold over six hours of footage. And the prices are falling rapidly.

Like most FireWire gear, these hard drives have several advantages over hard drives you may have known in the past. They're smaller and faster, can be plugged and unplugged from the computer without turning anything off, and don't require power cords of their own.

Tip: If you turn on your camcorder after iMovie is already running, the program conveniently switches into Camera Mode. (iMovie only does so the *first time* you power up the camcorder during a work session, however, to avoid annoying people who turn the camcorder on and off repeatedly during the editing process to save battery power.)

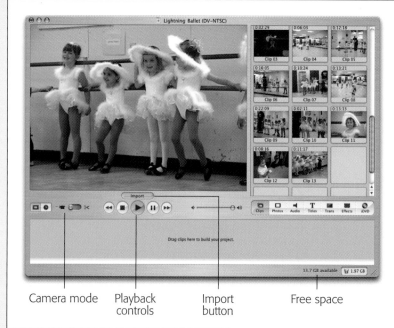

Camera mode   Playback   Import   Free space
                controls   button

Figure 4-6:
While you're importing footage, the time code in the upper-left corner of the clip on the Clips pane steadily ticks away to show you that the clip is getting longer. Meanwhile, the Free Space indicator updates itself, second by second, as your hard drive space is eaten up by the incoming footage. The square Stop button does exactly the same thing as clicking the Play button a second time. The Pause button also halts playback, but it freezes the frame instead of going to a blank screen.

The Monitor window becomes big and blue, filled with the words "Camera Connected." (If you don't see those words, check the troubleshooting steps in Appendix B.) This is the first of many messages the Monitor window will be showing you. At other times, it may say, "Camera No Tape," "Camera Fast Forward," "Camera Rewinding," and so on.

Now you can click the Play, Rewind, Fast Forward, and other buttons on the screen to control the camcorder (see Figure 4-6).

You'll probably find that you have even more precise control by using the mouse to control the camcorder than you would by pressing the actual camcorder buttons. (The Space bar turns the Import button on and off, as described below. Otherwise, though, no keyboard shortcuts control these buttons.)

Tip: The Rewind and Fast Forward buttons work a little strangely. If you *double-click* a button, playback stops and the rewinding or fast-forwarding begins at full speed. If you click and *hold* your mouse button down on a Rewind or Fast Forward button, playback continues with the tape moving at only twice its usual speed.

What you're doing now, of course, is scanning your tape to find the sections that you'll want to include in your edited movie.

The Monitor Window's Video Quality

After reading all the gushing prose about the high quality of digital-video footage, when you first inspect your footage in the Monitor window, you might wonder if you got ripped off. The picture may not look anything like DVD quality.

This video quality is *temporary* and visible only on the Mac screen. The instant you send your finished movie back to the camcorder, or when you export it as a Quick-Time movie or DVD, you get the stunning DV quality that was temporarily hidden on the Mac screen.

Still, you'll spend much of your moviemaking time watching clips play back, so it's well worth investigating the different ways iMovie can improve the picture.

- **Good.** If you have a fast Mac, a great way is to choose iMovie→Preferences, click the Playback tab, and then choose "Highest (field blending)." The only reason you'd want to choose one of the lower-quality settings, in fact, is if you experience hiccups during playback, usually in complicated movies on slowish Macs—400-megahertz G3 iMacs, for example.

Tip: iMovie HD's redesigned Preferences dialog box contains a slew of useful options. They're cited so frequently in this book that it's probably worth memorizing its keyboard shortcut: ⌘-comma.

As a bonus, that keystroke works to open the Preferences dialog box in all of the other iLife programs, too, not to mention Microsoft Word, Keynote, Safari, and others.

- **Better.** An even better solution is to choose iMovie→Preferences, click Playback, and turn on "Play DV project video through to DV camera." You've just told iMovie to play the video *through your camcorder*. In other words, if you're willing to watch your camcorder's LCD screen as you work instead of the onscreen Monitor window, what you see is what you shot: all gorgeous, all the time. (You hear the audio only through the camcorder, too.)

- **Best.** The ultimate editing setup, though, is to hook up a TV to your camcorder's analog outputs. That way, you get to edit your footage not just at full quality, but also at full size. The camcorder, still connected to the Mac via its FireWire cable, passes whatever you'd see in the Monitor window straight through to the TV set, at full digital-video quality. This is exactly the way professionals edit digital video—on TV monitors on their desks.

The only difference is that you paid about $99,000 less for your setup.

Capturing Footage

When you're in Camera Mode, an Import button appears just below the Monitor window. When you click this button (or press the Space bar), iMovie imports the footage you're watching, storing it as digital-video movie files on the Mac's hard drive.

You can ride the Space bar, tapping it to turn the Import button on and off, capturing only the good parts as the playback continues.

During this process, you'll notice a number of changes to your iMovie environment (Figure 4-6):

• The Import button lights up, as though illuminated by a blue spotlight.

• As soon as you click Import, what looks like a slide appears in the first square of the Clips pane, as shown in Figure 4-5. That's a *clip*—a single piece of footage that makes up one of the building blocks of an iMovie movie. Its icon is a picture of the first frame.

• Superimposed on the clip, in its upper-left corner, is the length of the clip expressed as "minutes:seconds:frames." You can see this little timer ticking upward as the clip grows longer. For example, if it says *1:23:10*, then the clip is 1 minute, 23 seconds, and 10 frames long.

Getting used to this kind of frame counter takes some practice for two reasons. First, computers start counting from 0, not from 1, so the very first frame of a clip is called 00:00. Second, remember that there are 30 frames per second (in NTSC digital video; 25 in PAL digital video). So the far-right number in the time code (the frame counter) counts up to *29* before flipping over to 00 again—not to 59 or 99, which might feel more familiar. In other words, iMovie counts like this: 00:28…00:29…1:00…1:01.

Tip: Standard DV camcorders record life by capturing 30 frames per second. (All right, 29.97 frames per second; see the box on page 298.)

That, for your trivia pleasure, is the standard frame rate for *television*. Real movies, on the other hand—that is, footage shot on film—roll by at only 24 frames per second. The European PAL format runs at 25 frames per second.

Killing the Sound-Delay Echo

When I'm capturing footage, I get this annoying echo in the sound, as though a delay unit is processing the soundtrack. What's going on?

You're probably trying to watch the footage on your camcorder's LCD screen and on the Mac screen at the same time. As a result, you're hearing the soundtrack twice—once from the camcorder's built-in speaker, and then, a fraction of a second later, from the Mac's speaker. (It takes that long for the sound to make its way through the Mac's sound circuitry and various layers of software.)

You can, of course, simply close the LCD screen, and presto! No more echo. If you still want to be able to watch the superior picture on the LCD screen, then mute (or fully turn down) either the camcorder's speaker or the Mac's. Now you get two ways to watch the movie play but only one sound source.

- iMovie HD is a Mac OS X–only program. As a result, you gain a huge perk: Your Mac doesn't have to devote every atom of its energy to capturing video. While the importing is going on, you're free to open other programs, surf the Web, crunch some numbers, organize your pictures in iPhoto, or whatever you like.

The Mac continues to give processor priority to capturing video, so your other programs may act a little drugged. But this impressive multitasking feat still means that you can get meaningful work or reading done while you're dumping your footage into iMovie in the background.

If you click Import (or press the Space bar) a second time, the tape continues to roll, but iMovie stops gulping down footage to your hard drive. Your camcorder continues to play. You've just captured your first clip(s).

Automatic scene detection

If you let the tape continue to roll, you'll notice a handy iMovie feature at work. Each time a new scene begins, a new clip icon appears in the Clips pane. The Clips pane scrolls as much as necessary to hold the imported clips.

What iMovie is actually doing is studying the *date and time stamp* that DV camcorders record into every frame of video. When iMovie detects a break in time, it assumes that you stopped recording, if only for a moment, and therefore that the next piece of footage should be considered a new shot. It turns each new shot into a new clip.

This behavior lets you just roll the camera, unattended, as iMovie automatically downloads the footage, turning each scene into a clip while you sit there leafing through a magazine. Then later, at your leisure, you can survey the footage you've caught and set about the business of cutting out the deadwood.

In general, this feature doesn't work if you haven't set your camcorder's clock. (JVC's high-definition camcorders are the exception; they don't time-stamp your footage, but iMovie *does* recognize their scene breaks anyway.) Automatic scene detection also doesn't work if you're playing from a non-DV tape using one of the techniques described on page 115.

Tip: If you prefer, you can ask iMovie to dump incoming clips into the Clip Viewer at the bottom of the screen instead of the Clips pane. You might want to do that when, for example, you filmed your shots roughly in sequence. That way, you'll have to do much less dragging to the Clip Viewer when it comes time to edit.

To bring this about, choose iMovie→Preferences and click Import. Where you see "Place clips in," click Movie Timeline. Click OK. Now when you begin importing clips, iMovie stacks them end to end in the Timeline instead of on the Clips pane.

If you would prefer to have manual control over when each clip begins and ends, iMovie is happy to comply. Choose iMovie→Preferences, click import, and proceed as shown in Figure 4-7.

Once you've turned off the automatic clip-creation feature, iMovie logs clips only when you click Import (or press Space) once at the beginning of the clip, and again at the end of the clip.

Tip: Tapping the Space bar is the same as clicking the Import button. In fact, if you tap Space when the camcorder is stopped, it begins to play *and* iMovie begins to capture the footage.

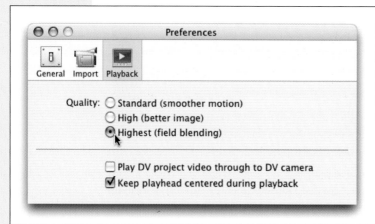

Figure 4-7:
The iMovie→Preferences dialog box gives you control over the automatic clip-logging feature. You can turn off this feature entirely by turning off the "Start new clip at each scene break" option.

How much footage to capture

For best results, don't attempt to use the footage-importing process as a crude means of micro-editing the footage on the fly. True, the ever-diminishing digits in the Free Space indicator may put you under pressure to limit the amount of footage you import. And it's OK to ride the Import button so that you block out the obviously unusable sections. But resist the temptation to do finer editing this way. You'll want to trim your clips with iMovie's accurate snipping tools later.

This doesn't mean that you must transfer *everything* from your camcorder (although many people do, just for the convenience). But when you come to a scene you want to bring into iMovie, capture 3 to 5 seconds of footage before and after the interesting part. Later, when you're editing, that extra leading and trailing video (called *trim handles* by the pros) will give you the flexibility to choose exactly the right moment for the scene to begin and end. Furthermore, as you'll find out in Chapter 6, you need extra footage at the beginnings and ends of your clips if you want to use crossfades or similar transitions between them.

The maximum clip length

iMovie veterans are used to a clip-length limit of 9 minutes, 28 seconds, and 17 frames (which is 2 gigabytes of hard drive space). But no more; in iMovie HD, a clip's length is limited only by the amount of space on your hard drive. You can easily import an entire 60-minute DV tape—if you've got enough hard drive space, of course—as a single icon on your Clips pane, if you like. (That would require, of course, that you've turned off automatic scene detection as described earlier.)

The Free Space readout

As noted earlier, the Free Space display (Figure 4-6) updates itself as you capture your clips. It keeps track of how much space your hard drive has left—the one onto which you saved your project.

This readout includes a color-keyed early warning system that lets you prepare for that awkward moment when your hard drive's full. At that moment, you won't be able to capture any more video. Look at the color of the text just beside the Trash (where it says, for example, "1.83 GB available"):

- If the words are **black,** you're in good shape. Your hard drive has over 400 MB of free space—room for at least 90 seconds of additional footage.

- If the text becomes **yellow,** your hard drive has between 200 and 400 MB of free space left. In about 90 more seconds of capturing, you'll be completely out of space.

- When the words turn **red,** the situation is dire. Your hard drive has less than 200 MB of free space left. About one minute of capturing remains.

- When the Free Space indicator shows that you've got less than 50 MB of free space left, iMovie stops importing and refuses to capture any more video. At this point, you must make more free space on your hard drive, either by emptying your Project Trash or by throwing away some non-iMovie files from your hard drive. (You don't have to quit iMovie while you houseclean; just hide it.)

Four Special Cases: iSight, HDV, USB, and Live Recording

Recorded footage from a MiniDV tape is by far the most popular source of iMovie video, but it's not the only one. iMovie is perfectly content to slurp in video from an iSight camera, from a DV camcorder with no tape in it, or from a high-definition, semi-professional camcorder. (That, after all, is where iMovie HD gets its name.)

Read on.

iSight Video

The Apple iSight is a compact silver tube, about the dimensions of a Hostess Ho-Ho, with a built-in microphone and video camera. Most people buy an iSight (about $150) for use with iChat AV, Apple's chat program, because iSight lets you conduct audio and video chats instead of typed ones.

But as it turns out, the iSight is also a darned fine capture device. No, it doesn't take tapes, so you can't prerecord something. But it's an excellent tool for recording live events directly into iMovie: interviews, meetings, travel adventures with your laptop, and so on.

The steps are almost the same. Start by connecting the iSight's FireWire cable to the Mac. Make sure that the iSight's shutter is open (turn the ring on the lens). Then continue as shown in Figure 4-8.

Live Camcorder Recording

iMovie is also happy to capture video straight from a camcorder that *doesn't* contain a tape. In other words, you can use your camcorder as though it were an iSight, sending whatever it "sees" directly into iMovie, live.

Figure 4-8:
When you move the Camera/Edit switch into the Camera position, you'll see a tiny down-pointing triangle next to it. From this pop-up menu, choose iSight. At this point, the Monitor window shows whatever the iSight camera is "seeing." Click Record with iSight to begin (and, later, to stop) recording. The video arrives in the Clips pane just like any other footage.

All you have to do is set its selector to Camera instead of VCR and take the tape out of the camcorder. Connect the camcorder to the Mac via FireWire, turn the camcorder on, and voilà: live, tapeless video capture.

USB Camcorders

These days, not all camcorders store their video on tape. There's a new breed of super-tiny, pants-pocketable microcorders that are capable of recording high-quality video directly onto memory cards. Panasonic, Fisher, Gateway, and other companies sell such gadgets.

iMovie, for the first time, lets you work with many of these "camcorders," or at least the ones that record in so-called MPEG-4 Simple Profile format. (You can find out by consulting the box, the Web page, or the manual.)

That's not to say that iMovie actually imports MPEG-4 video the same way it imports MiniDV footage; it doesn't. But when you connect one of these 'corders to your Mac's USB jack, the memory card shows up on your screen as though it's a disk. Double-click it to reveal its contents, which include a folder with all your video recordings in it. You can bring them into iMovie by simply dragging their Finder icons into the Movie Track or Clips pane of the open iMovie window.

HDV Camcorders

If Apple's marketing is to be believed, the big news in iMovie HD is the HD part. At its release, iMovie HD was by far the least expensive software capable of importing and editing video from high-definition camcorders. (It's about $750 less expensive than the next contender.)

POWER USERS' CLINIC

HDV, Apple Intermediate Codec, and You

If you've been merrily reading along, learning all kinds of new things about high-definition video, one apparent contradiction in this chapter might already be bugging your subconscious.

First you read that an HDV camcorder stores a full hour of high-definition video on a 60-minute Mini-DV tape—a cassette designed to hold 60 minutes of *standard*-definition video.

And then you read that HDV video takes up three or four times as much hard drive space as standard DV.

Which is it? Does HDV footage take up the *same* amount of disk space as standard DV, or does it take up much more?

Answer: It takes up much more, *unless* it's massively compressed. That's the most amazing part of the circuitry in today's HDV consumer camcorders: it manages to compress all of that information in real time, so that it fits in the same amount of tape as standard DV.

Your Mac, however, is not quite as dedicated a machine. Even the fastest Mac wouldn't be able to edit HDV footage in its original, super-compressed form. It'd be like: click to select a clip, wait; scroll to a later place in the clip, wait; hit the Space bar to play it, wait; and so on.

So Apple did something very clever in iMovie HD: when it imports video from an HDV camcorder, it *transcodes* (converts)

the signal into a much more lightly compressed format on your hard drive, using a new, virtually lossless compression scheme called the Apple Intermediate Codec (AIC). Once the footage is safely aboard your hard drive, you can edit it just as easily and quickly as you can regular DV video.

When you export your finished movie back to the HDV camcorder, iMovie *reconverts* it to the more compressed format that the camcorder expects.

During both of these transfers of video—from the camcorder, and later back to the camcorder—it's the transcoding that takes so much time. *That's* why importing HDV video isn't a real-time process in iMovie HD.

Now that you understand what transcoding is, here's a tip that exploits your new awareness.

If, during importing, you click the Stop button to stop the tape, iMovie continues transcoding the video it's already stored temporarily on the hard drive, right up until it catches up with the spot on the tape where you stopped. (A progress dialog box appears on the screen during this conversion process.)

But if you end the importing by clicking the Import button (to turn it off), iMovie stops right away. It throws away everything in its buffer, and keeps only what it has already transcoded.

But first, some definitions:

- High definition is a new video format that offers a stunning, high-resolution picture, clear enough to make you feel like you're looking out a window and wide enough to show you, in a single camera shot, the pitcher, the batter, and the runner on first.

  To see high definition, you need a high-definition TV set (an HDTV). You also need some source of HDTV programming, like an upgraded cable box or a special rooftop antenna.

  Or—and this is the exciting part—you can film your own. Read on.

- HDV camcorders capture the wide, super-clear picture of high definition—on ordinary MiniDV tapes. (HDV isn't a typo. That's the format these camcorders use to store high-def video on a MiniDV tape.)

  At the birth of iMovie HD, there were only two HDV camcorders: JVC's GR-HD1 ($1,700 and dropping) and Sony's much newer, three-chip HDR-FX1 ($3,300). Neither is what you'd call pocketable, unless perhaps you're the Jolly Green Giant. But for prosumers and independent filmmakers, these camcorders represent an insanely liberating development; until they came along, the least expensive HDTV camcorder cost $40,000.

In general, the process of importing and editing high-def video is exactly like working with any other kind of video. There are, however, a few differences.

Figure 4-9:
When you're importing video from an HDV camcorder, everything gets wide and rectangular. Otherwise, though, you should be able to work with it just as you would with standard-definition footage.

The one you'll notice first is the new shape of the iMovie monitor window, and the new shape of the captured clips. As you can see in Figure 4-9, they're wide instead of square. Welcome to the HDTV age, baby.

You'll notice another difference, too, once you start importing: Your Mac probably isn't fast enough to capture this massive amount of data in real time. (Remember, high-definition footage is three or four times as massive as standard DV.)

That's why, if you inspect Figure 4-9 carefully, you'll see the tiny notation "Capturing HD at 1/4 speed" just above the volume slider. This notation changes as the importing process chugs along; it may say "Capturing HD at 1/8 speed" or, if you're lucky, even "Capturing HD at full speed."

Tip: If you make your iMovie window smaller—small enough that the Monitor window is only a quarter its usual size—you get much better speed. iMovie, in that case, transcodes the high-def video at only a quarter of its normal size (see the box on page 103), and you get faster, smoother playback and quicker importing. (If your machine is anything slower than a dual-1 gigahertz G4 or G5 processor, in fact, you always get this quarter-sized video, unless you change the Playback settings in iMovie's Preferences dialog box.)

The bottom line, though, is that importing high-def footage isn't a real-time operation, as it is when you import standard-def footage. Even after the camera is finished playing the tape, iMovie takes a few more minutes to catch up; a message on the screen says, "Processing cached HDV data" until the post-processing is complete.

Note: If you want to stop before the end of the tape, note that there's a difference between clicking the Stop button and clicking the Import button; see the box on page 103.

Fortunately, it's worth the wait. Once the HDTV footage is inside iMovie, you can work with it with all the speed and fluidity of standard footage. And when the work is finished, you can export the result to iDVD to burn onto a DVD. No, the result won't be a high-definition disc; it will, however, be a widescreen disc (at your option), which will look absolutely spectacular on a widescreen TV.

Magic iMovie

Nobody disputes that music, titles, and crossfades make movies look a heck of a lot better. But let's face it: millions of people wind up taking camcorder movies, and then never looking at them again. Editing and spicing up those movies is great, but it's *work*. And it takes a lot of time.

In an effort to solve that problem, iMovie HD introduces something called the Magic iMovie—a *completely* automated movie-assembly feature. You literally connect the camcorder, choose File→Make Magic iMovie, choose the music and options you want, and then walk away. Without any further attention from you, the program rewinds the tape, creates an opening title, imports all the footage, adds a transition between shots (if you've opted for one), backs it all up with music that you choose (at a volume level you specify), and, if you like, hands off the result to iDVD for quick burning to disc.

Magic iMovie is ideal, in other words, in situations like these:

- The alternative is leaving the video untouched on the original tape. The simple grace notes added by magic iMovie—even adding an opening title to identify the footage—make the movie much more watchable than the unedited original.

- You've just captured footage of something—a wedding, a graduation, a school dance—and you want to put something together quickly that you can play at the reception afterward.

- You realize that Magic iMovie can serve as a starting point, with a lot of the grunt work done for you. Once it's done, you can pick through the scenes, deleting the ones you don't need, changing or removing the transitions that don't seem right, and adjusting music volume levels, without having to start from scratch.

- You feel that a DVD is a much better long-term storage depository than a tape, and you'd like Magic iMovie to automate the transfer for you.

Magic iMovie is, however, a fairly limited tool. It was designed to automate things for you, which means that it doesn't give you a lot of options. Here are some things you should be aware of:

- Magic iMovie creates a transition—for example, a crossfade—out of *every single* camcorder shot, even if there are several shots in a row of the same subject. (Of course, it's easy enough to delete these transitions later. Or just turn off the Transition checkbox if you don't want them.)

- You have little control over the specifics of the things the Magic iMovie feature adds, like the length of the duration, the font of the title, and so on. Here again, of course, you can always adjust these manually after the deed is done.

- Left to its own devices, Magic iMovie always imports the entire contents of the cassette; it rewinds the tape before it begins. (There is a workaround, though, as you'll read in a moment.)

Now that you understand what to expect from Magic iMovie, here's how it works:

1. **Choose File→Make a Magic iMovie.**

   From the top of the iMovie window, the options box shown in Figure 4-10 appears. (Incidentally, a Make a Magic iMovie button also appears on the Create Project dialog box described on page 89.)

2. **Type a name for the movie.**

   Whatever you type into the "Movie title" box is what will appear on the opening credit, as white text against a black background.

3. **Choose a transition style, if you like.**

If you like the idea of smooth crossfades between the shots of your video, make sure the first checkbox is turned on. And then choose the transition style you want from the pop-up menu. Your options are Circle Opening, Circle Closing, Cross Dissolve, Overlap, Push, Radial, Scale Down, and Random. (You can read much more about transitions, including descriptions of these effects, in Chapter 6.)

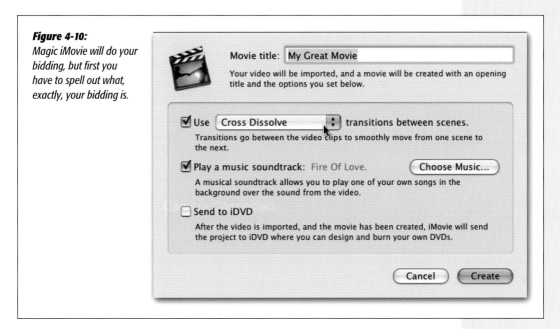

Figure 4-10:
Magic iMovie will do your bidding, but first you have to spell out what, exactly, your bidding is.

4. **Specify what music you want to play as the soundtrack, if you like.**

If you'd just like to use the audio captured by the camcorder, turn off the "Play a music soundtrack" checkbox. But if you want to try some background music (you can always remove or adjust it later), click Choose Music. Now the dialog box shown in Figure 4-11 appears, revealing the contents of your entire iTunes music library. Use the pop-up menu at the top to choose a playlist, if you like, from which to choose the songs you want.

In any case, Figure 4-11 shows you how to take it from here. Just remember that if you don't choose enough music to "cover" all the video, the music will just stop short in the middle. (If you choose too *much* music, the music will end with the video.) Click OK when you're finished setting up the music.

Tip: You don't have to choose your music from within iTunes. You can instead insert a music CD at this point, and choose from the list of songs that appear.

5. **Indicate whether or not you want a movie to send the completed Magic iMovie to iDVD in readiness for burning to disk.**

At that point, you'll still have to choose a DVD-menu design theme, preview the result, insert a blank DVD, and so on (see Chapter 15). But the work of adding chapter markers and opening a DVD itself—usually a minute-long wait—will at least be handled for you.

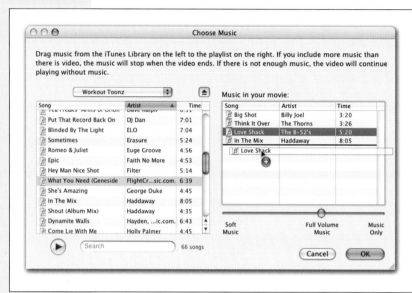

Figure 4-11:
Drag songs from the left-side list (your iTunes collection) to the right-side list (your Magic iMovie soundtrack). Drag them up or down to rearrange them in the right-side list. The volume slider beneath the list lets you control the volume of the music relative to the camcorder audio. At the far-right setting, you hear only the music, which can give your movie a sweet, emotional overtone.

And if you *don't* want a movie to hand off the result to iDVD, just turn off the "Send to iDVD" checkbox.

6. Click Create.

As shown in Figure 4-12, iMovie whirls into action.

Tip: If you don't want iMovie to import the entire tape, cue it up before you begin this process. Then, as soon as iMovie starts to rewind the tape, just hit Stop on the camcorder.

Similarly, you can stop the importing process before Magic iMovie reaches the end of the recorded portion of the tape just by turning off the camcorder at that spot.

By the way, each individual step of this process takes just as long as if you did it manually. iMovie must still import the video in real time, render (process) every transition, and so on.

The beauty of this method, though, is that you don't have to be there. You can be working in another program, or even another part of the house, as a movie chugs away unattended. (Then again, if you're a first-time iMovie maker, sticking around to watch the process may help to give you an idea of how the general iMovie workflow goes.)

The important thing to remember is that the resulting iMovie project is fully editable; there's nothing holy about any of the creative decisions that iMovie makes. You can still chop out clips you don't want, remove or edit some transitions, add or remove chapter markers, and so on.

Figure 4-12:
This handy cheat sheet helps you keep track of Magic iMovie's progress as it rewinds your camcorder, begins importing the footage, stops the camcorder when it reaches the end of the recorded portion, adds titles and transitions to the imported material, lays down the audio you selected (you'll even see a movie switch momentarily into the Timeline Viewer mode), and, if you requested it, hands off the result to iDVD.

Managing Project Files

In the iMovie HD era, your movie may appear on the hard drive in one of two formats:

- If it's a new iMovie HD project, it's represented on your hard drive by a single file icon (see Figure 4-13, top). Having a single-icon project document makes it very convenient to open, copy, delete, rename, or move a video project, because you have only one icon to worry about.

- If it's an older iMovie project that you've opened into iMovie HD, it remains just as it was: as a *folder* full of associated files (Figure 4-13, bottom).

You can read more about this distinction later in the chapter. But first, the basics of opening, switching, and converting movie projects.

Starting a New Project

To start a new project after you've been editing another one, choose File→New Project; indicate whether or not you want to save the changes to your outgoing movie (if you haven't already saved them); and off you go.

Switching Projects

To open a different iMovie Project, you can choose either of two routes:

- Close the current project's window. You return to the Create Project dialog box shown in Figure 4-3. Click Open Existing Project. Now you're shown the contents of your hard drive, so that you can find and open the iMovie project you want.

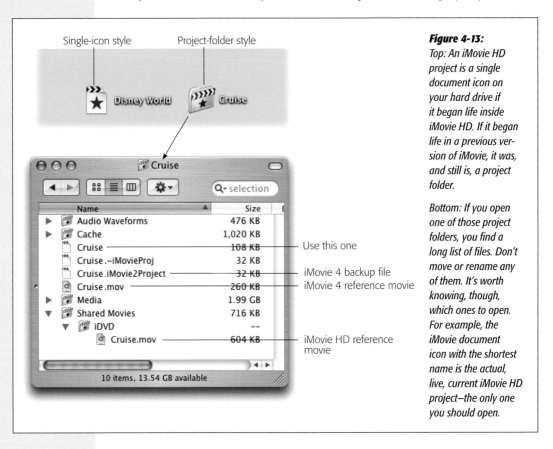

Single-icon style   Project-folder style

Use this one

iMovie 4 backup file
iMovie 4 reference movie

iMovie HD reference movie

Figure 4-13:
Top: An iMovie HD project is a single document icon on your hard drive if it began life inside iMovie HD. If it began life in a previous version of iMovie, it was, and still is, a project folder.

Bottom: If you open one of those project folders, you find a long list of files. Don't move or rename any of them. It's worth knowing, though, which ones to open. For example, the iMovie document icon with the shortest name is the actual, live, current iMovie HD project—the only one you should open.

- Choose File→Open Project. Once again, use the resulting dialog box to find the movie you want.

- Choose File→Open Recent, whose submenu lists the last few movies you've worked on.

In each case, if you've worked on the current movie but haven't saved the changes yet, iMovie asks you whether you'd like to save them or not. Click Save or Don't Save, as appropriate.

Tip: If you're a keyboard-shortcut fan, you can press ⌘-D instead of clicking Don't Save.

After a moment, the new movie's clips appear on the screen, and you're ready to go.

Converting Older Projects

When you open a project created by an older version of the program, iMovie asks permission to update its file format into the iMovie HD format, as shown in Figure 4-14. If you want to edit the project in iMovie HD, you have no choice; you must click OK. Doing so creates a new project file, and preserves a copy of the original with the filename suffix ".iMovie2Project" (see Figure 4-13, bottom).

Figure 4-14:
Top: When you open an older iMovie project, this message appears.

Bottom: Sometimes, opening an older project produces this message, which refers to clips that are still in the Trash. For details, see page 127.

> **Warning**
>
> The project "iPod" was saved with an older version of iMovie. Opening it in this version will cause it to be upgraded, which will make it unreadable by older versions. Are you sure you want to open it?
>
> Cancel   OK

> **Some stray files were found in the project, and were moved into iMovie's Trash.**
>
> Would you like to view the Trash contents?
>
> Don't View Trash   View Trash

Now, even if you click OK, your old iMovie project *folder* doesn't get turned into the new-style, single-icon project *file* as described earlier. Instead, iMovie HD leaves you with the original project folder, with a few new files and folders deposited there for safety. (See Figure 4-13 for an illustration.)

For example, suppose you try to open an iMovie 4 project called Cruise. You get the message shown in Figure 4-14. You click OK.

When the conversion is finished, you still have a document inside called Cruise. That's your new iMovie HD project file, the one you should double-click the next time you want to open it (identified in Figure 4-13 at bottom).

Your converted project folder *also* contains a copy of the old, untouched original, now called Vacation.iMovie2Project. That's a backup copy of your original, which iMovie HD thoughtfully deposits there just in case.

Note: Be careful, in the future, not to open the Vacation.iMovie2Project document by mistake. If you try, iMovie will offer to convert it to iMovie HD format again, you'll spin out a second backup copy, and you'll wonder why the editing you did in iMovie HD yesterday isn't showing up. Don't open the version with the ~ symbol, either (Vacation.~iMovieProj); that's your "Revert to Saved" copy, an older draft that iMovie maintains for its own backtracking purposes.

So what if you *do* want iMovie to convert the old project folder into the new-style, single-icon document? After you've opened it up, choose File→Save Project As. Type a name for the newly created package icon and then click Save. After a couple of minutes of file copying and hard drive filling, you wind up with *both* the old project folder *and* the new package icon. (If the conversion goes well, you can now delete the older project folder.)

How iMovie Organizes Its Files

Thousands of people will come to iMovie HD for the first time, observing that each movie is saved as a single document icon. They'll go on through life, believing that an iMovie project is a simple, one-icon file, just like a JPEG photo or a Microsoft Word document.

In fact, though, it's not.

What iMovie HD creates is not really a document icon. It's a *package* icon, which, to Mac OS X aficionados, is code for "a thinly disguised folder." Yes, it opens up like a document when double-clicked. But if you know what you're doing, you can open it instead like a folder and survey the pieces that make up an iMovie movie. If you *don't* know what you're doing, you can hopelessly mangle your movie. Still, now and then, doing just that can get you out of a troubleshooting jam.

GEM IN THE ROUGH

The No-Longer-Phantom "Save As" Command

iMovie versions 1 through 4 didn't have a Save As command. And without a Save As command, you couldn't save your project under a different name halfway through working on it, creating mid-project backups. You couldn't create multiple versions of the same movie—like short and long versions. And you couldn't spin out an intermediate version just before making some radical editing decision that you might regret later, so that you'd have a safe version to return to.

Clever iMovie disciples learned to duplicate the iMovie project folder on their desktops manually to achieve these purposes. But in iMovie HD, all of those workarounds are merrily forgotten.

Clearly, Apple was worried that its customers wouldn't be prepared for the amount of hard drive space that a Save As command would eat up, because each Save As process would duplicate all of the massive clip files in your project folder. One Save As could easily scarf down several gigabytes of data (and take a long time to execute).

But never mind all that. iMovie HD has a File→Save Project As command at long last. It does indeed wolf down disk space, because its function is to duplicate your entire iMovie project package. But as long as you're aware of that possibility, all the other blessings of a Save As command are now yours to enjoy.

To reveal the contents of this folder-pretending-to-be-a-document, use the Control-key trick revealed in Figure 4-15.

Once you've opened up a package into a folder, it looks and works almost exactly like the project *folder* of older iMovie versions, illustrated in Figure 4-13. Here's a rundown of the files and folders they have in common.

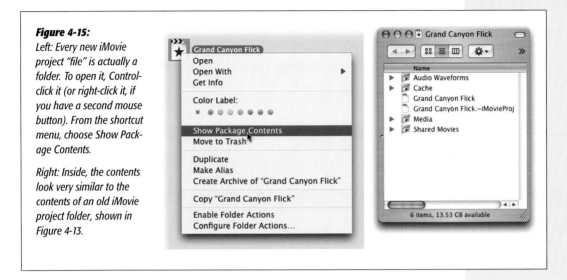

Figure 4-15:
Left: Every new iMovie project "file" is actually a folder. To open it, Control-click it (or right-click it, if you have a second mouse button). From the shortcut menu, choose Show Package Contents.

Right: Inside, the contents look very similar to the contents of an old iMovie project folder, shown in Figure 4-13.

The Project File

The actual iMovie project file—called Grand Canyon Flick at right in Figure 4-15—occupies only a few kilobytes of space on the disk, even if it's a very long movie. Behind the scenes, this document contains nothing more than a list of internal *references* to the QuickTime clips in the Media folder. Even if you copy, chop, split, rearrange, rename, and otherwise spindle the clips *in iMovie,* the names and quantity of clips in the Media folder don't change; all of your iMovie editing, technically speaking, simply shuffles around your project file's internal *pointers* to different moments on the clips you originally captured from the camcorder.

The bottom line: If you burn the project document to a CD and take it home to show the relatives for the holidays, you're in for a rude surprise. It's nothing without its accompanying Media folder. (And that's why iMovie now creates a package folder that keeps the document and its media files together.)

The Media folder

Inside the Media folder are several, or dozens, or hundreds of individual QuickTime movies, graphics, and sound files. These represent each clip, sound, picture, or special effect you used in your movie.

Caution: *Never* rename, move, or delete the files in the Media folder. iMovie will become cranky, display error messages, and forget how you had your movie the last time you opened it.

Do your deleting, renaming, and rearranging in *iMovie,* not in the Media folder. And above all, don't take the Media folder (or the project document) out of the package window. Doing so will render your movie uneditable.

(It's OK to rename the project folder or the project file, however.)

Shared Movies folder

This folder contains two items worth knowing about:

- **iDVD folder.** The reference movie is inside the Shared Movies folder called iDVD. The *reference movie* for your project bears the same name as the project. For example, if your movie is called Cruise, your Shared Movies→iDVD folder contains a file called Cruise.mov.

Note: As Figure 4-11 makes clear, projects converted from older iMovie versions contain a second reference movie, lying loose in the project folder. It's an older-style reference movie, left there in case you ever open up the movie in iMovie 4 again for editing.

Technically, this icon is called the reference movie not because you're supposed to refer to it, but because it *contains* references (pointers) to all of the individual movie and sound clips in the Media folder, just as the project file does. That's why the reference movie is so tiny, occupying only a few kilobytes of space.

The reference movie's primary purpose is to accommodate the direct-to-iDVD movie-burning feature described in Chapter 15. You may occasionally find the reference movie handy for your own purposes, though; it offers a great way to make a quick playback of a movie you've been working on. It's also a convenient "handle" for dragging your iMovie movie into iDVD, Toast Titanium, or other programs that use movies as raw materials.

When you double-click this icon, your iMovie movie appears in QuickTime Player, where a simple tap of the Space bar starts it playing. This method is quicker and less memory-hogging than opening it in iMovie. It's safer, too, because you don't risk accidentally nudging some clip or sound file out of alignment; in QuickTime Player, you can't do anything but *watch* the movie.

- **Other folders.** The File→Share command is the final step in almost every iMovie project. It's the last stop on your journey, where you export your masterpiece to another software or medium so it can reach an audience.

The Share command often hands off your work to some entity beyond itself. For example, when you tell iMovie that you want to burn a DVD, the program hands your work off to iDVD. When you say you want to send the movie to a Bluetooth device (like a cellphone), iMovie hands off to that wireless gadget. When you export your film to a .Mac Web page, you pass it on to that particular server.

In each case, iMovie stores the appropriately compressed version of your movie in a temporary folder inside the Shared Movies folder. Here, you'll find a folder called, for example, iDVD, Bluetooth, or HomePage.

The idea is that if you want to send the same movie out again later, you'll have a ready-to-transmit copy. You won't have to wait for iMovie to compress the movie all over again.

Cache Folder

This folder is where iMovie stores little scraps and bits it needs for its own use. For example:

- The Timeline movie is a lot like the reference movie described above, except that the Timeline.mov movie is primarily for iMovie's own use. It doesn't incorporate everything you might consider an important part of the movie (for example, it doesn't include DVD chapter markers).

- Thumbnails.plist and Timeline Movie Data.plist are special data files that store information about the status of your Clips pane (Thumbnails.plist) and the timeline at the bottom of the window (Timeline Movie Data.plist), like what zoom level you've selected and whether or not you've opted to display sound waves on the audio clips (see the following section). These .plist files are for iMovie's use, not yours.

Audio Waveforms Folder

Audio *waveforms* are visual "sound waves" that appear on audio clips. These visible peaks and valleys make it a lot easier to cue up certain video moments with the audio.

These graphic representations of your sound files don't appear by magic, though. First, you have to turn on this feature by choosing View→Show Clip Volume Levels. Then, iMovie has to compute the waveforms' shapes, based on the sonic information in each clip.

Because that computational task takes time, iMovie stores a copy of these visuals in the Audio Waveforms folder, which it creates on the fly. Thereafter, each time you open your iMovie project, you won't have to wait for the waveforms to appear. iMovie will retrieve the information about their shapes from the files in this folder and blast them to the screen in a matter of moments. (The .wvf files are the waveform graphics; .snp files store "snap to" information for Timeline snapping, as described and illustrated on page 217.)

Importing Footage from Non-DV Tapes

We live in a transitional period. Millions of the world's existing camcorders and VCRs require VHS, VHS-C, or 8 mm cassettes—that is, analog tapes instead of digital.

DV camcorders are rapidly catching up; they're the only kind people buy these days. But in the meantime, potential video editors face a very real problem: how to transfer into iMovie the footage they shot before the DV era. Fortunately, this is fairly easy to do if you have the right equipment. You can take any of these four approaches, listed roughly in order of preference:

Approach 1: Use a Recent Sony or Canon Camcorder

If you're in the market for a new digital camcorder, here's a great idea: Buy a Sony or Canon MiniDV camcorder. Most current models offer analog-to-digital *passthrough* conversion. In other words, the camcorder itself acts as a media converter that turns the signal from your old analog tapes into a digital one that you can record and edit in iMovie.

The footage never hits a DV tape. Instead, it simply plays from your older VCR or camcorder directly into the Macintosh. (Not all Sony and Canon camcorders have this feature, so ask before you buy. And on some models, you must use the camcorder's on-board menu system to enable the live passthrough.)

If you've got a drawerful of older tapes, such a camcorder is by far the most elegant and economical route, especially if you're shopping for a new camcorder anyway.

Approach 2: Record onto Your DV Camcorder

Even if your newish digital camcorder doesn't offer *real-time* analog-to-digital conversion, it may have analog inputs that let you record your older material onto a MiniDV tape in your *new* camcorder. If so, your problem is solved.

1. **Unplug the FireWire cable from the DV camcorder.**

   Most camcorders' analog inputs switch off when a FireWire cable is hooked up.

2. **Connect RCA cables from the Audio Output and Video Output jacks on the side of your older camcorder or VCR. Connect the opposite ends to the analog inputs of your DV camcorder.**

   Figure 1-3 illustrates this arrangement. Put a blank DV tape into your DV camcorder.

Tip: If both your old camcorder and your DV camcorder have S-*video* connectors (a round, dime-sized jack), use them instead. S-video connections offer higher quality than RCA connections. (Note that an S-video cable doesn't conduct sound, however. You still have to connect the red and white RCA cables to carry the left and right stereo sound channels.)

---

3. **Switch both camcorders into VTR or VCR mode.**

   You're about to make a copy of the older tape by playing it into the camcorder.

   By now, every fiber of your being may be screaming, "But analog copies make the quality deteriorate!" Relax. You're only making a single-generation copy. Actually, you're only making *half* an analog copy; it's being recorded digitally, so you lose only half as much quality as you would with a normal VCR-to-VCR duplicate. In other words, you probably won't be able to spot any picture deterioration. And you'll have the footage in digital format now forever, ready to make as many copies as you want with no further quality degradation.

4. **Press the Record button on the DV camcorder, and press Play on the older camcorder or VCR.**

You can monitor your progress by watching the LCD screen of your camcorder. Remember that the DV cassette generally holds only 60 minutes of video, compared with 2 hours on many previous-format tapes. You may have to change DV cassettes halfway through the process.

When the transfer is finished, you can rewind the newly recorded DV cassette in the DV camcorder and then import it into iMovie exactly as described in this chapter.

Approach 3: Use a Media Converter

If your DV camcorder doesn't have analog inputs, you can buy an *analog-to-digital converter*—a box that sits between your Mac and your VCR or older camcorder. It's an unassuming half-pound gray box, about 3 by 5 inches. Its primary features include analog audio and video (and S-video) inputs, which accommodate your older video gear, and a FireWire jack, whose cable you can plug into your Mac.

Your options include the Canopus ADVC-55 (*www.canopus.com,* $215, shown in Figure 4-16), and the Director's Cut Take 2 box *(www.miglia.com/products/index. html;* about $280).

In either case, you'll be very pleased with the video quality. And when it comes to converting older footage, the media-converter approach has a dramatic advantage over DV camcorders with analog inputs: You have to sit through the footage only once. As your old VCR or camcorder plays the tape through the converter, the Mac records it simultaneously. (Contrast with Approach 2, which requires you to play the footage *twice:* once to the DV camcorder, and then from there to the Mac.)

Figure 4-16:
The Canopus box requires no external power because it draws its juice from the Mac, via Fire-Wire cable. It also offers double sets of inputs and outputs, so you can keep your TV and VCR hooked up simultaneously. And it can handle both NTSC (North American) or PAL (European) video signals.

Unfortunately, you can't control these devices using iMovie's playback controls, as described in this chapter. Instead, you must transfer your footage manually by pressing Play on your VCR or old camcorder and then clicking Import on the iMovie screen. In that way, these converters aren't as convenient as an actual DV or Digital8 camcorder.

Approach 4: Use a Digital8 Camcorder

Sony's Digital8 family of camcorders accommodate 8 mm, Hi-8, *and* Digital8 tapes, which are 8 mm cassettes recorded digitally. (Low-end models may not offer this feature, however, so ask before you buy.) Just insert your old 8 mm or Hi-8 cassettes into the camcorder and proceed as described in this chapter. iMovie never needs to know that the camcorder doesn't contain a DV cassette.

Actually, a Digital8 camcorder grants you even more flexibility than that. Most Digital8 camcorders also have *analog inputs,* shown back in Figure 1-3, which let you import footage from your VCR or other tape formats, just as described in Approach 2.

Building the Movie

Whether on your Mac or in a multimillion-dollar Hollywood professional studio, film editing boils down to three tiny tasks: selecting, trimming, and rearranging *clips*. Of course, that's like saying that there's nothing more to painting than mixing various amounts of red, yellow, and blue. The art of video editing lies in your decisions about *which* clips you select, *how* you trim them, and *what* order you put them in.

At its simplest, iMovie editing works like this:

1. Trim your clips until they contain exactly the footage you want.

2. Drag your clips from the Clips pane to the storyboard area at the bottom of the screen, where iMovie plays them in one seamless pass, from left to right.

3. Rearrange the scenes by dragging them around.

4. Add crossfades, titles (credits), effects, music, and sound effects.

This chapter is dedicated to showing you the mechanics of the first three tasks. The following chapters cover the fourth step, and Chapter 10 offers tips for adding taste and artistry to these proceedings.

Navigating Your Clips

As you're building your movie, you can store your clips in either of two places: the Clips pane or the strip at the bottom of the window. You put clips on the Clips pane before deciding what to do with them, and drag them down to the storyboard area once you've decided where they fit into your movie.

This clip-assembly area at the bottom of the iMovie screen can appear in either of two ways:

- **Clip Viewer.** In this view, each clip appears as an icon, as though it's a slide on a slide viewer. Each is sized identically, even if one is 8 minutes long and the next is only 2 seconds.

- **Timeline Viewer.** This view also shows a linear map of your movie. But in this case, each clip is represented by a horizontal bar that's as wide as the clip is long. Short clips have short bars; long clips stretch across your screen. Parallel bars below the clips indicate the soundtracks playing simultaneously.

Grizzled iMovie veterans are used to switching between these two viewers by clicking the corresponding icon just above them (either the film strip or the clock) or by pressing the viewer-switching keystroke: ⌘-E.

But they might want to consider a different tactic in iMovie HD: not using the Clip Viewer *at all*. In iMovie HD, Apple gave the Timeline Viewer all of the drag-and-droppy talents once reserved for the Clip Viewer. Now, for example, you can drag clips to rearrange them in the Timeline Viewer, drag them back and forth to the Clips pane, drag them to the Finder or programs like iDVD, and so on. In short, there's very little reason left to use the Clip Viewer *at all*.

Note: You can read much more about these two views of your work at the end of this chapter. It's important now, however, to note that Apple hasn't given a name to this bottom-of-your-screen area as a *whole*. To prevent you from having to read about the "Clip Viewer/Timeline Viewer area" 47 times per chapter, this book uses the made-up term *Movie Track* to refer to this editing track, regardless of which view it's showing.

You can do several things to a clip, whether it's in the Clips pane or the Movie Track.

Select a Clip

When you click a clip—the picture, not the name—iMovie highlights it by making its border (the "cardboard" portion of the "slide") or its bar (in the Timeline) blue. The first frame of the selected clip appears in the Monitor window. (If you're in Camera Mode at the time, busily controlling your camcorder by clicking the playback

Figure 5-1:
iMovie HD no longer reveals, at the bottom of the window, the date and time a highlighted clip was originally recorded. You can still see those details, though, if you double-click the clip.

controls, iMovie immediately switches back into Edit Mode. The camcorder stops automatically.)

Once you've highlighted a clip, its name and duration appear at the bottom edge of the Movie Track, as shown in Figure 5-1.

To *de*select a clip (all clips, in fact), choose Edit→Select None, or press Shift-⌘-A, or Control-click any clip and choose Select None from the shortcut menu. If you're menu-phobic, just click anywhere *except* on a clip (on the metallic-looking iMovie background, say), or Shift-click the first or last in a series of highlighted clips.

Knowing these five ways to deselect your clips will save you frustration. Just after you create an effect or title, for example, iMovie leaves only that clip highlighted. You'll usually want to deselect it—and to play back what comes *before and after* the effect—to see your handiwork in context.

Select Several Clips

You can use a number of techniques to highlight several clips simultaneously. For example:

- In the Movie Track, click one clip, and then Shift-click the last one. All consecutive clips between them get selected.

- You can also select several clips that aren't next to each other using the same techniques you'd use to select nonadjacent icons in a Finder list view. To do so, click the first clip, then ⌘-click each additional clip. You can also ⌘-click a selected clip to deselect it.

- In the Clips pane, you can either Shift-click or ⌘-click several clips, one at a time. (You may as well learn to ⌘-click, though, so you can use the same shortcut in both the Clips pane and the Movie Track.)

- You can also choose a bunch of clips, either in the Clips pane or in the Movie Track, by *drag-selecting* them. This technique involves positioning the cursor in the gray area outside clips and dragging diagonally over the clips you want to select. As you drag, you create a faint gray selection rectangle. Any clips touched by, or inside, this rectangle become highlighted.

- In either the Clips pane or the Movie Track, you can select all of the clips by choosing Edit→Select All (⌘-A). Or Control-click any clip and choose Select All from the shortcut menu.

Tip: Once you've selected several clips, you can ⌘-click a clip to remove it from the selection, if you like. Also, like the corresponding trick in the Finder, you ⌘-click a stray clip to add it to a Shift-clicked group.

So why would you want to select several clips at once? Let us count the tricks:

- Delete them all by pressing the Delete key, or drag them all to the project Trash.

- Use the Cut, Copy, or Clear commands in the Edit menu to affect all of them at once. (Why not just choose these commands from the shortcut menu that appears when you Control-click a clip? Because Control-clicking simultaneously *deselects* all other selected clips, which sort of defeats the purpose.) You can paste copied clips either to another spot in the same movie, or even into a different iMovie HD project.

- Move them around the Movie Track or the Clips pane—or drag them from one of those locations to the other—by dragging any one of them. The remaining clips slide leftward to close the gaps.

- Drag them all to the Finder, where they appear as individual movie-clip icons, or into another program, like iDVD.

- Apply the same transition, special effect, or Ken Burns photo setting to all of them using the Apply button on the Trans, Effects, and Photo panes. Similarly, you can update them all using the Update button. (Details in Chapters 6 through 8.)

- Consolidate a batch of nonadjacent clips. For example, suppose you ⌘-click clips number 1, 3, 5, and 7. Now you can use Edit→Cut, click a different clip in the movie to pinpoint a landing site, and then choose Edit→Paste. The clips that you cut, which were once scattered, now appear adjacent to each other and in sequence.

Tip: Here's a secret little command that very few iMovie fans even know about: Select Similar Clips.

Here's how it works: Click a clip in the Movie Track, and then choose Edit→Select Similar Clips. (Alternatively, Control-click a clip and then, from the shortcut menu, choose Select Similar Clips.) iMovie thoughtfully selects all clips in the Movie Track that match: all black clips, all photos, all transition effects, all clips that were chopped out of the same original piece of footage, and so on. This command can be a quick, efficient way to delete, move, consolidate, or modify a lot of similar material en masse.

Whenever you've selected more than one clip (either in the Clips pane or the Movie Track), iMovie adds up their running times and displays the total at the bottom edge of the iMovie window. It says, for example, "3 items selected 2:12:01."

Play a Clip

You can play a highlighted clip in the Monitor window by pressing the Space bar (or clicking the Play triangle button underneath the Monitor window).

You can stop the playback very easily: Press the Space bar a second time, or click anywhere else on the screen—on another clip, another control, the Monitor window, the metallic iMovie background, and so on.

Jump Around in a Clip

Whether the clip is playing or not, you can jump instantly to any other part of the clip in one of two ways:

- Drag the Playhead handle to any other part of the Scrubber bar (see Figure 5-2).

- Click directly in the Scrubber bar to jump to a particular spot in the footage. Doing so while the movie is playing saves you the difficulty of trying to grab the tiny Playhead as it moves across the screen.

Tip: To play back a section repeatedly for analysis, just keep clicking at the same spot in the Scrubber bar while the clip plays.

Figure 5-2:
*While a clip plays, the Playhead
(the down-pointing triangle)
slides across the Scrubber bar.
If you can catch it, you can drag
the Playhead using the mouse,
thus jumping around in the
movie. Or you can simply click
anywhere in the Scrubber bar. Either way, the playback continues
at the new spot in the clip.*

Step Through a Clip

By pressing the right and left arrow keys, you can view your clip one frame at a time, as though you're watching the world's least interesting slideshow. Hold down these arrow keys steadily to make the frame-by-frame parade go by faster.

Adding the Shift key to your arrow-key presses is often more useful—it lets you jump *10* frames at a time. In time, you can get extremely good at finding an exact frame in a particular piece of footage just by mastering the arrow-key and Shift-arrow-key shortcuts. (These shortcuts work only when the clip isn't playing.)

Scan Through a Clip

The Rewind and Fast Forward keystrokes (left bracket and right bracket—that is, the [and] keys) let you zoom through your footage faster. Press once to start playback, a second time to stop. In iMovie HD, you even hear the audio as you rewind or fast forward (sped up, chipmunk-style).

You don't have to click Play first. The Rewind and Fast Forward keystrokes start your clip playing at double speed even from a dead stop.

Rename a Clip

When iMovie imports your clips, it gives them such creative names as *Clip 01, Clip 02,* and so on. Fortunately, renaming a clip on the Clips pane or Clip Viewer is very easy: Just click directly on its name ("Clip 11") to open the renaming rectangle, and then type the new name. All the usual Macintosh editing techniques work inside this little highlighted renaming rectangle, including the Delete key and the Cut, Copy, Paste, and Select All commands in the Edit menu.

You can also rename a clip in its Clip Info dialog box (see Figure 4-10), which is the *only* way to change a clip's name in the Timeline Viewer. To open this box, just double-click the clip. (Or, if you're billing by the hour, Control-click the clip and, from the shortcut menu, choose Show Info.)

An iMovie clip's name can be 127 letters and spaces long. Be aware, however, that only about the first eleven letters of it actually show up under the clip icon. (The easiest way to see the whole clip name is to double-click the clip icon and then drag your cursor through the Name field in the resulting dialog box.)

The clip renaming you do in iMovie doesn't affect the names of the files in your project's Media folder on the hard drive (see page 113). Files there remain forever with their original names: Clip 01, Clip 02, and so on. That's why, in times of troubleshooting or file administration, the Clip Info box that appears when you double-click a clip can be especially useful. It's the only way to find out how a clip that you've renamed in iMovie corresponds to a matching clip on your hard drive.

Tip: Because you can only see the first few letters of a clip's name when it's on the Clips pane, adopt clever naming conventions to help you remember what's in each clip. Use prefix codes like CU (for "closeup"), ES ("establishing shot"), MS ("medium shot"), WS ("wide shot"), and so on, followed by useful keywords ("wild laughter," "sad melon," and so on). If the clip contains recorded speech, clue yourself in by including a quotation as part of the clip's name.

Reorganize Your Clips

You can drag clips from cubbyhole to cubbyhole on the Clips pane. In fact, you can even drag a clip (or even a mass of highlighted clips) onto an *occupied* cubbyhole. iMovie automatically creates enough new cubbyholes to hold them all, and shuffles existing clips out of the way if necessary.

The freedom to drag clips around in the Clips pane offers you a miniature storyboard feature. That is, you can construct a *sequence* by arranging several clips in the Clips

---

UP TO SPEED

Secrets of the Save Command

As you work in almost any program, you're usually encouraged to choose File→Save (or press ⌘-S) frequently, thus preserving your latest efforts and protecting them against power-failure disaster.

Saving in iMovie is fairly quick; it doesn't require the long, disk-intensive wait that you might expect from a video-editing program. (You're saving only your Project file, not making any changes to the large, underlying DV files in your Media

folder.) Better yet, in iMovie HD, saving makes iMovie release unused memory and disk space, making the whole works run slightly faster.

Saving your document does, however, have a few downsides. Each time you save, you wipe out your entire Undo and Redo trail; you can no longer work backward to correct a mistake using the Undo command.

Apple giveth, and Apple taketh away.

pane. When they seem to be in a good order for your finished scene, drag the whole batch to the Movie Track at once.

Tip: See the little tiny icon next to the name of your project (top of the window)? If you drag that icon to any visible swatch of your Desktop, you create an alias of your project there—a handy, double-clickable launch pad to get you back into this project tomorrow.

Undo, Revert, and Other Safety Nets

As programs go, iMovie is a forgiving one. For starters, the Edit→Undo command is an *unlimited* Undo command, meaning that you can retrace (undo) your steps, one at a time, working backward all the way back to the moment when you created the project. (You can even unimport a clip from your camcorder!)

There's an Edit→Redo command, too, so you can undo your undoing.

Revert to Saved

But iMovie HD also offers, for the first time, a Revert to Saved command. If you *really* botch your work, choosing File→Revert to Saved takes the project all the way back to its condition the last time you used the Save command. It basically undoes every step you took since then.

Still, unlimited Undo, and even Revert to Saved, aren't always ideal. If you made a mistake eight steps ago, you can undo that step, but only by undoing the seven successful editing steps you took thereafter.

Even more important, you lose your entire Undo/Redo and Revert to Saved trails *every time you use the Save command!* That little quirk ought to throw cold water on any ⌘-S–happy frequent savers.

Revert Clip to Original

Even then, however, iMovie has one more safety net in store for you: the Advanced→ Revert Clip to Original command (called Restore Clip in iMovie 4).

Remember that every time you cut or crop a clip, iMovie doesn't actually disturb the clip itself (the file on your hard drive). Instead, it simply shifts around its own internal *pointers* to the portion of the clip that you want to use. As a result, it's a piece of cake for iMovie to say, "Oh, you want me to throw away those pointers and give you back the original clip as it came from the camcorder? No problem."

In short, the Revert Clip to Original command gives you a convenient safety net, a chance to start with a clean slate on a clip-by-clip basis. (You can also Control-click a clip and choose this command from the shortcut menu.)

When you choose Revert Clip to Original, iMovie displays the dialog box shown in Figure 5-3. If you click OK, iMovie returns the clip to its original, precut, precrop condition, even if you've already placed it into the Movie Track. In that case, the clip's bar in the Timeline Viewer grows correspondingly wider, shoving other clips to the right to make room.

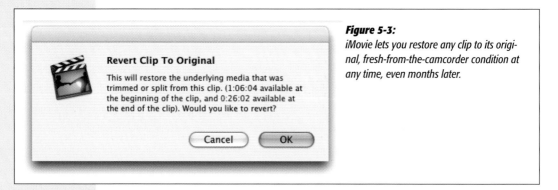

Revert Clip To Original

This will restore the underlying media that was trimmed or split from this clip. (1:06:04 available at the beginning of the clip, and 0:26:02 available at the end of the clip). Would you like to revert?

Cancel   OK

Figure 5-3:
iMovie lets you restore any clip to its original, fresh-from-the-camcorder condition at any time, even months later.

The Project Trash

You can get rid of a clip either by selecting it and then pressing the Delete key or by dragging it directly onto the project Trash icon (shown back in Figure 4-5). This iMovie feature is *radically* different than it was in previous versions, for better and for worse.

The iMovie Trash has a lot in common with the iPhoto Trash, the Finder's Trash, or the Windows Recycle Bin: it's a safety net. It's a holding tank for clips, photos, and sounds that you intend to throw out. They're not really gone, though, until you use the File→Empty Trash command.

In previous versions of iMovie, though, this Trash didn't *work* much like the standard Mac Trash. It didn't bulge when something was in it, you couldn't double-click it to open a window revealing its contents, and you certainly couldn't selectively rescue items from it.

All of that has changed in iMovie HD. Now, you can indeed open the Trash "folder," look over and even play back the clips inside, and rescue or delete *individual* audio and video clips without emptying the whole Trash.

To open the new Trash window, click the Trash icon or choose File→Show Trash. See Figure 5-4 for details.

Tip: If you just want to empty the whole Trash right now, without having to wait for the Trash contents window to open, press the ⌘ and Option keys as you click the Trash icon.

The fact that you can open the Trash window isn't the only startling change in iMovie HD. You should also be aware that:

- Whenever you choose File→Empty Trash (or double-click the Trash can), you *lose* your ability to undo your recent steps; the Undo command is dimmed. In fact, emptying the Trash also disables the Revert to Saved command and vaporizes whatever's on your Clipboard. (You can still use the Revert Clip to Original command, however.)

Figure 5-4:
Top: The first encounter most people have with the new iMovie HD Trash is this message, which often appears when you open up an iMovie project you made with a previous version. It's calling your attention to the fact that you can now open the Trash and look over its contents individually.

Middle: If you click the Trash icon (or click View Trash in the dialog box above), the Trash window opens. Click a clip to select it—and to make it appear, in tiny, QuickTime, playable form, at the right side of the box, so you can see what you're dealing with. If you decide you don't want to lose this clip after all, you can drag it right out of this box and back into the Clips pane or the Movie Track.

Bottom: On the other hand, if you don't want to hang onto the selected clip or clips, click Delete Selected Clip(s). Or click Empty Trash if you want to nuke the whole lot. Either way, a variation of this message appears, filling you in on the import of your decision.

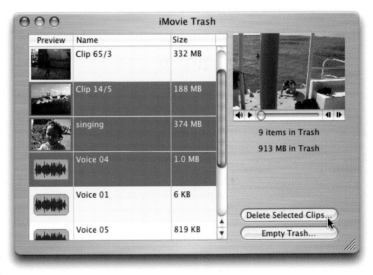

So when would you ever choose File→Empty Trash? The short answer is, only when you need to reclaim the hard-drive space it's taking up, and perhaps once when your project is finished.

- On the other hand, emptying the project Trash doesn't always restore free disk space, for technical reasons described in the box below.

- Emptying the Trash is no longer likely to corrupt your iMovie project—a rare but deeply upsetting occurrence in iMovie 4.

- Emptying the Trash is very fast in iMovie HD, even if there are thousands of clips in there.

Shortening Clips by Dragging

Almost nobody hits the camcorder's Record button at the precise instant when the action begins and stops recording the instant it stops. Life is just too unpredictable. That's why the first thing most people do when they get their clips into a movie is *trim* them—to chop the boring parts off the beginning and ending of each clip before dragging them onto the timeline.

In the earliest versions of iMovie, you trimmed your clips by splitting them apart, by chopping off their ends or lopping chunks out of the middle. That was OK, but things got messy if you later changed your mind; if, for example, you cut 10 seconds off the end and later decided you wanted 5 of them back.

UP TO SPEED

Why Emptying the Trash Doesn't Restore Disk Space

OK, this is so weird. I had a ton of stuff in my iMovie Trash. But when I emptied it, the little "free disk space remaining" counter didn't change at all! I had 532 megs available before I emptied the Trash, and the same amount after!

No doubt about it: iMovie HD's revamped editing-and-Trash features are a blessing and a curse.

Here's the blessing: In iMovie HD, you can use the Revert Clip to Original command *any time,* even after emptying the Trash, even months or years later. You can also add back a missing chunk from the middle of a clip that you'd previously lobotomized–again, even after emptying the Trash. You can chop, truncate, split, and shorten clips to your heart's content, and at any time, restore what you'd eliminated. (In previous iMovie versions, emptying the Trash meant that portions you cut from clips were gone forever.)

Here's the curse: These features work because iMovie quietly preserves the *entire* copy of every clip you import. If you split a clip in half, drag the second part to the Trash, and then empty the Trash, you don't get back one single byte of disk space. iMovie is hanging onto the *entire* original clip, just in case you change your mind someday.

The only time emptying the Trash actually frees up disk space, in fact, is if you've put an *entire clip* into it. If even one frame of it appears in the Timeline, iMovie still preserves the entire original clip on your hard drive.

So what if you've imported a 40-minute tape all in one clip and you intend to work with only the first 5 minutes' worth? Will that iMovie project occupy 40 minutes' worth of space on your hard drive forever?

Yes, unless you the somewhat drastic steps described on page 478. (In short, the process involves exporting the short clip to your hard drive as a full-quality DV movie, deleting all scraps of the original clip from iMovie, and emptying the Trash, which returns all that disk space to you. Finally, you drag the good part of the clip from the desktop *back into* the iMovie window. iMovie will be convinced that this 5-minute segment *is* the entire clip.)

Those time-honored techniques—and all of their related problems—still work in iMovie HD. You can read about them later in this chapter.

Most of the time, though, you'll want to adopt one of iMovie's sweetest features instead: *edge dragging.* Instead of chopping off the ends of your clips, you can just *hide* the ends by dragging them inward, as shown in Figure 5-5. (This kind of non-destructive edge-dragging also works with audio clips. It's a common technique in GarageBand, too.)

Tip: Here's a great way to use this technique. First, play back the sequence. Using the arrow keys, position the Playhead so that it pinpoints the precise frame where you want the clip to end. In other words, you're using the Playhead to mark the target for the drag-cropping you're about to perform.

Now grab the *end* of the clip and drag it up against the Playhead. Conveniently enough, the end you're dragging snaps against the ghosted Playhead line, as though it's a bookmark. As a result, you get individual-frame accuracy without having to remember precisely how far to drag. (This trick works only if "Snap to items in timeline" is turned on in iMovie→Preferences.)

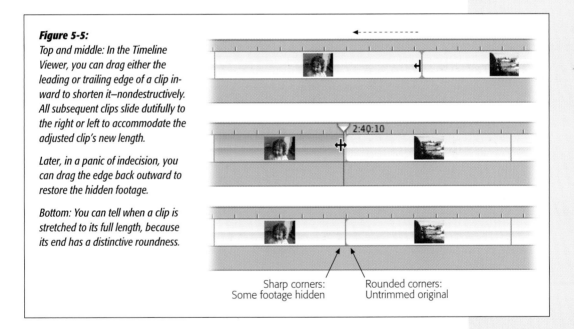

Figure 5-5:
Top and middle: In the Timeline Viewer, you can drag either the leading or trailing edge of a clip inward to shorten it—nondestructively. All subsequent clips slide dutifully to the right or left to accommodate the adjusted clip's new length.

Later, in a panic of indecision, you can drag the edge back outward to restore the hidden footage.

Bottom: You can tell when a clip is stretched to its full length, because its end has a distinctive roundness.

Sharp corners:
Some footage hidden

Rounded corners:
Untrimmed original

The beauty of this approach, of course, is its flexibility. After you crop a clip this way, you can play it back to gauge its impact on the flow of scenes. If you feel that you trimmed a little too much, simply grab the end of the clip and drag it outward a little more. If you don't think you cropped enough, drag it inward.

And now, three delicious tips pertaining to edge-dragging:

- In general, when you *shorten* a clip, all subsequent clips slide to the left to close up the gap. (That's what the pros call *ripple* editing.) Your overall movie gets shorter.

In some situations, though, you may want to shorten a clip *without* allowing any other clips to shift. Instead, you want to leave *empty space* behind as you shorten the clip, so that the overall movie stays exactly the same length.

To make it so, just press the ⌘ key as you drag the clip's edge inward. Now you're creating a gap that, when played back, appears as black space. Later, you can either convert the gap to a clip unto itself (page 140) or fill it with pasted footage.

- On the other hand, when you drag a clip's edge *outward* to expose previously hidden footage, iMovie generally shoves all subsequent clips to the *right* to make room. Your movie, as a result, gets longer.

Once again, though, the ⌘ key can stop the rippling. If you press ⌘ as you drag outward, you *cover up* some footage in the adjacent clip. Your movie remains exactly the same length.

- Want better precision? Try this technique.

First, play back the sequence. Using the arrow keys, position the Playhead so that it pinpoints the precise frame where you want the clip to end. In other words,

---

FREQUENTLY ASKED QUESTION

Nondestructive Confusion

OK, hold on a sec. You're saying that if I drag the end of a clip, I can stretch it outward to restore some hidden footage. Sounds great, except for one thing: when I drag the beginning of a clip leftward, it shortens the clip before it! I don't want that!

Patience is the path to happiness, grasshoppa.

First of all, it is true that dragging a clip's left edge to the left *looks* like it's eating into the clip before it, which gets shorter and shorter as you drag. But it's just an optical fake-out; the instant you release the mouse, you'll see the squished clip snap back to its original length, as shown here.

The first clip looks like it's getting shortened.

But when you release, the first clip snaps back to its original length.

OK, but I have another problem. Sometimes iMovie randomly refuses to let me do any edge-dragging at all. The little horizontal-arrow cursor just never appears.

It's true that iMovie sometimes doesn't let you do edge-dragging, but it's not at all random. You can't do edge-dragging when you've got audio levels turned on. Choose View→ Show Clip Volume Levels to turn off that feature; you can now drag clip edges as usual.

(Apple no doubt felt that you'd have too much trouble telling the program whether you were dragging an *edge* or an *audio level,* as described in Chapter 8.)

---

you're using the Playhead to mark the target for the drag-cropping you're about to perform.

Now grab the *end* of the clip and drag it up against the Playhead. Conveniently enough, the end you're dragging snaps against the ghosted Playhead line, as though it's a bookmark. As a result, you get individual-frame accuracy without having to remember precisely how far to drag. (This trick works only if "Snap to items in timeline" is turned on in iMovie→Preferences.)

There's only one limitation to this technique: It works only in the Timeline Viewer. You can't use it to pre-shorten clips while they're still in the Clips pane, or after you've dragged them into the Clips viewer. For those purposes, read on.

Three Ways to Trim a Clip

Trimming out the deadwood from your clips, so that you're left with only the very best shots from the very best scenes, is the heart of iMovie—and video editing.

Note: The following three techniques work as they did in previous versions of iMovie, with one huge exception: these are now nondestructive techniques, just like the edge-dragging business described earlier. For example, after you've shortened a clip by hacking a piece off the right end, you can later change your mind, even if you've emptied the Trash and let a year go by. You can restore some or all of the missing footage just by dragging the clip's right edge to the right in the Timeline Viewer.

Highlighting Footage

iMovie works just like other Mac programs: You highlight some footage, then use the Cut, Copy, or Paste commands to move it around. All three of the following footage-trimming techniques, for example, begin with *highlighting,* or selecting, a portion of your footage. Here's how you go about it:

1. **Click a clip to select it.**

   The clip can be either in the Clips pane or the Movie Track.

2. **Position your cursor just beneath the Scrubber bar.**

   See Figure 5-6.

3. **Drag horizontally until the triangle handles surround the footage you want to keep.**

   As soon as you push the mouse button down, the selection triangles jump to the position of your cursor. One remains where you clicked; the other follows your cursor as you drag. (In other words, don't waste time by dragging them painstakingly from the left edge of the Scrubber bar.)

   The Monitor window behaves as though you're scrolling the movie, so that you can see where you are as you drag the movable triangle. Also as you drag, the portion of the Scrubber bar between your handles turns yellow to show that it's highlighted.

Whatever Edit menu command you use now (such as Cut, Copy, Clear, or Crop) affects only the yellow portion.

Tip: Here's a quick trick for highlighting only the first portion of a selected clip: Shift-click within the Scrubber bar at the point where you'd like the selection to *end.* Instantly, iMovie highlights everything from the left end of the clip to the position of your click.

Figure 5-6:
Carefully drag horizontally until the triangles enclose only the scene you want to keep. Finally, when you choose the Edit→Crop command, everything outside of these handles is trimmed away.

After you've just dragged or clicked a handle, the arrow-key skills you picked up on page 123 come in extremely handy. You can let go of the mouse and, just by pressing the left and right arrow keys, fine-tune the position of the triangle handle on a frame-by-frame basis. (You can tell which triangle handle you'll be moving. It's darker, and it's marked by the Playhead, as shown in Figure 5-6. To move the *other* triangle handle, click it first.) Continue tapping the left and right arrow keys until the Monitor shows the precise frame you want—the first or last frame you'll want to keep in the clip.

Remember, too, that if you press *Shift-*right or -left arrow, you move the triangle handle 10 frames at a time. Between the 10-frame and one-frame keystrokes, you should find it fairly easy to home in on the exact frame where you want to trim the clip.

Tip: After you've highlighted a stretch of the Scrubber bar, you can adjust the selected portion—make it bigger or smaller—by clicking or dragging again beneath any unhighlighted portion of the Scrubber bar (to the right or left of the selected region). Either way, the end of the yellow bar jumps to your cursor as though attracted by a magnet. And either way, you avoid having to redo the entire selection, since one of your two endpoints remains in place.

As you drag the triangle handles, keep your eye on two readouts. First, your precise position within the clip or assembled movie appears just above your cursor, in seconds:frames format.

Second, a notation appears beneath the Movie Track that identifies the amount of footage between the handles. It might say, for example, "Frames selected 0:03:15 of 6:00:02 total." That is, you've selected 3.5 seconds of a 6-minute movie.

Being able to see exactly how much footage you're about to cut (or preserve) can be extremely useful when the timing of your movie is important, as when editing it to accompany a music track or when creating a movie that must be, for example, exactly 30 seconds long.

Tip: If you've really made a mess of your selection, click just *below* the Scrubber bar, on the brushed aluminum iMovie background. The program deselects your footage so that you can try again.

Snipping Off One End of a Clip

Having mastered the art of selecting a portion of a clip, as described in the previous section, you're ready to put it to work. Suppose, for example, that you want to shave off some footage from only one end of your clip:

1. **Highlight the footage you want to delete (at the beginning or end of the Scrubber bar).**

   The arrangement should look like Figure 5-7.

Figure 5-7:
To trim footage from one end of the clip, just highlight that much, using the triangle handles. The Monitor window shows you where you are in the footage as you drag the triangles. And once again, you can use the arrow keys to fine-tune the position of the triangle you've most recently clicked.

2. **Choose Edit→Cut.**

   iMovie promptly trims away whatever was highlighted between the triangles. As a bonus, your invisible Clipboard now contains the snipped piece, which you're welcome to paste right back into the Clips pane or Movie Track using the Edit→ Paste command, in case you might need it again.

Cropping Out the Ends of a Clip

If you want to trim some footage off *both* ends of a clip, it's quicker to highlight the part in the middle that you want to *keep*:

1. **Select the footage you want to keep.**

   Use any of the techniques described on page 131.

2. **Choose Edit→Crop (or press ⌘-K).**

   When you use this command, all of your signposts disappear, including the two triangle handles and the yellow part of the Scrubber bar. What used to be the yellow part of the Scrubber bar has now, in effect, expanded to fill the *entire* Scrubber bar. Your clip is shorter now, as a tap on the Space bar will prove.

Note: After you use the Crop command, the megabyte number underneath your project Trash icon usually increases. That's because, behind the scenes, iMovie hasn't actually thrown away the footage pieces you've just carved off. It's hanging onto them in case you decide to use the Edit→Undo command or the Advanced→ Revert Clip to Original command.

Chopping Out the Middle of a Clip

In this technique, you *eliminate* the middle part of a clip, leaving only the ends of it in your project.

You might not expect to encounter this situation very often, but you'd be surprised. The flexibility offered by this technique means that you can be less fussy when you're importing clips. You can import longer chunks of footage, for example, secure in the knowledge that you can always hack out the boring stuff that happens to fall in between two priceless moments:

1. **Select the footage you want to delete.**

   Again, you can use any of the tricks described on page 131.

2. **Choose Edit→Cut (or Edit→Clear), or press the Delete key.**

   If you're not prepared for it, the results of this technique can be startling—and yet it's perfectly logical. If you cut a chunk out of the middle of the clip, iMovie has no choice but to throw back at you the *two end pieces*—as two separate clips, side by side on the Clips pane or the Movie Track.

   Either way, the name of the newly created clip will help you identify it. If the original clip was called "Cut Me Out," the new, split-off clip is called "Cut Me Out/1."

Tip: Just a reminder: Whenever you cut material out of a clip, you can always restore it. Once the clip is placed in the Timeline, just tug outward on the edge where the cut occurred. iMovie smoothly "un-hides" the footage you had cut away.

Splitting a Clip

The techniques described in the previous section work well when you want to remove some footage from a clip. Sometimes, however, it can be useful to split a clip into two separate clips *without* deleting footage in the process. For example, suppose you want the title of your movie to appear 5 seconds into a certain piece of footage. In iMovie, the only way to accomplish that feat is to split the clip into three pieces—the first one being 5 seconds long—and superimpose the title credit on the middle piece. (More on titles in Chapter 7.)

The Split Video Clip at Playhead command is exactly what you need in that case.

1. **Click the clip to select it, whether in the Clips pane or the Movie Track.**

   This time, you'll click above the Scrubber bar, not below it.

2. **Click inside, or drag along, the Scrubber bar until you find the spot where you want to split the clip.**

Figure 5-8:
After you split a clip, iMovie cuts your clip in two and highlights both of the resulting clip icons (Clip Viewer, bottom). If the clip started out in the Movie Track, the Monitor window still lets you scroll all the way through the original clip. Only the telltale slashed number ("/1") on the second part of the clip lets you know that you're actually looking at two different clips side by side.

You can press the right- or left-arrow keys to nudge the Playhead one frame at a time to the right or left. Use Shift-arrow keys for *10*-frame jumps.

3. **Choose Edit→Split Video Clip at Playhead (or press ⌘-T).**

As shown in Figure 5-8, you wind up with two different clips, both highlighted. If the original was called "Split Me Up," iMovie calls the resultant clips "Split Me Up" and "Split Me Up/1." (To remove the highlighting, click anywhere else on the screen, or choose Edit→Select None.)

The Movie Track: Your Storyboard

When you're not trimming or splitting your clips, most of your iMovie time will be spent in the Movie Track—the horizontal strip at the bottom of the screen (see Figure 5-7). The idea is that you'll drag the edited clips out of the Clips pane and into the correct order on the Movie Track, exactly as though you're building a storyboard or timeline.

As noted at the beginning of this chapter, the Movie Track offers two different views: the Clip Viewer and the Timeline Viewer. Both are illustrated in Figure 5-9.

In either view, you can freely rearrange clips by dragging them. In the Clip Viewer, just drag them horizontally; in the Timeline Viewer, drag them *up and over* (or down and under) the adjacent clips, rather than directly to the side.

Tip: As you drag over them, the existing clips scoot out of the way, which can drive you crazy. In that case, hold down the ⌘ key until you're ready to let go of the clip you're dragging. They'll stay still.

Figure 5-9:
Top: When you click the film strip icon (indicated by the cursor), you see your camcorder footage.

Bottom: Click the clock icon to see the Timeline Viewer, which reveals your audio tracks and shows the relative lengths of your clips. You can even rearrange your clips in the Timeline Viewer, as long as you master the knack of dragging them up (or down) and around the adjacent clips.

Moreover, you can freely drag clips back and forth between the Clips pane and the Movie Track. (The ability to drag clips back and forth between the Clips pane and the Timeline Viewer is new in iMovie HD, and really useful.)

Remember, by the way, that you can switch the Movie Track between its two viewers by pressing ⌘-E. It corresponds to the second command in the new View menu, which says either "Switch to Clip Viewer" or "Switch to Timeline Viewer," whichever one you're *not* in.

Readouts in the Movie Track

iMovie identifies the name of your movie at the top of the window (and its format: DV-NTSC, for example, or HD-1080i-30 for "high-definition, 1080 interlaced scan lines, 30 frames per second").

At the very bottom of the window, you can see the name of the selected clip (or how many clips are selected), and how long it is relative to the whole movie.

Tip: The iMovie HD screen no longer tells you when a certain clip was filmed, as did previous versions. But that information is still easy to find: just double-click the clip you're wondering about. The resulting dialog box includes a line for Capture Date, which lets you know when you shot that clip. It's an extremely useful little statistic—like the date stamp on the back of a Kodak print.

Dragging to the Movie Track

There's not much to using the Movie Track: just drag a clip from the Clips pane directly onto it. For your visual pleasure, iMovie shows you a ghosted, translucent image of the clip's first frame as you drag.

Here are a few tips for making the most of this Clips pane–to–Movie Track procedure:

- If you want a clip placed at the *end* of the clips in the Movie Track, drop it in the slice of gray, empty space at the right end.

Tip: It can be difficult to drag a clip to the end of the *Timeline* Viewer, because no gray gap appears there. Depending on the mood of the technology gods, a gap may appear when your cursor actually approaches the right end of the display, making the existing clips scoot leftward to make room. But sometimes that doesn't happen.

If you're having trouble, remember that you can either (a) switch to the Clip Viewer view to tack a clip onto the end or (b) copy the clip from the Clips pane, click the last clip in the Timeline Viewer, and then paste. The clip pops neatly to the right of the last clip.

- If you want to put a clip *between* two clips on the Movie Track, drag your cursor between those clips, and watch as iMovie makes room by shoving existing clips to the right.

• You can also drag clips from the Movie Track *back* onto the Clips pane. You can take advantage of this feature whenever you decide that a sequence of clips isn't quite working, and you're going to postpone placing them into the movie.

• In the Movie Track, you can rearrange clips by dragging their icons horizontally. (Yes, this even works in the Timeline Viewer; see Figure 5-9.) Once again, iMovie makes room between existing clips when your cursor passes between them.

• In the Timeline Viewer, when you drag a clip directly to the right, iMovie leaves an empty gap. This is your opportunity to create a pure black clip (or, in fact, a clip of any solid color), as described on page 140.

• You don't have to drag one clip at a time; it's often more efficient to drag several clips simultaneously. Page 120 describes the various ways you can select several clips (like drag-selecting them or ⌘-clicking to select nonadjacent ones). For example, you might arrange several clips on your Clips pane into a mini-sequence that you then drop into your Movie Track as a unit.

Tip: As you're building your film on the Movie Track, think in terms of *sequences* of shots. By Shift-clicking, you can select, say, six or seven clips that constitute one finished sequence, and drag the selection (or cut and paste it) into a new location in the Movie Track to suit your artistic intentions.

That's an especially terrific tactic, since the *sequence of your Shift-clicking* determines the order of the clips when they get dumped onto the Movie Track. You now have a great way to pluck the best clips out of your video toolbox, no matter where they sit at the moment, and plunk them onto the Movie Track, already in the proper sequence.

Copying and Pasting Clips

Dragging isn't the only way to move footage around in iMovie; the Copy, Cut, and Paste commands can be more convenient. For one thing, you don't need the mouse.

For another, if you *copy* a clip from the Clips pane instead of dragging it, you leave a copy of the original behind. Later, if you've really made a mess of chopping up the clip in your Movie Track, you can return to the copy—your backup—without sacrificing the other editing work you've done since you made the copy. (Of course, the Revert Clip to Original command can do the same thing, but maintaining a whole, untouched original on the Clips pane is visual and easier to understand.)

For example, you can move a clip from the Clips pane to the Movie Track by clicking it, pressing ⌘-X, clicking in the Movie Track, and then pressing ⌘-V. (You can also *copy* the clip by beginning that sequence with ⌘-C instead.) You can move clips around within the Movie Track in the same way.

In fact, you can cut or copy clips out of one iMovie project and then paste them into a different one. The pasting process may take some time, because iMovie must move huge multimegabyte video files around on your hard drive. But this feature can come in very, very handy.

Note: When you copy and paste clips within a single project, you're never duplicating any files on your hard drive, so copying and pasting clips doesn't eat away at your remaining free space. But when you paste into a *different* project, you may be using far more disk space than you think; see page 478.

You may wonder how you're supposed to know where your cut or copied footage will appear when pasted. After all, there's no blinking insertion point to tell you.

The scheme is fairly simple:

- If there's a *highlighted* clip in the Clips pane or the Movie Track, the pasted clips appear *immediately to the right* of it. iMovie shoves all other clips to the right to make room for the new arrival. In other words, it's always a good idea to click a clip before pasting to show iMovie *where* to paste.

- If *no* clip is highlighted, iMovie pastes the cut or copied clips *at the Playhead position* in the Movie Track, even if that means chopping an existing clip in half to make room. (That's a change from previous iMovie versions.)

- If your intention is to *replace* the existing video in the Movie Track (instead of just shoving it to the right), don't use the Paste command at all. Instead, use the Paste Over at Playhead command, which is described on page 470.

Tricks of the Timeline Viewer

Everything you've read in the preceding pages has to do with the Movie Track in general. Most of the features described so far are available in either of the Movie Track's incarnations: the Clip Viewer or the Timeline Viewer.

But the Timeline Viewer is more than just another pretty interface. It's far more useful (and complex) than the Clip Viewer.

Many of the Timeline's super powers have to do with audio. Soundtracks, narration, music tracks, and sound effects all appear here as horizontal colored bars that play simultaneously with your video. You can read about these features in Chapter 8.

Some of the Timeline's features, however, are useful for everyday video editing—that is, if you consider playing footage in slow or fast motion everyday effects.

Zooming

The Timeline Viewer has a scroll bar, whose handle appears to be made of blue tooth gel, that lets you bring different parts of your movie into view. But depending on the length and complexity of your movie, you may wish you could zoom in for a more detailed view, or zoom out for a bird's-eye view of the whole project.

That's the purpose of the slider shown at lower left in Figure 5-9. It adjusts the relative sizes of the bars that represent your clips.

If you drag the slider handle all the way to the left, iMovie shows the entire movie in a single screen, without your having to scroll. The clip bars may be almost microscopic—you may not even be able to see the thumbnail picture on short clips—but at least you get a sense of the whole.

As you drag the zoom slider handle to the right, your clip bars expand in real time, widening to show you more detail. Finally, if the handle is all the way at the right side of the slider, only a few frames of video fill the entire width of the Timeline Viewer. You've zoomed in over 50 times!

There's no one best setting for the zoom level. You should adjust it constantly as you work, pulling back when you need to figure out why some sound effects are firing at the wrong moment, zooming in when you want to make fine adjustments to the sound volume in mid-clip (Chapter 8), and so on.

Sliding for Blackness

When you drag a clip to the right in the Timeline Viewer, you introduce a gap between the clip and the one to its left; iMovie automatically fills the gap with blackness and silence.

Tip: For greater precision, hold down the Control key and tap the arrow keys to move a clip right or left, making a wider or narrower black clip one frame at a time. Add the Shift key to nudge the clip 10 frames at a time.

You can turn this gap into a bona fide, clickable black clip in either of two ways:

• Flip back to the Clip Viewer. You'll see that iMovie has actually created a new clip, represented by its own icon in the Clip Viewer, called Black.

• Control-click anywhere inside the empty space in the Timeline Viewer. From the shortcut menu, choose Convert Empty Space to Clip.

Either way, you wind up with a new clip that's black and silent.

What you do with this gap is your business. You can leave it black, creating an effective "bookend" between scenes. You can switch to the Clip Viewer and drag the black clip up onto your Clips pane for future reuse. Or you can change its color, as described next.

Note: If there's a transition to the left of a clip (Chapter 6), dragging a clip to the right also drags everything attached to it, including the transition icon and the preceding clip, all in a merry little train.

Colorizing a Black Clip

Turning a black clip into a colored clip is a handy way to create a colored background for some titles or credits, for example. See Figure 5-10 for the secret.

Bookmarks

Navigating complex movies—or even simple ones—is a lot easier if you master the Bookmarks feature.

It works like this: Position the Playhead at an important spot in the movie, and then choose Markers→Add Bookmark (or just press ⌘-B, which is a lot quicker). iMovie responds by placing a tiny green diamond at that spot on the ruler (you can see a couple of them in Figure 5-11). Bookmarks are visible only in Timeline Viewer mode.

Figure 5-10:
When you double-click a black clip, this dialog box appears. (Other ways to get here: Control-click a clip and choose Show Info from the shortcut menu, or click a clip and choose File→Show Info.)

Click Color to open the Color Picker, where you can choose the color you want (page 189). The Duration box here lets you adjust the length of your color clip with frame-by-frame precision.

You'll see the real value of these markers once you've added a few of them to your movie. Now you can:

- Leap from one marker to the next using the Previous Bookmark and Bookmark commands (⌘-[and ⌘-], respectively).

- Align the Playhead with a bookmark by dragging it. You'll feel it—and even hear it—snap against the bookmark, assuming you've turned on Timeline Snapping (in iMovie→Preferences).

- Remove an individual bookmark by clicking it and then choosing Markers→ Delete Bookmark. Banish all of them at once by choosing Markers→Delete All Bookmarks.

Note: You can't move a bookmark once you've placed it. If you try to click its diamond, the Playhead jumps to the spot and covers up the bookmark, preventing you from dragging. Deleting the bookmark and installing a new one is your only alternative.

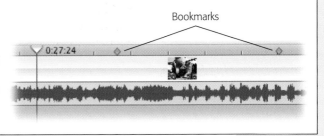

Figure 5-11:
When you drag a clip, a bookmark remains right where it was. As a result, you can bookmark a certain "hit" in the soundtrack and then fiddle with the video, dragging clips into alignment with the bookmark until you find the perfect visual jolt to go with the audio burst.

Playing the Movie Track

The Monitor isn't limited to playing clips; it can also play the Movie Track. That's handy, because one of iMovie's best features is its ability to show your movie-in-progress whenever you like (without having to *compile* or *render* anything, as you do in some more expensive editing programs).

Playing the Whole Movie

To play back your *entire* Movie Track, press the Home key on your keyboard, which in iMovie means "Rewind to beginning." As a timesaving bonus, the Home key *also* deselects all clips, as though it knows that you want to play back the entire Clip Viewer now.

Tip: On recent desktop Macs, the Home key is above the number keypad, or stationed together with a separate block of keys like Help, Delete, Page Up, and Page Down. On recent laptop Macs, you simulate the Home key by holding down the Fn key (in the lower-left corner of the keyboard) and tapping the left-arrow key.

Alternatively, you can click the Home *button*, which is beneath the Monitor just to the left of the Play button. Once again, iMovie deselects all clips in the process of rewinding.

When you tap the Space bar, iMovie plays your movie starting from the location of the Playhead in the Scrubber bar; if you've pressed Home, that's the beginning of the movie. iMovie plays one clip after another, seamlessly, from left to right as they appear in the Movie Track (Figure 5-12).

Playing your movie back is the best way to get a feeling for how your clips are working together. You may discover that, in the context of the whole movie, some are too long, too short, in the wrong order, and so on.

Figure 5-12:
When the Movie Track is ready to play, the Scrubber bar shows many different segments, one for each clip in it. Their relative lengths show you the lengths of the clips. You can use all of the navigating and editing tricks described in this chapter: pressing the arrow keys, splitting or trimming clips, and so on.

Playing a Segment of the Movie

You don't have to play the entire Movie Track. You can play only a chunk of it by first selecting only the clips you want. To do that, click the first clip you want to play, and then Shift-click the final one.

Now click the Play button or press the Space bar; iMovie plays only the clips you highlighted.

While the Movie is Playing

As the Movie Track plays, three simultaneous indicators show your position in the film. First, of course, the Playhead slides along the subdivided-looking Scrubber bar.

If the Timeline Viewer is visible, a duplicate Playhead slides along *it*. If the Clip Viewer is visible, on the other hand, a bright red, inverted T cursor slides along the faces of the clips themselves, which lets you know at a glance what clip you're seeing in the Monitor window *and* how much of it you've seen (Figure 5-13). You can't drag this cursor like a true scroll bar handle; it's purely an indicator.

Figure 5-13:
Because every clip icon is the same size but not every clip is the same length, the T indicator speeds up or slows down as it arrives at the left edge of each clip. (You can see it in the center clip here, approaching the right side of the frame.)

While the movie is playing, you can take control in several ways:

• Use the playback controls beneath the Monitor (or their keystroke equivalents) to pause, stop, rewind, and so on.

• Navigate the whole movie by clicking in the Scrubber bar or dragging the Playhead, exactly as when navigating a clip.

• Deselect the highlighted clips by clicking on any "brushed metal" spot in the iMovie window. This trick comes in very handy when you're doing a quick playback of a title, transition, or special effect you've just created. Ordinarily, iMovie would stop playback at the end of the new element, but often you want to see how the new effect flows into the next clip. If you see the end of the highlighted clip looming as the Playhead chugs along, you can click to deselect the clip without even interrupting the playback.

• Adjust the volume by pressing the up-arrow or down-arrow key.

• Jump into Play Full Screen mode by clicking the Play Full Screen button.

• Add a bookmark by pressing ⌘-B, or a DVD chapter marker by pressing Shift-⌘-M.

• Stop the playback by pressing the Space bar.

• Stop the playback *and* rewind to the beginning by pressing the Home key.

Editing Clips in the Movie Track

Fortunately, all of the editing tricks for trimming and splitting clips described in this chapter also work in the Movie Track. In other words, just because you see the segmented Scrubber bar (Figure 5-8) doesn't mean you can't click below it to produce the triangle handles, or click above it in readiness to use the Split Clip at Playhead command.

You can also perform many of the same clip-editing operations that you read about in their Clips pane context, earlier in this chapter. For example, you can rename a clip, delete it from the project, or use the Edit menu commands on it, exactly as you operate on Clips pane clips.

Full-Screen Playback Mode

Whenever you're tempted to play your movie-in-progress, consider clicking the Play Full Screen button (the darkened triangle to the right of the round Play button). It makes the playback—even if it's already under way—fill the entire computer screen.

To interrupt the movie showing, click the mouse or press any key on the keyboard. (The usual Macintosh "cancel" keystroke, ⌘-period, ironically, *doesn't* work in this context.)

Note: The quality of the full-screen playback still isn't the same pristine, crystal-clear playback you'll get when you transfer your finished movie back to your camcorder for TV playback. In fact, it's little more than a blown-up version of what you see in the Monitor window while editing your movie. If it's grainy there, it's enlarged-grainy in full-screen playback.

Transitions and Effects

This chapter is about two iMovie tools—Transitions and Effects—that can make your raw footage look even better than it is. Both of these tools are represented by buttons on the Clips/Effects/Sound panel that occupies the right side of your screen. This chapter covers both of these powerful moviemaking techniques.

About Transitions

What happens when one clip ends and the next one begins? In about 99.99 percent of all movies, music videos, and commercials—and in 100 percent of camcorder movies before the Macintosh era—you get a *cut*. That's the technical term for "nothing special happens at all." One scene ends, and the next one begins immediately.

Professional film and video editors, however, have at their disposal a wide range of *transitions*—special effects that smooth the juncture between one clip and the next. For example, the world's most popular transition is the *crossfade* or *dissolve,* in which the end of one clip gradually fades away as the next one fades in (see Figure 6-1). The crossfade is so popular because it's so effective. It gives a feeling of softness and grace

Figure 6-1:
The world's most popular and effective transition effect: a Cross Dissolve.

to the transition, and yet it's so subtle that the viewer might not even be conscious of its presence.

Like all DV editing programs, iMovie offers a long list of transitions, of which crossfades are only the beginning. You'll find an illustrated catalog of them starting on page 154. But unlike other DV editing software, iMovie makes adding such effects incredibly easy, and the results look awesomely assured and professional.

When Not to Use Transitions

When the Macintosh debuted in 1984, one of its most exciting features was its *fonts*. Without having to buy those self-adhesive lettering sets from art stores, you could make posters, flyers, and newsletters using any typefaces you wanted. In fact, if you weren't particularly concerned with being tasteful, you could even combine lots of typefaces on the same page—and thousands of first-time desktop publishers did exactly that. They thought it was exciting to harness the world of typography right on the computer screen.

You may even remember the result: a proliferation of homemade graphic design that rated very low on the artistic-taste scale. Instead of making their documents look more professional, the wild explosion of mixed typefaces made them look amateurish in a whole new way.

In video, transitions present exactly the same temptation: If you use too many, you risk telegraphing that you're a beginner at work. When you begin to polish your movie by adding transitions, consider these questions:

- **Does it really need a transition?** Sometimes a simple cut is the most effective transition from one shot to the next. Remember, the crossfade lends a feeling of softness and smoothness to the movie, but is that really what you want? If it's a sweet video of your kids growing up over time, absolutely yes. But if it's a hard-hitting issue documentary, then probably not, as those soft edges would dull the impact of your footage.

  Remember, too, that transitions often suggest the *passage of time.* In movies and commercials, consecutive shots in the same scene never include such effects. Plain old cuts tell the viewer that one shot is following the next in real time. But suppose one scene ends with the beleaguered hero saying, "Well, at least I still have my job at the law firm!"…and the next shot shows him operating a lemonade stand. (Now *that's* comedy!) In this case, a transition would be especially effective, because it would tell the audience that we've just jumped a couple of days.

  In other words, learning to have taste in transitions is a lot like learning to have taste in zooming, as described in Chapter 2. Transitions should be done *for a reason.*

- **Is it consistent?** Once you've chosen a transition-effect style for your movie, stick to that transition style for the entire film (unless, as always, you have an artistic reason to do otherwise). Using one consistent style of effect lends unity to your work. That's why interior designers choose only one dominant color for each room.

- **Which effect is most appropriate?** As noted earlier, the crossfade is almost always the least intrusive, most effective, and best-looking transition. But each of the other iMovie transitions can be appropriate in certain situations. For example, the Radial wipe, which looks like the hand of a clock wiping around the screen, replacing the old scene with the new one as it goes, can be a useful passage-of-time or meanwhile-back-at-the-ranch effect.

  The catalog of transitions on page 154 gives you an example of when each might be appropriate. Remember, though, that many of them are useful primarily in music videos and other situations when wild stylistic flights of fancy are more readily accepted by viewers.

Tip: The Fade In and Fade Out "transitions" in iMovie are exempt from the stern advice above. Use a Fade In at the beginning of *every* movie, if you like, and a Fade Out at the end. Doing so adds a professional feeling to your film, but it's so subtle, your audience will notice it subconsciously, if at all.

Creating a Transition

To see the list of transitions iMovie offers, click the Trans button, as shown in Figure 6-2. The Clips pane disappears, only to be replaced, in the blink of an eye, by a completely different set of controls.

Previewing the Effect

Like most video editing software, iMovie has to do a lot of computation to produce transitions, so it can't show you an instantaneous, full-speed, full-smoothness preview. Therefore, iMovie offers a choice of lower-quality (but instantaneous) previews:

- **The Preview window.** For a very small preview, shown in the tiny screen above the Transitions list, just click the name of a transition.

  This preview plays in real time, endeavoring to make the transition preview last exactly as long as the finished transition will. On slower Macs, you don't see all the frames in this little Preview window, making the transition appear jerky, but rest assured that the finished transition will be extremely smooth.

- **The Monitor window.** To see a preview in a much larger format—big enough to fill the Monitor window—click the Preview button.

Either way, you can drag the Speed slider just above the list to experiment with the length of each transition as you're previewing it. The numbers on this slider—*00:10* (10 frames) at the left side, *10:00* (10 seconds) at the right side—let you know the least and greatest amount of time that a transition can last.

Tip: For more precision, you can bypass the Speed slider. Instead, double-click the timing numbers that appear just above it, in the corner of the black Preview area. Once you've highlighted these digits, you can type new numbers to replace them. These numbers are in seconds:frames format.

When you release the slider, you see another quick preview in the miniature screen above it, and you also see, in the lower-right corner of the Preview screen, the actual length of the transition you've specified.

Tip: The program doesn't yet know which clips you'll want to "transish." Therefore, iMovie uses, for the purposes of this preview, whichever clip is currently highlighted in the Movie Track, into which it crossfades from the previous clip. If the very first clip is highlighted, iMovie demonstrates by transitioning that clip into the second clip.

If no clip is highlighted, iMovie is smart enough to seek out the "clip boundary" that's closest to the Playhead's current position. It uses the clips on both sides of that boundary for the preview—if it's a two-clip transition. If it's a one-clip transition, iMovie uses the clip to the right or left.

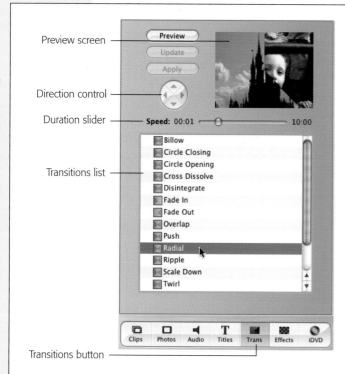

Preview screen

Direction control

Duration slider

Transitions list

Transitions button

Figure 6-2:
When you click the Transitions button, a list of the transitions available in iMovie appears. When you click a transition's name, the Preview screen above the list shows a simulation of what the effect will look like.

Once you've clicked a transition name, you can press the up or down arrow keys to "walk" through the list.

Applying the Effect—and Rendering

Once you've selected an effect and dragged the slider to specify how much time you want it to take, you can place it into the Clip Viewer or Timeline Viewer by dragging the *name or icon* of the effect out of the transitions list and down onto the Movie Track.

Either way, drag until your cursor is between the two clips that you want joined by this transition; iMovie pushes the right-hand clips out of the way to make room. (Most transitions must go *between* two clips, and so they can't go at the beginning or end of your Movie Track. The exceptions are the Fade and Wash effects.) Then a special transition icon appears between the clips, as shown in Figure 6-3.

Tip: The tiny triangles on a transition icon or bar let you know what kind of transition it is. A pair of inward-facing triangles is a standard transition that melds the end of one clip with the beginning of the next. A single, right-facing triangle indicates a transition that applies to the *beginning* of a clip, such as a fade-in from black (or wash-in from white). A single, left-facing triangle indicates a transition that applies to the *end* of a clip (such as a fade or wash *out*).

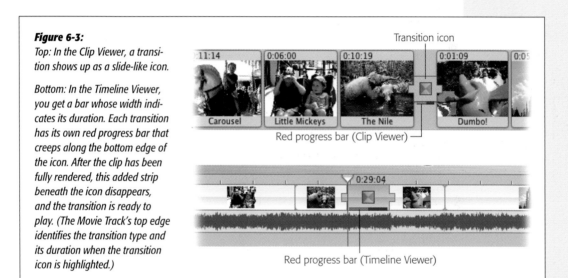

Figure 6-3:
Top: In the Clip Viewer, a transition shows up as a slide-like icon.

Bottom: In the Timeline Viewer, you get a bar whose width indicates its duration. Each transition has its own red progress bar that creeps along the bottom edge of the icon. After the clip has been fully rendered, this added strip beneath the icon disappears, and the transition is ready to play. (The Movie Track's top edge identifies the transition type and its duration when the transition icon is highlighted.)

[Figure labels: Transition icon; 11:14; 0:06:00; 0:10:19; 0:01:09; 0:0; Carousel; Little Mickeys; The Nile; Dumbo!; Red progress bar (Clip Viewer); 0:29:04; Red progress bar (Timeline Viewer)]

Almost immediately, a tiny red line begins to crawl, progress-bar-like, along the lower edge of this icon (see Figure 6-3). In the terminology of DV editors everywhere, the Mac has begun to *render* this transition—to perform the thousands of individual calculations necessary to blend the outgoing clip into the incoming, pixel by pixel, frame by frame.

Whether it's an iMovie transition or a scene in a Pixar movie, rendering always takes a lot of time. In iMovie, the longer the transition you've specified, the longer it takes to render. You should feel grateful, however, that iMovie renders its transitions in a matter of minutes, not days (which complex Hollywood computer-generated effects often require).

Furthermore, iMovie lets you *continue working* as this rendering takes place. You can work on the other pieces of your movie, import new footage from your camcorder, or even *play* your movie while transitions are still rendering. (If the transitions haven't finished rendering, iMovie shows you its preview version.)

In fact, you can even switch out of iMovie to work in other Mac programs. (This last trick makes the rendering even slower, but at least it's in the background. You can check your email or work on your screenplay in the meantime.)

Applying simultaneous clips

iMovie has always been able to render several transition effects simultaneously, albeit with some speed penalty. iMovie HD, though, offers an even more useful timesaver: you can apply the same transition to several pairs of clips at once. Figure 6-4 shows the idea.

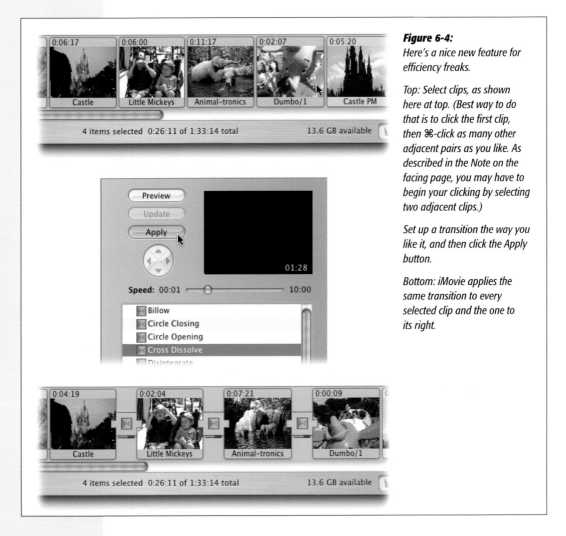

Figure 6-4:

Here's a nice new feature for efficiency freaks.

Top: Select clips, as shown here at top. (Best way to do that is to click the first clip, then ⌘-click as many other adjacent pairs as you like. As described in the Note on the facing page, you may have to begin your clicking by selecting two adjacent clips.)

Set up a transition the way you like it, and then click the Apply button.

Bottom: iMovie applies the same transition to every selected clip and the one to its right.

Note: In iMovie HD 5.0.1, there's a tiny bug. If you want to apply a transition to multiple clips, the first two you select must be adjacent clips (for example, Clips #1 and #2). After that, you can select isolated clips (like Clip #5, Clip #10, and so on). The Apply button will add a transition between each selected clip and the one to its right.

And what if you didn't want a transition out of Clip #2? After iMovie applies the multiple transition, you'll have to manually delete the Clip #2 transition.

When rendering is complete

When the rendering is complete, you can look over the result very easily.

- To watch just the transition itself, click the transition's icon or bar in the Movie Track (it changes color to show that it's highlighted) and then press the Space bar.

- To watch the transition *and* the clips that it joins together, Shift-click the two clips in question. Doing so also highlights the transition between them. Press the Space bar to play the three clips you've highlighted.

- It's a good idea to watch your transition by "rewinding" a few seconds into the preceding footage, so that you get a sense of how the effect fits in the context of the existing footage. To give yourself some of this "preroll," choose Edit→Select None (or just click anywhere but on a clip) to deselect all the clips. Then click a spot on the Scrubber bar somewhere in the clip before the transition, and press the Space bar to play the movie from that point.

- If you don't care for what you've done, choose Edit→Undo.

- If it's too late for the Undo command, you can return to the transition at any time, highlight its icon, and press the Delete key. Your original clips return instantly, exactly as they were before you added the transition.

How Transitions Affect the Length of Your Movie

As you can see by the example in Figure 6-5, most transitions make your movie shorter. To superimpose the ends of two adjacent clips, iMovie is forced to slide the right-hand clip leftward, making the overall movie end sooner.

Under most circumstances, there's nothing wrong with that. After all, that's why you wisely avoided trimming off *all* of the excess "leader" and "trailer" footage (known as *trim handles*) from the ends of your clips. By leaving trim handles on each clip—which will be sacrificed to the transition—you'll have some fade-in or fade-out footage to play with.

Sometimes, however, having your overall project shortened is a serious problem, especially when you've been "cutting to sound," or synchronizing your footage to an existing music track, as described in Chapter 8. Suppose you've spent hours putting your clips into the Movie Track, carefully trimming them so that they perfectly match the soundtrack. And now, as a final touch, you decide to put in transitions. Clearly, having these transitions slide all of your clips to the left would result in chaos, throwing off the synchronization work you had done.

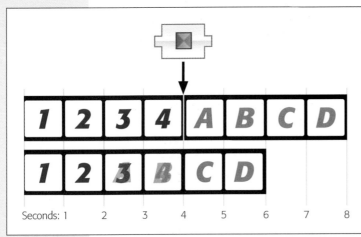

Figure 6-5:
When you insert a 2-second transition (top) between two clips, iMovie pulls the right-hand clip 2 seconds to the left so that it overlaps the end of the left-hand clip. The result (bottom): The entire movie is now 2 seconds shorter.

Now you can appreciate the importance of iMovie's Advanced→Lock Audio Clip at Playhead command, which marries a piece of music or sound to a particular spot in the video. If all of your added music and sound elements are attached in this way, adding transitions won't disturb their synchronization. See page 231 for details on locking audio into position.

Tip: Certain transitions—Overlap, Fade In, Fade Out, Wash In, and Wash Out—don't shorten the movie. As described at the end of this chapter, each of these five special transitions affects only *one* clip, not two. They're meant to begin or end your movie, fading in or out from black or white.

How Transitions Chop Up Clips

After your transition has been rendered, you'll notice something peculiar about your Scrubber bar: The transition has now become, in effect, a clip of its own. (In fact, if you open your project "package" icon [page 112] and look in the project's Media folder, you'll even see the newly created clip file represented there, bearing the name of the transition you applied.)

If you click the first clip and play it, you'll find that the playback now stops sooner than it once did—just where the transition takes over. Likewise, the clip that follows the transition has also had frames shaven away at the front end. Both clips, in other words, have sacrificed a second or two to the newly created transition/clip between them. Figure 6-5 illustrates this phenomenon.

Tip: You can rename a transition icon, if it helps you to remember what you were thinking when you created it. To do so, double-click its icon or bar. The Clip Info dialog box appears, in which you can change the name the transition icon displays in your Movie Track.

Editing the Transition

You can edit the transition in several ways: You can change its length, its type, its direction (certain effects only), or all three. To do so, click the transition icon, and then click the Trans button (if the Transitions pane isn't already open). You can now adjust the Speed slider, click another transition in the list, or both. (For the Push and Billow effects, you can also change the direction of the effect.)

When you click Update—a button that's available *only* when a transition icon is highlighted in the Movie Track—iMovie automatically re-renders the transition.

Tip: You can also adjust the effect on several clips simultaneously. Just select the ones that you want to edit (⌘-click each one)—or, to select all transitions in the whole movie, click one and then choose Edit→Select Similar Clips. (The selected transition clips don't have to have matching transition types; you can click one Disintegrate, one Twirl, and one Push, and then change them all to the same Cross Dissolve.)

Now make the changes you want, and then click the Update button shown in Figure 6-4.

Deleting a Transition

If you decide that you don't need a transition effect between two clips after all, you can delete it just as you would delete any Movie Track clip: by clicking it once and then pressing the Delete key on your keyboard (or by choosing Edit→Clear). Deleting a transition clip does more than eliminate the icon—it also restores the clips on either side to their original conditions. (If you change your mind, Edit→Undo Clear brings back the transition.)

Transition Error Messages

Transitions can be fussy. They like plenty of clip footage to chew on, and once they've begun rendering, they like to be left alone. Here are some of the error messages you may encounter when working with transitions.

When you delete a clip

For example, if, in the process of editing your movie, you delete a clip from the Movie Track that's part of a transition, a message appears (Figure 6-6) that says: "This action will invalidate at least one transition in the project. Invalid transitions will be deleted from the project. Do you want to proceed?"

iMovie is simply telling you that if you delete the clip, you'll also delete the transition attached to it (which is probably just what you'd expect). Click OK. If you first click "Don't ask me again," iMovie will henceforth delete such clips *without* asking your permission.

When the transition is longer than the clip

If you try to add a 5-second crossfade between two 3-second clips, iMovie throws up its hands with various similarly worded error messages (Figure 6-6, left). In all cases, the point is clear: The two clips on either side of a transition must *each* be longer than the transition itself.

Put another way, iMovie can't make your transition stretch across more than two clips (or more than one clip, in the case of the Fade and Wash effects).

When you quit while rendering

Creating transitions requires a great deal of iMovie's concentration. If you try to save your project, close it, or empty its Trash, you'll be advised to wait until the rendering is over, as shown in Figure 6-6 at right.

The clip before that title or transition is too short; it must be at least 0:02:17.

A transition must be deleted.
This action will invalidate at least one transition. Invalid transitions will be deleted. Would you like to proceed?

☐ Don't ask me again

You cannot apply a transition between two very short clips. They must each be at least 0:02:18 long.

Rendering In Progress
An effect is still rendering and cannot be saved in the file. Okay to stop rendering and remove these clips?

This title or transition must be placed after an existing clip.

Unable To Empty Trash
You have titles, transitions or effects currently rendering. Please wait until they complete before emptying the Trash.

Figure 6-6:
Left: Three messages that tell you there's not enough footage for the transition.

Right: Messages that appear when you delete a clip to which you've attached a transition (top); when you try to quit or save your project during rendering (middle); and when you try to empty the project Trash before the transitions have finished rendering.

Transitions: The iMovie Catalog

Here, for your reference, is a visual representation of each transition, and what editing circumstances might call for it.

Billow

Billow is one of three new transition styles in iMovie HD. It might also be called "Polka-Dot," "Acid Drops," or "Expanding Swiss Cheese." As the clip progresses, a fleet of, well, flying holes descends on the first clip; you can see the second clip through

Billow

the holes. The holes gradually grow until they occupy the entire frame—and presto, you're now in a new scene. (You can use the directional arrows to specify a general direction for the flurry of UFH's [unidentified flying holes].)

It's kind of hard to imagine when this transition would feel natural, except perhaps in documentaries about cellular reproduction.

Circle Closing

This effect, called *iris close* or *iris in* in professional editing programs, is a holdover from the silent film days, when, in the days before zoom lenses, directors used the effect to highlight a detail in a scene.

It creates an ever-closing circle with the first clip inside and the second clip outside. It's useful at the end of the movie, when the second clip is solid black and the subject of the first clip is centered in the frame. In that setup, the movie ends with an ever-shrinking picture that fades away to a little dot. (If the subject in the center waves goodbye just before being blinked out of view, this trick is especially effective.)

Circle Opening

This effect is much like Circle Closing, except it's been turned inside out. Now the circle grows from the center of the first clip, with the second clip playing inside it, and expands until it fills the frame. (This effect is also called *iris open* or *iris out.*)

Here again, this effect is especially useful at the beginning of a movie, particularly if the subject of the second clip is at the center of the frame. If the first clip in your movie is a solid black frame, your film begins as though the camera's sleepy eye is opening to reveal the scene.

Circle Opening

Cross Dissolve

The crossfade, or dissolve, is the world's most popular and effective transition. The first clip gradually disappears, superimposed on the beginning of the second clip, which fades in. If you must use a transition at all, you can't go wrong with this one.

Tip: You can use a very short cross dissolve to create what editors call a "soft cut." When the footage would jump too abruptly if you made a regular cut, put in a ten-frame cross dissolve, which makes the junction of clips *slightly* smoother than just cutting. Soft cuts are very common in interviews where the editors have deleted sections from a continuous shot of a person talking.

Disintegrate

Ever see a film projector get stuck? One frame of film gets stuck in front of the hot projection bulb—and, after a few seconds of heating up, literally melts away to a blank white movie screen?

Imagine your first clip melting away in several spots at once, revealing the second clip beneath, and you've got the idea behind Disintegrate. It looks very, very cool, and is sure to become an everyday effect—among monster-movie makers.

Cross Dissolve

Disintegrate

Fade In

Use this effect at the beginning of your movie, or the beginning of a scene that begins in a new place or time. Unlike most transition effects, this one makes no attempt to smooth the transition between two clips. The fade-in overlaps only the clip *to its right*, creating a fade-in from complete blackness.

This transition affects only the clip that follows it, so it doesn't shorten your movie or throw subsequent clips out of alignment, like genuine crossfade-style transitions.

Tip: In general, iMovie doesn't let you place one transition next to another.

The exceptions are the Fade (In and Out) and Wash (In and Out) transitions. Each of these affects only one clip, not two. By placing an In immediately after an Out, you create an elegant fade out, then in to the next shot—a very popular effect in movies and commercials.

Placing an Out just after an In isn't quite as useful, because it reveals only a fleeting glance of the footage in between. But when you're trying to represent somebody's life flashing before his eyes, this trick may be just the ticket.

Fade Out

This effect, conversely, is best used at the *end* of a movie, or the end of a scene that requires a feeling of finality. Like its sister, the Fade In, this one doesn't involve two clips at all; it affects only the end of the clip to its left. As a result, it doesn't affect the length or synchronization of your movie.

It's worth noting, by the way, that a fade-out is almost always followed by a fade-*in,* or by the closing credits. You'll blast your audience's eyeballs if you fade out, sweetly and gracefully—and then cut directly into a bright new clip.

Both Fade In and Fade Out are very useful, and frequently used, effects.

Tip: If you'd rather fade to black and then hold on the black screen for a moment, add a few seconds of blackness after the fade. To do so, switch to the Timeline Viewer and create a pure black clip, as described on page 140. Switch to the Clip Viewer, cut the black clip to the Clipboard, and paste it at the end of the movie. Now iMovie will fade out to black—and hold on to that blackness.

Fade Out

Overlap

Overlap is almost exactly the same as the Cross Dissolve, illustrated earlier. The sole difference: The outgoing clip freezes on its last frame as the new clip fades in. (In a Cross Dissolve, the action continues during the simultaneous fades.) Use it in situations where you might normally use a Cross Dissolve, but want to draw the eye to the second clip right away.

Tip: Unlike the Cross Dissolve, the Overlap transition doesn't change the duration of your movie, which makes it a good choice for movies where you've spent a lot of time synchronizing audio and video. In those cases, a Cross Dissolve might knock things out of sync.

Push

In this transition, the first clip is shoved off the frame by the aggressive first frame of the second clip. This offbeat transition effect draws a lot of attention to itself, so use it extremely sparingly. For example, you could use it to simulate an old-style projector changing slides, or when filming a clever, self-aware documentary in which the host (who first appears in the second clip) "pushes" his way onto the screen.

When you select this transition in the list, the four directional arrows—which are dimmed for most transition types—become available. Click one to indicate how you want the incoming clip to push onscreen: up, down, to the left, or to the right.

Push Right

Radial

You probably saw this one in a few movies of the seventies. What looks like the sweep-second hand on a watch rotates around the screen, wiping away the first clip and revealing the second clip underneath. This transition suggests the passage of time even more than most transitions, clueing the audience in that the scene about to begin takes place in a new location or on a different day.

Radial

Ripple

This effect is gorgeous, poetic, beautiful—and hard to justify.

Ripple

Ripple invokes the "drop of water on the surface of the pond" metaphor. As the ripple expands across the screen, it pushes the first clip (the pond surface) off the screen to make way for the incoming new clip (the expanding circular ripple). It's a soothing, beautiful effect—but unless you're making mascara commercials, it calls a little too much attention to itself for everyday home movies.

Scale Down

Scale Down, known to pro editors as the *picture zoom* effect, is a peculiar effect, whereby the end of the first clip simply shrinks away. Its rectangle gets smaller and smaller until it disappears, falling endlessly away into the beginning of the second clip, which lies beneath it. The rectangle seems to fly away into the upper-left corner of the second clip, not into dead center.

This kind of effect occasionally shows up on TV news, in documentaries, and so on, after you've been watching a closeup of some important document or photograph. By showing the closeup flying away from the camera, the film editor seems to say, "Enough of that. Meanwhile, back in real life…"

Scale Down

Twirl

Here's your basic *Batman* TV-show transition: The first clip spins away, receding into the black abyss, and then the next clip spins in from the same vanishing point.

Tip: If you transition out of a black clip, you're left with the spinning-in appearance of the second clip without the spinning-away of the first one. In other words, you've just created the spinning-newspaper-headline effect of many an old movie.

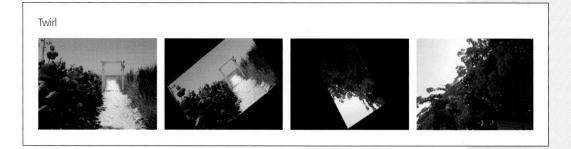

Twirl

Warp In

This effect is very similar to Scale Down, except that as the first clip flies away, it seems to fold in on itself instead of remaining rectangular. That characteristic, combined with the fact that it flies away into dead center of the second clip's frame, makes it look as though the first clip is getting sucked out of the center of the picture by a giant video vacuum cleaner.

It's hard to think of *any* circumstance where this effect would feel natural, except when you're deliberately trying to be weird.

Warp Out

You might think that this effect would be the flip side of the Warp In effect, but it's quite different. This time, the second clip intrudes on the first by pushing its way, as an ever-growing sphere, into the frame. What's left of the first clip gets smashed outward, bizarrely distorting, until it's shoved off the outer edges of the picture.

Warp Out

Wash In, Wash Out

These two effects work exactly like Fade In and Fade Out, described earlier, with one big difference: They fade in from, and out to, *white* instead of black.

Fading in and out to white, an effect first popularized by Infiniti car commercials in the early eighties, lends a very specific feeling to the movie. It's something ethereal, ghostly, nostalgic. In today's Hollywood movies (including *The Sixth Sense*), a fade to white is often an indication that the character you've been watching has just died.

Wash Out

Fading out to white and then in from white—that is, putting two of these transitions side by side in your Movie Track—is an extremely popular technique in today's TV commercials, when the advertiser wants to show you a series of charming, brightly colored images. By fading out to white between shots, the editor inserts the video equivalent of an ellipsis (…like this…), and keeps the mood happy and bright. (Similar fade-outs to black seem to stop the flow with more finality.)

Downloading More Transition Choices

Simple cuts, cross dissolves, and fade-ins/fade-outs are all the transitions many professionals ever need. But if you're feeling hemmed in by the limited number of built-in transitions, you can download plenty more to expand the list.

Here's a quick look at some of the leading contenders in the blossoming Commercial iMovie Plug-ins category:

- **GeeThree.** At *www.geethree.com*, you can preview and buy plug-in collections that add over 200 new transitions to iMovie's list. They offer a huge number of different shapes that open up to reveal a new piece of footage: hearts, barn doors, checkerboards, zigzags, page turns, swirls, explosions, drips from the top of the screen, and so on. You can even find picture-in-picture, morphing, and even image-stabilizing plug-ins that take the shake out of unsteady footage.

Note: Be sure you also download the free Slick Transitions updater, a little program that makes the older GeeThree transitions compatible with iMovie HD. Otherwise, mysterious bugs will seem to plague unrelated areas of iMovie.

- **Virtix.** Check out *www.virtix.com* to view this impressive set of effects and transitions. Burn Through makes it look like the first piece of film is melting on the projector, revealing the second clip behind it. Dream should be familiar to David Letterman or "Wayne's World" fans: it creates a soft-focused, warpy, zig-zaggy strip down the center of the frame that melts into the second clip. Fog and Smoke reveal the second clip through a passing haze. If you've shot one clip of an empty space (using a tripod) and another containing a person, Materialize creates a convincing simulation of the *Star Trek* transporter beam. And so on.

- **cf/x.** The transition effects at *www.imovieplugins.com* are very nicely done; some, like a *soft-edged* wipe, are even more useful than some of Apple's included transitions. What's especially nice is that you can buy these transitions individually (usually $3.50 or $4.50) instead of having to buy a whole package.

Tip: Most of these products come with installers that put the plug-in files where they belong: in your Home→Library→iMovie→Plug-ins folder. Knowing where they live also makes it easy to remove them—which may come in handy in times of troubleshooting. Note, too, that older plug-ins not specifically identified as iMovie HD-compatible can cause all kinds of mysterious problems in apparently unrelated areas of the program.

The Effects Pane

The Effects button summons a panel full of visual effects that you can apply directly to your footage: slow motion, backward, black-and-white, and so on. Some are designed to adjust the brightness, contrast, or color tints in less-than-perfect footage. Most, though, are designed to create actual special effects that simulate fog, rain, earthquakes, lightning, flashbulbs, and bleary-eyed bad LSD.

And if these don't satisfy your hunger for effects, other software companies have had a field day dreaming up new special effects that you can buy and install as plug-ins.

As with transitions, most of these are so out-there and distracting, you should use these only on special occasions.

Selecting the Footage

Before you apply an effect, specify which lucky region of footage you want to be affected:

- **One clip.** Click a clip in the Movie Track or Clips pane; the effect will apply to the entire clip.

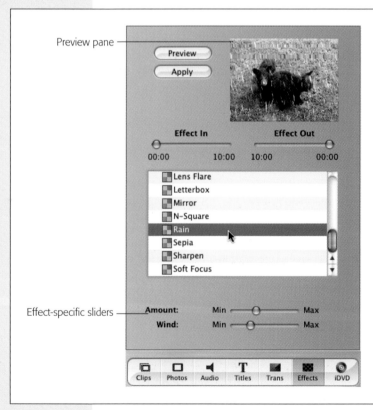

Preview pane

Effect-specific sliders

Figure 6-7:
Several of the effects in the Effects panel offer additional controls, which take the form of sliders beneath the list. You can drag the small blue handle of such sliders, or simply click anywhere in its track.

When it's not showing footage, the Preview pane shows numbers in the corners. They reflect the timings you've selected by dragging the Effect In and Out sliders.

- **Multiple clips.** If you highlight several clips in the Movie Track, your selected effect will apply to all of them, treating them as one giant clip. When you click the Apply button, you'll see multiple progress bars marching across the faces of the affected clips in the Movie Track. (Unfortunately, some effects, like the rocketing sparkler of Fairy Dust, aren't smart enough to continue across more than one clip. If you select several clips, the effect starts over at the beginning of each one.)

Tip: Don't forget that you can select several nonadjacent clips. At that point, you can apply an effect to all of them at once.

- **Part of a clip.** If you use the Scrubber bar's selection handles to highlight only a portion of a clip, iMovie will split the clips at the endpoints of the selection, and then apply the effect to the central clip. (iMovie can apply effects only to *entire* clips, which is why this automatic splitting takes place.)

- **Parts of multiple clips.** If you choose Edit→Select None, you can use the Scrubber bar's selection handles to enclose any stretch of clips (or portions of clips) you like. If necessary, iMovie will again split the end clips at the locations of your handles.

Surveying Your Options

Now click the Effects button. Portions of this panel (Figure 6-7) should look familiar. The list of effects, the Preview button, and the Preview pane all work exactly as they do for transitions. (For example, when you click an effect name, the small Preview pane shows a crude, jerky representation of what it will look like; if you click the Preview *button,* you see the same preview in the Monitor window.)

But you'll also find other controls that don't exist anywhere else in iMovie:

- **Effect In, Effect Out.** If you want the chosen effect to start and end exactly at the boundaries of your selection, leave these sliders at their zero points (the far left for Effect In, the far right for Effect Out).

  If you like, however, you can make these effects kick in (and kick out) gradually, after the clip has already begun (and before it has ended). That's the purpose of these two sliders: to give you control over when they begin or end.

  For example, if you drag the Effect In slider for a Black & White effect to 5:00, the clip will begin playing in full color. After playing for 5 seconds, however, the color will begin to leach out, leaving the rest of the clip to play in black-and-white (a useful effect if you're trying to depict someone slowly going color-blind). You can set the Effect In and Out points no more than 10 seconds from the beginning or ending of a clip.

  For example, here's how to make a knockout, professional-looking effect to open your film: Create a still clip from the first frame of a movie, as described on page 256. Split it in half. Convert the first half to black and white, then create a Cross Dissolve between it and the second half. The result: What appears to be a black-

and-white photograph "coming to life" as it fades into color and then begins to play normally.

Tip: Instead of using the Effect In and Effect Out sliders, you can gain more precision by double-clicking the timing numbers that appear in at the bottom of the Preview area. (You have to wait until the Preview area is black—that is, until the preview itself has finished playing.) Once you've highlighted these digits, you can type new numbers to replace them. These numbers are in seconds:frames format.

• **Effect-specific controls.** As you click the name of each effect in the list, additional sliders may appear above the Effects panel. They're described in the effect-by-effect descriptions later in this chapter.

• **Apply.** When you click Apply, iMovie begins to render the selected clip—to perform the massive numbers of calculations necessary to bring each pixel into compliance with the effect you've specified. As with transitions, effect rendering telegraphs its progress with a subtle red line, a miniature progress bar that crawls from left to right beneath the selected clip (see Figure 6-8).

Number of effects
Effect indicator

Progress bar

Figure 6-8:
The thin red progress bar lets you know how much longer you have to wait. You can tell at a glance that a clip has had an effect applied, thanks to the checkerboard brand in the upper right. And if there's a digit beside the checkerboard, you've applied more than one effect to the same clip.

Rendering effects works exactly like rendering transitions: You can continue working on other parts of your movie, but things can bog down if you've got several effects rendering at once. Actually, rendering effects takes much longer than rendering transitions, in part because you apply each effect to an entire clip instead of just the last couple of seconds. Press ⌘-period to cancel the rendering.

It's important to note, by the way, that iMovie actually applies the selected effect to a *duplicate* copy of the clip's DV file on your hard drive. iMovie creates the behind-the-scenes duplicate as a safety net for you. It gives you the option of removing or adjusting the effect at any time. (If you're curious, switch to the Finder; open your project package as described on page 112; and open its Media folder. Inside, you'll find a new clip called, for example, Earthquake 01, which represents the modified clip.)

So what happens to the original clip? iMovie puts it into your project Trash. As long as you don't empty your trash, you can recover the original clip (and remove the effect) at any time.

Removing an Effect

If you click a clip and then press the Delete key, you're saying: "Throw away the effect. Bring back my original, unmodified clip." Much though it may feel like you're instructing iMovie to delete the *clip itself,* you're not. (You would have to press Delete a *second time* to achieve that purpose.)

In any case, when you delete an effect in this way, iMovie pulls your original footage out of the project Trash and reinstates it. That is, it does so *if* you haven't *emptied* the Trash. Remember that once you empty your project Trash, you throw away your opportunity to adjust or remove effects forever.

Note: If you do empty the Trash, you'll notice something weird: The little Effect indicator shown in Figure 6-8 *vanishes* from all of your effects clips! That's because as far as iMovie is concerned, those effects are now part of the original clips, married to them forever.

Adjusting an Effect

Despite what the iMovie online help says, there's no Update button on the Effects pane. To adjust the start time, stop time, or other parameters of a special effect, you must first delete the effect altogether, as described above, and then reapply it using new settings.

Superimposing Effects

It's perfectly possible to combine effects by applying first one, and then another. For example, after using the Black & White effect, you may want to use the Brightness & Contrast control to adjust its gray tones. You can even apply a single effect repeatedly, intensifying its effect; for instance, you could apply Fairy Dust several times to make it appear as though multiple fireworks are going off. Or you could apply Rain twice at different intensities to add depth to your simulated deluge.

Once you've applied more than one effect to a certain clip, iMovie thoughtfully adds a "number-of-effects" number next to the effects symbol, as shown in Figure 6-8. When it comes time to *remove* some of your layered effects, you'll appreciate that indicator. It will keep you sane as you peel away one effect after another.

For example, suppose you're making a disaster movie. To one climactic clip, you've applied two Rains, three Earthquakes, an Electricity, and a pair of Fogs.

If you decide that perhaps you've laid it on a bit thick, you can click the clip and then start tapping the Delete key. With each tap, you remove one effect, in reverse chronological order, until only the original clip remains. (Be careful not to press Delete that last time; you'll remove the clip itself!)

Effects: The iMovie Catalog

iMovie HD comes with 23 built-in effects, including five new ones. The following list describes them all.

Adjust Colors

This powerful effect adjusts the actual color palette used in your clip footage. If your footage has an unfortunate greenish tint, you can color-correct it; if you're hoping for a sunset look, you can bring out the oranges and reds; if it's a sci-fi flick taking place on Uranus, you can make it look blue and spooky.

The special sliders for this effect affect the hue, saturation, and brightness of your footage. Hue, saturation, and brightness are cornerstones of color theory; you can read much more about them on the Web, or in books and articles about photo editing. In the meantime, here's a brief summary:

- **Hue Shift (Left—Right).** Adjusts the overall color tint of the clip. What iMovie is actually doing is rotating the hue around the hue circle, either to the left or the right. In practice, this effect doesn't do anything predictable to an image; you're meant to play with it until you find something you like.

- **Color (B&W—Vivid).** This slider lets you control the intensity of a color, or its *saturation.* If it's blue, you control *how* blue it is: increasing toward Vivid makes the blue more intense.

- **Lightness (Dark—Bright).** Use this slider to adjust the overall brightness or darkness of the *colors* in your clip. There's only a subtle difference between these effects and the Brightness/Contrast effect described below; this slider adjusts the brightness of the colors, rather than the overall brightness.

Aged Film

Here you've just spent $500 on a camcorder and a couple thou on a Macintosh, all in the name of attaining perfect purity of video—and then this effect comes along. It's designed to make a clip look like an old, flickering, dusty film, complete with horrible scratches along the celluloid.

Using the Exposure, Jitter, and Scratches sliders, you can control just how faded, shaky-in-the-projector, and scratched up the footage looks (Figure 6-9, top).

Combine this one with Black & White, described next, and you've got yourself something that looks authentically like a horribly preserved reel you dug up from somebody's attic.

Black & White

This effect does one thing very well: It turns your clip into a black-and-white piece of footage, suitable for simulating security-camera footage or TV from the 1950s.

Brightness & Contrast

Footage that's too dark is one of the most common hallmarks of amateur camcorder work. If you're filming indoors without extra lights, you may as well accept the fact that your clip will be too dark.

The Brightness & Contrast controls can help, but they're no substitute for good lighting in the original footage. When you drag the Brightness and Contrast sliders in very small amounts, you may be able to rescue footage that's slightly murky or washed out. Dragging the sliders a lot, however, may make the too-dark footage grainy and weird-looking.

Tip: Using the Effect In and Out sliders, you can control which *parts* of the clip are affected by the Adjust Colors and Brightness & Contrast effects. If you need the colors or brightness to shift several times over the course of a clip, consider chopping up the clip into several smaller clips, each of which is an opportunity to reset the effect settings and timings.

Figure 6-9:

Top: Modern museum? No— thanks to the Aged Film effect, it's ancient edifice circa 1938.

Middle: Georges Seurat's take on a coffeehouse: a pointillistic mosaic, courtesy of the Crystal- lize effect.

Bottom: Earthquake! (For a better simulation of what iMovie really does, shake this book rapidly in front of your face.) This effect looks really great when you adjust the Effect In and Effect Out sliders so that the shaking begins gradually and intensifies. (Better yet, apply the effect several times, to make the intensity of the shaking appear to fluctuate.)

Before

After

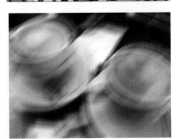

Crystallize

This effect makes your footage look like you shot it through a stained-glass window, or perhaps a translucent honeycomb (Figure 6-9, middle). As you drag the Size slider toward Max, the size of the individual "crystal" facets gets so large, it's more like you're looking at a living stained-glass window. At the Max end, you can't even identify what you're looking at; it's as though you've got an abstract painting that's come to life. This is not, ahem, an effect you'll use often.

Earthquake

Talk about an effect you'll use only rarely!

This one (Figure 6-9, bottom) is designed to simulate *camera shake,* the jittery, shuddering, handheld, no-tripod, stabilizer-off look that you'd get if you felt the earth move under your feet, and felt the sky come tumblin' down. You can use the two sliders to specify *how* the earthquake is tossing your camera around: sideways or vertically, and to what degrees.

Edge Work

Here's another effect that's new in iMovie HD. Its peculiar mission: to reduce the scene to black-and-white moving blobs, as though the entire clip had been constructed of bad Xerox copies.

iMovie creates this effect by setting every *edge* that it detects—borders between light and dark areas—in fat "boldface." The Max slider governs the chunkiness of the rendered black and white blobs. You could easily imagine Edge Work finding a home in music videos, homemade animated movies, or courtroom scenes where you want to mask a witness's identity.

Edges

Again, think "music-video weirdness." This new, amazing-looking iMovie HD effect reduces the entire scene to an *inverted* photocopy. That is, the scene goes black except for the moving edges of things, which are white (Figure 6-10, top). You can still tell what you're looking at, especially if you move the Intensity slider to the right, but the whole thing has a weird, ghostly, "erased" look to it.

Electricity

Unlike most of the other effects, which apply equally everywhere in the video frame, this one (Figure 6-10, middle) actually superimposes an image—in this case, a purplish, flickering bolt of lightning—onto any spot of the footage you want. You can use this one to great comic effect; when attached to the end of somebody's wand or walking stick, the electricity looks like it's shooting out. When attached to somebody's head or rear end, the electricity looks like it's zapping that hapless person.

You can probably figure out that the Rotate slider lets you change the lightning bolt's angle (CW = Clockwise, CCW = Counter-Clockwise). But what you may not realize is that you can *click* inside the Preview window to specify the landing (or starting) point of the sparkler. By using the rotation and position controls in combination,

you have complete freedom in designing the placement of the zap within the frame.
(Alas, you can't make the bolt move *during* a clip. It stays put, crackling away right
in place, so it's primarily useful for adding to a tripod shot that you filmed expressly
for the purpose of doctoring later in iMovie.)

Fairy Dust

Like Electricity, this effect (Figure 6-10, bottom) is designed to superimpose a professional-looking sparkler effect on your footage. In this case, you get a shooting firework
that follows a specified arc across the frame; the net effect is something like a burning
fuse, except that the path, although visible in the Preview window for your reference,
doesn't actually appear once you apply the effect.

Here again, you can click within the Preview frame to position the arc, thereby adjusting the sparkler's trajectory. Use the Direction slider to specify whether the fire
flies left to right across the frame, or right to left. (It really has no business being a

Figure 6-10:
*Top: The Edges effect, which
might be better named "Bad
drug trip," "Hangover,"
or "After the surgery."*

*Middle: Lightning strikes as
often as you feel like making it
strike, thanks to the Electricity
effect.*

*Bottom: The Fairy Dust ef-
fect might be better named
Fireworks Sparkler, or perhaps
Burning Fuse on an Invisible
String. The trajectory and angle
are up to you.*

Before

After

slider. It has only two positions: left or right. Dragging the handle to an intermediate point does nothing.)

The Trail slider, meanwhile, governs the size of the sparkler.

Fast/Slow/Reverse

If you're a veteran of iMovie, you may remember that the Fast, Slow, and Reverse controls used to be at the bottom edge of the Timeline Viewer. It occurred to somebody at Apple that this placement really made very little sense; those are, after all, special effects. Why should they work differently from all the other effects? So Fast/Slow/Reverse is now a card-carrying occupant of the Effects list—and each component has been improved and upgraded in the process.

Reverse Direction

When you hear that iMovie can play clips backward, you might assume that this feature is a gimmick that's primarily useful for applying to footage of people jumping into swimming pools or jumping off of walls. To be sure, iMovie does a great job at creating these comic effects, even if their novelty does wear off quickly.

But reverse motion can be useful in much less obvious situations—cases where your original footage needs some help. For example, you can use this feature to create a zoom out when all you filmed was a zoom in, or a pan to the right when you shot a pan to the left. You can make your star's head turn away from the camera instead of toward it. Even reversing the playback of a slow-motion eye blink can make all the difference in the emotional impact of a certain shot.

To make a clip play backwards, click its icon, click the Effects button, click Fast/Slow/Reverse, and then turn on Reverse Direction.

The video in a reverse-motion clip plays back beautifully; even the audio gets reversed, offering hours of fun to the kind of people who look for secret messages in Beatles albums. (Of course, you can always turn off the clip's sound, if that backward-audio effect isn't what you want.)

FREQUENTLY ASKED QUESTION

The Time-Lapse Trick

I want to speed up my banana-slug footage beyond the scope of the speed slider—really fast. How can I do it?

The following technique involves a bit more effort than most iMovie projects. But as long as the camcorder was on a tripod during the initial filming, here's a great way to create true time-lapse movies:

Crank up the clip speed to its highest setting, and then export the clip to tape on your camera (see Chapter 11).

Then reimport the same clip into iMovie, which considers the reimported clip to be at "normal" speed. Use the speed slider again—and repeat the whole procedure as necessary—until you get the extreme speed changes you want.

Slow Motion, Fast Motion

Slow motion is extremely effective when you're going for an emotional, nostalgic, warm feeling, especially when you delete the original soundtrack and replace it with music (see Chapter 8). On the more pragmatic side, it's also useful when analyzing your tennis swing, golf stroke, or sleight-of-hand technique.

Fast motion is generally useful only for comic effects—kids wrasslin' on the living-room floor is a sure winner—but can also help with time-lapse effects, as described on the facing page.

To produce one of these effects, use the Speed slider at the bottom of the Fast/Slow/Reverse effect panel. You can drag this slider to the left or right to make the clip play faster or slower.

This slider has been enhanced in one very important way since its iMovie 4 incarnation: you're no longer limited to positioning the slider handle directly on the slider notches. That is, you're no longer obligated to make your footage play exactly two, three, four, or five times faster or slower. Now you can make a clip play just *slightly* faster by parking the little blue handle *between* the slider notches.

When you adjust this slider and click Apply, the clip's blue bar grows or shrinks in the timeline to indicate its new duration. iMovie also speeds up and slows down the sound to match the video. Dialogue in sped-up clips takes on an "Alvin and the Chipmunks" quality, as though you're fast-forwarding through a tape; slowed-down clips sound like the dying computer HAL in *2001: A Space Odyssey*.

Tip: If the distortion of slow- or fast-motion audio bothers you, you may find it wise to split the audio from the video *before* applying a slow- or fast-motion effect, so that the sound will be unaffected (see page 239). Of course, the sound will no longer match the length of the video clip, but you may be able to solve this by cropping some of the audio or video.

Flash

This effect simulates flash bulbs going off. You won't have much call for this effect in everyday filmmaking; but when that day arrives that you're trying to depict a movie star arriving at opening night—or somebody getting electrocuted—iMovie stands ready.

- **Count (One—Max).** This slider controls how many flashes will go off in the scene. (The maximum number depends on your Speed slider setting and the length of the clip, but the most you'll get is about one every seven frames, or about four per second.)

- **Brightness (Min—Max).** Controls the intensity of each flash. For true flashbulb effects, you'll want the slider at, or close to, its Max. For storm lightning or nuclear-bomb-watching effects, use lower settings.

- **Speed (Fast—Slow).** Governs how far apart the flashes appear.

Fog

You already knew that by letting you edit and add music to your movies, iMovie lets you fiddle with the emotional overtones of your own memories. What you may not have realized is that it also lets you retroactively change the weather.

The Fog effect (Figure 6-11, top) creates a mist that seems to float in front of the camera lens. It's suitable for atmospheric effects, simulated fire or crash footage, comical hangover clips, and so on.

The Amount slider controls the opacity of the fog, the Wind slider governs how quickly it drifts, and the Color slider lets you specify the color.

Ghost Trails

This effect makes moving portions of the video leave behind "visual echoes." In addition to blurry-vision effects, it can also be handy when you're trying to depict a runner as a superhero with blinding speed.

On clips without much motion, this effect does nothing at all.

The sliders let you control the intensity of the effect:

- **Trail (Short—Long).** Governs the length of the ghost images that follow a rapidly moving object in your scene.

- **Steps (Small—Large).** Controls how closely the ghost image follows the object.

- **Opacity (Clear—Opaque).** Lets you specify the transparency of the ghost image.

Glass Distortion

Those nutty Apple programmers must start to go a little stir-crazy after too many long days and sleepless nights. Why else would they introduce, in iMovie HD, a new effect that makes it look like you shot the scene through, ahem, the textured glass of a *bathroom window?*

Anyway, that's exactly what Glass Distortion does (Figure 6-11, middle). It's incredibly realistic—as long as you are, in fact, going for that public-restroom-window look. (The Scale slider affects the size of the "wrinkles" in the "glass" of the "window.")

Lens Flare

When you aim the camera toward the sun, sunshine can strike the anti-reflective coating on the inside of each lens, resulting in a reflection—a bright spot, or (on complex lens systems) a trail of bright spots—called lens flare.

Ordinarily, photographers try to avoid lens flare. But hey, as long as Apple is on a quest to let you deliberately make your footage look damaged (see Aged Film and Earthquake), why not?

Click within the Preview window to set the rotation point for the lens flare. Then use the Sweep slider to control how broadly the flare line sweeps across the frame, as happens when the camera moved during the shot. (If it did not, in fact, move, do your best to position the Sweep slider handle squarely in the middle of the slider to prevent the flare from moving at all.)

The Intensity slider adjusts the size of the primary sunshine blob. (You'll get it as soon as you try it.) Figure 6-11, bottom, shows the result.

Figure 6-11:
Top: Weather not cooperating? Now you're the weatherman! Make it as foggy as you like, using the Fog effect.

Middle: The World As Seen Through a Public Restroom Window, otherwise known as Glass Distortion.

Bottom: The Lens Flare creates an effective impersonation of an actual lens flare, especially if the angle of the shot changes to match the motion of the flare.

Before

After

Letterbox

This filter adds black letterbox bars above and below the frame, creating the look of movies (which have 16:9 proportions) as they sometimes appear when presented on a TV (which has 4:3 proportions). You may have seen this look on the Bravo channel, on a Woody Allen video, on some DVDs, or in artsy TV commercials.

The paradox, of course, is that your footage was *already* correctly shaped for a 4:3 TV screen. So to make it look as though the original was movie-shaped, iMovie has no choice but to *chop off* the top and bottom slices of your movie. It works, therefore, only when the subject matter is already vertically centered.

Fortunately, you can use the Shift slider to nudge the original footage upward or downward in the gap between the black bars, or use the Size slider to make the bars themselves more or less intrusive (thinner or fatter).

Mirror

This completely freaky effect makes iMovie split the video picture down the middle—horizontally, vertically, or both (in quadrants). It then fills the left half of the screen with a mirror image of the right half, or the top half with a mirror of the bottom. There's no seam to indicate what's going on; the result is an Alice-in-Wonderland hybrid.

- **Vertical (Top—Bottom).** This slider moves a horizontal "mirror" up and down the frame. At the Top setting, the footage doesn't look any different. At far right, you've flipped the entire frame upside-down.

Tip: If you drag the Vertical slider all the way to Bottom, and the Horizontal slider to Left, you neatly flip your clip upside-down—an iMovie first.

- **Horizontal (Left—Right).** This slider moves a vertical "mirror" left and right across the frame. Pushing this slider all the way to Left removes the horizontal reflections altogether. At far right, you've flipped the entire frame right-for-left. (While the Mirror effect in general doesn't seem to be very practical for most filmmaking, the ability to flip the frame horizontally can be terrifically useful. It can make the actor look left instead of right, make the fire engine drive west instead of east, and otherwise fix continuity problems.)

If you drag both sliders to their center positions, all four quadrants of the picture are, in fact, upside-down and/or horizontally flipped copies of the lower-right quadrant of the original footage.

The Effect In and Effect Out sliders make the mirrors fly in from the top and side of the frame as the clip plays. (Memo to music-video makers: The effect can be truly creepy.)

Tip: Be careful of *signs* (such as road signs) in footage you've mirrored. Their reverse-image type is a dead giveaway that you've rewritten history.

N-Square

If you've been secretly burning to remake *The Fly* from the insect's point of view, this is your effect. It "echoes" the video frame over and over again in miniature, like tiles of a mosaic (Figure 6-12, top).

The **Squares** (**Min—Max**) controls how many panes the frame contains, each showing the same image. At the Min position, you get four copies; at Max, you get literally hundreds. (Talk about *The Matrix*!)

Tip: If you use the Effect In and Effect Out sliders, you get an interesting variation on the N-Square effect. The clip starts out looking normal; as it plays, the grid of duplicates flies in from the lower right, sliding into its final matrix.

Rain

Here's one of iMovie's most realistic efforts. It makes your clip look as though it was filmed in a driving rainstorm (Figure 6-12, middle).

Figure 6-12:
Top: The N-Square effect at a low setting looks like this. Higher settings make the video look like Hollywood Squares *gone berserk.*

Middle: Be grateful. The Rain effect is about the only time you'll ever be able to control the rain, at least in this lifetime.

Bottom: The Soft Focus effect is great for anything misty, nostalgic, or filmed through a nylon stocking.

Before

After

How driving? You determine that by adjusting the Amount slider (which controls the lengths of the raindrop slashes) or the Wind slider (which specifies how much the drop directions change over time).

Tip: You can create a better depth simulation by stacking this effect onto a clip twice: once with small droplets (farther) and once with long ones (closer). Try throwing in a little Fog, too.

Sepia

You might think of this effect as a more nostalgic version of the Black & White effect. Once again, the color drains out of your clip, but instead of black-and-white, you get brown-and-white, which conveys the feeling of memory (thanks to its resemblance to the look of antique photographs). Don't forget to follow up with the Brightness/ Contrast effect, if necessary, to fine-tune the effect.

Sharpen

You might guess that this effect could help to repair out-of-focus scenes. In practice, however, the Sharpen effect isn't very effective in that role. Instead, it adds a fine grain to your footage, often creating a "solarized" color-banding effect, to the degree you specify using the Amount slider.

Soft Focus

Soft-focus lenses are often used when filming TV commercials that feature aging movie stars, because the fine netting or Vaseline coating on such lenses blurs fine wrinkles. (Soft-focus lenses also give everything a faintly blurry, fuzzy-edged look, but that's the price the stars pay for wrinkle obfuscation.)

Now you, too, can hide your subjects' wrinkles, by applying this soft-focus effect after the filming is complete (Figure 6-12, bottom). This effect is also good for suggesting dreams, memory, summertime nostalgia, or other hazy situations. At the sliders' extreme positions, the whole frame looks like the nuclear-holocaust scene in *Terminator 2* (especially if you use the Effect In slider to make the glow creep in over time).

Use the Softness slider to adjust the amount of Vaseline on the lens, Amount to specify what percentage of the frame is smeared, and Glow to govern just how radioactive the bright spots look.

Installing More Effects

The effects that come with iMovie certainly aren't the only ones available. For $25 or $30 you can buy dozens of additional effects like Mosaic, Emboss, X-ray, and so on. A quick Google search for *iMovie plug-instrument* will reveal to you a full array of companies that sell these effects online, but here's a sampler:

- **GeeThree.** This is the same company (*www.geethree.com*) that makes additional transitions, as described earlier in this chapter. Its eight packages of iMovie add-ons come with effects like film grain (attempts to make your video look more like film), various *vignetting* effects (which frame your footage inside the cutout shape of a heart, oval, star, and so on), and Rotate & Scale (which let you rotate your footage, say, 90 degrees, or resize it within the frame).

Two of the most interesting volumes are Volume 4 (picture-in-picture and *compositing* effects, which let you create special effects using blue screen or green screen backgrounds, just like they do in Hollywood) and Volume 8, which offers a unique image-stabilization fixer, a more powerful Ken Burns effect for photos, morphing, warping, and 100 animated backgrounds.

- **Stupendous Software.** This company (*www.stupendous-software.com*) offers an absolutely enormous array of effects plug-ins, from color-adjustment to video overlays, smoke, glass refraction, scratches and dirt, time effects, and many more. The Web site offers a number of free plug-ins to whet your appetite, as well as demo movies that show what all the other plug-ins do. (See Figure 6-13.)

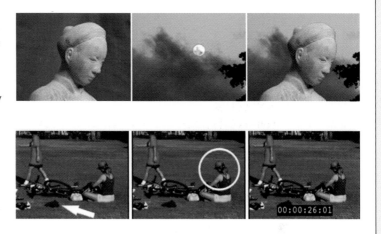

Figure 6-13:
These samples, from Stupendous Software, show you the power of plug-ins.

Top: Bluescreen is a common technique in Hollywood, and now on your own Mac. Shoot one image against a blue backdrop, and the plug-in superimposes it on any other clip you like.

Bottom: These plug-ins let you draw or type right on top of the video.

- **Virtix.** Visit *www.virtix.com* to see a complete list and illustrations. Among them, various effects let you add thought bubbles to the characters in your footage; add heat waves, lightning, or laser beams to your footage; create simulated rain, smoke, or snow; tweak colors in various ways; create an artificial zoom into a piece of moving footage; and superimpose "witness protection" rectangles on people to protect their identities.

Virtix also offers an "effect" called 16x9 Converter, which is designed to convert footage taken (accidentally or not) in widescreen format and convert it to fit a normal 4:3, squarish TV screen.

- **cf/x.** At *www.imovieplugins.com,* you'll find a staggering array of effects plug-ins of every sort: picture-in-picture, zooming, cropping, color correction, snow, "witness protection" blurring, annotation (you can *write* right on the picture), and so on (as well as transitions and title effects). One of them actually lets you *paint* onto your movies, frame by frame, to eliminate unwanted background elements, for example.

The nice part about the cf/x effects is that you can apply them to only a part of the screen; you just drag across the area you want the effect to affect. The other nice part is that you can buy only the plug-in you want (at prices like free, $1.50, or $10) without having to buy a whole package.

Tip: If you have more time than money, you can create a number of fantastic special effects in QuickTime Player Pro, including picture-in-picture effects, "video wall" simulations, and so on. See the end of Chapter 14 for an introduction to this concept of multiple video tracks in a single clip.

Note, too, that QuickTime itself offers a wealth of special effects, including blur, color balance, emboss and edge detection, and many more. They all await in the Filter box that appears when you export a movie from iMovie, as described in Chapter 12. If you're aching to use one of those filters in your iMovie project, export the clip as a full-quality DV QuickTime movie, process it with those Filters, and then reimport it into your iMovie project.

Titles, Captions, and Credits

Text superimposed over footage is incredibly common in the film and video worlds. You'd be hard-pressed to find a single movie, TV show, or commercial that doesn't have titles, captions, or credits. In fact, it's the *absence* of superimposed text that helps identify most camcorder videos as amateur efforts.

In iMovie, the term *title* refers to any kind of text: credits, titles, subtitles, copyright notices, and so on. You use them almost exactly the way you use the transitions or effects described in Chapter 6: by choosing a text-animation style from a list, adjusting its duration using a slider, dragging it into your Movie Track, and waiting while iMovie renders the effect.

But you don't need to be nearly as economical in your use of titles as you are with transitions. Transitional effects and visual effects interfere with something that stands perfectly well on its own—the footage. Transitions and special effects that aren't purposeful and important to the film may well annoy or distract your audience. When you superimpose text, on the other hand, the audience is much more likely to accept your intrusion. You're introducing this new element for its benefit, to convey information you couldn't transmit otherwise.

Moreover, as you'll soon see, most of iMovie's text effects are far more focused in purpose than its transition and effect selections, so you'll have little trouble choosing the optimum text effect for a particular editing situation. For example, the Scrolling Credits effect rolls a list of names slowly up the screen—an obvious candidate for the close of your movie. Another puts several consecutive lines of text in a little block at the lower-left corner of the screen—exactly the way the text in MTV music videos appears.

Tip: Using the Titles feature described in this chapter isn't the only way to create text effects. Using a graphics program like AppleWorks or Photoshop Elements, you can create text "slides" with far more flexibility than you can in the Titles feature. For example, the built-in Titles feature offers you a choice of only 16 colors and limited choice of type size. But using a "title card" that you import as a graphic, you're free to use any text color and any font size. You can even dress up such titles with clip art, 3-D effects, and whatever other features your graphics software offers.

Credits that you import as still graphics in this way can't do much more than fade in and fade out. When you bypass iMovie's built-in titles feature, you give up the ability to use the fancy animations. Still, the flexibility you gain in the look, color, and size of your type may be worth the sacrifice. For details on this technique, see Chapter 9.

Setting Up a Title

Adding some text to your movie requires several setup steps:

1. Choose a title effect.

2. Type the text.

3. Specify the duration and timing.

4. Choose a font.

5. Specify the size of the lettering.

6. Choose an animation direction.

7. Turn on the "Over black" checkbox, if desired.

8. Choose a color for the lettering.

9. Add a backdrop.

Here are these same steps in more detail:

Choose a Title Effect

Start by clicking the Titles button. The effects list and the other elements of the Titles palette appear, as shown in Figure 7-1.

Tip: If your mouse has a built-in scroll wheel, you can turn it to scroll the list of title effects, even without clicking the clicker, whenever the cursor is in the list area.

When you click an effect's name, you see a short preview in the Preview screen. (Use the catalog at the end of this chapter to guide you in choosing a text effect.) To view the same preview on the full-size Monitor, click the Preview button.

Incidentally, the items in the list with flippy gray triangles next to their names aren't actually titles. They're title *categories*. Click a category name to expand the triangle and see what's inside, as shown in Figure 7-1.

Tip: When showing you the preview, iMovie superimposes the text over whatever Movie Track clip is currently showing in the Monitor window. Drag the Playhead anywhere you like to specify which footage you'd like to see behind this preview. (If you haven't put any clips into the Movie Track, your preview displays only a black background, as though you'd turned on the "Over black" checkbox.)

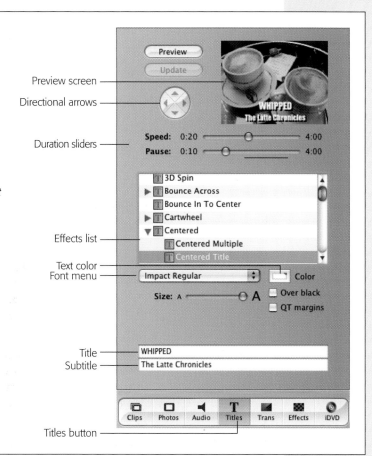

Figure 7-1:
Apple has organized the list by clumping related effects into categories. To expand a title category, you don't have to click the little triangle. Instead, you can click the category name, like Bounce Cross, which gives you a broader target. Click the name a second time to collapse the list of titles.

Each time you start a new iMovie project, the proposed title and subtitle aren't very stimulating. The first title is "My Great Movie," and its subtitle is your name (or whatever you've typed into the Sharing pane of System Preferences). The second title is "Starring," and its subtitle is "Me." You get the idea.

Fortunately, these are quick enough to change: Click in the text box, press ⌘-A to select all of the dummy text, and then type right over it.

Type the Text

Beneath the list of text effects, you'll find a place to type the actual text you want to appear in this credit, caption, or title. Just click the box once to highlight the proposed text and then begin typing. (You don't have to backspace over the factory-installed dummy text first.)

The way this text box looks and acts depends on the kind of title you've selected in the list. They fall into three categories (see Figure 7-2): text blocks, title/subtitle pairs, and pair sequences.

Text blocks

When you choose the Music Video or Scrolling Block text effects, you get a simple text box, into which you can type any text you want. At the end of each line, you can press Return to create a new line or press Return twice to create a blank line, exactly as you would in a word processor. (You can use the Cut, Copy, and Paste commands in the Edit menu to edit this text, too.)

The maximum amount of text you can type or paste here is just under 256 characters—one short paragraph. (See "Music Video" and "Scrolling Block" in the catalog section at the end of this chapter for more details.)

Tip: You don't have to settle for the proposed placement of the text when you choose one of the animation styles described below. By adding spaces before your text, or Returns after it, you get much more flexibility over where the text appears in the frame.

For example, if you add enough spaces and Returns to your text in the Music Video effect, you can place your text virtually anywhere on the screen.

Title/Subtitle pairs

When you click the names of most effects, you're shown only two narrow boxes into which you can type text, as shown in Figure 7-2 at center. Whatever you type into the top box often appears in larger typeface than the one in the bottom box.

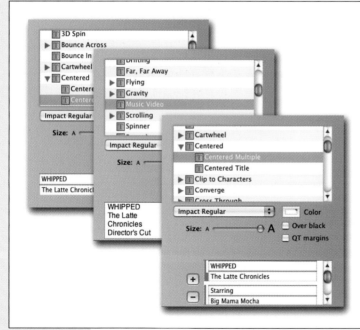

Figure 7-2:
The area into which you can type your text depends on the kind of text effect you've selected. You'll be offered either two lines for a title and subtitle (top left), one big text box (middle), or a virtually unlimited number of two-line pairs (bottom right), suitable for credit sequences at the end of your movie.

Such effects as Bounce In to Center, Centered Title, Flying Letters, Flying Words, Scroll with Pause, Stripe Subtitle, Subtitle, Typewriter, and Zoom fall into this category.

Tip: You don't have to type text into both of these boxes. In fact, *most* of the time you'll probably type into only the top box. The subtitle box underneath is there solely for your convenience, for those occasions when you need a second, usually smaller, line of type underneath the larger credit.

Pair sequences

When you're creating the credits for the end of a movie, you usually want two columns of text: on the left, the list of roles; on the right, the actors who portrayed them. In these situations, you need iMovie to offer *pairs* of slots—enough to accommodate the names of everybody who worked on your movie. It's easy to spot the text effects that offer these two-line pairs because they're the ones with the words "Multiple" or "Rolling" in their names.

After clicking one of these title effects, you see not one but two different text-box pairs. The window offers a scroll bar, plus a + button, so that you can add more pairs and scroll through them (Figure 7-3).

Figure 7-3:
You can rearrange the credits in your sequence by dragging the left edge of a credit pair up or down in the list, and waiting patiently as iMovie scrolls the list (arrow). You can also remove a credit by clicking the – button.

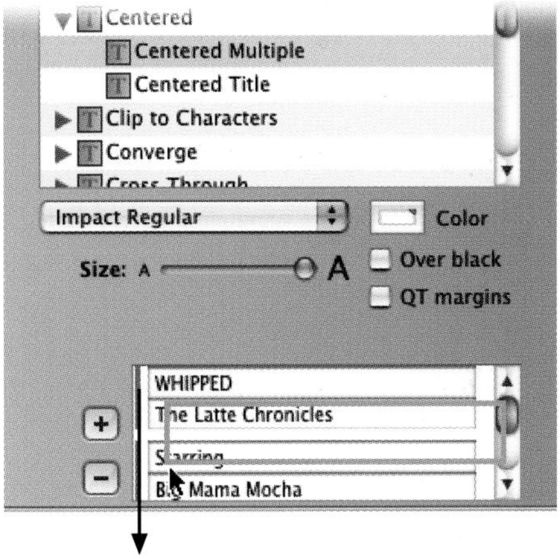

Start by clicking the top box. Drag across the dummy text ("My Great Movie"), or press a quick ⌘-A to highlight it, and then type the first character's name (*Raymond,* for example). Press Tab to highlight the lower box, and then type the actor's name (*Dustin Hoffman,* for example). If there's another empty pair of boxes beneath the one you've just filled, press Tab again, and fill in those boxes, too.

Don't worry, you'll know when you've filled up all the available boxes: You'll either discover that you can't scroll down any more, or that when you press Tab, you'll circle around and wind up in the *first* box you filled in. At that point, click the + button beside the text boxes to add another pair of boxes. Keep going this way—clicking +, typing a pair of names, clicking + again—until you've typed in the names of everybody you want in the list of credits.

Specify the Timing

You have a lot of control over the timing of your titles' animation. Most of the title styles offer two sliders just below the Preview screen:

- The **Speed** slider has different results with different titles. Setting a faster Speed setting makes the Centered Title fade in/out faster, Flying Words fly faster, Typewriter types faster, and so on. For title styles involving motion, it controls the text speed; for title styles that remain still (such as Centered Title), it controls the total amount of time the text spends onscreen. The catalog of title styles at the end of this chapter identifies the Speed slider's effect for each style.

- The **Pause** effect depends on the style, too. For titles that fade in and out, it controls the amount of time the text will be fully manifested onscreen, readable and at full size and brightness, between its fade in and fade out segments. For titles whose text flies or rolls into place (such as Typewriter or Flying Words), Pause controls how long the finished title hangs around after it's complete.

As you adjust these sliders, the readout at the bottom of the preview screen shows you, in the seconds:frames format, the time settings you've specified. (You have to wait until the preview is finished playing before these numbers appear.) For example, if it says "05:20 + 01:08 = 6:28," iMovie is trying to tell you, in its own way:

"You've set the Speed slider to 5:20—that is, you've allotted 170 frames for fading in and out. So I'll make the text fade in over half of that time: 2 seconds, 15 frames. Then you've set the Pause slider to 1:08, so I'll make the text sit there onscreen for 1 second, 8 frames. Finally, I'll take another 2 seconds, 15 frames to fade out."

Tip: When precision counts, don't use the Speed slider. Instead, double-click directly on those numbers in the Preview rectangle, the numbers that make up the "05:20 + 01:08 = 6:28" display. Once highlighted, you can type in new numbers with frame-by-frame accuracy (these numbers are in seconds:frames format).

Take into account your viewers' reading speed. There's only one thing more frustrating than titles that fly by too quickly to read, and that's titles that sit there on screen forever, boring the audience silly. Many video editors use this guideline: Leave the words onscreen long enough for somebody to read them aloud twice.

Note: Not all of the effects offer a Pause slider. Drifting, Music Video, the Rolling Credits effects, and the Subtitle effects, for example, have no motion/pause sequence to speak of. Either they move steadily or they don't move at all.

In these cases, the time readout is affected only by the Speed slider and simply means, "Total time onscreen."

Preview the Effect

As with the transitions described in the previous chapter, iMovie offers two kinds of preview for titles:

- **Preview box.** If you click a title style's name, you see a real-time preview of your title animation in the small Preview box above the list of titles. It's very tiny, but it lasts as long as the finished title will last, giving you a good idea of your title's readability. (The Speed and Pause sliders affect these previews.)

- **Monitor window.** If you click the Preview *button,* iMovie shows another kind of preview in the Monitor window. This time, you get to see every single frame of the animation, no matter how long it takes your Mac to spew out these images. On slow Macs, you may not see the animation play at real-world speed; you're getting, in essence, a slow-motion version of the full effect.

Choose a Font

Using the pop-up menu just below the list of effects, you can choose a typeface for your text. Consider these guidelines:

- **Use only TrueType or PostScript fonts.** Just don't use *bitmapped* fonts. And if you have no idea what these terms mean, don't worry. *All* the fonts that come preinstalled on your Mac are TrueType fonts, and will look terrific in your iMovie production. You need to worry about the font type only if you've manually installed some additional ones (probably very old ones) onto your Mac.

Note: The beauty of iMovie's titling feature is that the fonts you choose become embedded into the actual digital picture. In other words, when you distribute your movie as a QuickTime file, you don't have to worry that your recipients might not have the same fonts you used to create the file. They'll see on their screens exactly what you see on yours.

- **Be consistent.** Using the same typeface for all of the titles in your movie lends consistency and professionalism to the project.

- **Remember the QuickTime effect.** If you plan to distribute your finished movie as a QuickTime file—an electronic movie file that you can distribute by email, network, CD, disk, or Web page—use the biggest, boldest, cleanest fonts you have. Avoid spindly delicate fonts or script fonts. When your movie is compressed down to a 3-inch square, what looks terrific in your Monitor window will be so small it may become completely illegible. (Look at each illustration in the catalog discussion at the end of this chapter. If the text is hard to read there, you won't be able to read it in a small QuickTime movie either.)

  If your movie is going to be a QuickTime movie, turn on the QT Margins checkbox, too. Doing so increases the maximum font size you're allowed to select using the text-size slider. (See the box on the next page for the explanation.)

  Come to think of it, you might want to choose big, bold, clean fonts even if you're going to play the finished movie on a TV whose resolution is far lower than that

---

of your computer screen. Be especially careful when using one of the text effects that includes a subtitle, as iMovie subtitles often use an even smaller typeface than the primary title font, and may lose legibility if the font has too much filigree.

Finally, favor *sans serif* fonts—typefaces that don't have the tiny *serifs*, or "hats and feet," at the end of the character strokes. The typeface you're reading now is a serif font, one that's less likely to remain legible in a QuickTime movie. The typeface used in the Tip below is a sans serif font.

Tip: Some of the standard Mac fonts that look especially good as iMovie fonts are Arial Black, Capitals, Charcoal, Chicago, Gadget, Helvetica, Impact, Sand, Techno, and Textile.

Some of the fonts whose delicate nature may be harder to read are Monaco, Courier, Old English, Swing, Trebuchet, Times, Palatino, and Verdana.

The TV-Safe Area, Overscanning, and You

Millions of TV viewers every day are blissfully unaware that they're missing the big picture.

In its early days, the little cathode-ray guns inside the TV worked by painting one line of the TV picture, then turning around and heading back the opposite direction. To make sure that the screen was painted edge to edge, these early TVs were programmed to overshoot the edges of the screen—or, to use the technical term, to *overscan* the screen.

TV technology is much better now, but even modern TVs exhibit overscanning. The amount varies, but you may be missing as much as 10 percent of the picture beyond the left and right edges (and often the top and bottom, too).

TV producers are careful to keep the action and titles in the part of the frame that's least likely to be lost in the overscan. But as a film editor, the *TV-safe area* is suddenly your concern, too. The overscanning effect means that when you show your iMovie productions on a TV, you'll lose anything that's very close to the edges of the frame.

Most of the time, that's no problem; only when you're adding titles does the overscanning effect become a worry.

Fortunately, avoiding text-chopping problems is supremely easy: Just turn *off* the QT Margins checkbox. Doing so makes iMovie shrink the text enough so that it won't get chopped off on a TV—guaranteed.

This business of the TV-safe area *isn't* an issue if you plan to convert your iMovie work into QuickTime movies, which have no such complications. That's why this checkbox is worded as it is: "QT Margins" means "Assume that this movie will be shown as a QuickTime movie, and therefore won't have chopped-off margins." When the QT Margins checkbox is turned *on*, the text-size slider lets you crank your font sizes a few notches higher.

Specify the Size of the Lettering

iMovie is extremely conservative with its font-size choices. Even with the Size slider (just to the right of the Font pop-up menu) all the way to the right, and even with "QT Margins" turned on, iMovie doesn't let you make titles that fill the screen. (Keeping your text short may help. If the phrase is very long, iMovie further reduces the point size enough to fit the entire line on the screen, even if the type-size slider is at its maximum. In other words, you can make the font for the credit *PIGGY* much larger than you can *ONE HAM'S ADVENTURES IN MANHATTAN.*)

If you feel hemmed in by the font-size limitations, consider using a still-image "title card" with text as large as you like, as described on page 244.

Choose an Animation Direction

Most of iMovie's text effects are animated. They feature words flying across the screen, sliding from one edge of the frame to the other, and so on. Some feature directional arrows (seen in Figure 7-1, for example) that let you control which direction the text flies or slides in. By clicking the appropriate arrow, you can specify which direction the text should fly. (The directional controls are dimmed and unavailable for other text effects.)

Note: In the case of the Music Video effect, the arrow specifies which *corner* the text block should sit in, motionless.

The catalog of text effects at the end of this chapter identifies those that offer a direction control, and what it does in each case.

The "Over Black" Checkbox

Under normal circumstances, the text you've specified gets superimposed over the video picture. Particularly when you're creating opening or closing credits, however, you may want the lettering to appear on a black screen—a striking and professional-looking effect. In those cases, turn on the "Over black" checkbox.

It's important to note that when you do so, you *add* to the total length of your movie. Adding the "Over black" title is like inserting a new clip, in that you force the clips to the right of your text effect to slide further rightward to accommodate the credit you just inserted. (When the "Over black" checkbox *isn't* turned on, adding a text effect doesn't change the overall length of your movie.)

The "Over black" option is attractive for three reasons. First, it looks extremely professional; it's something people who don't have an editing program like iMovie can't even do. Second, the high contrast of white against black makes the text very legible. Third, the audience will *read* it, instead of being distracted by the video behind it.

Tip: You don't have to limit yourself to adding text over black; you can just as easily superimpose your titles over blue, over red, or over fuschia. The trick is to create a colored clip as described on page 140, and add your titles to *it*. In that case, do *not* turn on "Over black", since you want your lettering to float on top of the existing video, which happens to be a solid, unchanging color.

Choose a Color for the Lettering

By clicking the tiny square beside the word Color, you get a little dialog box known as the Mac OS X Color Picker. (The box on the facing page describes it in detail.) For now, the important thing is to choose a color that *contrasts* with the footage behind the lettering. Use white against black, black against white, yellow against blue, and so on.

Note: iMovie doesn't limit you to TV-safe colors. But be careful. If colors are too bright (saturated), the edges of the letters can smear and tear when played back on a TV.

Add a Backdrop

If you left your education to the Apple online help, you might assume that there are only two kinds of images that can underlie your titles: video footage or a solid black frame. Fortunately, there's a third option that greatly expands your creative possibilities: superimposing your text on a still image, such as a photo or some gradient fill you've created in, say, Photoshop Elements.

Figure 7-4:
When you hand-build a title using a graphics program like Photoshop Elements or AppleWorks, you lose the ability to animate the words and letters. The results can be much more interesting than plain white text on a black background, yet less distracting than text superimposed over footage.

Another option is to just add color bars (lower left) to make people think you really work in television.

Tip: One of the still backgrounds you can download from the "Missing CD" page at *www.missingmanuals. com* is called Color Bars. It lets you begin and end your movie with the standard, broadcast-TV color bar chart like the one shown (in shades of gray) at lower left in Figure 7-4. In professional video work, about 20 seconds of color bars are always recorded at the beginning of a tape. They give the technicians a point of color reference for adjusting their monitors and other reproduction equipment to ensure that the footage looks the same on their gear as it did on yours. Their goal is to adjust the knobs until the white bars look white, not pink, and the black ones don't look gray.

If you intend your movie to be used for TV broadcast, the color bars may actually be required by the station. If not, the color bars make your homemade production look and feel as though you edited it in a $600-per-hour New York editing facility.

The Color Picker

Here and there—not just in iMovie, but also in System Preferences, TextEdit, Microsoft Office, and many other programs—Mac OS X offers you the opportunity to choose a *color* for some element, like your desktop background, a window, and so on.

The Colors dialog box offers a miniature color lab that lets you dial in any color in the Mac's rainbow. *Several* color labs, actually, arrayed across the top, are each designed to make color-choosing easier in certain circumstances:

Color Wheel. Drag the scroll bar vertically to adjust the brightness, and then drag your cursor around the ball to pick the shade.

Color Sliders. From the pop-up menu, choose the color-mixing method you prefer. *CMYK* stands for Cyan, Magenta, Yellow, and Black. People in the printing industry will feel immediately at home, because these four colors are the component inks for color printing. (These people may also be able to explain why *K* stands for *black*.)

RGB is how a TV or computer monitor thinks of colors: as proportions of red, green, and blue. And *HSV* stands for Hue, Saturation, and Value—a favorite color-specifying scheme in scientific circles.

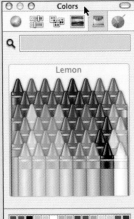

In each case, just drag the sliders to mix up the color you want, or type in the percentages of each component.

Color Palettes presents canned sets of color swatches. They're primarily for programmers who want quick access to the standard colors in Mac OS X.

Image Palettes offers the visible rainbow arrayed yet another way—cloudy, color-arranged streaks.

Crayons. Now *this* is a good user interface. You can click each crayon to see its color name: "Mocha," "Fern," "Cayenne," and so on. (Some interior decorator in Cupertino had a field day naming these crayons.)

In any of these color pickers, you can also "sample" a color that's *outside* the dialog box—a color you found on a Web page, for example. Just click the magnifying-glass icon and then move your cursor around the screen. You'll see the sliders and numbers automatically change inside the dialog box when you click.

Finally, note that you can store frequently used (or frequently admired) colors in the mini-palette squares at the bottom. To do that, drag the big rectangular color swatch (next to the magnifying glass) directly down into one of the little squares, where it will stay fresh for weeks.

To use one of these backdrops, import it into your project as you would any graphics file, as described on page 245. That discussion also explains how to control the length of time a still image appears in your movie. From there, you should have little difficulty superimposing titles as described in this chapter.

Inserting and Rendering a Title

When you've taken into consideration all the options described so far in this chapter, you probably have a good feel for how this title is going to look once it's inserted into your movie. Now it's time to commit it to digital film.

Dragging the Title into the Movie Track

To place the title you've selected into Movie Track, proceed as follows:

1. **Decide where you want the title to begin.**

   Begin by pressing the Home key on your keyboard, which simultaneously deselects all clips and rewinds the Playhead to the beginning of the Movie Track. Now you can drag the playhead along the Scrubber bar. As you do, a bright red, inverted "T" cursor slides along your Clip Viewer (or a duplicate Playhead slides along your Timeline Viewer) to indicate your position.

   Consider the location of your title carefully. If you're superimposing it on a solid-colored background or a still image, no problem. But if you're planning to

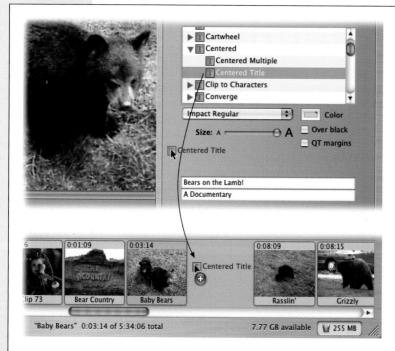

Figure 7-5:
Drag the name of the title you want out of the Titles list directly into the Movie Track.

The clips in the Clip Viewer or Timeline Viewer scoot to the right to make room for the title you're inserting.

superimpose it on moving video, choose a scene that's relatively still, so that the video doesn't distract the audience from the words onscreen. (The exception: If you're using one of iMovie's "see-through" lettering styles, you may want to choose active video to deliberately call attention to the "cutouts.")

Be particularly careful not to superimpose your titles on an unsteady shot; the contrast between the jiggling picture and the rock-steady lettering on the screen will make your audience uncomfortable.

Sometimes, such as when you've selected a title style that fades in from nothing, it's OK to put the title squarely at the beginning of a clip. At other times, you'll want to position the title a few seconds into the clip.

2. **If you've selected a starting point for a title that's in the middle of the clip, position the Playhead there and then choose Edit→Split Video Clip at Playhead.**

   It's a fact of iMovie life: A title can begin only at the *beginning* of a clip, never the middle. To make the title seem as though it's starting partway through a clip, therefore, you must *turn* that spot into the beginning of a new clip by chopping the clip in half.

   This is not the only time the title feature will be chopping your clips into smaller clips, as Figure 7-6 illustrates.

3. **Drag the name or icon of your chosen title style from the list of titles directly onto the Movie Track, as shown in Figure 7-5.**

   Drag it just to the left of the clip you'll want to play underneath the title text. All clips to the right scoot rightward to make room for your cursor.

Rendering Begins

Now iMovie begins to *render* the title effect. In other words, it creates a new clip that incorporates both the original footage and the text you're superimposing.

In some ways, this title-rendering process resembles the transition- or effect-rendering process described in the previous chapter. For example, you can stop it by pressing either the Esc key (in the upper left of your keyboard) or ⌘-period.

POWER USERS' CLINIC

Behind-the-Scenes Undo Magic

iMovie can restore an original clip when you delete a title that you've superimposed on it, even weeks later.

Yet as noted in this chapter, iMovie creates titles by *modifying* the original clips—by changing the actual pixels that compose the image. So where is iMovie storing a copy of the original, for use when you decide to delete the title?

In the project's Media folder, that's where (see page 113). There you'll find the original clip from the camcorder (called "Clip 1," for example), untouched. There you'll also find a new clip (called "Typewriter 1," for example), bearing the name of the title style you used. *This* clip contains the modified portion of your original clip.

The longer the title is to remain onscreen, the longer the rendering process takes. But exactly as when rendering transitions, you can continue to do other work in iMovie (or even in other programs) while the title is rendering. In fact, you can play titles before they're fully baked, to see what they'll look like in your final movie —another handy preview feature that doesn't require you to wait until the rendering is finished. You can even have several titles rendering simultaneously, although iMovie slows down quite a bit if you have more than, say, three titles rendering at once.

The bright red progress bar creeps along the bottom of the clip, as shown in Figure 7-6. In other words, a title in the Movie Track doesn't have its own icon, as a transition does. Instead, you get to see a miniature illustration of what it's going to look like. (Tiny lettering appears directly *on* the superimposed clip icon to help you identify it as a title clip.)

As soon as you've finished dragging a title into the Movie Track, the affected clip's name instantly changes. It takes on the words of your actual title (or as much as will fit; if the name is wider than the clip icon, you see an ellipsis "like … this"). If the clip was called, for example, "Chris closeup," iMovie renames it "Shoestring Productions

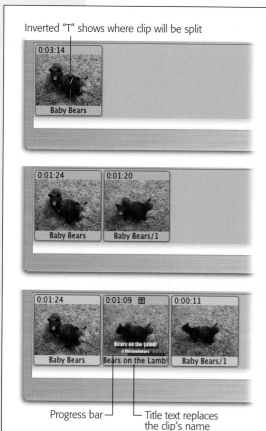

Inverted "T" shows where clip will be split

Progress bar

Title text replaces the clip's name

Figure 7-6:
If you want a title to begin partway into a clip (top) instead of at the very beginning, you must first chop the clip into two pieces (middle). During rendering, a progress bar keeps track of the rendering progress (bottom).

After the title has finished rendering, you'll find that iMovie has automatically made yet another clip split—at the end of the title (bottom). The result: After you're done inserting a title, that portion of your movie occupied by the title has become a clip unto itself.

presents," or whatever your title says. (You can see this effect, too, in Figure 7-6.) As a bonus, a tiny letter T appears in the upper-right corner of the "slide" in the Clip Viewer, a friendly reminder that you've applied a title to it.

How Titles Chop Up Your Clips

As Figure 7-6 illustrates, it's not enough that you split your clip if you want the title to begin partway into the footage. iMovie may chop up your clips on its own, according to this scheme:

- If the title you've specified is shorter than the clip, iMovie splits the clip in two. The first portion gets the title text embedded into it; the second portion is left alone.

- If the title is *longer* than the clip, iMovie *steals footage* from the next clip to the right (see Figure 7-7). In fact, it continues to eat up as many additional clips as necessary to fulfill the duration you've specified for it. This powerful feature means that you can make a single title sequence extend across a series of short clips, still images, transitions, and so on. (By contrast, the transitions and effects described in Chapter 6 limit their appetites to single clips.)

iMovie may still chop up the final clip in the sequence, however, to accommodate the tail end of the title sequence.

Figure 7-7:
If your title is longer than its clip, iMovie steals however many seconds of footage it needs from the next clip and incorporates it into the first clip. If you look carefully at the durations of these two clips before (top) and after the title has been applied, you'll see that the second clip has been shortened by one second, and the first clip lengthened, when the stealing process is over (middle).

If you try to apply your title to a too-short clip when there's no subsequent clip from which iMovie can steal frames, on the other hand, you get the error message shown at bottom.

Tip: If the title is long enough, it can gobble down a number of individual clips—and turn them into a *single* title clip in your Movie Track. This can be a sneaky way to organize your movie, as described in the box on the facing page.

Checking the Result

When the rendering process is complete—or even before it's complete—check out the effect. Click the title clip in the Movie Track and press the Space bar to view the title clip, or Shift-click the clips before and after the title clip (and then press the Space bar) to see how the title looks in the context of the clips around it. Or just drag the Playhead back and forth across the title to see how it looks.

If the title isn't quite what you wanted—if it's the wrong length, style, or font, or if there's a typo, for example—you can change its settings as described in the next section. If the title wasn't *at all* what you wanted—if it's in the wrong place, for example—you can undo the entire insertion-and-rendering process by highlighting the title clip and pressing the Delete key (or choosing Edit→Undo, if you added the title recently). The original footage returns, textless and intact.

Editing a Title

Editing a title is easy. Click the title clip's icon in the Movie Track. Then click the Titles button, if the list of titles isn't already open.

POWER USERS' CLINIC

Multiple Simultaneous Superimposed Titles

If you've read this chapter carefully, you may have discovered an intriguing aspect of titles: After iMovie creates one, you don't wind up with a special TV icon in your Movie Track, as you do when you create a transition (see Chapter 6). Instead, the clip that now has your superimposed title is just an ordinary clip—one that you can treat like any other clip. You can move it around in the movie, put it back onto the Clips pane, and so on.

As a result, there's nothing to stop you from applying *another* title to the same clip…and another, and another. Each can have its own style, animation, duration, color, font, and text. By carefully splitting each title clip in the Movie Track before applying the next title to it, you can stagger the entrance of each title, so that your words fly onto the screen exactly when, and how, you specify.

Furthermore, by combining these titles so that they don't crash into each other—or *do* crash into each other in artistic ways—you can come up with extremely complex title sequences that rival some of the fanciest opening-credit sequences Hollywood has ever dreamed up.

Now you can adjust the title style, the text of the title itself, the title's timing, the direction of motion, or any other parameters described in the first part of the chapter. When you're finished, click the Update button just below the Preview button. iMovie begins the rendering process again, putting in place a brand-new title, and splitting the superimposed footage in a different place, if necessary.

Note: The good news is that your ability to edit the title isn't subject to the availability of the Undo command. In other words, you can revise the settings for a title at any time, even if you've saved the project (and therefore wiped out your Undo trail).

But if you've applied *multiple* superimposed titles, as described in the box below, you can revise only the most recent title you've applied to a particular clip.

Deleting a Title

As noted previously, a title clip is just a clip. You might wonder, therefore, how you can remove a title without also deleting the footage it affects.

Blank Titles and Uni-Clips

If you begin a 6-second title at the start of three 2-second clips, you'll wind up with just one clip on your Movie Track: a 6-second title clip. Instead of three icons on your Movie Track, you'll wind up with just one uni-clip.

This is business as usual for iMovie, but a unique opportunity for you. You can use the titling feature to deliberately knit together multiple clips into one icon—a great way to simplify your movie in progress. As you complete a section of your film, you can freeze and consolidate its component clips into a single icon. Having fewer clips instead of lots of tiny ones makes it easier to get an overview of your movie as well as do any restructuring work.

Of course, this is not to suggest that you should superimpose the words "Bat Dogs from Hell: The Return" across all of your clips just to enjoy the uni-clip feature. You can use *blank* titles and get the icon-consolidation effect without adding text.

Suppose, for example, that you have three 2-second clips, as shown here at top. To knit them into a single frozen icon, you'd create a 6-second title—but you'd leave its text boxes empty. (If you need a longer title, use one of the Multiple titles, like Centered Multiple. Make as many pair sequences as you want, making sure that all of them are empty.) Once you apply that title, the three 2-second clips magically turn into a single 6-second clip, as shown here at bottom.

The best part of all of this is that you can now drag your uni-clips around on the Movie Track, each actually composed of multiple clips. At any time—for example, once you've got the basic structure of your movie intact—you can restore the original component clips. Just click the uni-clip and press the Delete key (as though to remove the title). Boom: It sproings apart into its component pieces.

Yet sure enough, iMovie remembers what your clips looked like before you overlaid a title. You can click a title clip at any time, press the Delete key, and then watch iMovie restore the original footage. True, pressing Delete on a conventional clip deletes it, but pressing Delete on a title clip simply deletes its "titleness." The clip to its right merges back into its formerly text-overlaid portion, leaving only one clip instead of two.

Now, if you've *moved* the clip that follows the title clip, and you *then* delete the title clip, iMovie will still put back the underlying footage that it consumed, but it may no longer be where you expect it to be. The program can't "splice" the footage back onto the beginning of a clip from which it was split, because iMovie doesn't know where that clip is (you might even have deleted it). If you move the clips back into their original sequence after deleting the title, the footage will still be continuous, but there might now be a cut or break where the title ended, as if you had split the clip at that point.

The iMovie Titles Catalog

This discussion describes and illustrates each of the title effects available in iMovie. Along the way, you'll find out several useful pieces of information about each title:

- How the Speed slider affects the effect.
- Which directions you can make the text move, if any.
- When you might find each effect useful.

Note: Despite the smooth, professional look of iMovie's text effects, many of them may become tiny and illegible when you export your finished movie as a QuickTime movie (see Chapter 12). They may look terrific in your Monitor window or when played on your TV; however, in a small QuickTime movie frame, especially the kind you might post on a Web page or send by email, the text may shrink away to nothing.

If you have time to experiment with different versions of your movie, exporting each to a QuickTime movie until you find a text effect that's legible, then great. If not, use the notations in this section as a guide. They assume that you've set the text slider to its maximum and turned on the QT Margins checkbox.

3D Spin

Speed slider: *Controls duration*
Direction control: *None*

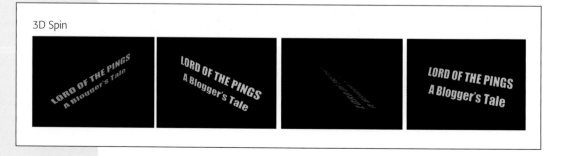

3D Spin

This twisty title effect sends your title text spinning crazily in all three dimensions, as though it were typeset on a piece of transparent confetti that's tumbling down from the sky. It's not especially easy to read, since for most of the time onscreen, you're reading it in mirror-image, upside-down, or squished. (It never does come to a stop.) Its transparency also fluctuates, permitting more or less of the background video (or background black) to show through the letters.

Bounce Across

Speed slider: *Controls flying-on speed*
Direction control: *Left, right*

Don't use this effect for anything serious or hard-hitting. It's a light-hearted, almost comical animation in which your title and subtitle come rolling in on invisible roller-coaster tracks, bouncing up and down as they come to rest in the center of the screen. You get an additional control—a Wave slider that controls how high the bounces are, and therefore how dramatic the effect.

The Bounce Across Multiple variation (which appears when you open the Bounce Across category name) brings on a second and then a third title or title pair, each coming to rest in the center of the screen and then disappearing to make way for the next wave.

Bounce In to Center

Speed slider: *Controls flying-on speed*
Direction control: *Up, down, left, right*

In this animated effect, the title slides down from the top of the frame and comes to rest, with a little springy bounce, in the center. If you've specified a subtitle, it floats upward simultaneously from the bottom of the frame. Use it for quirky or comic opening credits—it's not very subtle, but reasonably useful. (The illustration on the previous page shows the direction control set to Right.)

Cartwheel

Speed slider: *Controls flying-on speed*
Direction control: *Left, right*

iMovie includes several text effects that involve spinning or tumbling words or letters. You'll probably want to avoid most of them except in special situations. The picture below shows the first of this family.

In this version, all of the letters of your title and subtitle fly onto the screen from one side, each spinning as though pierced on its own axle. You can't actually read the titles until they're finished with their spinning and land in the center.

Read quickly, however, because the letters stand still only for a moment (the moment you specify with the Pause slider), and then spin away again, cartwheeling their way offscreen. If you chose the Cartwheel Multiple version, the next pair of credits now cartwheels on.

Cartwheel

Centered Title

Speed slider: *Controls fade in/fade out speed*
Direction control: *None*

The Centered Title is one of the most useful of all the iMovie text effects. iMovie shows a single line of text (or two lines, if you take advantage of the subtitle option), fading in, staying onscreen for a moment, then fading out, making this effect ideal for displaying the title of your movie.

The Centered Multiple variation is ideal for opening credits, because each name (along with an optional subtitle) fades professionally onto the screen, remains there for a moment, and then fades away again. The next name fades in to repeat the cycle. (If you haven't seen this particular opening-credit style used at the beginning of a million TV shows and movies, you haven't watched enough TV.)

This is a tasteful, professional, powerful effect.

Tip: By using several consecutive Centered Titles, you achieve exactly the same effect as the Centered Multiple sequence, except with individual control over the timing of each text pair.

Centered Title

Clip to Characters

Speed slider: *Controls fade in/fade out speed*
Direction control: *None*

Over and over again in Apple's history, its designers have noticed the masses flocking to a certain piece of shareware that fills a feature hole in Apple's own software. In this case, the iMovie team observed how many people were buying add-on title effects from other companies, and decided to spare them that expense by introducing, back in iMovie 4, this powerful title category. All four new text effects described here were once available only as shareware add-ons. (They're called Clip to Characters because the actual letter outlines serve as cookie cutters that clip out video or pictures behind them. You'll get the idea in a moment.)

Animated Gradient

Animated Gradient

Man, if you're into making mystery movies, you've got your opening credits right here. In this two-toned extravaganza, a moving searchlight seems to be shining out at you from behind the screen, turning the insides of the letters bright yellow as it passes from left to right. It's particularly striking when you turn on the "Over black" checkbox.

Clip Image

Here's a wild new effect with infinite possibilities. In this variation, iMovie fills the hollow outlines of your lettering with a still image—a graphic or photo. You specify which graphic you want to use by clicking the little File button that magically appears below the Size slider, and then using the Open File dialog box to peruse the contents of your hard drive.

If you're just looking for some quick graphic interest, you can choose an interesting photo of texture—a close-up of sandpaper, clouds, or diamonds, for example. If you're aiming for Sundance, you could conceivably spend a few hours in Photoshop creating a more elaborate graphic whose elements are strategically placed to peek out from inside the letters of your title. These could be little silhouetted spy characters, mischievous monkeys, or even tiny words that appear *inside* the larger letters.

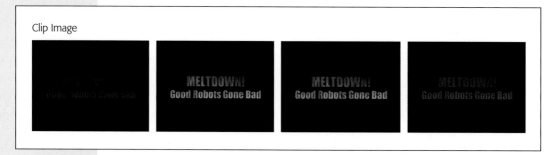

Clip Video

This titling effect wins the award for Most Likely to Save You $30 on Shareware Title Styles. Once again, it makes your letters transparent—but instead of permitting a background still photo to peek through, it actually permits your own video to play inside the lettering. The rest of the screen is black (which is why the "Over black" checkbox is automatically turned on and dimmed when you choose this effect). The Color checkbox has no effect in this case, either.

You can use this title style to create some truly brilliant visuals, video puns, or double meanings. Maybe the title of your short film is "Energy Drink," but we see what appears to be dripping blood inside the lettering. Maybe you've made a movie about a Fourth of July picnic, and you've got some waving-flag video that fills in the hollow letters. Or maybe you're editing a home movie called "Off to Topeka," and a jet plane takes off behind the words, unforgettably appearing and disappearing through and between the letters of the words.

Starburst

Like Clip Image, this effect fills in your lettering with a single image that stretches across the entire title. In this case, though, you don't get to choose which image you get. Like it or not, it's a sunburst, bright yellow in the middle and fading out, with visible radiating lines, toward the outer edges.

The Color box is very important in this case, as it specifies what color the yellow central sunball becomes as its rays reach the outer edges of your words.

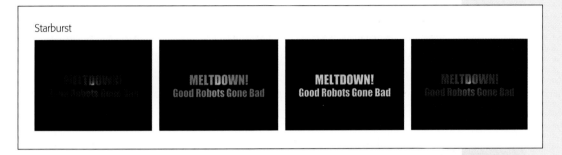

Converge

Speed slider: *Controls letter-movement speed*
Direction control: *Left, right (Converge and Converge Multiple only)*

As seen on TV—or in any number of artsy serial-killer movies. The title appears with its letter spacing far too wide—and as you watch, the letters slowly glide inward until they're correctly spaced.

You get four variations. In Converge (for one line) and Converge Multiple (several pairs), the letters on the right or left side remain essentially stationary during the animation, leaving the letters on the opposite side to do all the movement. In the Multiple version, each completed title blinks out of sight to make way for the next title pair.

In Converge to Center and its Multiple variation, the text appears instantly onscreen—but spaced so widely that the right and left parts of it may even be chopped off by the borders of the frame. They immediately float inward to the center until they're

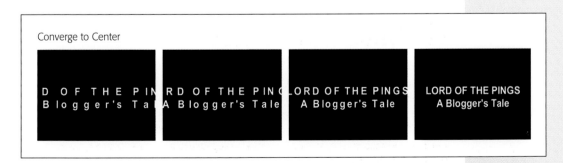

readable. Once again, this form of credits has been used now and again during the openings of scary thrillers.

In all four cases, the effect is vaguely menacing and very slick.

Cross Through

Speed slider: *Controls letter-movement speed*
Direction control: *None*

The Cross Through Center title (and its Multiple variant) appears perfectly normal—centered and nicely spaced. There's only one thing wrong with it: every word is spelled backwards, sihT ekiL hcuM ytterP.

As you watch, iMovie straightens things out for you. The letters fly through the center point of the frame and out the other side, until they're in the proper order. (This one is best suited for movies about spelling bees or mirror manufacturers.)

Drifting

Speed slider: *Controls total time onscreen*
Direction control: *Up, down, left right*

This effect duplicates the opening credits of many a recent Hollywood movie, not to mention TV commercials for the *New York Times* and various over-the-counter drugs. Your text fades in at center screen, and the first and second lines subtly float in opposite directions before fading out again. The effect is eye-catching, although it can be annoying to try to read lines of text that are slipping apart. (The Pause slider is dimmed—because the text never pauses!)

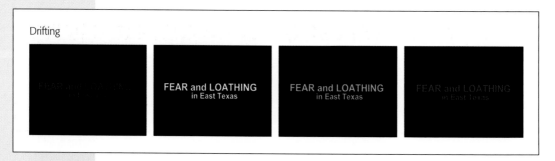

Far, Far Away

Speed slider: *Controls flying-on speed*
Direction control: *None*

Star Wars geeks, rejoice! Now you, too, can simulate the legendary prologue text of the Star Wars movies. Your text appears in a block, huge at the bottom of the screen, and then scrolls up and away, in severe perspective, fading out to blackness in the distance as it approaches the top of the screen.

You can't really get away with using this effect for anything but spoofs of the Star Wars movies and tributes to them, because it's so instantly recognizable to just about everyone who's ever been to the movies. But in the right context, and when filled with just the right text, it can be truly hilarious. ("Long, long ago, in a dead-end job far, far away, Larry first saw Charlene, bent over the Xerox machine as she changed the toner cartridge. Thus began the story of their courtship…")

Far Far Away

Flying

Speed slider: *Controls flying-on speed*
Direction control: *Up, down*

In the Flying Letters effect, the letters of your title (and subtitle, if you've specified one) fly onto the screen one at a time from the upper-right or lower-right corner of the frame (depending on the directional arrow you click), gradually assembling the phrase you've specified. If nothing else, this effect is certainly offbeat, but it can quickly get boring if you use it more than once.

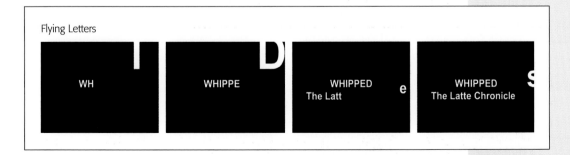

Flying Letters

The Speed slider's maximum time grows according to the length of your title. At its maximum, you and your audience could be sitting there for nearly a full minute while your letters plod onto the screen.

The Flying Words effect is similar, except that entire words fly onto the screen instead of letters. It may be less tedious for your audience to watch, but you should still use it sparingly.

Flying Words

Gravity, Gravity Multiple

Speed slider: *Controls overall title timing*
Direction control: *Up, down, left, right*

This time, the letters of your title and subtitle begin at the top of the screen, fading into a horizontal jumble of mixed-up letters. Then, as you watch, they slide down the screen into position, much like snowflakes or melted ice on a windowpane. It's too bizarre to be generally useful, but looks pretty cool when superimposed over snow-flurry footage.

Using the direction arrows, you can specify that your jumbled letters begin at the bottom of the screen and slide upward instead (something to remember if you ever get involved with producing grass-growing videos). You can also click the left or right direction arrows, although these don't produce any visible difference from the down and up versions.

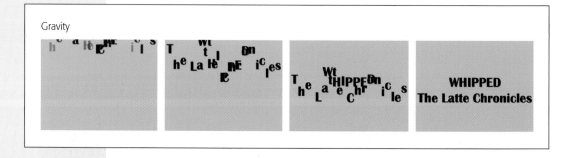

Gravity

Music Video

Speed slider: *Controls total time onscreen*
Direction control: *Left, right*

If you've ever seen a music video on MTV or VH1, you'll recognize this effect instantly. It places the block of text you've typed—a short paragraph of it, anyway—into the lower-left or lower-right corner of the screen, depending on which directional arrow you select.

The authenticity of this effect is unassailable. It looks *exactly* like the credits that appear at the beginning of actual music videos. Be careful not to make the type too small, though, especially for videos you intend to distribute by email or on the Web.

Tip: The Music Video title is one of the most useful text styles, as it's the only iMovie text style that gives you complete freedom over placement of your text. You can make your title appear off-center, in any corner of the frame, and so on.

The trick is to use "white space" to position the text. By pressing the Space bar before typing each line, you can push your text to the middle or right side of the frame; by pressing Return after the text, you can force the text upward to the middle or top of the frame. Combine these techniques with the left/right directional buttons for various wacky placement effects.

Music Video

Scrolling

Here they are: four variations of the closing-credits effect that wraps up every Hollywood movie you've ever seen. It creates what the pros call a *roll*—text that slides up the screen from the bottom, as though on an endless roll of clear plastic, showing the names of the characters and the actors who played them.

Rolling Credits, Rolling Centered Credits

These effects give you text pairs, like Director/Steven Speilberg and Writer/Robert Towne, or character name/actor name. (The Rolling Credits effect is identical to the Rolling Centered Credits except for the formatting; that is, instead of straddling an invisible "gutter" of empty space, the two columns are separated by a dotted line.)

You can opt to have the text scroll down from the top instead (by clicking the directional arrow), although it looks very weird. (A *crawl*, on the other hand, slides onto the screen from side to side, like the tornado-warning notices that sometimes appear during a TV show. At this writing, iMovie offers no method for creating crawls, much to the disappointment of TV stations in Iowa.)

Be careful when using this effect for two reasons. First, remember that 45 seconds is the longest scroll you can create, and iMovie automatically adjusts the speed of scrolling to fit all the names you've typed into the duration you've specified. You couldn't fit even 10 percent of the closing credits of *Titanic* into 45 seconds, at least not without scrolling them too fast to read. (On the other hand, you can always use multiple *sets* of Rolling Credits titles, superimposed if necessary [page 194].)

Second, the type is very small, which could be a problem if you intend to save your movie as a QuickTime file.

Scroll with Pause

Speed slider: *Controls scroll-in/scroll-off speed*
Direction control: *Up, down, left, right*

The title and subtitle (if you've specified one) slide, as a pair, from the edge of the screen you've specified (by clicking the directional arrows), pause at the center of the screen for the audience to read, and then continue sliding on their merry way off the screen.

Sure, this isn't an effect you're likely to use often, but it can look quirky and charming if the speed and typeface are right. For example, when your credits slide from left to right, you suggest an old-time slide projector changing slides.

Scrolling Block

Speed slider: *Controls total time onscreen*
Direction control: *Up or down*

This text style is a lot like Far, Far Away, in that a long block of introductory text scrolls slowly upward from the bottom of the screen. In this case, however, it doesn't shrink as it rolls up the screen.

This roll effect is extremely common in commercial theatrical movies. You can use it at the beginning of your movie to explain the plot setup. At the end of the movie, you can use it to provide a postscript or update to the events the audience has just witnessed (like the postscripts at the end of *October Sky* or *A Beautiful Mind*).

You can also tack one scrolling block onto the end of another, although this tactic is less necessary now that a single Scrolling Block can contain well over 4,000 typed characters. You can also tack a Scrolling Block onto one of the other iMovie scrolling-text effects (it can follow the Rolling Credits effect, for example) to provide a neatly centered copyright, an "in memoriam," or some disclaimer information. As far as the audience is concerned, it will be just one more part of the same smooth scroll.

Furthermore, you don't have to begin this follow-up block after the regular credits (or the preceding Scrolling Blocks) have completely disappeared off the top of the screen.

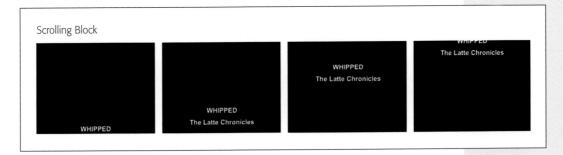

You can make the additional Scrolling Block appear at any moment, even while the previous crawl is still finishing up its movement; see the box on page 194.

The directional arrows let you control whether this roll proceeds downward from the top or upward from the bottom. You're welcome to make your text block scroll downward, but do so with the knowledge that you're doing something unconventional, even unheard of, in the world of filmmaking.

Spinner

Speed slider: *Controls spinning-on/spinning-off time*
Direction control: *None*

It's taken four versions of iMovie, but at last you can simulate the spinning-newspaper-headline effect made popular by many an old black-and-white movie, not to mention the old *Batman* TV show of the '60s. Each line of your credits comes spinning out of a dot at the center of the screen, finally stopping at full size at center so that you can read it. (The Spins slider even lets you control how many times it spins before coming to rest.) At that point, it retreats, spinning right back into the distance again.

Tip: The Spinner effect might be more familiar-looking if it would come to a stop and then *stay there* until the next line spun onto the screen, rather than spinning away again. Of course, if that's what you want, go ahead and render the effect—and then just chop out the spinning-away-again section of the resulting title clip.

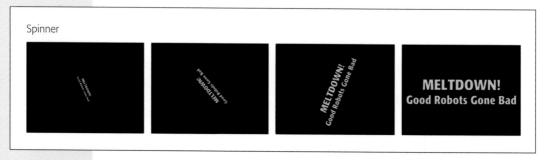

Spinner

Spread

Speed slider: *Controls total time onscreen*
Direction control: *None*

The Spread from Center effect was clearly written by the same programmer who created Converge. Once again, it's all about letter spacing—but this time, all of the letters on each line of your title begin in the center of the frame, superimposed in a chaotic, unreadable jumble. As the title rolls on, the letters drift outward and into their rightful places.

If you choose the Multiple version, they hold in place for a moment and then vanish just in time for the next set of titles to appear and blossom.

Stripe Subtitle

Speed slider: *Controls total time onscreen*
Direction control: *None*

This effect creates what the pros call a *lower third*—a stripe across the bottom of the picture where the text identifies, for example, the name and affiliation of the person being interviewed. The tinted background is an unusual touch.

Oddly enough, clicking the Color swatch here *doesn't* let you change the color of the text, as it usually does. (Stripe Subtitle text is always white.) Instead, it specifies the background color of the stripe itself.

Odder still, the stripe always stops just shy of the screen's right edge.

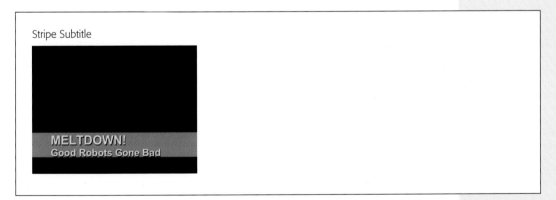

Subtitle

Speed slider: *Controls total time onscreen*
Direction control: *None*

This effect gives you the more traditional look for a "lower third" title, one that identifies the person or place being shown in the footage. The text quietly fades in, centered at the bottom of the screen, and then fades out again. (If you choose the Multiple variation, the next pair of lines now fades on.) It's a very useful, professional-looking effect.

As the name implies, you can also use this effect to provide captions that translate, say, an opera performance, although that may be a less frequent requirement in your moviemaking career.

Subtitle

Twirl

Speed slider: *Controls time for text to complete rotation*
Direction control: *Left, right*

You'll really have to scratch your head to figure out the point of this one. The letters of your title appear at full size, dead center, and then begin to spin in place (either clockwise or counterclockwise, depending on your selection on the Direction control). When they complete one rotation, they stop so you can read them. Overall, the effect looks a little bit like each letter has been fastened to a hotel-room door with only one nail—at the bottom—and they're swinging freely.

Twirl

Typing

Speed slider: *Controls time for text to fully appear*
Direction control: *None*

Typewriter

You occasionally see the Typewriter effect in the credits of TV police dramas (especially *JAG* and *Homicide*). The letters spill across the screen from left to right, as though being rapidly typed in a word processor.

Tip: When this title style was under development at Apple, it was called *X-Files*—a reference to the animated titles in *The X-Files* that establish the time and date of each new scene. Before iMovie was officially unveiled, the name was changed to Typewriter for obvious reasons (obvious to lawyers, anyway).

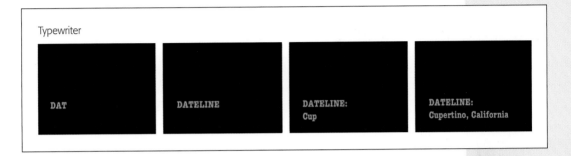

Video Terminal

Video Terminal is only slightly different. It adds a blinking insertion-point cursor that gets pushed along as you type—not the vertical one that's familiar to millions of Mac and PC fans, but instead a horizontal underline character like the one on ancient, pre-mouse video terminals. (For some inexplicable reason, Hollywood movies generally depict text appearing on *any* computer screen using this effect, even if it's popping up in a dialog box or error message. The accompanying teletype sound makes Hollywood computers seem even less like the real-world kind.)

The Video Terminal effect is especially useful when you want to recreate the "I'm summing up my day in sentimental, bittersweet prose on my word processor" effect that concluded every episode of *Doogie Howser, M.D.*

Unscramble

Speed slider: *Controls speed of unscrambling*
Direction control: *Left, right*

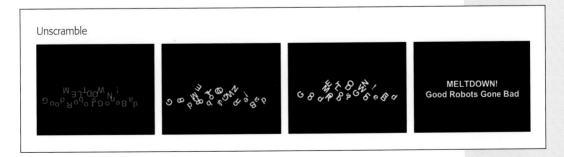

Here's yet another relative of Cartwheel, Gravity, and Twirl. This time, all the letters begin both out of place and upside down, scattered on an invisible horizontal line like pieces of a jigsaw puzzle that have been dumped out of the box. They seemed to wake up, shake it off, right themselves, and dance into proper position.

The only difference between the left and right directional arrows is which way the letters spin: clockwise or counterclockwise. (Not one audience member in one million would be able to tell the difference.)

Wipe

Speed slider: *Controls speed of reveal*
Direction control: *Left, right, up, down*

The Wipe effect is among the most practical of title styles. Your text is revealed by a soft-edged "spotlight" that, unlike the Animated Gradient effect, reveals the entire width or height of the text at once. (You can direct the wiper to reveal your text from any direction: left, right, up, or down.) The effect is smooth, intriguing, and not overbearing.

During the pause while the audience reads the title, a hint of the shadow is still there, slightly obscuring one edge of the words. Then the wiper moves on, its trailing edge concealing the text that the forward edge revealed a moment earlier.

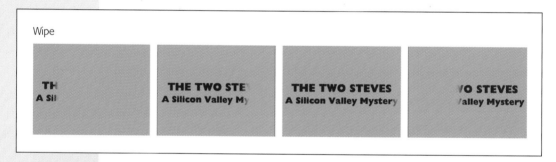

Zoom

Speed slider: *Controls zoom-in speed*
Direction control: *None*

When you select this effect, your text begins as a dot in the center of the screen, growing larger as it approaches, eventually becoming large, bold type (if the typed phrase is short). It holds for a moment, then fades out gracefully.

This effect is dramatic and punchy. Use it to get attention when the name of your movie finally appears onscreen, and to differentiate it from the opening credits that may have preceded it.

Use the Zoom Multiple variation for opening credits, especially those accompanied by rock music and exciting footage shot through the windshield of a fast-moving car. (If you know what's good for you, don't use either Zoom effect to introduce soft, sweet, or nostalgic flicks.)

Narration, Music, and Sound

I f you're lucky, you may someday get a chance to watch a movie whose soundtrack isn't finished yet. You'll be scanning channels and stumble across a special about how movies are made, or you'll see a tribute to a film composer, or you'll rent a DVD of some movie that includes a "making of" documentary. Such TV shows or DVDs sometimes include a couple of minutes from the finished movie as it looked *before* the musical soundtrack and sound effects were added.

At that moment, your understanding of the film medium will take an enormous leap forward. "Jeez," you'll say, "without music and sound effects, this $100 million Hollywood film has no more emotional impact than…my home movies!"

And you'll be right. It's true that in our society, the *visual* component of film is the most, well, visible. The household names are the directors and movie stars, not the sound editors, composers, *foley* (sound effects) artists, and others who devote their careers to the audio experience of film.

But without music, sound effects (called SFX for short), and sound editing, even the best Hollywood movie will leave you cold and unimpressed.

The Two iMovie Soundtracks

Much like traditional film cameras, iMovie separates the audio and video into separate tracks, which you can view and edit independently. In iMovie, you can view the contents of your soundtracks with a single click on the clock icon shown in Figure 8-1.

As noted in Chapter 5, the top horizontal band of the Timeline Viewer displays the *video* component of your movie. It shows tiny thumbnails that help you identify which clips you've placed in which order. For the most part, you won't do much with this strip when you're editing audio; its primary purpose is to show where you are in the movie.

The two horizontal strips underneath it are your playground for audio clips. Both audio tracks are equivalent and each of them can hold sound from any of these sources, which you're free to drag between the two tracks anytime:

- **iTunes tracks.** This, of course, is an example of what makes iLife a suite and not just a handful of separate programs: iMovie's integration with the other Apple programs. As described later in this chapter, iMovie displays your complete iTunes music collection, playlists and all. Adding background music to your flick is easy as can be.

- **Narration.** This can be anything that you've recorded with your microphone.

- **Sound effects.** Choose these from iMovie's Audio palette (gunshots, glass breaking, applause, and so on).

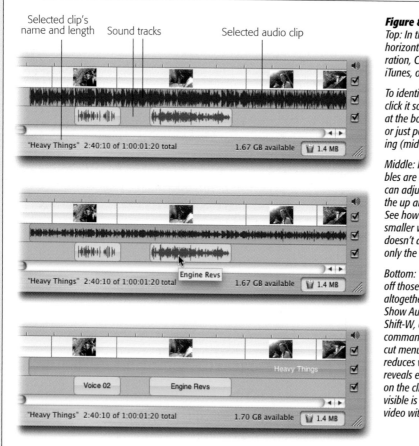

Selected clip's name and length   Sound tracks   Selected audio clip

"Heavy Things" 2:40:10 of 1:00:01:20 total   1.67 GB available   1.4 MB

Engine Revs

"Heavy Things" 2:40:10 of 1:00:01:20 total   1.67 GB available   1.4 MB

Voice 02   Engine Revs   Heavy Things

"Heavy Things" 2:40:10 of 1:00:01:20 total   1.70 GB available   1.4 MB

Figure 8-1:
Top: In the Timeline Viewer, horizontal strips represent narration, CD tracks, music from iTunes, or sound effects.

To identify a sound clip, either click it so that its name appears at the bottom of the window, or just point to it without clicking (middle).

Middle: If the soundwave scribbles are a little distracting, you can adjust their size by tapping the up and down arrow keys. See how the top audio clip has smaller waveforms now? (This doesn't affect the volume level, only the onscreen graphics.)

Bottom: You can also turn off those visual soundwaves altogether by choosing View→ Show Audio Waveforms (⌘- Shift-W, or choose the same command from the clip's shortcut menu). Hiding waveforms reduces visual clutter and reveals each clip's name right on the clip—but leaving them visible is a great way to align video with audio "hits."

- **MP3, WAV, AIFF, and AAC files.** iMovie can directly import files in these popular music formats. You can drag them in from the Finder, use the File→Import command, or bring them in from iTunes.

- **Music from a CD.** You can insert a standard audio CD and transfer a song into iMovie to serve as the music for a scene.

- **Your camcorder audio.** You can turn the ordinarily invisible audio portion of a video clip into an independent sound clip, which you can manipulate just like any other kind of sound clip.

This chapter covers all of these sound varieties.

Tip: Ordinarily, when playing your movie, iMovie plays the sound in both audio tracks. But you can use the three checkboxes at the right end of these tracks to control which ones play back. When you want to isolate only one track, turn off the other two checkboxes (Figure 8-2). (These checkboxes also govern which soundtracks are exported when you send your finished iMovie production back to tape or to a QuickTime movie.)

Figure 8-2:
A view of the right end of the Timeline Viewer. Drag the Playhead so that the vertical line beneath it strikes the piece of sound you want to listen to. Then turn off the track checkboxes to isolate the track you want. Press the Space bar to begin listening.

Hint: If you've turned on "Snap to items in Timeline" in iMovie→Preferences, the Playhead snaps neatly against the beginnings and ends of audio clips–and bookmarks, chapter markers, and video clips–when you drag it. In fact, it even snaps against bursts of sound within an audio clip, which helps you find the start or end of silent bits. (You can Shift-drag to override the snapping setting.)

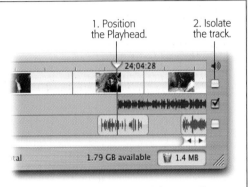

1. Position the Playhead.

2. Isolate the track.

3. Press the Space bar.

Audio Clips

In many regards, working with sound files is much like working with video clips. For example, each piece of sound appears as a horizontal colored bar in the Timeline Viewer. You can move a clip around in the movie by dragging horizontally; cut, copy, and paste it; delete it by selecting it and then pressing the Delete key; and so on.

As you work, remember to use the Zoom slider (at the lower-left corner of the Timeline Viewer) to magnify or shrink your audio clips as necessary.

Renaming Sound Clips (or Not)

When you click an audio clip, iMovie intensifies its color to show that it's highlighted. The bottom edge of the Timeline Viewer displays the audio clip's name and duration, as shown in Figure 8-1. (You can also see a clip's name by pointing to it without clicking, as shown at middle in Figure 8-1.)

To rename an audio clip, double-click it. The Clip Info box appears, where you can type a new name into the Name box.

Listening to a Sound Clip

To isolate and listen to a particular audio clip, proceed as shown in Figure 8-2.

Tip: Once your movie is playing, you can *loop* a section of audio (play it repeatedly as you study the effect) by clicking repeatedly in the same spot on the Scrubber bar, keeping the mouse very still. With each click, the Playhead snaps back to replay the segment from the position of your cursor.

Recording Narration

If anyone ever belittles iMovie for being underpowered, point out an iMovie feature that isn't even available in most expensive video-editing programs: the ability to record narration while you watch your movie play. If your Mac has a microphone, you can easily create any of these effects:

- **Create a reminiscence.** As the footage shows children playing, we hear you saying, "It was the year 2005. It was a time of innocence. Of sunlight. Of children at play. In the years before the Great Asteroid, nobody imagined that one 6-year-old child would become a goddess to her people. This, then, is her story."

  This technique of superimposing an unseen narrator's voice over video is called a *voice-over*. It's incredibly popular in TV, commercials, and movies (such as *Saving Private Ryan, American Beauty,* and of course, the *Look Who's Talking* movies).

- **Identify the scene.** Even if your movie isn't one with a story line, iMovie's narration feature offers an extremely convenient method of identifying your home movies. Think about it: When you get photos back from the drugstore, the date is stamped across the back of each photo. In years to come, you'll know when the photos were taken.

  Video cameras offer an optional date-stamp feature, too—a crude, ugly, digital readout that permanently mars your footage. But otherwise, as they view their deteriorating VHS cassettes in 2025, most of the world's camcorder owners will never know where, why, or when their footage was shot. Few people are compulsive enough to film, before each new shot, somebody saying, "It's Halloween 2003, and little Chrissie is going out for her very first trick-or-treating. Mommy made the costume out of some fishnet stockings and a melon," or whatever.

  Using iMovie, thought, it's easy to add a few words of shot-identification narration over your establishing shot. (To find out the time and date when the footage was shot, just double-click the clip.)

- **Provide new information.** For professional work, the narration feature is an excellent way to add another continuous information stream to whatever videos or still pictures are appearing on the screen. Doctors use iMovie to create narrated slideshows, having created a Movie Track filled with still images of scanned slides (see Chapter 9). Realtors feature camcorder footage of houses under consideration, while narrating the key features that can't be seen ("Built in 1869, this house was extensively renovated in 1880…"). And it doesn't take much imagination to see how lawyers can exploit iMovie.

Preparing to Record

Your Mac's microphone takes one of two forms: built-in or external. The built-in mike, a tiny hole in the facade of the iMac, eMac, or PowerBook, couldn't be more convenient—it's always with you, and always turned on.

If your Mac doesn't have a built-in microphone, you can plug in an external USB microphone (see the Apple Products Guide at *www.guide.apple.com*) or a standard microphone with the help of an adapter (like the iMic, *www.griffintechnology.com*).

Making the Recording

Here's how you record narration:

1. **Click the clock icon so that you're looking at the Timeline Viewer.**

   You'll do all your audio editing in Timeline view.

2. **Drag the Playhead to a spot just before you want the narration to begin.**

   You can use all the usual navigational techniques to line up the Playhead: Press the Space bar to play the movie, press the right and left arrow keys to move the Playhead one frame at a time, press Shift-arrow keys to make the Playhead jump 10 frames at a time, and so on.

3. **Open the Audio panel, if it's not already open.**

   You do so by clicking the Audio button, shown in Figure 8-3.

Figure 8-3:
To summon the narration controls, click the Audio button. If your microphone is correctly hooked up, the round, red Record Voice button is available. (Otherwise, it's dimmed.) Just beside the Record button is a live "VU" level meter. Test your setup by speaking into the microphone; if this meter twitches in response, you're ready to record.

4. **Click the round, red Record Voice button and begin to speak.**

You can watch the video play as you narrate.

Note: If the level meter isn't dancing as you speak, the problem may be that your Mac is paying attention to the wrong audio input. Choose ⌘→System Preferences, and click the Sound icon. Click the Input tab, then click the microphone input that you want to use. When you're done, quit System Preferences.

If the level meter bars are dancing, but not farther than halfway across the graph (see Figure 8-3), then your narration isn't loud enough. On playback, it'll probably be drowned out by the camcorder audio track.

To increase the volume, open System Preferences, click Sound, and click the Input tab to make sure that your input volume slider is at maximum. If that's not the problem, your only options are to lean closer to the microphone, speak louder, or use an external microphone. (You can learn tricks for boosting the volume of audio tracks later in this chapter, but it's much better to get the level right the first time.)

5. **Click Stop to complete the recording.**

Now a new stripe appears in the upper soundtrack, already highlighted, bearing the name Voice 01, like the one shown in Figure 8-1. Drag the Playhead to the left—to the beginning of the new recording—and then press the Space bar to listen to your voice-over work.

If the narration wasn't everything you hoped for, it's easy enough to record another "take." Just click the stripe representing your new recording and then press Delete to get rid of it. Then repeat the process.

Choosing from Separate Takes

If you like what you recorded, but think that you might be able to do better, you don't have to delete the first one forever. You can record the new take and then compare the two. In fact, iMovie offers four different ways to do so:

• **Use a temporary "shelf."** Drag the newly recorded audio clip (the stripe) to another spot in the Timeline Viewer. For example, if you drag it far to the right, beyond any other existing sound clips, you've just stashed it on a makeshift "shelf." Now move the Playhead back to the correct spot and rerecord the narration. By dragging the two resulting sound clips around, or by using the Cut and Paste commands, you can try out one, then the other.

• **Cut and paste.** Alternatively, after recording the first take, click its clip and then choose Edit→Cut. Record the new take. If you don't like it, you can always delete it and then paste the original one—which has been on the invisible Clipboard all this time—back into place.

• **Park it elsewhere.** You can also drag the narration clip onto the other audio track, where you can mute it either by turning off the track's checkbox or by setting the clip's volume to zero.

- **Use the Undo command.** Finally, don't forget that you can always use the Edit→ Undo command several times in succession. If you delete the first take, rerecord, then decide that you preferred the original take, just choose Edit→Undo Record from Microphone, and then choose Undo Clear. In fact, if you can keep your takes straight, you can utilize the unlimited Undo command to try *several* different takes.

You can edit and adjust the resulting sound clip just as you can other sounds in iMovie. See "Editing Audio Clips" later in this chapter for details.

Importing iTunes Music

Nothing adds emotional impact to a piece of video like music. Slow, romantic music makes the difference between a sad story and one that actually makes viewers cry. Fast, driving music makes viewers' hearts beat faster—scientists have proven it. Music is so integral to movies these days that, as you walk out of the theater, you may not even be aware that a movie *had* music, but virtually every movie does, and you were emotionally manipulated by it.

Home movies are no exception. Music adds a new dimension to your movie, so much so that some iMovie fans *edit to music.* They choose a song, lay it down in the audio track, and then cut the video footage to fit the beats, words, or sections of the music.

Tip: Even if you don't synchronize your video to the music in this way, you might still want to experiment with a music-only soundtrack. That is, *turn off* the camcorder sound, so that your movie is silent except for the music. The effect is haunting, powerful, and often used in Hollywood movies during montage sequences.

If you've been using the free iTunes jukebox software to manage your music collection, you're in for a real treat. iMovie is well integrated with the other programs in its iLife software suite—including iTunes. You can view, and even play, your entire music library, complete with its individual playlists, right in iMovie, making it easy to choose just the right piece of music to accompany your video.

(If you've created homemade songs in GarageBand, this feature is your ticket to importing them into iMovie, too. They show up in the iTunes playlist named after you.)

Tip: You can use iTunes to build a music library by converting the songs on your audio CDs into MP3 files on your hard drive, by buying individual pop songs from the iTunes Music Store, or by importing digital audio files you found on the Internet. See *iPod & iTunes: The Missing Manual* for complete instructions.

Here's how you go about choosing an iTunes track for your movie:

1. **Click the Audio button, if necessary (Figure 8-3).**

   The panel changes to reveal your iTunes music collection. (If you don't see your list of songs, choose iTunes Library from the pop-up menu above the panel.)

---

2. Find just the right song.

The panel is filled with useful controls to help you find the right music. For example, if you've organized your iTunes music into *playlists* (subsets), you can use the pop-up menu above the list to choose the playlists you want to look over. (All other songs are temporarily hidden.)

You can also use the Search box at the bottom of the list, as shown in Figure 8-4.

Figure 8-4:
Left: Choose any of your playlists to navigate your massive music collection.

Right: You can also click in the Search box. As you type a song or performer's name, iMovie hides all songs whose names don't match, so that you can quickly home in on a certain song or group of songs from among thousands. (To restore the entire list and delete what you've typed, click the little X button at the right end of the Search box.)

To listen to a song, click its name and then click the round Play button beneath the list. Or, if you think life is too short already, just double-click a song name. (To interrupt playback, either double-click a different song, double-click the same one, or click the round Play triangle button to turn it gray once again.)

You can sort the list alphabetically by song name, artist name, or song length, just by clicking the appropriate heading above the list. (Ordinarily, you wouldn't think that it would be very useful to sort the list by track length. But remember that in the context of a video-editing program, finding a song that's exactly the right length for your video might wind up being more important than which band plays it.)

Tip: The playback controls in the Audio palette are independent of the playback controls in the Monitor window. You may find it useful, therefore, to play your movie in progress *as* you listen to the different songs, so that you can preview how the music might sound when played simultaneously with the video.

The easiest way to experiment in this way is to click the Play button in the Audio panel at precisely the same instant that you press the Space bar to begin the movie playback.

---

3. Place the music into one of your audio tracks.

You can go about this in either of two ways. If the Playhead is already parked where you want the music to begin (you can take this opportunity to move it, if you like), just click the song name and then click the Place at Playhead button beneath the song list. iMovie takes a moment to deposit the entire song, beginning at the point you've indicated.

You can also drag the song name directly out of the list and down into the Timeline Viewer. As long as you don't release the mouse button, and as long as the cursor is in one of the two audio tracks, you'll see that you can simultaneously move the Playhead and position the beginning of the song at just the right spot. Release the mouse when the song looks like it's in the right place.

(On the other hand, you can always adjust the starting point of the music after you've placed it, by dragging its audio-clip stripe horizontally.)

Depending on the length of the song you've selected, the importing process can take 30 seconds or more. That's how long it takes for iMovie to copy the iTunes track into a new audio file (in your project's Media folder). When it's complete, a new colored bar appears in the audio track, labeled with the song name.

FREQUENTLY ASKED QUESTION

Fun with Copyright Law

Don't I break some kind of law when I copy music from a commercial CD, or use iTunes Music Store music in one of my movies?

Exactly what constitutes stealing music is a hot-button issue that has tied millions of people (and recording executives) in knots. That's why some iMovie fans hesitate to distribute their iMovie films in places where lawyers might see them—like the Internet.

Frankly, though, record company lawyers have bigger fish to fry than small-time amateur operators like you. You're perfectly safe showing your movies to family and friends, your user group, and other limited circles of viewers. In fact, Apple encourages you to use iTunes Music Store purchases in your movies; after all, Apple is the one who made them available right in iMovie.

You'll risk trouble only if you go commercial, making money from movies that incorporate copyrighted music.

Still, if your conscience nags you, you could always use one of your GarageBand compositions. And even if you're not especially musical, the world is filled with *royalty-free music*—music that has been composed and recorded expressly for the purpose of letting filmmakers add music to their work without having to pay a licensing fee every time they do so.

Some of it's even free. For example, check out *www.freeplaymusic.com*, a Web site filled with prerecorded music in every conceivable style, that you're welcome to use in your movies at no charge.

If that's not enough for you, visit a search page like *www.google.com*, search for *music library* or *royalty-free music*, and start clicking your way to the hundreds of Web sites that offer information about (and listenable samples of) music that you can buy and use without fear. (Many of these sites require a RealAudio plug-in, an add-on for your Web browser that you can download and install from *www.real.com*.)

Try dragging the Playhead back to the beginning of the music bar and pressing the Space bar to play it. If it doesn't have quite the effect you thought it would, click the newly placed music's bar and then press the Delete key, to make room for your next experiment.

CD Music

If you don't use iTunes to organize your music, you can also snag a track or two directly from an audio CD. You just insert your favorite music CD (Carly Simon, Rolling Stones, the Cleveland Orchestra, or whatever), choose the track you want to swipe, and the deed is done.

Here's the procedure:

1. **Open the Audio panel, if it isn't already open.**

   Do so by clicking the Audio button shown in Figure 8-3.

2. **Insert the music CD into your Mac.**

   After a moment, a list of songs on the CD appears in the list (Figure 8-5).

Figure 8-5:
The list in the Audio palette identifies the different songs (tracks) on your CD, along with the play length of each one. You can sort the list, audition different songs, or search the list just as you do your iTunes library (Figure 8-4). Drag an entire song into your movie, or click Place at Playhead.

Clicking that little triangle button at upper right, by the way, ejects the CD.

At first, they're probably called Track 1, Track 2, and so on. Unfortunately, audio CDs were invented before the advent of computers that could read them, and so the text of their track names isn't stored on the disc. Clearly, it would be a lot easier to find the music you want if you could see the *actual names* of the songs on the CD.

That's why, after a moment, iMovie automatically begins to download the list of songs on your CD, assuming that you're online. (iTunes may also open automatically, depending on how you've set up the CDs & DVDs panel in System Preferences.) Behind the scenes, it's consulting the Gracenote Internet CD database—a worldwide repository of track and album information. After a few moments, switch back into iMovie. You'll see that both the track names and the name of the album have now been typed in for you.

You'll also notice that the pop-up menu above the Audio palette has changed to identify the name of the album.

3. Find the song you want.

To do so, double-click one of the songs in the scrolling list (or click a song and then click the Play triangle button below the list). Click the Play triangle again to stop the music. Unfortunately, there's no way to fast-forward.

4. Insert the song into one of your audio tracks.

You can use either of the techniques identified in the previous step 3 (page 223). Either click the Place at Playhead button beneath the song list, or drag the song name out of the list and into position on one of your audio tracks.

A progress bar appears as iMovie copies the song file off the CD and into your project's Media folder. When it's finished, you'll see a new colored bar in your audio track representing the imported song and bearing its name.

When you're finished importing music, you're free to eject the CD (by holding down the Eject button on your keyboard, for example), insert another one, and nab another selection of music. iMovie no longer requires the first CD.

Sound Effects

There's more to a movie soundtrack than music, goodness knows. Fortunately, iMovie also comes with a juicy collection of sound effects, suitable for dropping into your movies. If you choose iMovie Sound Effects from the pop-up menu at the top of the Audio palette, you'll find two flippy triangles, each denoting a collection of professional sound effects. (You don't have to click the triangle to see its contents; you can click directly on the collection's name.)

One, called Skywalker Sound Effects, is named for the Hollywood sound studio from which Apple licensed the effects (Birds, Cold Wind, Creek, and so on)—a list that's been expanded in iMovie HD. The other, Standard Sound Effects, contains the sounds that began life in iMovie 3 (Alarm, Bark, Crickets, and so on).

Across from each sound's name, you see its length, expressed in the minutes:seconds format.

Using a Sound Effect

You add a sound to your audio tracks exactly the way you add an iTunes tune—either by clicking the Place at Playhead button or by dragging the effect's name into either of the audio tracks in the Timeline Viewer. As your cursor moves over a track, the Playhead—accompanied by a cool, fading-out purple stripe—helps you see precisely where the sound will begin. Once placed there, the sound effect appears as a horizontal purple bar, just like any other sound clip. (If the sound effect is very short, you may have to zoom in to see it as a bar, using the Zoom slider at the left edge of the screen.)

A sound-effect clip behaves like any other sound clip. You can edit its volume in any of the ways described in "Editing Audio Clips," later in this chapter. You can slide it from side to side in the track to adjust where it begins, and even shorten, crop, or split it.

Adding or Removing Sound Effects

The list of sound effects in the Sounds palette isn't magical. It's simply a listing of the sound files that came with iMovie. If you know the secret, you can open a special folder and delete, move out, or rename your sound effects—or even install new ones.

1. **Quit iMovie. In the Finder, open your Applications folder. Control-click the iMovie icon; from the contextual menu, choose Show Package Contents.**

   The iMovie *package window* appears. You've just discovered, if you didn't already know, that many Mac OS X program icons are, in fact, thinly disguised folders (called *packages*) that contain dozens or hundreds of individual support files. You've just opened up iMovie for inspection.

2. **Open the Contents→Resources folder.**

   Welcome to the belly of the beast. Before you, sit hundreds of individual files, most of them the little graphics that make up the various iMovie buttons, controls, and so on. (If you're really feeling ambitious, you can actually open up these graphics and edit them, completely changing the look of iMovie.)

   The icon you want is the folder called Sound Effects. It's a folder full of individual sound files—in MP3 format—that make up the list you see in the Audio palette (Figure 8-6).

Tip: *MP3 files* are extremely popular among music fans, since they're compact and sound great. Plus, all kinds of computers can read them.

Looking for even more sound effects? The Internet is filled with downloadable MP3 files that you can use in your iMovie projects. You might start your search at *www.google.com*. Perform a search for *free sound effects*. Many are already in MP3 format; many others are in AIFF format, which you can convert to iMovie-friendly MP3 files using iTunes.

   Feel free to reorganize these files. For example, you can throw away the ones you never use. You can also create new folders in the Sound Effects window to create new categories of sound effects in the Audio palette.

3. **Open iMovie. Click the Audio button. From the pop-up menu above the list, choose iMovie Sound Effects.**

Each folder in the Sound Effects folder forms its own subcategory of effects here.

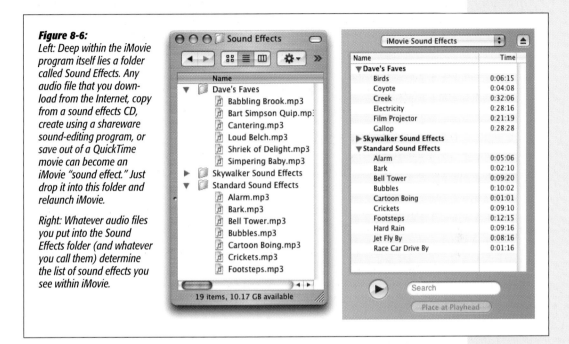

Figure 8-6:
Left: Deep within the iMovie program itself lies a folder called Sound Effects. Any audio file that you download from the Internet, copy from a sound effects CD, create using a shareware sound-editing program, or save out of a QuickTime movie can become an iMovie "sound effect." Just drop it into this folder and relaunch iMovie.

Right: Whatever audio files you put into the Sound Effects folder (and whatever you call them) determine the list of sound effects you see within iMovie.

Editing Audio Clips

Fortunately, you can do more with your audio clips than just insert them into the Timeline Viewer. You can lengthen them or shorten them, make them fade in or out, shift them to play earlier or later in time, and even superimpose them. Best of all—and here's one of the most useful features in iMovie—you can make their volume rise and fall over the length of the clip.

Making Whole-Clip Volume Adjustments

To make a particular clip louder or quieter relative to the other tracks, click its representation in the Timeline Viewer to select it. The clip darkens to show that it's highlighted.

Having selected an audio (or video) clip in this way, you can affect its overall volume level by using the "Clip:" volume pop-up menu shown in Figure 8-7. You can make it so quiet that it's absolutely silent, or you can actually make it 50 percent louder than the original.

Here are some pointers in this regard:

- You can also type a percentage number into the "Clip:" text box. This isn't a feature only for the obsessively precise; it's a useful way to make sure that each of several audio clips are boosted to the same degree.

- iMovie stores your Volume pop-up menu settings independently for every audio clip. That's why the Volume setting may seem to jump around as you click different audio clips.

- If even 150 percent isn't enough of a volume boost, you can always open the audio clip in GarageBand for a quick boost. Drag the clip from the Finder into a waiting Real Instrument (blue) track, bump up the track's volume, export the result to iTunes, and then reimport the newly amplified file into iMovie.

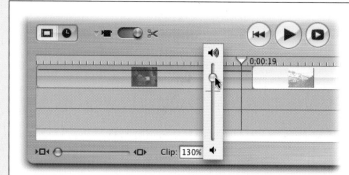

Figure 8-7:
If you set the volume pop-up all the way to 0, you mute the sound completely—for this clip only. If you drag it all the way to the top, you actually boost the volume up to 150%—a terrific way to compensate for weak camcorder microphones.

In any case, adjusting the pop-up menu makes the horizontal volume-level line temporarily appear on the selected clips.

Volume Adjustments Within a Clip

Being able to make the volume of a clip rise and fall along its length, as you can in iMovie, comes in handy in a multitude of ways:

- It's a rare documentary or news show that doesn't begin a story with a full-volume, attention-getting shot (protesters shouting, band playing, airplane landing, and so on), whose audio fades to half volume after a few seconds, just in time for the reporter to begin speaking.

- Similarly, you can "pull back" the musical soundtrack whenever somebody on camera is speaking, and then bring it back to full volume in between speeches. This technique is incredibly common in movies, TV shows, commercials, and just about every other form of professional video.

- Suppose that the last second of a clip caught the unseemly off-camera belch of a relative at the dinner table. In a flash, you can edit it out, simply by silencing the audio just before the belch.

- You can compensate for the volume drop that occurs whenever your interview subjects momentarily turn their heads away from the camera.

- If you're a parent filming small children, your footage often winds up peppered with parental instructions recorded at a very high volume level, because you're right next to the microphone. ("Honey, stand over there by your brother," or "Watch out for the car!") These parental voice-overs often ruin a clip—but you can rescue them by adjusting the original audio from the camcorder, which you can edit just as easily as imported audio.

- You can make create smooth fade-ins or fade-outs of your music (or the sound from the original video).

Volume "Rubber Bands"

The key to this feature is the new Show Clip Volume Levels command (⌘-Shift-L) in the View menu. (The same command appears in the shortcut menu when you Control-click an audio clip.) When you turn on Show Clip Volume Levels, a horizontal line appears on every audio and video clip, edge to edge. It's an audio-volume graph, which you can manipulate like a rubber band. Here's how it works (consider zooming in for greater control):

- Click directly on the line and drag upward or downward (Figure 8-8, top). The original click produces a small spherical handle, and the drag produces a curve in the line from its original volume level. (Actually, you can simultaneously drag left or right to adjust the timing of this volume change.) Each "knot" in the line (the round handle) represents a new volume level that sticks until the end of the clip or the next volume level, whichever comes first.

- After you create such a curve, the point where the audio deviated from its original volume is denoted by a tiny square handle (Figure 8-8, third from top). To make the volume increase or decrease more or less gradually, drag that tiny square handle left or right, closer to your round adjustment handle or farther from it.

- To make the volume take another dip or swoop, click elsewhere on the volume line and drag again. You've just created a second round orange handle, which you can position independently (Figure 8-8, bottom).

- To remove a volume change, click the orange "knot" to select it, and then press the Delete key. (Or just drag it to the original volume level.) The knot disappears, and the "rubber band" line snaps back to the previous knot, stretched tight.

- To make a volume change extremely sudden, click a knot to highlight it, and then drag the tiny square just to its left. You'll find that you can drag this little square until it's directly above or below the knot—an instantaneous volume change.

- Consider making your volume adjustments *while* the movie plays back. Each time you make an adjustment, the Playhead jumps to that spot. As you keep clicking and adjusting, clicking and adjusting, the Playhead keeps jumping back to that spot, saving you the trouble of having to rewind and play, rewind and play, as you fine-tune the fluctuation.

- To restore the original, straight-line condition of a clip's volume, click each of the orange knots and press Delete until none of them remains.

Tip: When you're finished editing volume fluctuations, you can turn off the View→Show Clip Volume Levels command again. iMovie will remember all of the changes that you've made, and you'll still hear the volume changes on playback. But iMovie hides all of the handles and rubber-band graph lines, making it possible once again to drag clip edges to shorten them (which you can't do while volume graphs are visible).

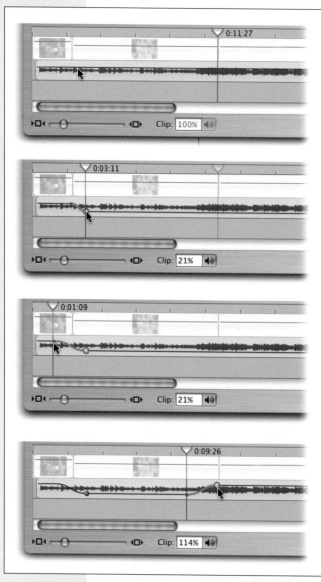

Figure 8-8:

Top: The horizontal line represents the audio clip's standard, 100% volume level. Suppose, in this case, that it's drowning out the spoken dialog in the video track above it. (That's a pretty common occurrence when you add, say, a pop song to your movie as a soundtrack.)

Second from top: As you drag the little "knot" vertically, you have two sources of feedback on how much you've increased or decreased the volume at that spot: the height of the line segment itself (in which the purple clip itself is the piece of graph paper, from 0% to 150%), and the number in the "Clip:" percentage box.

In any case, the orange handle tells you how much volume fluctuation you've introduced, but it doesn't let you specify how gradually you want the change to occur.

Third from top: For that purpose, drag the tiny square (indicated by the cursor) in any direction to control where the volume change begins—both when, and at what level.

Bottom: Repeat the process in reverse when you want to bring the music back up after the dialog portion is over.

Adjusting Many Clips at Once

You can adjust the volume levels of more than one clip simultaneously—a technique that comes in handy more often than you might think. For example, you may decide that *all* of the music excerpts you've grabbed from a CD are too loud compared to the camcorder audio. In one fell swoop, you can make them all softer.

You can select as many as you want, even if they're on different audio tracks. Start by selecting the clips you want to affect:

- To select several non-consecutive clips, Shift-click them in any order: clip 1, clip 3, and so on. (Actually, ⌘-clicking works, too.)

- To select several connecting clips, drag-select. That is, begin dragging in any empty part of a track. As you drag, iMovie selects any audio clip that even partly falls within the light gray rectangle you're creating.

- To select *all* of the clips in both audio tracks, highlight *one* clip there. Then choose Edit→Select All.

- To unhighlight a selected clip, Shift-click or ⌘-click it.

Now when you adjust the "Clip:" volume pop-up menu, you're affecting all of the highlighted clips at once. (If you've fiddled around with the clips' rubber-band volume lines, adjusting the volume slider scales the volume of the whole thing up or down proportionally, maintaining the relative sizes of the fluctuations.)

Note: When several audio clips are highlighted, the volume pop-up menu reflects whichever clip has the *highest* volume level.

Locking Audio Clips to Video

Figure 8-9 illustrates a serious problem that results from trying to line up certain video moments (like Bill-Gates-getting-hit-with-a-pie footage) with particular audio moments (like a "Splat!" sound effect). In short, when you insert or delete some video footage *after* lining up audio clips with specific video moments, you shove everything out of alignment, sometimes without even realizing it. This syndrome can rear its ugly head in many video-editing programs.

You may wind up playing a frustrating game of find-the-frame, over and over again, all the way through the movie, as you try to redo all of your careful audio/video alignments.

In iMovie, the solution is especially elegant. Whenever you place an audio clip that you'd like to keep aligned with a video moment, get it into position and then *lock* it by choosing Advanced→Lock Audio Clip at Playhead (or press ⌘-L). What happens next depends on how you've set things up:

- If you've dragged or nudged the Playhead to the frame you care most about, iMovie locks the audio to the video at that frame, as indicated by the little pushpin (see Figure 8-9). Even if you later trim away some footage from the beginning part of the video clip, the sync moment remains intact.

- If the Playhead isn't anywhere near the highlighted audio clip, iMovie simply locks the beginning of the highlighted audio clip to the video frame it's currently aligned with.

- If you've highlighted several audio clips, once again, iMovie "pushpins" the beginning of each clip at its present video location.

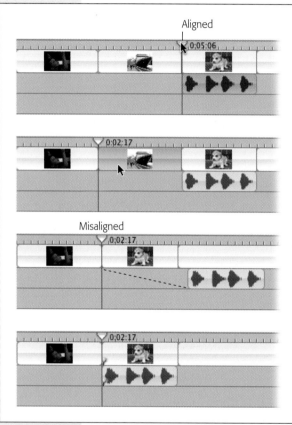

Aligned

Misaligned

Figure 8-9:
Top: You've carefully lined up a barking sound effect with the beginning of the dog clip.

Second from top: Uh-oh. You've selected the clip right before the dog, in preparation for deleting it.

Third from top: Now you've done it. You've deleted the clip that was just to the left of the dog. The dog clip slides leftward to close the gap—and leaves the barking sound behind, now hopelessly out of alignment with the video above it.

Bottom: If you had remembered to lock the barking clip to the video above it, as indicated by the tiny pushpins, the sound effect would have slid to the left along with the dog clip, remaining perfectly in sync.

Once you've locked an audio clip to its video, you no longer have to worry that it might lose sync with its video when you edit your video clips. Nothing you do to the video clips to its left in the Timeline Viewer—add, delete, insert, or trim them—will affect its synchronization.

It's important to understand, however, that locking an audio clip freezes its position only relative to the video clip above it. The audio clip isn't locked into a particular *time* in the movie (such as 5:23:12). Put another way, "Lock Audio" actually means "*Don't* Lock Audio (to one spot in the Movie Track); Let It Slide Around as Necessary."

Nor does locking an audio clip prevent *you* from shifting it. Dragging the audio clip will *not* drag the "attached" video clip along with it. You're still welcome to slide the audio clip left or right in its track, independent of any other clips. Doing so simply makes iMovie realign the clip with a new video frame, lining up the pushpin accordingly. (If you *cut* the audio clip and then paste it into a new location, it forgets both its original video-clip spouse and the fact that it was ever "married" to begin with. After pasting, it's pushpin-free.)

To unlock an audio clip, highlight it and then choose Advanced→Unlock Audio Clip (or press ⌘-L again).

Cropping an Audio Clip

As you may remember from Chapter 5, the ability to *crop*, or chop the ends off a video clip, is one of the key tools in video editing. As it turns out, you can adjust the beginning or ending points of any audio clip even more conveniently.

Tip: If you use the Extract Audio command described on page 239, you can even crop the original camcorder audio in this way, without cropping the video clip in the process. Doing so is a convenient way to trim out an audio glitch that appears at the beginning or end of a shot without having to crop the video clip.

You can shorten one of your music or narration clips from either the beginning or the end, just by dragging the corresponding end inward, as shown in Figure 8-10.

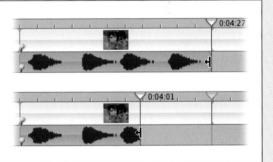

Figure 8-10:
You can shorten an audio clip without actually deleting any of it, just by dragging the edges inward (shown here before and after). Does this sound familiar? It should...you can do the same thing with video clips.

At any time, you can restore the original length, or part of it, by dragging the edge outward again. (Note, though, that edge dragging doesn't work if Show Clip Volume Levels is turned on in the View menu.)

For finer adjustments, click one of the clip ends, so that the Playhead snaps to your cursor. Then press the right or left arrow key to move the handle in one-frame increments, or—if you press Shift as you do so—in *10*-frame increments. You might want to zoom in, using the Zoom slider at the left side of the window, if you're finding it hard to see the effects of your cropping maneuvers.

Note: As you drag the audio-clip crop handles inward or outward, any volume fluctuations you've added remain exactly where they were—which means that they might just wind up in nowhere-land. You might drag the end point of a clip so far to the left that you'll never hear the fluctuations you had programmed for the very end of the clip. If your volume fluctuations seem to be missing, turn on View→Show Clip Volume Levels to make your volume graph reappear. You'll see the problem right away.

Splitting an Audio Clip

When you drag an audio clip's ends inward, you're not actually trimming the clip. You're simply shortening the *audible portion* of the full-length clip. At any time in your project's lifetime, if you decide that you've overshot, you can slide the clip ends back outward again.

However, you may have good reason to make the cropped-clip arrangement permanent. First, in complex audio tracks, your clips can become cluttered and difficult to "read," thanks to the duplicate clip ends. Second, dragging the ends of clips inward doesn't reduce the amount of disk space that your audio file uses, since iMovie hangs onto the full original in case you decide to uncrop it.

There is an alternative, however. You may remember reading about the power of the Edit→Split Clip at Playhead command, which uses the current Playhead location as a razor blade that chops a video clip in two. In the Timeline Viewer, the equivalent command is called Split Selected Audio Clip at Playhead. As you'd expect, it breaks the *audio* clip beneath the Playhead into two independent clips.

Tip: If your Edit menu doesn't list a command called Split Selected Audio Clip at Playhead, it's because your Playhead isn't in the middle part of a *highlighted* audio clip. If no audio clip is selected, or if the Playhead's vertical insertion point isn't running through it, the command says Split Video Clip instead (and has a very different effect).

Being able to split an audio clip is useful in a number of ways. For example:

- You can use it as another form of the Crop command. Split off the unwanted end of some imported CD music, for example, and then delete the segment you don't need.

- You can separate statements in a voice-over (narration by an unseen speaker). This is an extremely common requirement in professional editing.

  Suppose, for example, that you've got a voice recording of a guy recounting his days at the beginning of Apple Computer. One line goes, "We lived in a rundown tenement on the Lower East Side of Cupertino, but nobody cared. We loved what we were doing."

  Now suppose you've also got a couple of terrific still photos of the original Apple building, plus a photo of the original Apple team, grinning like fools in their grungy T-shirts and beards. After using the Split Audio Clip command, you can place the first part of the recording ("We lived in a rundown tenement on the Lower East Side of Cupertino") beneath the campus photos, and then *delay* the second utterance ("But nobody cared. We loved what we were doing") until you're ready to introduce the group photo.

Tip: You can't split a clip and then immediately move one of the halves. After the Split command, both clips remain in position, side by side, both highlighted. Whatever you do will affect both pieces, as though you'd never split them at all. Shift-click the piece you *don't* want before trying to drag or cut anything.

Moving an Audio Clip

You can drag audio clips around in their tracks just as you would video clips, or even back and forth between the two audio tracks.

In fact, because precision is often so important in positioning audio relative to the video, iMovie harbors a few useful shortcuts.

For example, whenever you drag an audio clip, the Playhead magnetically attaches itself to the beginning of the clip. As you drag, therefore, you get to watch the video in the Monitor window, corresponding to the precise moment where the sound begins.

Once the clip is highlighted, don't forget that you can press the left and right arrow keys to move it one frame at a time, or Shift-arrow keys to slide it 10 frames at a time. Even then, you'll see your exact position in the video by watching the Monitor window.

As a matter of fact, you can combine these two tricks. Once the Playhead is aligned with either end of a clip, you can press the arrow keys, or Shift-arrow, to move the Playhead *and* drag the audio clip along with it. You'll feel like the audio is somehow Velcroed to the Playhead.

Superimposing Audio Clips

iMovie may seem to offer only two parallel audio tracks, but that doesn't mean you can't have more layers of simultaneous sound. There may be only two horizontal strips on the screen, but there's nothing to stop you from putting audio clips *on top of each other*. By all means, drag a sound effect onto your already-recorded narration clip, or superimpose two or more different CD music recordings, if that's the cacophonous effect you want. When playing back your project, iMovie plays all of the sound simultaneously, mixing them automatically (Figure 8-11).

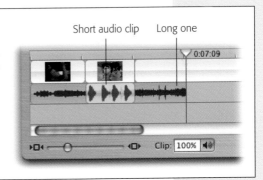

Figure 8-11:
The first time you drag or paste a new audio clip onto an existing one, the situation is fairly clear, thanks to iMovie's tendency to put shorter clips on top of longer ones. It's impossible for a clip to become covered up entirely.

Short audio clip   Long one

If you're having trouble sorting out several overlapping sound clips, consider selecting one and then choosing Edit→Cut. Often, just getting one clip out of the way is enough for you to understand what's going on in its original location. Once you've got your bearings, you can choose Edit→Undo to put it right back where it was.

Another tactic: When you click a clip, iMovie always selects the shortest one in the stack. If you have two overlapping audio clips, therefore, and you intend to select the longer one, click one of its visible ends.

Remember, too, to glance at the top of the Timeline Viewer as you click each audio clip. You'll see its name (if you've turned off the soundwaves, that is), which is another helpful clue when clips collide.

Scrubbing Audio Clips

Scrubbing once meant rotating reel-to-reel tapes back and forth manually, in an effort to find a precise spot in the audio (to make a clean splice, for example). In iMovie HD, you can scrub by Option-dragging your mouse back and forth across an audio clip. iMovie plays the sound under your cursor.

(This technique is extremely useful, but it works best when you're zoomed in and dragging very slowly. Note that Option is called Alt on some non–U.S. keyboards.)

Overlaying Video over Sound

One of the most popular editing techniques—both with editors and audiences—is the *video overlay*. (On the Internet, you may hear this technique called an *insert edit*, but that actually has nothing to do with pasting video over audio.)

As shown in Figure 8-12, a video overlay is where the video cuts away to a new picture, but you continue to hear the audio from the original clip.

Figure 8-12:
When you overlay video over sound, you can illustrate what the speaker is saying without losing her train of voice.

"What did I love about Edenville? Well, not the odor, that's for sure. And not the plant. No, what I loved most was the   old canoe lake. Oh, sure, it was all foamed up with nitrates, and you didn't dare touch the water. But without a doubt, those were   some of the happiest days of my life. I'd give almost anything to take one more look at that old lake."

Suppose, for example, that you've got footage of an old man describing his first love. As he gets to the part where he describes meeting her, you want to cut to a closeup of her portrait on his mantelpiece.

The "Extract Audio in Paste Over" Checkbox

It's a piece of cake to paste a piece of video without disturbing the original audio track. First, though, choose iMovie→Preferences, click General, and make sure "Extract audio when using 'Paste Over at Playhead'" is selected.

If this checkbox is turned *on,* you'll paste only the video, preserving whatever audio is already on your audio tracks. If the checkbox is turned *off,* you'll wipe out both the audio and the video in the spot where you paste.

Close the Preferences window. You're now ready to paste over.

Performing the Overlay

To perform the video overlay, follow these steps:

1. **Select the footage you want to paste.**

   If it's a complete clip, just highlight its icon on the Clips pane or in the Movie Track. If it's a portion of a clip, use the crop markers to specify the part you want, as described on page 131.

2. **Cut or copy the selected footage.**

   Use the Edit→Cut or Edit→Copy commands.

   Now you have to make an important decision. You're about to paste some copied video *over* some existing video. But how much of it do you want to paste? You can either "paste to fit" so that the pasted video begins and ends at precise frames, filling a hole in the existing footage of a particular length; or you can paste it all, without worrying about where the end of the pasted material falls. In this second scenario, you don't want to have to specify a cutoff point (where the existing video cuts in again).

   These two cases are illustrated in Figure 8-13.

3. **If you want to paste the entire copied chunk, position the Playhead in the Timeline Viewer exactly where you want the insert to appear. Then choose Advanced→ Paste Over at Playhead (or press Shift-⌘-V).**

   The video you've pasted wipes out whatever was already there, even if it replaces multiple clips (or parts of clips). If the "Extract audio when using 'Paste Over at Playhead'" checkbox is turned on, as described above, your edit is complete. You've got a cutaway to new video as the original audio track continues.

GEM IN THE ROUGH

The Invisible Audio "Shelf"

When you're editing video, the Clips pane provides a handy temporary working space where you can set aside clips that you haven't yet placed into the movie. If you've ever worked with a page-layout program like InDesign, you're already familiar with this "pasteboard" effect.

Unfortunately, iMovie doesn't come with any pane or pasteboard where you can temporarily park *audio* clips.

If you think it might be handy to have such a workspace as you manipulate your audio clips, the solution is simple: Drag them, or paste them, far off to the right of the Timeline Viewer, beyond the right edge of your video. Then, just drag them back into place when you're ready for them. (Just don't leave any stray audio clips there by accident. You'll look pretty silly when your movie premieres at Cannes.)

---

4. **If you want to paste to fit, highlight the portion of the movie that you want the pasted video to replace. Then choose Advanced→Paste Over at Playhead.**

To select the region that your paste will replace, you can use any of the techniques described in Chapter 4. If you want to knock out only a portion of a single clip, for example, click the clip in the Movie Track and then use the Scrubber bar crop handles to isolate the section that will be replaced (Figure 8-13, bottom). If you want to paste into a segment that spans multiple clips (or parts of clips), choose Edit→Select None, and then use the cropping handles on the entire Scrubber bar map of your movie.

When you paste, one of three things may happen. If the pasted material is *precisely* the same length as the region you've highlighted, great…the pasted chunk drops perfectly into the hole. If the pasted material is longer than the highlighted region, however, iMovie chops off the pasted portion, using as much of the first portion as possible to fit the area you've designated. And if the pasted material is too *short* to fill the reserved space, iMovie creates a "black" clip (see page 140) to fill the remaining highlighted area.

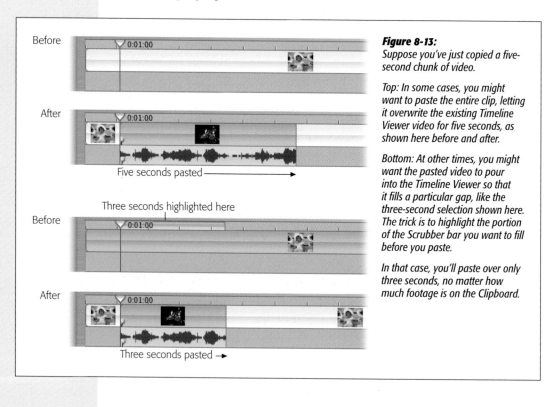

Figure 8-13:
Suppose you've just copied a five-second chunk of video.

Top: In some cases, you might want to paste the entire clip, letting it overwrite the existing Timeline Viewer video for five seconds, as shown here before and after.

Bottom: At other times, you might want the pasted video to pour into the Timeline Viewer so that it fills a particular gap, like the three-second selection shown here. The trick is to highlight the portion of the Scrubber bar you want to fill before you paste.

In that case, you'll paste over only three seconds, no matter how much footage is on the Clipboard.

Extracting Audio from Video

iMovie is perfectly capable of stripping the audio portion of your footage apart from the video. All you have to do is click the video clip in question and then choose Advanced→Extract Audio.

As shown in Figure 8-14, the recorded audio suddenly shows up in your first audio track as an independent audio clip; its pushpins indicate that it's been locked to the original video.

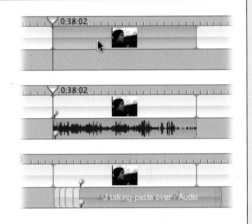

Figure 8-14:
Top: Highlight a camcorder clip and choose Advanced→Extract Audio.

Middle: The camcorder audio appears as an independent clip, which you can manipulate exactly as though it's any ordinary audio clip.

Bottom: You can create a reverb or echo effect by overlaying the same extracted audio several times. (The "soundwave" images have been turned off here for clarity.)

This command unleashes all kinds of useful new tricks that are impossible to achieve any other way:

- **Make an echo.** This is a cool one. Copy the extracted clip and paste it right back into the audio track—and then position it a few frames to the right of the original, as shown at bottom in Figure 8-14. Use the slider at the bottom of the Timeline Viewer to make it slightly quieter than the original. Repeat a couple more times, until you've got a realistic echo or reverb sound.

- **Boost the audio.** The Volume slider at the bottom of the Timeline Viewer is a terrific help in boosting feeble camcorder audio. It does, however, have its limit: it can't crank the volume more than 50 percent above the original level.

Sometimes, even that's not enough to rescue a line of mumbled dialog, or the distant utterances of eighth-graders on the school stage 100 yards away.

When all else fails, try this crazy technique: Copy the extracted clip and paste it *right back on top of itself.* iMovie now plays both audio tracks simultaneously, giving an enormous boost to the volume. In fact, you can stack two, three, four, or even more copies of the same clip on top of each other, all in the same spot, for even more volume boosting.

Now, there's a pretty good reason the Volume slider doesn't go higher than 150%. As you magnify the sound, you also magnify the hiss, the crackle, and whatever other underlying sonic noise there may have been in the audio. When you try this pasting-on-top trick, you may run into that problem, too. Even so, for insiders who know this technique, many an important line of dialog has been saved from oblivion.

- **Reuse the sound.** You can copy and paste the extracted audio elsewhere in the movie. (You've probably seen this technique used in dozens of Hollywood movies: About 15 minutes before the end of the movie, the main character, lying beaten and defeated in an alley, suddenly pieces together the solution to the central plot mystery, as snippets of dialog we've already heard in the movie float through his brain, finally adding up.)

- **Crop the scene's audio.** Trim out an unfortunate cough, belch, or background car honk by cropping the audio. Now the video can begin (or end) in silence, with the audio kicking in (or out) only when required. (Of course, complete silence isn't generally what you want either, as described next.)

- **Grab some ambient sound.** In real movie-editing suites, it happens all the time: A perfect take is ruined by the sound of a passing bus just during the tender kiss moment—and you don't discover it until you're in the editing room, long after the actors and crew have moved on to other projects.

  You can eliminate the final seconds of sound from the scene by cropping or splitting the clip, of course. But that won't result in a satisfying solution; now you'll have three seconds of *silence* during the kiss. The real world isn't truly silent, even when there's no talking. The air is always filled with *ambient sound,* such as breezes, distant traffic, the hum of fluorescent lights, and so on. Even inside in a perfectly still room, there's *room tone.* When you want to replace a portion of the audio track with "silence," what you usually want, in fact, is to replace it with ambient sound.

  Professionals always record about 30 seconds of room tone or ambient sound just so that they'll have material to use in case of emergency. You may not need to go to that extreme; you may well be able to grab some sound from a different part of the same shot. The point is that by importing that few seconds of scene into iMovie, extracting the audio, and then *deleting* the leftover video clip, you've got yourself a useful piece of ambient-sound "footage" that you can use to patch over unwanted portions of the originally recorded audio.

- **Add narration.** The technique described on page 218 is ideal for narration that you record at one sitting in a quiet room. But you can add narration via camcorder, too. Just record yourself speaking, import the footage into iMovie, extract the audio, and then throw away the video. You might want to do this if you're editing on a mike-less Mac, or if you want the new narration to better match the camcorder's original sound.

It's important to note that iMovie never actually *removes* the audio from a video clip. You'll never be placed into the frantic situation of wishing that you'd never done the extraction at all, unable to sync the audio and video together again (which sometimes happens in "more powerful" video-editing programs).

Instead, iMovie places a *copy* of the audio into the audio track. The original video clip actually retains its original audio—but iMovie sets its volume slider to zero, thereby muting it. As a result, you can extract audio from the same clip over and over again, if you like. iMovie simply spins out another copy of the audio each time. (When you extract audio, the video clip, too, sprouts a pushpin, but don't let that fool you. It's perfectly legal to extract the audio again.)

If you intend to use the extracted audio elsewhere in the movie *without* silencing the original clip, no problem. Just click the video clip and then drag the volume pop-up menu back up to 100% once again.

Still Pictures and QuickTime Movies

T he DV camcorder is the source of iMovie material you'll probably use the most often, but it's not the only source. You can also bring in still images and existing QuickTime movies from your hard drive. In addition, you can *export* still frames from your movie, a much more direct method of producing still images than having to use your camcorder's built-in "digital camera" feature.

Importing Still Images

You might want to import a graphics file into iMovie for any number of reasons. For example:

- You can use a graphic, digital photo, or other still image as a backdrop for iMovie's titling feature (Chapter 7). A still image behind your text is less distracting than moving footage.

- You can use a graphics file *instead* of using the iMovie titling feature. As noted in Chapter 7, iMovie's titling feature offers a number of powerful features, including animation. However, it also has a number of serious limitations. Namely, you can't specify any type size you like, you can't use more than one font per title, and you have only rudimentary control over the title's placement in the frame.

  Preparing your own title "slides" in, say, Photoshop Elements or AppleWorks gives you a lot of flexibility that the iMovie titling feature lacks. You get complete control over the type size, color, and placement, for starters. You can also add graphic touches to your text or to the "slide" on which it appears (see Figure 9-1).

- One of the most compelling new uses of video is the *video photo album*: a smoothly integrated succession of photos (from your scanner or digital camera), joined by crossfades, enhanced by titles, and accompanied by music. Thanks to iMovie's ability to import photos directly—either from your hard drive or from your iPhoto collection—creating this kind of video show is a piece of cake.

Note: Of course, iPhoto can create video photo albums, too. And in iPhoto, you can opt to loop a slideshow (which iMovie can't do); rearranging and regrouping your photos is much easier than in iMovie, too. But building them in a movie has several advantages. First of all, your music options are much greater; you can import music straight from a music CD, for example, or record narration as you watch the slideshow. You have a full arsenal of tools for creating titles, credits, and special effects, too.

As your life with iMovie proceeds, you may encounter other uses for the picture-importing feature. Maybe, when editing a home movie of your kids tussling in the living room, you decide it would be hilarious to insert some *Batman*-style fight-sound title cards ("BAM!") into the footage. Maybe you need an establishing shot of, say, a storefront or apartment building, and realize that you could save production money by inserting a still photo that passes for live video in which there's nothing moving. And maybe you want to end your movie with a fade-out—not to black, but to maroon (an effect described later in this chapter).

You have a delicious choice of two methods for bringing still photos into a project. The first and most convenient method is to choose the photo from among those you've organized in iPhoto, using iMovie's window into your picture collection. If you're not using iPhoto to organize your digital photos, you can also use the older method of importing pictures directly from the hard drive.

Figure 9-1:
Preparing your "title cards" in a graphics program gives you far more typographical and design flexibility than iMovie's own titling feature gives you. Using separate graphics software, for example, you can enhance your titles with drop shadows, a 3-D look, or clip art.

Snagging Pictures from iPhoto

The more you work with iMovie and iDVD, the more you appreciate the convenience of the way Apple has linked them to the other i-programs, like iTunes and iPhoto. Here's a classic case:

When you click the Photos button (Figure 9-2), you're shown what amounts to iPhoto Lite: a scrolling panel of thumbnail images reflecting the contents of your entire iPhoto Library. Using the pop-up menu just above the thumbnails, you can even limit your view to the contents of one iPhoto *album* or *folder*.

Tip: Albums are the category "containers" that you can create in iPhoto by choosing File→New Album (or by clicking the + button at the lower-left corner). You can drag a single picture into as many of these albums as you like. Folders are larger structures that let you group albums together. Complete details in *iPhoto 5: The Missing Manual.*

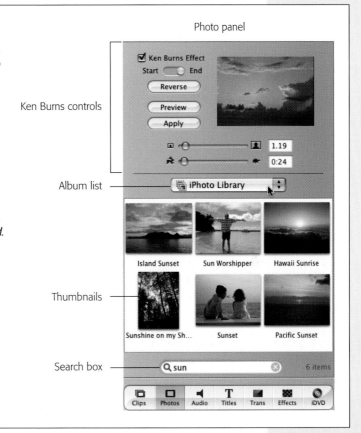

Figure 9-2:
The photo panel shows all the pictures you've imported into iPhoto. Use the Album list pop-up menu to limit the photo display to those in a certain album or folder.

(The dark gray readout at the lower right tells you how many pictures are in that album or folder—or in your entire library, if that's what you're seeing.)

Note the Search box, which debuts in iMovie HD. As you type into it, iMovie smoothly hides all photos except the ones whose names contain matching text. It's an amazingly quick way to pinpoint one photo out of several thousand.

To clear the search box and return to viewing all photos, click the circled X button at the right end of the box.

Photo panel

Ken Burns controls

Album list — iPhoto Library

Island Sunset   Sun Worshipper   Hawaii Sunrise

Thumbnails —

Sunshine on my Sh...   Sunset   Pacific Sunset

Search box — sun   6 items

Clips   Photos   Audio   Titles   Trans   Effects   iDVD

Once you've pinpointed the picture you want, you install it in your movie like this:

Phase 1: Specify the duration

Because you're importing a still image, it doesn't have a *duration*, as a movie clip might. (Asking "How many seconds long is a photograph?" is like asking, "What is the sound of one hand clapping?")

Still, it's a clip, so iMovie has to assign it *some* duration. You can make your graphic appear on the screen for as little as three frames (a favorite of subliminal advertisers) all the way up to 30 seconds (a favorite of all other advertisers).

There's a fast way and a precise way to change this number. The fast way is to drag the rabbit/turtle slider shown in Figure 9-3.

Tip: When you get right down to it, 30 seconds is plenty of time for looking at one particular photo, no matter how good it is. Still, if you need it to last longer—perhaps because you're using it as a background for a series of opening credits—you can always overcome the 30-second limit by placing the same photo into the Movie Track over and over again, side by side, 30 seconds long each.

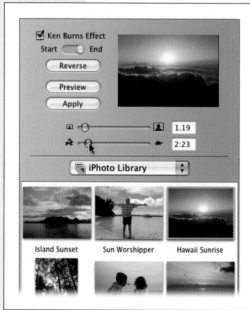

Figure 9-3:
To edit the duration of a still image, click it, either in the Photos panel or in the Movie Track.

Now you can use the rabbit/turtle slider to adjust the photo's duration—that is, the amount of time the picture will appear on the screen, in seconds:frames format.

Or, for greater precision, double-click the actual numbers and then type new numbers over them.

When more precision is required, you can also type the number of seconds and frames into the Duration box to the right of the slider. You can use a number of shortcuts to edit the numbers in this tiny box:

- Press the arrow keys to walk your cursor from one number to the next. Press the Delete key to backspace over the number to the left of the insertion point, or the forward-delete (Del) key (if your keyboard has one) to delete the number to the right of it.

- Double-click the *portion* of the number you want to change. For example, if a clip's Duration box says 10:00 (10 seconds), double-click the 10 to highlight it, type the new number (such as *07*), and press Enter. (You must type a leading zero in front of a single-digit number, or else you'll get an error message.)

   In other words, when efficiency counts, don't waste your time deleting the numbers that are already in the Duration box. Instead, double-click only the portion of it you want to change, and then type right over the highlighted digits.

- Similarly, if you want to change both the seconds and the frames, drag directly across the right pair of numbers in the box. Type the new duration—seconds, a colon, and then frames—and then press Enter.

- If you highlight the entire Duration box (by pressing ⌘-A, for example, or by choosing Edit→Select All), you can rapidly specify the new duration by just typing up the whole thing, including the colon, like this: *05:15*.

Phase 2: Specify the Ken Burns effect

If you turn on the Ken Burns Effect checkbox at the top of the Photos panel, you unleash a wild and arresting feature: the ability to pan and zoom smoothly across photos, in essence animating them and directing the viewer's attention. Details on page 251.

If you'd rather have your photo just pop onto the screen and remain stationary, make sure that the Ken Burns checkbox is turned off. (If you plan to export the movie to iDVD, however, you might want to read page 489 to find out why you'd want to apply Ken Burns to *every* photo, even motionless ones.)

Phase 3: Insert the photo

At last you're ready to put the picture into the movie (a phrase that would hopelessly confuse Hollywood executives who already refer to movies *as* pictures). You can do so in either of two ways:

- Drag a photo out of the thumbnail palette and into the Movie Track. The other clips scoot out of the way to make room, and the photo becomes, in effect, a new silent video clip with the duration you specified. (If you turned on the Ken Burns effect, iMovie takes a few moments to render the animation. The familiar red progress bar inches across the face of the clip.)

- If you want the photo to drop into the end of the movie—as you might when assembling a slideshow, one photo at a time—click the Apply button.

Tip: Speaking of slideshows: You can also drop a whole bunch of photos into the Movie Track at once. Select them in the Photos palette just as you would clips (page 120), then drag them en masse down to the Movie Track. Or click Apply to drop them all at the end of the Movie Track.

You may notice, by the way, that black bars appear above and below (or along both sides of) certain photos, creating the traditional letterbox effect. That happens when a photo doesn't have the proportions that quirkly old iPhoto expects. See the next pages for the fix.

Importing Photos from the Hard Drive

If you want to incorporate graphics that aren't in iPhoto, begin by making sure that no thumbnails are selected in the Photos palette. (If one thumbnail remains highlighted, ⌘-click it.) Then specify the duration for the incoming photo, as described on page 246. If you don't intend to animate or crop your photo, make sure the Zoom slider is set to 1.0, and that the Ken Burns checkbox is turned off.

Finally, choose File→Import File (or just press Shift-⌘-I). When the standard Open File dialog box opens, navigate your way to the desktop (or wherever you put your graphics file), and double-click the file itself. Actually, because you're using Mac OS X, you can select a whole batch of photos to import simultaneously, using the Shift-clicking and ⌘-clicking techniques described on page 120.

The new photo shows up instantly in the Clips pane or the Movie Track, depending on where you've directed incoming clips to go in iMovie's Preferences box. Once again, if black bars appear on the sides or top and bottom of the photo, see page 250.

Tip: iMovie can import graphics in any format that QuickTime can understand, which includes PICT, JPEG, GIF, Photoshop files, and even PDF files, for when an IRS form is exactly what you want to illustrate in your movie. Avoid the GIF format for photos, which limits the number of colors available to the image. But otherwise, just about any format is good still-image material.

After you've imported a graphics file into your project, it's OK to delete, rename, or move the original graphics file you imported. iMovie doesn't need it anymore.

And if you've been lying awake at night, wondering *how* iMovie can display your graphic even after the original file is gone, look no farther than the Media folder inside your movie's project file (or project folder). There you'll find copies of your imported graphics files, with their original names and at full resolution (so that the Ken Burns effect, if turned on, will have enough "margin" to animate your photo). You'll also find clip icons called Still 01, Still 02, Still 03, and so on; these are the rendered video clips, at 640 x 480 resolution, that iMovie made.

Working with Photos

Once you've installed them in the Movie Track, photos behave a lot like standard movie clips. You can rename them, drag them around, click them to view them in the Monitor window, drag them back and forth from the Clip Viewer and Clips pane, delete them, incorporate them into titles or transitions, and so on.

You can also adjust the timing of an imported picture. Just highlight its icon, adjust the Duration slider (or type new numbers into the Duration box), and then click the

Update button just above those controls. (The Update button appears only when a single photo is selected. You can't change the timings of multiple photos at once.)

If you haven't applied the Ken Burns effect (described later in this chapter), you can also change a photo's duration by double-clicking it and then typing a new duration into the Clip Info box. Using this method, you save yourself a click on the Photos button.

Tip: If you've used still images in your movie, don't even think about turning your project into a DVD until you've read the troubleshooting steps on page 489. Otherwise, you'll wind up with very jagged photos.

The Dimensions of an iMovie Photo

On the iMovie discussion forums of the Web, the question comes up over and over again: "What resolution should my iMovie-bound photos be?"

Figure 9-4:
If the dimensions of your graphic aren't in the exact width-to-height ratio that iMovie demands, you'll get letterboxed bars like these.

Top: A portrait-orientation photo.

Bottom: A landscape-orientation photo that's not quite the right aspect ratio.

That question implies that you're thinking of *changing* them—reducing their resolution from their multi-megapixel original state—and that's generally a bad idea. iMovie can use all the resolution it can get, especially if you intend to give the photos the Ken Burns treatment or edit them for HDTV.

A better question is: "What *proportions* should my photo have?" If your photos don't have precisely the dimensions iMovie expects, you'll get letterbox bars, as shown in Figure 9-4.

Until iMovie HD came along, iMovie expected photos to have 4:3 width-to-height proportions to avoid letterboxing. That was just fine for most people, because 4:3 is exactly how photos come from most digital cameras.

As of iMovie 5.0.1, though, something strange is going on. A perfect 4:3 photo does not perfectly fill the standard-definition 4:3 iMovie screen. Instead, it leaves tiny vertical letterbox bars on the sides. To make the bars go away, you have to use the Ken Burns effect to enlarge the photo slightly—1.06 on the Size slider (for standard DV projects), to be exact.

Note: To make this technique work, click the photo in the Photos pane, then use the Size slider to specify 1.06—don't try typing it into the little box. (The type-into-the-box thing only sometimes works, as thousands have unhappily discovered.)

Even then, you'll see thin letterbox bars in the tiny Preview window—but don't worry. When you proceed by clicking Apply, the photo will neatly fill the standard TV-shaped window.

If you'd rather crop your stills in a program like Photoshop or iPhoto before bringing them into iMovie, you'll have to put up with some pretty peculiar ratios. For example, for NTSC (North American), standard-definition projects, you have to crop photos a width-to-height ratio of *1.364 to 1* if you want them to fit the screen neatly! (For other video formats, see the following table.)

Graphics from Scratch

What if you intend to design a graphic from scratch? Maybe it's going to be a simple colored square, which you'll fade into between movie segments. Maybe it's going to be a title card that you intend to dress up in a graphics program.

Technically, images 640 pixels wide and 480 pixels tall ought to be perfect for standard TV (assuming you don't intend to zoom or pan with Ken Burns), because that's the resolution of a standard TV screen. Here again, though, iMovie HD has some funny ideas of its own. To prevent letterboxing on a standard-def, NTSC TV, for example, your iMovie-bound graphics files should be at least *720 x 528* pixels!

Confused yet?

Here's the point: If you're going to crop your photos before bringing them into iMovie, look up the "Aspect Ratio for Photos" in the table below. Crop your photos to those width:height proportions to make them fit iMovie's screen perfectly.

And if you're going to create graphics from scratch, consult the "Minimum Graphics Dimensions" in the table below. That, in pixels, is the lowest resolution you should feed iMovie to fit the screen neatly. (If you plan to use the Ken Burns effect, of course, you'll want to use much greater resolution to avoid ugly pixellation—twice the listed resolution, for example, for a 2X zoom effect.)

NTSC Projects (North America, Japan)

Project Format	Screen Dimensions	Aspect Ratio for Photos	Minimum Graphics Dimensions
Standard DV	720 x 528	1.364:1	720 x 528
DV Widescreen	869 x 480	1.818:1	874 x 480
HDV (720p)	1280 x 720	16:9	1280 x 720
HDV (1080i)	1440 x 1080	16:9*	1440 x 1080

PAL-Format Projects (Europe)

Project Format	Screen Dimensions	Aspect Ratio for Photos	Minimum Graphics Dimensions
Standard DV	784 x 587	1.364:1	788 x 576
DV Widescreen	1040 x 576	1.823:1*	1050 x 576
HDV (720p)	1280 x 720	16:9	1280 x 720
HDV (1080i)	1440 x 1080	16:9*	1440 x 1080

* These figures are for Photoshop editing. For some reason, the numbers are different if you're editing in iPhoto. The HDV 1080i aspect ratio should be 16:9.02 (NTSC and PAL). And for PAL widescreen DV, the aspect ratio should be 1.818:1 and the minimum import size should be 1048 x 576.

The Ken Burns Effect

The only problem with using still photos in a movie is that they're *still*. They just sit there without motion or sound, wasting much of the dynamic potential of video.

For years, professionals have addressed the problem using special sliding camera rigs that produce gradual zooming, panning, or both, to bring photographs to life.

But this smooth motion isn't just about adding animation to photos for its own sake. It also lets you draw the viewer's attention where you want it, when you want it. For example: "Little Harry graduated from junior high school in 1963"—slow pan to someone else in the school photo, a little girl with a ribbon in her hair—"little suspecting that the woman who would one day become his tormentor was standing only a few feet away."

Among the most famous practitioners of this art is Ken Burns, the creator of PBS documentaries like *The Civil War* and *Baseball*—which is why Apple, with his permission, named the feature after him.

You can endow any still graphics file with this kind of motion, either at the moment when you place it or import it from your hard drive, or anytime thereafter.

Applying the Ken Burns Effect

In this example, you'll animate a photo that's in the iPhoto palette.

1. **Select the photo.**

   Actually, you can select more than one, to process all of them in the same way.

2. **Turn on the Ken Burns Effect checkbox at the top of the window. Specify how long you want the picture to remain onscreen.**

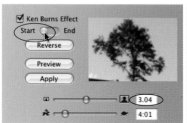

Zoom out Pan and zoom in Diagonal pan

Figure 9-5:
Top: To set up the Ken Burns effect, establish the position and zoom level of the Start and End points separately. (At top right, you can see the little grabby hand cursor that lets you shift the photo within the frame.)

Bottom: Here are three possibilities. The zoom-out pictured at left results from the Ken Burns settings shown above. The center example makes the camera appear to zoom in on the woman holding the pine-apple, even as the photo shifts position to center the pineapple. At right, the Zoom setting was the same (2.0) for both the Start and End points. The only thing that changes over time is the left-to-right position of the photo in the frame.

Use the Duration controls, just as described on page 246.

3. **Click Start. Use the Zoom controls until the photo is as big as you want it at the** *beginning* **of its time on screen. Drag inside the Preview screen to adjust the photo's position (Figure 9-5).**

In other words, you're setting up the photo the way it appears at the beginning of the shot. Often, you won't want to do anything to it at all. You want it to start on the screen at its original size—and then zoom in from there.

But if you hope to create a zooming *out* effect, then drag the Zoom slider to the right (or type a larger number into the box), magnify the photo in the Preview screen, and finally drag the picture itself to center it properly.

Tip: It's actually possible to drag the photo partially or completely *out of the frame,* leaving an empty black void in its place. If you've done this accidentally, just nudge the Zoom slider slightly right, then left. The photo smartly snaps back into centered position.

On the other hand, there are certain creative possibilities here. You can make a photo begin offscreen and then slowly slide into place, for example—or even exit the screen by sliding off the opposite side.

4. **Click End. Use the Zoom controls to set up the picture's final degree of magnification. Drag inside the Preview screen to specify the photo's final position. (Shift-drag to constrain your dragging to perfect vertical or horizontal adjustments.)**

In short, you've set up the starting and ending conditions for the photo.

Take a moment now to click the Preview button. The animated photo goes through its scheduled motion within the Preview box, so that you can check the overall effect. Repeat steps 3 and 4 as necessary.

Tip: At any time, you can click the Reverse button to swap the settings of the Start and End positions. What was once a slow zoom in, left to right, becomes a slow zoom out, right to left.

5. **Drag the thumbnail image out of the Photos palette and into the Movie Track.**

Or click the Apply button; iMovie plunks the image at the end of the movie.

Either way, iMovie now begins rendering your photo effect. You specified the beginning and ending positions of the photo; now iMovie is interpolating, calculating each intermediate frame between the starting and ending points you've specified. The red progress bar crawls across the face of the clip, showing you how much longer you have to wait. (Of course, you're free to work on other aspects of your movie in the meantime, although you may notice a slowdown.)

After the rendering is complete, click the photo clip in the Movie Track and press the Space bar to play your Ken Burns-ized "photo movie" in the Monitor window.

Editing or Removing the Ken Burns Effect

If a photo clip requires adjustment, touching it up is easy enough. Select it in the Movie Track (or wherever it is). Click the Photos button (if the Photos pane isn't already open). Click Start or End, and reprogram the Ken Burns effect just as you did the first time around. (Feel free to edit the duration, too.) When you're finished, click Update. iMovie dutifully re-renders the clip with its new settings.

And what if you want the photo to return to its original, virginal condition? In that case, click the Start button. Drag the Zoom slider all the way to the left, which both re-centers the photo and restores it to its original size. Click the End button and repeat. Finally, click the Update button.

Cropping or Moving a Photo Without Animating It

If you decide that a certain still photo really should be still, click the clip in the Movie Track, turn off the Ken Burns Effect checkbox, and then click Update. The photo is now frozen at its first frame, at the same zoom and position it had when the Ken Burns checkbox was still turned on.

What's neat is even when the Ken Burns effect is turned off, the Zoom slider and the little "move my photo around the frame" cursor still work. In other words, you can use the Ken Burns control to enlarge, crop, or shift a still photo *without* animating it.

Still Images as Titles

As noted at the beginning of this chapter, one of the best reasons to get to know the still-image importing feature is so that you can supplement, or replace, iMovie's built-

---

GEM IN THE ROUGH

The Ken Burns Cropping Effect

You already know that the Ken Burns effect can animate a photo over time, slowly (or quickly) zooming, panning, or both, depending on where the picture is when you click the Start and End buttons.

But you can also zoom or shift the photo *without* animating it. In effect, you can use the Ken Burns tools to crop a photo as you place it into your Movie Track. This is a great trick for dealing with a vertical photo that you want to use in the horizontal orientation of a standard television. By zooming in until the black bars disappear, you've chopped off some of the top and bottom of the picture.

To try this out, click a photo, make sure the Ken Burns checkbox is turned off, specify the duration, and then zoom in. Lastly, drag to shift the photo the way you like it.

Here's a related trick that you may find useful. Suppose you've just Ken Burns-ized a photo. You change your mind. You want it to be still, but you like the way it *ends*.

In that case, Option-click the Start button (in the Photos panel), and then click Update.

Option-clicking copies the End position and zoom level into the Start position. The result is a clip that doesn't move or pan at all, but instead maintains the same zoom level and position for its entire duration. (You can Option-click the End button, too, if the Start position and zoom level are what you want to use for the entire clip.)

---

in titling feature. By using still images as your titles, you gain the freedom to use any colors, type sizes, and positions you want.

The only disadvantage to this approach is that you sacrifice the professional-looking animation styles built into the iMovie titling feature.

Even so, imported graphic title cards don't have to be still and static by any means. For one thing, there's nothing to stop you from animating your still-image titles by applying the Ken Burns effect to them—to make the title zoom in from nothing, for example, or slide from left to right. (Just remember to prepare the title as a graphic with high enough resolution for Ken Burns to work with.)

Furthermore, consider the following title tricks.

The Freeze-Frame Effect

If you were a fan of 1970s action shows like *Emergency!,* you may remember how the opening credits looked: You'd be watching one of the starring characters frantically at work in some lifesaving situation. As she looked up from her work just for a moment, the picture would freeze, catching her by lucky happenstance at her most flattering angle. At that instant, you'd see her credit flashed onto the screen: "JULIE LONDON as Dixie McCall, RN." (*Queer Eye for the Straight Guy* does the same kind of thing.)

That's an easy one to simulate—and nobody will guess that it was created using a still image. To pull this off, you must first export the still frame from your footage that you'll want to use as the freeze-frame. (You'll find instructions for exporting a still

---

POWER USERS' CLINIC

The Fade-to-Black (or Fade-to-Puce) Secret

As noted in Chapter 6, it's easy to create a professional-looking fade-out at the end of your movie. Unfortunately, while iMovie does a great job at taking your film from the final footage to a black frame, it ruins the mood created by its own effect–by *ending the movie.* Unlike professional movies, which fade to black *and then hold* for a moment, iMovie fades to black at the end of the movie and then stops playing, sending your viewers back to iMovie, your desktop, the football game, or whatever was on the computer or TV screen before you played the movie.

The solution is very simple, and well worth making a part of your regular iMovie repertoire. Here's the drill:

Just after the final fade-out, create a black clip. (Recap: Paste a random clip after the final shot of your movie, drag it rightward in the Timeline Viewer to make a black clip

appear, Control-click the gap, choose Convert Empty Space to Clip, and then delete the random clip, leaving the freshly minted black clip behind.)

Then, instead of using the Fade Out transition described in Chapter 6, use Cross Dissolve. iMovie fades smoothly from the final footage of the clip into your black box.

As noted in Chapter 6, whenever you use a transition, iMovie splits the clip into two pieces–one that includes the transition animation, and the unaffected half. Change the duration of the unaffected half of your black square to make the moment of blackness as long as you desire.

Nor should you be content to fade to *black.* In fact, you can fade out to whatever color you desire–white, blue, gray, anything. Just change the black clip's color as explained on page 140.

---

frame in the next section.) Import the frozen shot into your graphics program, like AppleWorks or Photoshop Elements. Then add the text you want.

Finally, import this touched-up image into iMovie as a still image. Place it at the precise frame in your footage from which you exported the still frame to begin with, and you've got your freeze-frame title effect.

Tip: If you don't need the added typographical flexibility of your graphics program, you can simplify this procedure by simply creating a freeze-frame, as described on the previous page, and then using iMovie's built-in title feature to add the text over it.

The Layered Effect

In many cases, the most creative use of still-image titles comes from using *several* of them, each building on the last. For example, you can make the main title appear, hold for a moment, and then transition into a second still graphic on which a subtitle appears.

If you have more time on your hands, you can use this trick to create simple animations. Suppose you were to create ten different title cards, all superimposed on the same background, but each with the words in a different size or position. If you were to place each title card on the screen for only half a second (15 frames), joined by very fast crossfades, you'd create a striking visual effect. Similarly, you might consider making the *color* of the lettering shift over time. To do that, create two or three different title cards, each with the text in a different color. Insert them into your movie, join them with slow crossfades, and you've got a striking, color-shifting title sequence.

Creating Still Images from Footage

iMovie doesn't just take still photos; it can also dish them out. It can grab selected frames from your footage, either for use as frozen frames in your movie or for exporting as graphics files. (You might want a still frame to end a Ken Burns zoom, for example, so that the camera seems to hold still for a moment after the zoom.)

Creating a Still Frame

The Edit→Create Still Frame command creates a still image, in the Clips pane, of the frame currently indicated by the Playhead. You can use the resulting still clip just as you would any still clip: Drag it into your Movie Track, apply effects or transitions to it, change its name or duration, and so on.

One of the most obvious uses of this feature is the *freeze-frame* effect, in which the movie holds on the final frame of a shot. It's a terrifically effective way to end a movie, particularly if the final shot depicts the shy, unpopular hero in a moment of triumph, arms in the air, hoisted onto the shoulders of the crowd. (Fade to black; bring up the music; roll credits.)

Here's how you do it. (These steps assume that you're creating a still frame from a clip that you've already placed in the Movie Track. It's possible, however, to create a still frame from a clip that's still in the Clips pane.)

1. **Position the Playhead on the frame you want frozen.**

   If it's the last shot of a clip, use the right and left arrow keys to make sure you're seeing the final frame.

2. **Choose Edit→Create Still Frame (Shift-⌘-S).**

   iMovie places a new clip either in your Clips pane or at the end of the Movie Track, depending on how you've set up the iMovie→Preferences dialog box.

   It's a still image, set to play for five seconds—but it's not the same kind of still photo you're used to. None of the controls in the Photos palette, for example, has any effect on a *Still,* as iMovie calls it. You can't apply the Ken Burns effect to it, for example.

   If you created this still clip from the *final frame* of a clip, proceed to the next step. If you created this clip from the *middle* of a clip, however, you should now choose Edit→Split Clip at Playhead. You've just chopped up the clip at the precise source of the still clip, resulting in two side-by-side clips in your Movie Track. Delete the right-hand clip.

3. **Drag the still clip just to the right of the original clip (Figure 9-6).**

   If you play back the result, you'll be impressed at how smoothly and professionally iMovie joins the frozen frame onto the moving footage; there's not even a hint of a seam as the Playhead slides from clip to still.

Figure 9-6:
A creative way to end a movie: Chop up the final clip and slow down each piece, finally coming to rest on your still image.

Near the Finish | Crowd Shot | Slow Mo | Freeze Frame | End Credits

4. **Adjust the still's playback duration, if necessary.**

   Fortunately, iMovie HD treats still frames the same way it treats video clips. You can change its duration just by dragging its edges in the Timeline Viewer.

   Or, for more precision, double-click the still frame. In the Clip Info dialog box, change the number in the Duration box, and then click OK.

Figuring out how to handle the *audio* in such situations is up to you, since a still frame has no sound. That's a good argument for starting your closing-credits music *during* the final clip and making it build to a crescendo for the final freeze-frame.

Exporting a Still Frame

While it's convenient to be able to grab a frame from your footage for use in the same movie (as a freeze-frame, for example), you may sometimes find it useful to export a frame to your hard drive as a graphics file. You can use such exported images in any way you use graphics—for emailing to friends, installing on your desktop as a background picture, posting on a Web page, and so on. An exported frame also makes a neat piece of "album art" that you can print out and slip into the plastic case of a homemade DVD.

This feature is, after all, the reason that most iMovie fans don't really care about the built-in still-photo features of DV camcorders. Basically, iMovie can create still images from *any* frame of regular video footage.

It's worth noting, however, that the maximum *resolution* for a digital video frame—the number of dots that compose the image—is 640 across, 480 down. (By this time in the chapter, these numbers have probably become engraved into your cerebrum.) As digital photos go, that's pretty pathetic, on a par with the photos taken by camera phones these days. That's one-third of a megapixel—a pretty puny number compared with the shots from today's three- to eight-megapixel cameras.

The resolution problem

The standard DV resolution is probably good enough for viewing your captured frames onscreen—that is, for use in Web pages and sending by email. But printing is a different story. You'll notice a certain coarseness to the printouts of frames you export from iMovie (see Figure 9-7).

Figure 9-7:
Digital still frames you export from your DV footage suffers from two disadvantages. First, the resolution is comparatively low. Second, the horizontal scan lines of the original video may sometimes create subtle stairstepped, jagged edges in the still.

The low resolution of the video frame is only half the reason your captured pictures look so bad. Most camcorders capture images the same way television displays images: as hundreds of fine horizontal stripes, or *scan lines*. You don't actually see all of the scan lines at any one instant; you see odd-numbered lines in one frame, even-numbered lines in the next. Because the frames flash by your eyes so quickly, your brain smooths the lines together so that you perceive one continuous image.

This system of *interlacing* may work OK for moving video images, but it presents an unpleasant problem when you capture just one frame. Capturing a still image from this footage gives you, in essence, only half of the scan lines that compose the image. iMovie does what it can to fill in the missing information. But as shown in Figure 9-7, there's still a jaggedness problem involving the horizontal scan lines.

Exporting a frame

Now that your expectations have been duly lowered, here's how you capture a frame in iMovie:

Open the project from which you want to grab a still photo. Make sure that no individual clips are selected, and then locate the frame you want to capture. Drag the Playhead along the Scrubber bar, for example. Remember that you can press the left and right arrow keys to step through the movie one frame at a time, or Shift-arrow keys to jump ten frames at a time, in your quest for the precise moment you want to preserve as a still image.

When the image you want appears in the Monitor window, choose File→Save Frame (or press ⌘-F). The Save As dialog box (sheet) slides down from the top of the iMovie window (Figure 9-8).

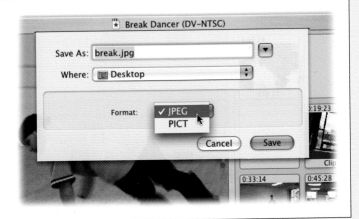

Figure 9-8:
The Save Frame sheet lets you choose a graphics-file format: JPEG or PICT. When the process is over, the saved frame appears with its own icon on your desktop (or wherever you happened to save it).

Use the Format pop-up menu to specify the file format you want for your exported graphic: PICT or JPEG (the better choice if you intend to email it to someone or use it on a Web page). Navigate to the folder where you want this graphic saved (or press ⌘-D to save it onto the desktop). Click Save.

Importing QuickTime Movies

iMovie can import more than still images. It can also import existing digital movies, which you can then incorporate into your footage.

Maybe you've created such QuickTime movies yourself, using other Macs or other software. Maybe you've grabbed a QuickTime movie from a CD-ROM or Web site. Or maybe you've used a digital still camera's Movie mode to grab some short scenes.

Movies from iPhoto

Figure 9-9:
Any digital movies that you've imported using iPhoto show up right here among the still photos in the Photos panel. The little camera icon lets you know which ones are movies.

You can double-click one of the thumbnails to play the movie right in place—a neat trick.

Of course, you can't apply the Ken Burns effect to one of these digital-camera movies. You can, however, drag one of these into place on your Movie Track, where it becomes a standard video clip.

FREQUENTLY ASKED QUESTION

Capturing the Screen

I want to use iMovie to make a software training course. How do I make movies of what I'm doing on the Mac screen?

Use SnapzPro X (available from *www.missingmanuals. com*), a remarkable shareware program. It lets you specify which area of the screen you want to capture—or the whole screen, for that matter. (For best results in iMovie, make the iMovie window as small as possible by dragging the

lower-right corner up and to the left.)

Then, when you press a keystroke that you've specified, Snapz starts recording all the onscreen action: the movement of your cursor, windows and menus opening, and so on. All of it gets saved into a QuickTime movie, which you can then import into iMovie, as described in this chapter.

In any case, here are three ways to get digital movies into an iMovie project:

- If they're lying on your hard drive, choose File→Import (Shift-⌘-I). In the Open File dialog box, navigate to and open the QuickTime movie you want to import.

- If you used iPhoto 5 to import the movies, you'll find them nestled among the still photos in iMovie's Photos pane. See Figure 9-9 for details.

- With movies stored in iPhoto, you can also drag the thumbnails out of that program's window and into the Clips pane or Movie Track of iMovie. (Of course, you have to first position the windows so that you can see both at once.)

It may take iMovie some time to process the incoming movie. Behind the scenes, it's converting the QuickTime movie into DV format, just like the clips that come from your camcorder. A progress bar keeps you posted.

When it's complete, a new clip appears in your Clips pane, which you can manipulate just as you would any movie clip.

Using the Imported QuickTime Clip

It's worth noting that most of the world's QuickTime movies aren't big enough, in terms of frame size, to fill your entire monitor. In fact, most of the world's QuickTime movies—like all the ones on the Web—play in a window only a couple of inches square.

Therefore, when you play back an imported QuickTime movie, iMovie does what it hopes is the right thing: It blows up the QuickTime movie until the footage fills the entire iMovie playback screen (640 x 480 pixels).

As you probably know by now, however, enlarging *any* graphic on the computer usually winds up degrading its quality, because each pixel that composes the image must be enlarged. The bottom line: QuickTime movies you import into iMovie may look coarse and blotchy unless they were at least 640 x 480 to begin with.

Grabbing Clips from Other Projects

It's worth a reminder: You can also grab clips from one iMovie project and use them in another. Forget all the workarounds you once knew; in iMovie HD, reusing a clip is as simple as highlighting it in Project A, choosing Edit→Copy, opening Project B, choosing Edit→Paste, and then waiting patiently as iMovie, behind the scenes, duplicates the massive video file. (See page 478 for more caveats regarding the Copy command and disk space.)

Professional Editing Techniques

T he preceding chapters have covered the *technical* aspects of editing video in
iMovie: where to click, what keys to press, and how iMovie's various controls
operate. This chapter is about the *artistic* aspects of video editing: when to
cut, what to cut to, and how to create the emotional impact you want.

Put another way, this chapter is a continuation of the film-theory crash course that
began in the first three chapters of this book. Chapter 2, for example, describes filmmaking techniques that you must think about at the time you're *shooting*. This chapter
offers some tricks in *editing*.

The Power of Editing

The editing process is crucial in any kind of movie, from a home movie to a Hollywood thriller. Clever editing can turn a troubled movie into a successful one, or a
boring home movie into one that, for the first time, family members don't interrupt
every three minutes by lapsing into conversation.

You, the editor, are free to jump from "camera" to "camera," angle to angle, to cut
from one location or time to another, and so on. Today's audiences accept that you're
telling a story; they don't stomp out in confusion because one minute, James Bond
was in his London office, but showed up in Venice a split second later.

You can also compress time; that's one of editing's most common duties. (That's for-
tunate, because most movies tell stories that, in real life, take days, weeks, or years to
unfold.) You can also *expand* time, making ten seconds stretch out to six minutes—a
familiar effect to anyone who's ever watched a final sequence involving a bomb connected to a digital timer (and heroes racing to defuse it).

Editing boils down to choosing which shots you want to include, how long each one lasts, and in what order they should play.

Modern Film Theory

When you're creating a rock video or an experimental film, you can safely chuck all the advice in this chapter—and in this book.

But if you aspire to make good "normal" movies, ones that are designed to engage or delight your viewers rather than shock or mystify them, then you should become familiar with the fundamental principles of film editing that shape virtually every Hollywood movie (and even most student and independent films) of the last 75 years. For example:

Tell the story chronologically

Most movies tell the story from beginning to end. This part is probably instinct, even when you're making home movies. Arrange your clips roughly in chronological order, except when you're representing your characters' flashbacks and memories or deliberately playing a chronology game, as in *Pulp Fiction*.

DV ETHICS

The Home-Movie Dilemma

As you edit your footage, you're altering reality; you're showing the audience only what you want it to see. When you create movies that have a story line, that's no problem—the audience knows perfectly well that what it's seeing didn't actually happen the way they're seeing it.

When you edit home movies, however, you have a dilemma. How true should you be to real life? iMovie 2 came with a tutorial movie, in which you worked with footage that showed a muddy dog being unsuccessfully washed by two noncommunicative children. In real life, those events might have constituted an unpleasant experience involving a ruined carpet and yelling parents. But with the help of a little sweet guitar music and some selective editing, the entire affair becomes a sunlit, nostalgic snapshot of idyllic childhood.

In a way, you've *already* pre-edited your life, simply in selecting what to film. Most people don't film the family bickering at dinnertime, the 20 minutes when the baby screams inconsolably, or the uneventful hours family mem-

bers spend sleeping or watching TV. You're probably more likely to film the highlights—the laughter, the successes, the special events.

But when you edit this footage in iMovie, you'll probably weed out even more of the unpleasant, the boring, and the mundane. You may even be tempted to *rearrange* events, making the movie funnier, more entertaining, and more cohesive. When it's all over, you'll have a DV cassette filled with sunny, funny, exciting footage that may have come a long way from the much less interesting reality it was meant to capture—*especially* if you add music to your movies. (Music gives footage enormous emotional overtones that weren't there at all when the scene was originally filmed.)

All of this introduces a fascinating ethical challenge that's new to the iMovie era. In the past, few people could edit their home movies, so every home movie was pure documentary. With your DV camcorder and iMovie, you must decide whether you're a documentary maker, a storyteller, or both—and in what combination.

Try to be invisible

These days, an expertly edited movie is one where the audience isn't even aware of the editing.

This principle has wide-ranging ramifications. For example, the desire to avoid making the editing noticeable is why the simple cut is by far the most common joint between film clips. Using, say, the Circle Opening transition between alternate lines of the vows at somebody's wedding would hardly qualify as invisible editing.

Within a single scene, use simple cuts and no transitions. Try to create the effect of seamless real time, making the audience feel as though it's witnessing the scene in its entirety, from beginning to end. This kind of editing is more likely to make your viewers less aware that they're watching a movie.

Develop a shot rhythm

Every movie has an editing *rhythm* that's established by the lengths of the shots in it. The prevailing rhythm of *Dances with Wolves,* for example, is extremely different from that of *Natural Born Killers.* Every *scene* in a movie has its own rhythm, too.

As a general rule, linger less on closeup shots, but give more time to establishing and wide shots. (After all, in an establishing shot, there are many more elements for the audience to study and notice.) Similarly, change the pacing of the shots according to the nature of the scene. Most action scenes feature very short clips and fast edits; most love scenes include longer clips and fewer changes of camera angle.

Maintaining Continuity

As a corollary to the notion that the audience should feel that they're part of the story, professional editors strive to maintain *continuity* during the editing process. This continuity business applies mostly to scripted films, not home movies; still, knowing what the pros worry about makes you a better editor no matter what kind of footage you're working with.

Continuity refers to consistency in:

- **The picture.** Suppose we watch a guy with wet hair say, "I'm going to have to break up with you." We cut to his girlfriend's horrified reaction—but when we cut back to the guy, his hair is dry.

  That's a continuity error, a frequent by-product of having spliced together footage that was filmed at different times. Every Hollywood movie, in fact, has a person whose sole job it is to watch out for errors like this during the filming process.

- **Direction of travel.** In the effort to make the editing as seamless as possible, film editors and directors try to maintain continuity of direction from shot to shot. That is, if the hero sets out crawling across the Sahara from right to left across the scene to be with his true love, you better believe that when we see him next, hours later, he'll still be crawling from right to left. This general rule even applies to much less dramatic circumstances, such as car chases, plane flights, and even people walking to the corner store. If you see her walk out of the frame from left to right in Shot A, you'll see her approach the corner store's doorway from left to right in Shot B.

- **The sound.** In an establishing shot, suppose we see hundreds of men in a battlefield trench, huddled for safety as bullets and bombs fly and explode all around them. Now we cut to a closeup of two of these men talking—but the sounds of the explosions are missing.

  That's a sound continuity error. The audience is certain to notice that hundreds of soldiers on both sides were issued an immediate cease-fire just as these two guys started talking.

- **The camera setup.** In scenes of conversations between two people, you may notice that, even when the camera cuts from one person to the other, the degree of zoom, lighting, and positioning in the frame is roughly the same from shot to shot. It would look really bizarre to show one person speaking only in closeup, and his conversation partner filmed in a medium shot. (Unless, of course, the first person were filmed in *extreme* closeup—just the lips filling the screen—because the filmmaker is trying to protect his identity.)

- **Gesture and motion.** If one shot begins with a character reaching down to pick up the newspaper from her doorstep, the next shot—a closeup of her hand closing around the rolled-up paper, for example—should pick up from the exact moment where the previous shot ended. And as the rolled-up paper leaves our closeup field of view, the following shot should show her straightening into an upright position. Unless you've made the deliberate editing decision to skip over some time from one shot to the next (which should be clear to the audience), the action should seem continuous from one shot to the next.

Tip: For this reason, when filming scripted movies, directors always instruct their actors to begin each new scene's action with the same gesture or motion that *ended* the last shot. Having two copies of this gesture, action, or motion—one on each end of each take—gives the editor a lot of flexibility when it comes time to piece the movie together.

This principle explains why you'll find it extremely rare for an editor to cut from one shot of two people to another shot of the *same* two people (without inserting some other shot between them, such as a reaction shot or a closeup of one person or the other). The odds are small that, as the new shot begins, both actors will be in precisely the same body positions they were in as the previous shot ended.

When to Cut

Some Hollywood directors may tell their editors to make cuts just for the sake of making the cuts come faster, in an effort to pick up the pace.

The more seasoned director and editor, however, usually adopts a more classical view of editing: Cut to a different shot when it's *motivated*. That is, cut when you *need* to cut, so that you can convey new visual information by taking advantage of a different camera angle, switching to a different character, providing a reaction shot, and so on.

Editors look for a motivating event that suggests *where* they should make the cut, too, such as a movement, a look, the end of the sentence, or the intrusion of an off-camera sound that makes us *want* to look somewhere else in the scene.

Choosing the Next Shot

As you've read elsewhere in this book, the final piece of advice when it comes to choosing when and how to make a cut is this: Cut to a *different* shot. If you've been filming the husband, cut to the wife; if you've been in a closeup, cut to a medium or wide shot; if you've been showing someone looking off-camera, cut to what she's looking at.

DV ETHICS

The Internet Continuity-Screwup Database

It's fine to say that the film editor's job is to attempt continuity of picture, sound, direction, and so on throughout a movie. The trouble is, that's not nearly as easy as it sounds. Remember that the editor works by piecing together individual clips from many different camera shots that may have been filmed on different days. When the production is as complicated as a Hollywood movie, where several different film crews may be shooting simultaneously in different parts of the world, a few continuity errors are bound to slip in—and sometimes they're hilarious.

Catching continuity errors in Hollywood movies has become a beloved pastime for thousands of movie fans. *Premiere* magazine, for example, carries a monthly feature called Gaffe Squad, in which readers point out continuity errors in popular commercial movies. An Internet search for *film continuity errors* yields hundreds of Web sites dedicated to picking apart the movies. Among these, the Internet Movie Database Goofs page *(http://us.imdb.com/Sections/Goofs*–capitals count) is Ground Zero; it's probably the largest collection of viewer-submitted movie errors ever assembled. They run along these lines:

Raiders of the Lost Ark: "During the firefight in Marion's bar, Indy's gun changes from a .38 revolver to the Colt .45, back to a .38, then back once again to a .45. This might be the reason that he is able to fire his gun seven times with every loading."

Back to the Future: "When talking to George at the clothesline, both of Marty's shirt pocket flaps are out, but in the next shot one of them is tucked in."

Pulp Fiction: "When young Butch is receiving the watch from the Army guy, the time changes twice as it is flipped over in his hand."

Jurassic Park: "As the helicopter lands on the island, we get a nice overhead view of the landing area, featuring a waterfall and two Jeeps waiting to take the passengers to the visitors' center. But when we see the ground-level view of the helicopter landing in the next shot, we see the Jeeps backing up to the position they were already in three seconds earlier."

Titanic: "When Capt. Smith orders, 'Take her to sea, Mr. Murdoch—let's stretch her legs,' they're standing to the right of the wheelhouse looking forward with the sun coming from their left. When Murdoch walks into the wheelhouse to carry out the order, the sun's behind him."

The Shining: "We see Jack Nicholson chop apart only one of the door's panels with his axe—and yet after we see him listen to the arrival of the Snow-Cat, both panels are chopped."

In other words, making a perfect movie is almost impossible. Of course, as an increasingly experienced film editor yourself, you already knew that.

Avoid cutting from one shot of somebody to a similar shot of the same person. Doing so creates a *jump cut,* a disturbing and seemingly unmotivated splice between shots of the same subject from the same angle. (Figure 3-3 shows a deliberate jump cut, used as a special effect.)

Video editors sometimes have to swallow hard and perform jump cuts for the sake of compressing a long interview into a much shorter sound bite. Customer testimonials on TV commercials frequently illustrate this point. You'll see a woman saying, "Wonderglove changed … [cut] our lives, it really did … [cut] My husband used to be a drunk and a slob … [cut] but now we have Wonderglove." (Inevitably, a fast cross dissolve is applied to the cuts in a futile attempt to make them less noticeable.)

As you can probably attest if you've ever seen such an ad, however, that kind of editing is rarely convincing. As you watch it, you can't help wondering exactly *what* was cut out and why. (The editors of *60 Minutes* and other documentary-style shows edit the comments of their interview subjects just as heavily, but conceal it much better by cutting away to reaction shots—of the interviewer, for example—between edited shots.)

Popular Editing Techniques

Variety and pacing play a role in every decision the video editor makes. Here are some common tricks and techniques professional editors use, which you can adopt for your use in iMovie editing.

Tight Editing

One of the first tasks you'll encounter when editing your footage is choosing how to trim and chop up your clips, as described in Chapter 5. Even when editing home movies, consider the Hollywood guideline for tight editing: Begin every scene as *late* as possible, and end it as *soon* as possible.

In other words, suppose the audience sees the heroine receiving the call that her husband has been in an accident, and then hanging up the phone in shock. We don't really need to see her putting on her coat, opening the apartment door, locking it behind her, taking the elevator to the ground floor, hailing a cab, driving frantically through the city, screeching to a stop in front of the hospital, and finally leaping out of the cab. In a tightly edited movie, she would hang up the phone—and then we'd see her leaping out of the cab (or even walking into her husband's hospital room).

You might keep this principle in mind even when editing your own, slice-of-life videos. For example, a very engaging account of your ski trip might begin with only three shots: an establishing shot of the airport; a shot of the kids piling on to the plane; and then the tumultuous, noisy trying-on-ski-boots shot the next morning. You get less reality with this kind of tight editing, but much more watchability.

Variety of Shots

As described in Chapter 2, variety is important in every aspect of filmmaking—variety of shots, locations, angles, and so on. Consider the lengths of your shots, too:

In action sequences, you might prefer quick cutting, where each clip in your Movie Track is only a second or two long. In softer, more peaceful scenes, longer shots may set the mood more effectively.

Establishing shots

As noted in Chapter 2, almost every scene of every movie and every TV show—even the nightly news—begins with an *establishing shot:* a long-range, zoomed-out shot that shows the audience where the action is about to take place.

Now that you know something about film theory, you'll begin to notice how often TV and movie scenes begin with an establishing shot. It gives the audience a feeling of being there, and helps them understand the context for the medium shots or closeups that follow. Furthermore, after a long series of closeups, consider showing *another* wide shot, to remind the audience of where the characters are and what the world around them looks like.

As with every film editing guideline, this one is occasionally worth violating in special circumstances. For example, in comedies, a new scene may begin with a closeup instead of an establishing shot, so that the camera can then pull back to *make* the establishing shot the joke. (For example, closeup on main character looking uncomfortable; camera pulls back and flips over to reveal that we were looking at him upside down as he hangs, tied by his feet, over a pit of alligators.) In general, however, setting up any new scene with an establishing shot is the smart, and polite, thing to do for your audience's benefit.

Cutaways and Cut-ins

Also as described in Chapter 2, *cutaways* and *cut-ins* are extremely common and effective editing techniques. Not only do they add some variety to the movie, but they let you conceal enormous editing shenanigans. By the time your movie resumes after the cutaway shot, you can have deleted enormous amounts of material, switched to a different take of the same scene, and so on. Figure 10-1 shows the idea.

The *cut-in* is similar, but instead of showing a different person or a reaction shot, it usually features a closeup of what the speaker is holding or talking about—a very common technique in training tapes and cooking shows.

Reaction shots

One of the most common sequences in Hollywood history is a three-shot sequence that goes like this (Figure 10-1 again): First, we see the character looking off screen; then we see what he's looking at (a cutaway shot); then we see him again so that we can read his reaction. This sequence is repeated so frequently in commercial movies that you can feel it coming the moment the performer looks off the screen.

From the editor's standpoint, of course, the beauty of the three-shot reaction shot is that the middle shot can be anything from anywhere. That is, it can be footage shot on another day in another part of the world, or even from a different movie entirely. The ritual of character/action/reaction is so ingrained in our brains that the audience believes the actor was looking at the action, no matter what.

In home-movie footage, you may have been creating reaction shots without even knowing it. But you've probably been capturing them by panning from your kid's beaming face to the petting-zoo sheep and then back to the face. You can make this sequence look great in iMovie just by snipping out the pans, leaving you with crisp, professional-looking cuts.

Otherwise, it's safe to say that iMovie 3 fans create reaction shots far more often than they did when using, say, iMovie 1; now it's easy to cut to a listener's reaction as the sound of the speaker's voice continues. Creating this effect requires nothing more than a video overlay, as described on page 239.

Figure 10-1:

Top: You've got a shot of your main character in action.

Middle: We cut away to a shot of what he's looking at or reacting to.

Bottom: When you cut back to the main character, you could use a different take on a different day, or dialog from a much later part of the scene (due to some cuts suggested by the editor). The audience will never know that the action wasn't continuous. The cutaway masks the fact that there was a discontinuity between the first and third shots.

Parallel cutting

When you're making a movie that tells a story, it's sometimes fun to use *parallel editing* or *intercutting*. That's when you show two trains of action simultaneously; you keep cutting back and forth to show the parallel simultaneous action. In *Fatal Attraction*, for example, the intercut climax shows main character Dan Gallagher (Michael Douglas) downstairs in the kitchen, trying to figure out why the ceiling is dripping, even as his psychotic mistress Alex (Glenn Close) is upstairs attempting to murder his wife in the bathtub.

You may not have much call for intercutting if you're just making home movies, especially because it's deliberately artificial. Everybody knows you've got only one camcorder, and therefore the events you're depicting couldn't have taken place simultaneously. But even if you're making movies that tell a story, you'll find this technique an exciting one when you're trying to build suspense.

Part Three:
Finding Your Audience

3

Back to the Camcorder

Unless you edit your movies while keeping your eyes on the camcorder's screen or a TV attached to your camcorder (as recommended on page 97), you've been editing your work in the Monitor window. But the Monitor window doesn't show you the real thing. It's only an approximation of the smooth, clear video image that your camcorder caught to begin with.

Fortunately, behind the scenes, every shred of crisp, clear, smooth-motioned video is intact on your hard drive. When you export the movie back to your DV camcorder, it appears in all its original, high-resolution glory.

Why Export to Tape

There are any number of reasons you might want to send your finished product back to the camcorder. The following pages outline some of the most popular scenarios.

To Watch It on TV

Once your iMovie creations are back on the camcorder's tape, you can then pass them along to a television. To pull this off, you must connect the camcorder to your TV, using one of the following cables, listed here in order of preference:

- **Component video.** If you're editing high-definition video, sending the result back to your HDTV camcorder is just about the *only* way to play it on a TV. After all, the era of commonplace high-definition DVDs has not yet arrived.

  Your HDTV camcorder came, therefore, with a special cable that ends with three small round jacks colored green, blue, and red. These are *component* video cables, and they must be connected to matching inputs on a high-end (if not high-definition) TV. You'll have to use an additional cable for audio (RCA cables).

- **S-video.** If both your camcorder and your VCR or TV have *S-video* connectors, use an S-video cable to join the two (see Figure 11-1). You'll still have to use the red- and white-ended RCA cables for the audio.

- **RCA cables.** Most TVs and VCRs don't have S-video connectors, but almost all have *RCA phono* jacks, usually labeled Audio In and Video In. Connect them to the double- or triple-ended cable that came with the camcorder, like the one shown in Figure 11-1. (If it has *three* connectors at each end, the yellow one is for the video signal, and the red and white ends are for left and right stereo sound.)

Tip: If your TV is very old, it may not have auxiliary input jacks. In this case, plug your camcorder into the VCR's auxiliary inputs instead. It will patch the signal through to the TV.

Figure 11-1:
Most camcorders come with a special, proprietary cable. The miniplug end goes into a special output jack on the camcorder; the far ends are RCA cables (or, on HDTV camcorders, component cables) for your TV or VCR. If your TV accepts only one sound cable (and not stereo inputs), plug the camcorder's left-channel connector (usually the red one) into the sole TV audio jack.

(This camcorder also has an S-video connector. It's the large, round, black jack at the top of the connector panel. S-video transfer produces better transfer quality between your DV camcorder and non-DV equipment than RCA cables.)

- **Coax inputs.** TVs of a certain era (or price) don't have the RCA-style cables shown in Figure 11-1, but do have a cable-TV (*coaxial*) input—a round connector about the size of a 24-point capital O, with a single pin in the center. You can buy an adapter (at Radio Shack, for example) that lets you connect your camcorder's output cables to this kind of jack.

- **RF modulator.** If your TV doesn't even have that connector, it probably has two screws to which you can attach a "rabbit ears" antenna. You can buy an adapter called an *RF modulator* for this kind of connector, too.

- **Special patch cable.** Most camcorder models (including those from Sony and Canon) come with a special input/output cable with RCA or component connectors at one end and a special miniplug at the camcorder end (see Figure 11-1, bottom). Plug this skinny end into the appropriate camcorder jack, often labeled "Audio/Video ID2" or "AV In/Out."

To Transfer It to Your VCR

The glorious thing about DV tape, of course, is that its picture quality and sound quality are sensational. Unfortunately, most of the world's citizens don't *have* DV camcorders or DV decks. They have standard VHS VCRs or DVD players.

Chapters 15 and 16 guide you through turning iMovie masterpieces into DVDs—but that's a stunt you can pull off only if your Mac has a built-in DVD burner. For everyone else, the best way to get your movies to the TV screens of your adoring fans is to transfer them (the movies, not the fans) to VHS cassettes.

You lose a lot of picture and sound quality when you transfer footage to a VHS cassette, whose lines-of-resolution capacity is lower than any other kind of tape reproduction. Still, your viewers will most likely remark how *good* your movies look, not how bad. That's because most people are used to playing back VHS recordings they've made from television, which (unless it's a satellite system) has its own low-resolution problems. The transfers you make from your Mac, even when played back on VHS, look terrific in comparison.

To make a transfer to your VCR, you have a choice: You can either copy the movie back onto a DV cassette in the camcorder, so that you'll have a high-quality DV copy, and then play it from the camcorder onto your VCR; or you can pour the video directly from the Mac, through the camcorder, into the VCR. Both of these techniques are described in the coming pages.

To Offload Footage from Your Mac

Another great reason to transfer your iMovie work back to the camcorder is simply to get it off your hard drive. As you know, video files occupy an enormous amount of disk space. After you've made a couple of movies, your hard drive might be so full that you can't make any more iMovies.

Offloading the movie to your DV camcorder is the perfect solution, thanks to a key advantage of digital video: the ability to transfer footage back and forth between the camcorder and your Mac as many times as you like with *no deterioration in quality*. You can safely unlearn the years of experience you've had with VHS and 8 mm video and feel free to transfer video between your Macintosh and DV camcorder whenever and however you like.

Note: When you transfer an iMovie back to your camcorder–to a fresh tape, if you're wise–the footage remains in perfect, pristine condition. Remember, however, that there's a downside to doing so: Once you've thrown away the digital video files from your Mac, you've lost the ability to adjust titles, effects, transitions, and soundtracks. For best results, therefore, transfer footage back to the camcorder either when you're finished editing the movie, or haven't edited it much at all.

Offloading video to reclaim disk space

After transferring the movie to a DV cassette in your camcorder, you can throw away the corresponding files on your hard drive, which frees up an enormous amount of disk space. The space-consuming digital-video clips sit in the Media folder that lurks within the folder for your project (page 103). In other words, the Media folder is the one taking up all the disk space. Still, you may as well throw away the *entire* project folder (after "backing it up" onto the camcorder), because without the Media files, the actual iMovie document file, and the accompanying *.mov* reference-movie file, are useless.

Transferring Footage to the Camcorder or VCR

The actual steps of transferring the project from iMovie back to the camcorder are fairly simple. The results are almost always satisfying, especially if you've had to look at your footage in its relatively coarse Mac rendition for hours or days. Finally, you get to see your masterpiece at full digital quality. Most people are particularly thrilled by the professional look of iMovie's transitions and titles when they see it on the actual TV (or camcorder LCD panel).

In early iMovie versions, you had to begin the transfer process by sending your finished movie to a DV camcorder as a first step. Now, however, a new possibility awaits: You can play the finished movie directly from the Mac to a VCR, using the camcorder only as a passthrough adapter that doesn't actually record anything. The following discussions cover both methods.

First to DV Tape, Then to VCR

If you'd like your finished movie on DV tape, preserving 100 percent of its original quality, proceed like this:

1. **Insert a blank cassette into your camcorder.**

   Confirm that the tape is unlocked (see page 284), and—*this is important*—that it's cued up to a part of the tape you're willing to record over.

   This may sound like an obvious step, but complacency on this point has led camcorder owners to the accidental erasure of many a precious piece of footage. Sooner or later, everyone finds out: A camcorder has no Undo command.

2. **Put the camcorder into VTR or VCR mode (refer back to Figure 2-1).**

Confirm that its FireWire cable is plugged into your Mac. Unless you're willing to risk running out of battery power in midtransfer, plug your camcorder into a power outlet, too.

Open your iMovie project on the Mac, if it isn't already open.

3. **Choose File→Share (Shift-⌘-E, a keystroke designation that's left over from iMovie 3, when this command was called Export).**

   The Share dialog box appears, as shown in Figure 11-2.

Figure 11-2:
The Share dialog box lets you specify whether you're sending your finished movie to a tape, QuickTime movie, DVD, Bluetooth phone, Palm organizer, or whatever.

(Technically, this type of box, which slides down from the iMovie title bar, is known as a sheet.)

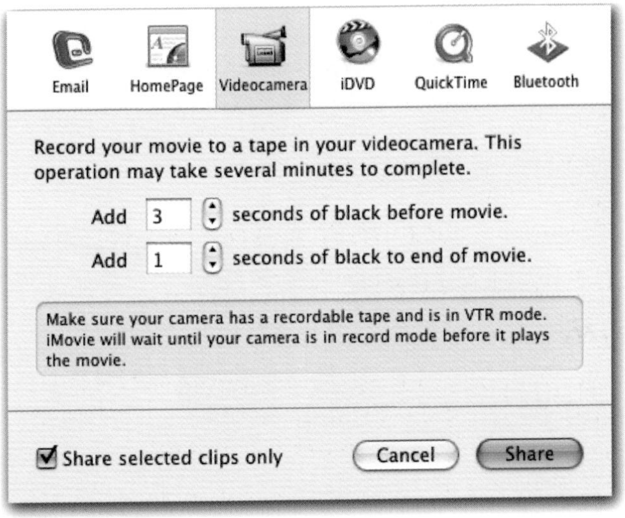

4. **At the top of the dialog box, click Videocamera. Change the "seconds of black" numbers in the dialog box, if necessary.**

   The "seconds of black" numbers specify how many seconds of blackness you want to appear on the tape before the movie begins or after it ends; three or four seconds is about right. Without a black "preroll," the movie would begin instantly. Your audience would be deprived of the customary "settle down and start paying attention" moment that precedes every TV show, movie, and commercial throughout the world. And without a moment of blackness at the end, the mood created by your movie might be shattered too soon.

   You can also take this opportunity to turn on "Share selected clips only," if you like. This feature lets you split up a long movie into smaller chunks by preselecting only the clips you want before you invoke the Share command. (See page 485 for tips on troubleshooting this feature.)

5. **Click Share.**

If your project contains certain special effects, iMovie takes this opportunity to say "Your movie contains still, slow motion, and/or reverse clips which need to be rendered for export to iDVD or tape." In that case, click "Render and Proceed." You're instructing iMovie to generate smoother, more professional looking versions of these scenes—not the quick-and-dirty, temporary ones it's been showing you during editing.

Either way, after a moment, iMovie commands the camcorder to begin recording, and then begins pumping your finished video over the FireWire cable to the tape, from the very beginning of the movie (Figure 11-3). (There's no way to begin playing from the middle of your movie.)

While this process is taking place, you might want to open the LCD panel on the camcorder so that you can watch the transfer and listen to the audio. iMovie plays

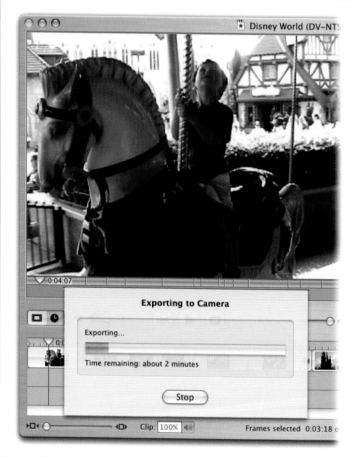

Figure 11-3:
While iMovie sends your finished production back to the camcorder from whence it came, a progress bar shows how much longer you have to wait. Also, you see the playhead ride along your Movie Track to show where you are in the transfer.

You can interrupt the transfer process at any time by clicking Stop. The camcorder stops automatically, having recorded your movie up to the part where you stopped.

the movie simultaneously in its Monitor window, but the camcorder screen's quality is generally superior.

When the transfer is complete, the camcorder automatically stops recording. Your finished production is now safely on DV tape.

Tip: After the transfer is complete, drag the Camera/Edit switch on your iMovie screen (at the left edge of the screen, just below the Monitor) to its Camera position. Doing so puts iMovie into "I'm controlling your camcorder now" mode. Click Rewind, then Play to watch your newly transferred production.

At this point, you can connect your camcorder to a VCR for transfer to a standard VHS cassette (or any other non-DV format). Connect the camcorder to the Audio and Video input jacks on the VCR. These jacks were once found exclusively on the *backs* of VCRs, but appear on the front panels of many recent VCR models for convenience at times like this.

Make sure that the VHS tape is blank and not protected by its erase tab. If you're smart, you'll label it, too—*now,* before you even record it, so that you won't forget. Put it into the VCR and cue it up to the right spot. Cue up the camcorder, too.

Finally, put your camcorder into VCR or VTR mode, start the VCR recording, and then press Play on the camcorder. If your TV is on, you can watch the footage as it plays into your VCR. Press Stop on both the camcorder and VCR when the transfer is complete.

From Mac Directly to VCR

If your aim is to get your movie onto VHS tape, you don't have to transfer it to your camcorder first. Hook the camcorder to the Mac via the FireWire cable, if it isn't already, and then hook the VCR to the camcorder as described above.

The trick here is to turn on the "Play DV project video through to DV camera" option in the iMovie→Preferences→Playback dialog box, as described on page 97.

Press Record on your VCR, then play your movie from the beginning (or from whatever spot you like). iMovie sends the full-quality video through the camcorder and into the connected VCR.

When you reach the end of playback, hit Stop on the VCR.

Tip: If you have an analog-to-DV converter box like those described on page 117, use precisely the same steps. The converter replaces the camcorder in the setup described here.

Of course, this technique bypasses the Export dialog box shown in Figure 11-2, and with it the ability to "lay down" some nice blackness before and after the footage. If you really want those bookends, just add black clips to the movie itself (page 140).

Notes on DV Tapes

As noted in Chapter 1, DV cassettes present the promise of immortality for your video. Because you can transfer the footage nearly indefinitely from camcorder to computer (or to camcorder) without ever losing quality, there's no reason your footage can't stick around forever.

The tapes themselves are not immortal, however. Although you can record and rerecord them dozens of times, you can't do so indefinitely, as most people assume. You'll know when a particular cassette is starting to go when you begin to notice *dropouts* in the video—pops in the picture, tiny rectangular pixels of the wrong color. At that point, it's time to retire that cassette.

Tip: Following the advice on the little set of label stickers that comes in each tiny DV cassette box will delay this cassette death as long as possible. It recommends that you keep the tapes in their boxes, away from dust, heat, magnets, electricity, marauding children, and so on.

Here are a few other cassette pointers that may surprise you:

The Two-Cassette System

Consider conceiving of each iMovie project as a two-cassette affair. Designate one cassette (or set of cassettes) as your raw-footage tapes, and a second set as the finished-movie tapes. (Video editors call these the *original* and *master* tapes, respectively.)

Doing so, and labeling the tapes carefully, makes it less likely that you'll accidentally record over some important movie that you slaved at for days. It also makes life simpler when friends come over and suddenly say, "Hey, let's see what you did with your Mac!" If you keep all of your iMovie creations on a single special cassette, you won't have to hunt for a particular tape to show them your prize-winning creations.

Labeling and Logging

DV cassettes are so tiny that you'll find it almost impossible to write more than a few words onto their little white labels. If you want to write down the list of finished movies you've recorded on such a cassette, you'll have to use the fold-out cardboard index card that comes inside the cassette's little plastic box.

Tip: As noted earlier, it's a good idea to label your DV cassettes *before* you record them, especially if you'll be filming an event that requires multiple tapes (such as weddings or shows). Your annotation doesn't have to be elaborate (*1, 2, 3,* and so on is fine), just something to prevent you from shoving an already-recorded cassette into the camcorder, forgetting, in the heat of the moment, that it's not a blank.

That's a real problem if you intend to create movies that are any more elaborate than simple home movies. While shooting, professional film and video makers keep careful track of which cassette contains which shots, and which *takes* of those shots were useful. In fact, they typically write "G" (*good*) or "NG" (*no good*) on the log sheet as they complete each shot.

This kind of logging is enormously useful even for the amateur. It can save you lots of time when you sit down to transfer the footage from camcorder to Mac, because you don't have to sit there watching the entire hour of tape. You already know that the first 15 minutes were fantastic, followed by 15 minutes of lousy stuff that you can fast-forward past, and so on.

Long Play Mode

Most DV camcorders let you squeeze 90 minutes of video onto each 60-minute cassette by using Long Play (LP) mode, in which the tape travels more slowly through the camcorder electronics. On a DV camcorder, LP mode doesn't bear the same stigma of lousy picture quality that it does on VHS equipment. In fact, there's absolutely *no difference* in quality between LP and Standard Play mode on a DV camcorder. The data is stored as a stream of numbers; the computer doesn't care how fast they're slipping through the camcorder innards.

You should, however, be aware of several LP side effects:

- You lose the ability to dub in a second soundtrack after having recorded some video. That's not much of a sacrifice, however, since you can do the same thing and more in iMovie.

- In theory, LP mode also increases the *chance* of getting dropouts. Most people report no such occurrence, but it's more likely to occur when recording at LP speed. Experiment with your camcorder before recording some once-in-a-lifetime event in LP mode.

- Avoid recording LP and standard-speed footage on the same cassette. Camcorder makers warn that doing so is a recipe for scrambled footage.

- Use LP-recorded tapes only in the camcorder that recorded them. Swapping LP tapes among different camcorder models—or even different units in the same camcorder line—invites dropouts and other video noise, because the playback heads in each camcorder are aligned differently. LP recordings use a much narrower stripe of tape to record video information (6.7 microns wide, instead of 10 microns wide in Standard Play mode), so even minor differences in the position of the heads in different camcorders can result in LP playback problems.

Clearly, LP recording is something of a black art. For the smoothest sailing in your DV career, avoid it except when getting 90 minutes in a single pass is crucial to your project.

Tip: If you have a Sony Digital8 camcorder, another option is open to you: Buy 180-minute Hi-8 tapes, such as Sony E6-180HME cassettes. You won't find them at your local drugstore, that's for sure, but *www. bhphotovideo.com,* for example, carries them. These tapes let you fit 90 minutes of high-quality footage on a single cassette, without the downsides of LP mode. (They're a good way to return finished iMovies that are over an hour long back to tape, too.)

The Protect-Tape Tab

In the old days of audiocassettes and VHS tapes, you could prevent an important recording from being accidentally erased by a clueless family member. You simply had to pry out or break off a tiny, plastic, square "protect" tab on the top edge of the cassette. Doing so left a hole that prevented the recorder from recording.

The trouble with that system, of course, was if you changed your mind, the only way you could "unlock" the tape to permit recording again was to cover the little hole with a piece of tape. This tape trick was an inelegant solution, and often a risky one, because tape peeling off inside a VCR was a one-way ticket to the repair shop.

DV and Hi-8 cassettes (for Digital8 fans) are far more sophisticated. They have a sliding shutter that covers the "can't record" hole (see Figure 11-4), making it much easier to prevent recording on a particular tape and then change your mind.

Note: The record-lock tab on Digital8 (Hi-8) tapes works backwards from mini-DV cassettes. The little red slider *covers* the hole to prevent recording, and must be *open* to record.

Figure 11-4:
You need a sharp fingernail, pocket knife blade, or other implement to slide this very small shutter (top right). But at least you'll never need tape to cover the hole.

From iMovie to QuickTime

For the best and most cinematic viewing experience, play your finished iMovie productions on TV, via VHS tape or DVD. That way, your public gets to see the full-sized picture that your camcorder captured.

But when you want to distribute your movies electronically, convert them into Quick-Time files instead. Both Mac and Windows machines can play these files right on the screen with little more than a double-click.

Your distribution options for QuickTime files are far greater than for videocassette or DVD, too. You can email a QuickTime file to somebody or post it on the Web for all the world to see (Chapter 13). You can put bigger QuickTime files onto a disk, like a recordable CD, a Zip disk, or an Apple iPod, to transport them.

This chapter covers all of these techniques, step by step.

Saving a QuickTime Movie

After you've finished editing your iMovie production, save it onto a DV cassette (as described in Chapter 11) as a backup, even if your primary goal in creating the movie is to save it as a QuickTime file. Relative to the time you've probably spent editing your movie, the cost of making this backup is trivial, and it gives you flexibility if someday, somehow, you want to show that same movie on a TV or re-edit it in iMovie.

Once that's done, you're ready to proceed with the QuickTime creation process:

1. **Choose File→Share.**

   The Share dialog box appears.

2. **Click the QuickTime icon at the top.**

   Now the dialog box looks like Figure 12-1.

3. **Using the Formats pop-up menu, choose one of the preset export formats such as Email, Web, CD-ROM, or Expert Settings.**

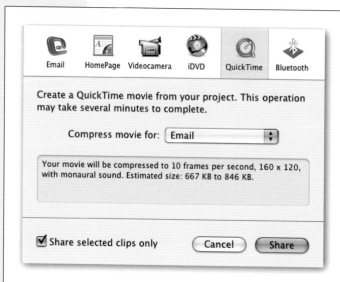

| Email | HomePage | Videocamera | iDVD | QuickTime | Bluetooth |

Create a QuickTime movie from your project. This operation may take several minutes to complete.

Compress movie for: [Email ▼]

Your movie will be compressed to 10 frames per second, 160 x 120, with monaural sound. Estimated size: 667 KB to 846 KB.

☑ Share selected clips only   (Cancel) (Share)

Figure 12-1:
Using the pop-up menu in this dialog box, you can indirectly specify how much compression you want applied to your movie, and what the dimensions of the finished movie frame will be. The small print below the pop-up menu warns you that many of these settings will reduce the size and quality of the finished product.

This decision dramatically affects the picture quality, motion smoothness, file size, and window size of the finished QuickTime movie.

Making a smart choice in this step requires some comprehension of the QuickTime technology itself, so although "Understanding QuickTime" in the next section is many pages long, it's well worth absorbing. It's critical to your grasp of QuickTime movies, what they are, and what they can do.

That section also describes the choices in this pop-up menu one by one.

4. **Click Share.**

   Now the standard Save File dialog box appears, sprouting from the title bar of the iMovie window.

5. **Type a name for your movie.**

   (Unless, of course, you really do want to call your movie "My Great Movie," as iMovie suggests.)

   Don't remove the letters *.mov* from the end of the file's name, especially if it might be played on Windows computers. That suffix is a requirement for machines who aren't savvy enough to know a movie file when they see one.

6. **Navigate to the folder where you'll want to store the resulting QuickTime file.**

   You can just press ⌘-D if you want your QuickTime Movie saved onto the desktop, where it'll be easy to find.

7. **Click Save.**

Now the time-consuming exporting and *compression* process begins. As you can read in the next section, compression can take a long time to complete—from a minute or two to an hour or more, depending on the settings you selected in step 3, the length of your movie, and the speed of your Mac. Feel free to switch into other programs—check your email or surf the Web, for example—while iMovie crunches away in the background.

A progress bar lets you know how much farther iMovie has to go.

When the exporting is complete, the progress bar disappears. Switch to the Finder, where you'll find a new QuickTime movie icon (see Figure 12-2). Double-click it to see the results.

Tip: You can click Stop anytime during the export process, but you'll wind up with no exported movie at all.

Figure 12-2:
When you double-click the resulting QuickTime movie on your hard drive (left), it opens into your copy of QuickTime Player, the movie-playing application described in Chapter 14. Press the Space bar to make the movie play back (right).

Understanding QuickTime

A computer displays video by flashing many still images in rapid succession. But if you've ever worked with graphics, you know that color graphics files are data hogs. A full-screen photograph file might occupy 5 or 10 MB of space on your hard drive and take several seconds to open up.

Unfortunately, most computers are far too slow to open up 30 full-screen, photographic-quality pictures per second. Even if they could, full-screen, full-quality QuickTime movies would still be mostly useless. Each would consume hundreds of gigabytes of disk space, requiring days or weeks to download from the Web or by email—a guaranteed way to annoy citizens of the Internet and doom your movie-making career to obscurity.

That's why most QuickTime movies *aren't* full-screen, photographic-quality films by any stretch of the imagination. In fact, most QuickTime movies are much "smaller"—in three different dimensions:

- **The window is much smaller.** It's rare to see a QuickTime movie that, when played back, fills the computer screen. Instead, most QuickTime movies today play in a much smaller window (see Figure 12-3), therefore requiring far less data and resulting in far smaller files.

- **The frame rate is lower.** Instead of showing 30 frames per second, many QuickTime movies have far lower frame rates; even fifteen frames per second produces smooth motion. On the Web, especially during live QuickTime "broadcasts," still lower frame rates are common, such as two or five frames per second. This kind of movie is noticeably jerky, but sends so little data that people using telephone-line modems can watch live events in this format.

- **The video is *compressed*.** This is the big one—the technical aspect of QuickTime movies that gives you the most control over the resulting quality of your movie. In short, when iMovie uses QuickTime to compress your video, it discards infor-

Figure 12-3:
Here's the same movie in two standard playback sizes (with the menu bar showing so you can gauge its size). Movies designed for playback from the hard drive are often 640 pixels wide, 480 tall (640 x 480). Movies intended for the Web email are smaller—often 320 x 240. (Movies sent by email are often as tiny as 160 x 120.) The common denominator: Almost all QuickTime movies have the same relative dimensions—a 4:3 width-to-height ratio, which is exactly the same ratio as the picture produced by your TV and your camcorder.

mation that describes each frame. True, the picture deteriorates as a consequence, but the resulting QuickTime movie file is a tiny fraction of its original size. The following section describes this compression business in much greater detail.

The bottom line is that by combining these three techniques, iMovie can turn your 10 GB DV movie into a *3 MB* file that's small enough to email or post on your Web page. The resulting movie won't play as smoothly, fill as much of the screen, or look as good as the original DV footage. But your viewers won't care. They'll be delighted to be able to watch your movie at all, and grateful that the file didn't take hours to download. (And besides, having already been exposed to QuickTime movies, most know what to expect.)

Tip: The later the QuickTime version your Mac contains, the better and faster the movie-exporting process becomes. Mac OS X's Software Update feature is supposed to alert you every time a new version becomes available (if you have it turned on in System Preferences).

A Crash Course in Video Compression

The following discussion explores some technical underpinnings of QuickTime technology. It may take you a few minutes to complete this behind-the-scenes tour of how a computer stores video. But without understanding the basics, iMovie's QuickTime-exporting options will seem utterly impenetrable.

Spatial compression

Suppose you overhear a fellow Mac fan telling her husband, "Would you mind running to the grocery store? We need an eight-ounce box of Cajun Style Rice-A-Roni, and an eight-ounce box of Cajun Style Rice-A-Roni, and also an eight-ounce box of Cajun Style Rice-A-Roni."

You'd probably assume that she's enjoyed a little too much of that new-computer smell. Why didn't she just tell him to pick up "three boxes" of it?

When it comes to storing video on a hard drive, your Macintosh faces the same issue. When storing a picture file, it must "write down" the precise color of *each pixel* of each frame. It could, of course, store the information like this:

- *Top row, pixel 1:* Beige

- *Top row, pixel 2:* Beige

- *Top row, pixel 3:* Beige

…and so on. Clearly, this much information would take a lot of space and a lot of time to reproduce.

Fortunately, when Apple engineers were designing QuickTime in the 1980s, it occurred to them that the individual dots in solid-colored areas of the picture don't need to be described individually. That top row of pixels could be represented much more efficiently, and take up a lot less disk space, if the Mac were simply to write down:

- *Top row:* 60 consecutive pixels of beige

This simplified example illustrates the power of *compression software,* whose job it is to make graphics files smaller by recording their pixel colors more efficiently. This kind of compression explains why a JPEG file always takes up far less space on your hard drive (and less time to download by email) than, for example, the Photoshop or AppleWorks document that created it; the JPEG file has been compressed.

This form of file-size reduction is called *spatial* or *intraframe* compression. iMovie analyzes the picture on each individual frame and reduces the amount of information needed to describe it.

Temporal compression

But there's another way to reduce the size of a QuickTime file, too. Not only is there a lot of redundant color information from pixel to pixel on a single frame, but also from *frame to frame.*

Suppose, for example, that you've captured some footage of a man sitting behind a desk, talking about roofing materials. Picture the first pixel of the back wall in that piece of footage. Chances are good that this pixel's color remains absolutely consistent, frame after frame, for several seconds at least, especially if the footage was shot using a tripod. Same thing with the rug, the color of the desk, the fern in the pot beside it, and so on. These elements of the picture don't change at all from one frame to the next.

Here again, if it were your job to record what's on each frame, you could choose the slow and laborious method:

- *Frame 1:* The upper-left pixel is beige.

- *Frame 2:* The upper-left pixel is still beige.

- *Frame 3:* The upper-left pixel is *still* beige.

... and so on. This time, however, a clever QuickTime movie would record the details of only the *first frame.* "The upper-left pixel on the first frame is beige," it might begin. In filmmaker terminology, that first, completely memorized image is called the *key frame.*

Thereafter, rather than memorizing the status of every pixel on the second frame, the third frame, and so on, the Mac might just say, "On the next 60 frames, pixel #1 is exactly the same as on the first one." That more efficient description just made the resulting QuickTime file a *lot* smaller, as shown in Figure 12-4. (The subsequent, shorthand-recorded frames are often called *delta frames* by the geeks.)

This kind of shorthand is called *temporal* or *interframe* compression, because it refers to the way pixels change over time, from one frame to the next.

About Codecs

As shown in Figure 12-1, at the moment you save your QuickTime movie, iMovie asks you which of several schemes you want to use for compressing your footage. To use the technical terminology, it asks you to choose a *codec* from a long list. That term is short for compressor/decompressor, the software module that translates the pixel-by-pixel description of your DV footage into the more compact QuickTime format—and then *un*translates it during playback.

Each QuickTime codec works differently. Some provide spatial compression, some temporal, some both. Some are ideal for animations, and others for live action. Some work well on slower computers, others on faster ones. Some try to maintain excellent picture quality, but produce very large QuickTime files on the disk, and others make the opposite tradeoff. Later in this chapter, you can read about each of these codecs and when to use them.

In the meantime, all of this background information should help explain a few phenomena pertaining to converting DV movies into QuickTime files:

- **Saving a QuickTime movie takes a long time.** It's nothing like saving, say, a word processing document. Comparing every pixel on every frame with every pixel on the next frame involves massive amounts of number crunching, which takes time.

Figure 12-4:
When iMovie saves a QuickTime movie, it doesn't bother writing down the description of every pixel on every frame. If there are a lot of areas that remain identical from frame to frame, the QuickTime movie doesn't remember anything more than, "Same as the previous frame."

In this example, the faded portions of the picture are the areas that the QuickTime movie data doesn't describe—because they're the same as on the first (key) frame. (At last you understand why, as you may have read in Chapter 2, using a tripod for your footage doesn't just give your movies a more professional look. By ensuring that most of the picture stays exactly the same from frame to frame, a tripod-shot video helps to produce smaller QuickTime files.)

(Some codecs take longer than others, however.)

- **QuickTime movies don't look as good as the original DV.** Now you know why: In the act of shrinking your movie down to the file size that's reasonable for emailing, copying to a CD-ROM, and so on, a codec's job is to *throw away* some of the data that makes a movie look vivid and clear.

- **QuickTime is an exercise in compromise.** By choosing the appropriate codec and changing its settings appropriately, you can create a QuickTime movie with excellent picture and sound. Unfortunately, it will consume a lot of disk space. If you want a small file on the hard drive *and* excellent picture and sound, you can make the QuickTime movie play in a smaller window—160 x 120 pixels, for example, instead of 320 x 240 or something larger—or at a slower frame rate. The guide in this chapter, some experimentation, and the nature of the movie you're making all contribute to helping you make a codec decision.

The Share Presets: What They Mean

iMovie offers several ready-to-use QuickTime compression settings that govern the quality, file size, and playback-window size of the movie you're exporting. Here's a guide to these presets to help you choose the one that's appropriate for your movie-distribution plans.

Each of the descriptions below includes the following information:

- **Video codec.** As noted earlier, iMovie offers access to QuickTime's long list of codecs, each offering a different tradeoff in compression speed, file size, picture quality, and so on. These codecs are described in detail in the next section.

- **Size.** These dimensions, in pixels (of which there are 72 per inch on your computer screen), indicate how big the finished QuickTime movie "screen" window will be. Use Figure 12-3 to guide you.

- **Frame rate.** This number tells you how many frames (individual pictures) you'll see per second when the QuickTime Movie plays back. Thirty frames per second is standard NTSC television quality (in PAL countries, it's 25 per second). Ten to fifteen frames per second begins to look less smooth, and anything under ten yields a flickering, old-time movie effect.

Trivia: Old-time silent movies actually played at *eighteen* frames per second.

- **Audio codec.** This statistic is the sonic equivalent of the frame rate, in that it tells you what kind of sound quality you'll get. At 44.1 kHz, the quality is exactly the same as that of a commercial music CD. At 22 kHz, it's half as good, but you won't hear any difference except when you listen through headphones or stereo speakers. When the sound plays through the *built-in* speaker on the standard Macintosh, most people can't tell the difference between 44.1 and 22 kHz.

Tip: All of the canned export presets preserve the stereo sound present in your original camcorder footage. Unfortunately, most computers don't *have* stereo speakers. (Only certain Mac models come with built-in stereo speakers.) Meanwhile, saving two independent soundtracks makes your QuickTime file larger than it would be if it were saved in mono.

Therefore, if creating a compact QuickTime Movie file is important to you, consider using the Expert settings, described later in this chapter, to eliminate the duplicate soundtrack.

- **Time to compress one minute of video.** The "Time to Compress" statistic provided below indicates how long it took a PowerBook G4 to compress a standard sample movie that's exactly one minute long. (Compressing a 10-minute movie, of course, would take about ten times as long.) Of course, the time it will take your movie to get compressed and saved depends on the codec you've chosen, the length of the movie, how much motion is visible on the screen, and your Mac's speed, but the next section offers a rough guide.

- **File size.** The final statistic provided for each option shows you how big the resulting QuickTime file might be (in megabytes). These numbers, too, refer to the sample one-minute DV movie described in the previous paragraph.

Email

Video codec: *H.263*
Size: *160 x 120*
Frame rate: *10 per second*
Audio codec: *QDesign Music 2, mono, 22 kHz*
Time to compress one minute of video: *1 minute*
File size: *1.2 MB*

The movie you export with these settings is fairly blurry, and the size of the QuickTime screen is closer in size to a Wheat Thin than a Cineplex.

Still, the H.263 video codec has two important benefits. First, it makes the exporting much faster than if you used, say, the Sorenson 3 codec (which takes nearly twice as long). Second, the resulting QuickTime file is relatively tiny; at just over 1 MB for a minute-long movie, it's actually within the realm of possibility that you could email this thing to somebody without incurring their wrath. (The Sorenson 3 codec produces a better-looking movie. But its movies are 3.3 MB per minute—far too large for casual emailing.)

Web

Video codec: *H.263*
Size: *240 x 180*
Frame rate: *12 per second*
Audio codec: *QDesign Music 2, stereo, 22 kHz*
Time to compress one minute of video: *1 minute, 35 seconds*
File size: *2.4 MB*

This kind of movie is much more satisfying to watch than the Email type. The image is over twice as big, and the higher frame rate produces smoother motion.

Once again, the Sorenson Video codec could provide far better image quality; but at 2.4 MB per minute, the product of the H.263 codec is small enough to download from a Web page without a high-speed Internet connection.

Web Streaming

In quality and size, this preset is identical to the Web preset described above. The only difference is that this kind of movie comes set up for *streaming* delivery from the Web, meaning it's played on your audience's screens *as* it's being sent from the Web. In other words, your viewers don't have to download the entire movie before playing it.

Streaming means that your movies can be extremely long, even if they're therefore extremely large files. Only a tiny bit at a time is sent to your spectators' computers.

For details on putting your QuickTime movies on the Web, see Chapter 13.

CD-ROM

Video codec: *H.263*
Size: *320 x 240*
Frame rate: *15 per second*
Audio codec: *IMA 4:1, Stereo, 44.1 kHz*
Time to compress one minute of video: *1 minute, 30 seconds*
File size: *6 MB*

As you can see by the specs above, a movie with the CD-ROM setup generally contains too much data to be suitable for live Web delivery. But saving your QuickTime productions into this kind of QuickTime file is ideal if you plan to play it from a hard drive or a CD-ROM that you record yourself, as described later this chapter. The high frame rate means that motion will seem smooth, and the 320 x 240 dimensions of the window mean that the movie will fill a decent fraction of the computer screen. That's big enough to see a good amount of detail.

Tip: If you're willing to endure more compressing time and a larger resulting file, you can give your CD-ROM movies a dramatic picture-quality upgrade by substituting the Sorenson Video 3 codec for the H.263 codec. (Use the Expert settings described on the next page to do so; duplicate the settings described here, but choose the Sorenson Video 3 codec instead of H.263.)

The only down side is that the resulting QuickTime movie contains too much data for older, slower CD-ROM drives, such as those rated below 12X, to deliver to the computer's brain. The movie will *play* on slower CD-ROM drives, but it will skip a lot.

Full Quality DV

Video codec: *DV*
Size: *720 x 480*
Frame rate: *29.97 per second (for NTSC; 25 for PAL)*
Audio codec: *No compression; stereo, 32 or 48 kHz (depending on source audio)*
Time to compress one minute of video: *1 minute*
File size: *411 MB*

As the numbers (and the example in Figure 12-3) show you, this is the QuickTime format for people whose equipment doesn't mess around. The file size is massive—much too large for playback from a CD-ROM drive.

That's because this setting isn't intended for playback; it's intended to offer you a means of *storing* your iMovie production without sacrificing any video quality. The Full Quality DV setting applies *no compression at all* to your audio or video.

Yet preserving your iMovie work as a giant, single DV clip on the hard drive is still a useful exercise. It can save hard drive space, for one thing, since the resulting Quick-Time file is still far smaller than the collection of DV clips in your project's Media folder from which it was made. After creating a Full Quality DV movie, you could delete the project folder to free up some disk space, confident that you've got your entire movie safely preserved with 100 percent of its original DV quality intact.

The Expert Settings

The canned presets aren't the only ways you can turn your iMovie project into a QuickTime movie. By choosing Expert Settings from the pop-up menu shown in Figure 12-1, and then clicking the Share button, you embark on a tour of crazy nested dialog boxes. Along the way, you'll be offered control of every aspect of the compression process, including which codec it uses, the degree of sound compression, how many frames per second you want, and so on.

The first dialog box to appear is the "Save exported file as" box, where you can type a name and choose a folder location for the file you're about to save (Figure 12-5, top). Resist the temptation, for now.

The real power lies in the buttons and pop-up menus elsewhere in this little box. For starters, the Export pop-up menu (shown at top in Figure 12-5) offers a wealth of conversion options. This is your opportunity to save your film as:

- An AVI file to give to your Windows PC-using friends. (Choose **Movie to AVI**.)

- A huge folder full of still images, one per frame of your movie. (Choose **Movie to Image Sequence.** Click Options to specify the file format—like JPEG or Photoshop—and how many stills per second you want.)

• A soundtrack. Here's a great opportunity to convert the audio tracks of your movie into standalone sound files. (Choose **Sound to AIFF, Sound to Wave,** or whatever format you want.)

You'll find this feature very handy in two situations. First, you can use iMovie as a quick-and-dirty piece of *sound-recording* software (see Chapter 8), and use this feature to export the recording as a sound file.

Second, certain troubleshooting situations, described in Chapter 8 and elsewhere, call for your exporting and reimporting your finished soundtrack—in essence, temporarily splitting it apart from the video. (You can even edit the soundtrack

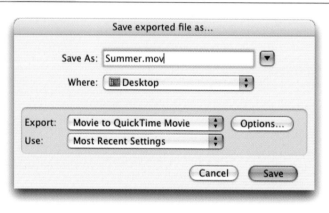

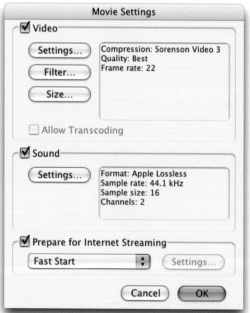

Figure 12-5:
You're about to burrow down through several nested dialog boxes, only the first two of which are shown here. (See Figure 12-6 for some of the others.)

Top: Use the Export pop-up menu when you want to save just your audio track, or when you want to convert your movie into another movie format (like AVI for Windows machines). Most of the time, though, you'll click Options.

Bottom: The Movie Settings box is just a summary screen for the dialog boxes that hide behind it: Settings, Filter, Size, and so on.

file in a sound-editing program along the way, if you're so inclined. That's one way to get rid of the occasional pop or crackle.)

But most of the time, you'll ignore this Export pop-up menu. Most of the time, you'll want to leave it set to "Movie to QuickTime Movie," and then click the Options button to make some settings changes.

As illustrated in Figure 12-5, that Options button opens a very important dialog box: the Movie Settings box. Here's where you can export your finished product with *exactly* the size-smoothness-speed compromise you want.

You'll notice that this box offers three buttons for video: Settings, Filter, and Size. Below that, you get one Settings button for Sound; and at the bottom of the box, you get options for *Internet streaming*. All of these settings are covered in the next few pages.

The Settings Button

The Settings button takes you to the powerful Compression Settings dialog box (Figure 12-6), the heart of the entire Expert software suite. Here's what the controls do:

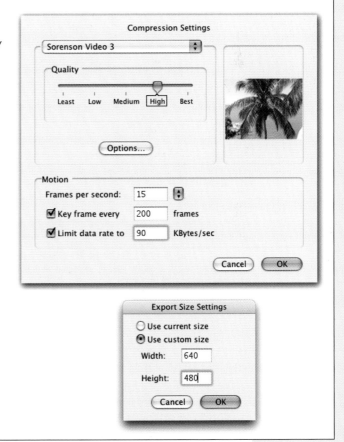

Figure 12-6:
Top: This dialog box gives you point-by-point control over the look, size, and quality of the QuickTime movie you're exporting. Not all of these controls are available for all codecs. That is, depending on what you choose using the top pop-up menu, some of the controls here may be dimmed and unavailable. Furthermore, only some of the codecs offer an Options button in the middle of the dialog box.

In the Sorenson 3 codec controls, shown here, the "Limit data rate to ___" option is useful when you're trying to produce a movie that will stream from the Web. Note, however, that this setting overrides the Quality slider setting. (Many people have been baffled by a crummy-looking Sorenson movie that they'd set to Best quality. Now you know why.)

Bottom: Here's where you can specify the dimensions of the movie you're saving, in pixels. (This box appears when you click the Size button shown at bottom in Figure 12-5.)

Compressor pop-up menu

The unlabeled pop-up menu at the top lets you choose one of 27 codecs—or None, which means that iMovie won't compress your project at all. Each codec is useful in a different situation; each compresses your footage using a different scheme that entails different compromises. You can read "The Video Codecs: A Catalog" on page 305 to learn about the codecs listed in this pop-up menu. For now, it's enough to note that for live video that will be played on modern computers, the Sorenson Video 3 codec almost always produces the highest quality at reasonably small file sizes.

Quality slider

This slider offers another tradeoff between the size of the resulting QuickTime file and the quality of its picture. In general, the proposed value (usually Medium or High) offers the best balance between file size and picture quality. But on important projects, by all means experiment. Export a representative sample of your movie several times, moving the slider each time, so that you can compare the results.

Frames per second

The number you specify here makes an enormous difference in the smoothness of the QuickTime movie's playback. As always, however, it's a tradeoff—the higher the number, the larger the QuickTime file, and the more difficult it is to email, store, or transfer.

You can type any number between 1 and 29.97 in this box, or you can use the pop-up menu to the right of the "Frames per second" box. Here's what you can expect from these settings:

- **8, 10.** These movies are very compact, and make good candidates for transmitting over the Internet. They also look very jerky.

- **12,15.** These are by far the most common frame rates for today's QuickTime movies. By playing only half as many frames as you'd see on a TV show, the QuickTime movie saves itself a lot of data, making it smaller on the disk and more likely to

---

RARELY ASKED QUESTION

30 fps Drop-Frame

OK, I'll bite. Why on earth did the USA, which is supposed to be so technically advanced, settle on a TV standard that plays at such an oddball frame rate? Why is it 29.97—why couldn't it be rounded off to 30?

The 29.97 frame rate, known in the TV business as *30 fps drop-frame,* dates back to the dawn of color TV. As they prepared to launch color TV broadcasts in January 1954, network engineers wanted to make sure that the expensive black-and-white TV sets of the day could receive the color

shows, too. (Talk about backward-compatible software!)

Trouble was, when they tried to broadcast a color signal at the then-standard 30 frames per second, the extra color information wound up distorting the audio signal. Eventually, they hit upon a discovery: If they slowed down the frame rate just a hair, the distortion disappeared. The video, meanwhile, looked just as good at 29.97 frames per second as it did at 30.

A standard was born.

---

succeed when played on slower computers. And yet this many frames per second tricks the eye into perceiving satisfying, smooth motion; most people can sense that they aren't seeing quite the motion quality they'd see on TV, but don't miss the other fifteen frames each second.

- **24, 25.** An actual Hollywood movie plays 24 frames per second, and the European television signal (PAL) plays at 25. These settings, in other words, are provided for situations where you want excellent motion quality, without going all the way to the extreme of 29.97 frames per second of the American TV standard (NTSC). You save a little bit of disk space, while still showing as many frames as people are accustomed to seeing in motion pictures.

- **29.97.** If you're wondering how this oddball number got into the pop-up menu, you're not alone. As it turns out, every source that refers to television broadcasts as having 30 frames per second (including other chapters in this book) is rounding off the number for convenience. In fact, a true television broadcast plays at *29.97* frames per second. (iMovie can reproduce that rate for you, if it's important to do so. In fact, this is iMovie's top frame rate.)

FREQUENTLY ASKED QUESTION

Oddly Shaped Movies

I'm doing a project where I need my movie to be perfectly square, not in a 4:3 width-to-height ratio. But every time I try to specify these dimensions in the Expert QuickTime Settings dialog box, I get a distorted, squished iMovie movie. What can I do?

What you're really asking is how to *crop* your movie. Remember that iMovie creates DV movies, which have a 4:3 aspect ratio. If you want any other proportions without squishing the picture, you have to *trim off* some of the edges, thus cropping it.

Unfortunately, neither iMovie nor QuickTime Player Pro (Chapter 14) offers any simple method of cropping the picture. There is software that can do so, however: Cleaner 6 (*www. discreet.com*), the $500, professional QuickTime-compression software. As shown here, it lets you

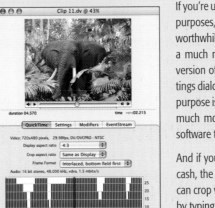

draw a dotted-line rectangle that indicates how you'd like the picture to be cropped.

If you're using iMovie for professional purposes, a program like Cleaner is a worthwhile investment. Think of it as a much more powerful and flexible version of the Expert QuickTime Settings dialog box (Figure 12-5). Its sole purpose is to compress movies, using much more efficient and intelligent software than that built into iMovie.

And if you have more expertise than cash, the freeware program ffmpegX can crop video, too. You have to do it by typing in coordinates (rather than adjusting a visual cropping frame), but it works. (You can download ffmpegX from the "Missing CD" page at *www. missingmanuals.com*.)

• **30.** Don't fall for it—this choice is for suckers. NTSC (North American) digital video itself is 29.97 frames per second, so asking it to save a QuickTime movie with an even *higher* rate is like thinking you'll be wealthier if you exchange your dollar bills for quarters.

If you *do* try choosing 30 from this pop-up menu, when you click OK, you'll be scolded, told you're out of line, and then returned to the dialog box to make another choice.

As described under "Quality slider" in the previous section, you don't have to export your movie in its entirety, just to see the effects of different frame-rate settings. Create a dummy project that contains only a few seconds of your movie, and try exporting it at each frame rate. Then play back the short QuickTime movies. You'll get a self-instruction course in the effects of different frames-per-second settings.

Key frame every __ frames

You can read about *key frames* earlier this chapter—they're the full frames that get "memorized" in your QuickTime movie, so that the QuickTime file can store less data for subsequent frames (see Figure 12-4).

Additional key frames make your QuickTime file bigger, so you have an incentive to make them appear infrequently (that is, to type in a higher number in this box). But if the resulting QuickTime movie is something that your viewers might want to *skip around* in, key frames are very useful. Somebody might scroll back into the movie to a spot with no key frame. When playback begins at that point, the image might be scrambled for a fraction of a second, until the next key frame appears.

In most cases, one key frame per second is about right. In movies that will be played back from beginning to end and never rewound or scrolled, it's safe to increase the number in this box.

Limit data rate

Each delivery mechanism—a CD-ROM, a cable modem, a 56 K modem, and so on—delivers information at a different rate. If you want to ensure that no frame-skipping or jerkiness occurs when somebody plays your movie, turn this checkbox on and type a number into the box.

The precise number to type depends on your goals for the movie you're exporting. In other words, it depends on what kind of gadget will be playing the movie data. Here are some guidelines for the Sorenson codec:

If the movie will be played by:	Use this maximum data rate:
56 K modem	5 K/second
T1 or cable modem	20 K/second
CD-ROM	100 K/second
Hard drive	250 K/second

iMovie automatically adjusts the picture quality as necessary, on a moment-by-moment basis, so that the QuickTime movie will never exceed this rate.

Options

When you choose the names of certain codecs from the Compressor pop-up menu—Motion JPEG, Photo-JPEG, PNG, Sorenson Video, or TIFF, to be precise—an Options button magically appears in the dialog box shown in Figure 12-6, top.

In general, you can ignore this button and the extremely technical dialog box that appears when you click it. The "options" for the Sorenson codec aren't options at all—only a summary of your settings. And the options that appear for the other codecs offer only one useful option—"Optimize for Streaming." You'd use this checkbox if you intended to prepare your movie for *streaming Internet video,* as described in the next chapter. Trouble is, you'd be foolish to use the JPEG, PNG, or TIFF codecs for this purpose to begin with. Codecs like Sorenson and H.263 offer far better quality, smaller size, and better compatibility.

The Filter Button

Chapter 6 details a number of special effects you can apply to clips *in* iMovie. But unbeknownst to nine out of ten iMovie fans, you can apply a second suite of special effects to your movie on its way *out* of iMovie. Simply click the Filter button (Figure 12-5) as you export a QuickTime movie.

The dialog box shown in Figure 12-7 appears. By opening the various flippy triangles, you'll find a lot of effects you've seen before in iMovie (color balance, brightness and contrast, lens flare, fake old-film grain)—and a few you haven't (blur or sharpen, emboss, edge detection).

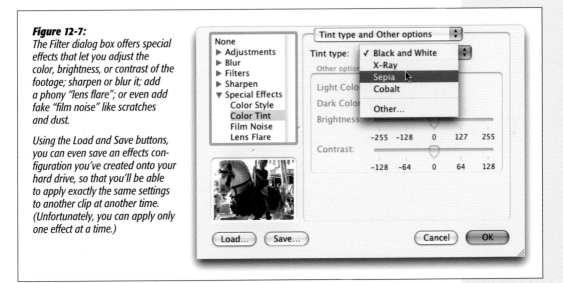

Figure 12-7:
The Filter dialog box offers special effects that let you adjust the color, brightness, or contrast of the footage; sharpen or blur it; add a phony "lens flare"; or even add fake "film noise" like scratches and dust.

Using the Load and Save buttons, you can even save an effects configuration you've created onto your hard drive, so that you'll be able to apply exactly the same settings to another clip at another time. (Unfortunately, you can apply only one effect at a time.)

The list of effects appears in the scrolling list at top left; a preview of the result appears in lower left. Use the controls on the right side of the dialog box to affect the intensity and other settings of the effect.

As you work, remember that whatever filter you apply here applies to the *entire movie* you're about to export.

You might be inclined to pooh-pooh this whole feature, in that case. Really, when would you ever want to apply the same degree of blur to an entire movie? But with a little forethought, you can still apply an effect to just one clip (or one section of your movie, using the invisible-title trick described on page 195). The trick is to create a new iMovie project containing only that clip. Export it using the DV/DVCPRO-NTSC or DV-PAL compressor (page 307) to make sure that you retain all your digital-video size and quality—and apply the filter you want in the process. When it's all over, you can reimport your exported, processed clip into the original iMovie file.

Caution: iMovie preserves your Expert settings from export to export, even if weeks or months elapse in between. That's an especially treacherous feature when it comes to these filters; you may sit through a 45-minute export the next time, only to find that the resulting movie is all Embossed and color-shifted because those are the settings you used last time. The only way to escape this nightmare is to reopen the Filter dialog box and choose None.

The Size Button

And now, back to your tour of the dialog box shown in Figure 12-5.

The Size button summons the dialog box shown at bottom in Figure 12-6, where—after clicking "Use custom size"—you can specify the dimensions for the playback window of your QuickTime movie. See Figure 12-3 for some examples of these different sizes.

Of course, the larger the window you specify, the longer the movie will take to save, the slower it will be transmitted over the Internet, and the larger the resulting file will be.

Keeping the dimensions you specify here in a width-to-height ratio of 4:3 is important. (In the business, they call the width-to-height ratio the *aspect ratio* of the picture.) The QuickTime software plays back most smoothly if your movie retains these relative proportions. Furthermore, if the width and height you specify *aren't* in a 4:3 ratio,

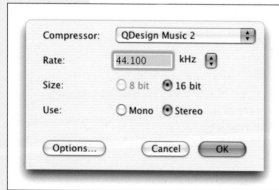

Figure 12-8:
It probably goes without saying that the better the audio quality you specify, the larger your QuickTime movie will be. In any case, this is the dialog box where you make such decisions. Audio isn't nearly as data-greedy as video, so compressing it isn't nearly as urgent an issue (unless you want your movie to play over the Internet).

iMovie will have to squish the picture accordingly, which may lend a funhouse-mirror distortion effect to your film.

The huge majority of QuickTime movies play in at one of several standard sizes, such as 160 x 120, 240 x 180, or 320 x 240. All of them maintain this 4:3 aspect ratio. Still, there are dozens of other possible sizes that maintain the correct proportions.

Audio Settings

At the bottom of the dialog box shown in Figure 12-5 is a second button called Settings. This one lets you specify how—and how much—your soundtrack is compressed in the exported QuickTime movie (see Figure 12-8).

Compressor

When most people think of codecs—those who've even *heard* of codecs, that is—they think of *video* compression. But iMovie offers a choice of audio codecs, too. This pop-up menu lets you specify which one you want to use.

Many of them aren't, in fact, appropriate for movie soundtracks. Remember that these codecs are provided by QuickTime, not by iMovie, and that QuickTime is designed to be an all-purpose multimedia format. It's supposed to be just as good at creating pictureless sound files as it is at creating movies. For best results in most movies, use the QDesign or IMA setting. For the benefit of trivia fans, here's the complete list:

- **24-bit Integer, 32-bit Floating Point, 32-bit Integer, 64-bit Floating Point.** If you don't already know what these are, then you're not a hardware or software engineer who traffics in this kind of audio file. These formats are high-quality, no-compression file formats that aren't appropriate for movie soundtracks.

- **ALaw 2:1.** Use this low-quality, low-compression European standard only when requested, such as when you're exporting audio-only files for people who require ALaw as an exchange format.

- **AMR Narrowband.** This item, which debuted in QuickTime 6.3, stands for Adaptive Multi-Rate, meaning that it thins out its stream of data whenever possible (as opposed to using the same number of bits per second throughout the movie). It's intended for movies in the 3GPP format (a standard developed for cell phones).

  Use it if you have a 3GPP-compatible phone. For other phones, use the Qualcomm PureVoice codec (page 304), click Options, and turn on the Half Rate option.

- **Apple Lossless.** This item, also part of QuickTime 6.3 and later, is the only truly *lossless* audio codec available to you. "Lossless" means that although this codec cuts the audio track's file size in half, it doesn't lose *any* of the sound quality in the process. The resulting files are too big for the Web or emailing, but Apple Lossless is a great alternative to "None" when you're saving a movie for best-quality playback from a hard drive.

- **IMA 4:1.** This codec was one of the first QuickTime movie audio compressors. It provides excellent audio quality—you *can't* change it to a sample size less than 16-bit—and plays back equally well on Windows and Macintosh.

It's great for movies that will be played from a hard drive or CD-ROM. Be aware, however, that the resulting disk-space savings aren't very great. For example, the compression isn't good enough for QuickTime movies that will be played over the Internet.

- **MACE 3:1, MACE 6.1.** These options are included for people who want to swap sound files with very old Macs. They feature high compression, but very low quality. Playback works only on Macs.

- **MPEG-4 Audio.** If you choose this audio codec, you'll save your soundtrack in AAC format—the same one used for songs you buy from the iTunes music store.

The sound quality is superb, although it depends on the settings you make when you click Options. (Choose, for example, 128 kbits/second from the Bit Rate pop-up menu to match the quality of iTunes songs.) The file size, meanwhile, is only a fraction of the original. It's a welcome and useful choice for movies not intended to be played over the Internet.

- **QDesign Music 2.** An engineering breakthrough, this is the sound codec to use for online or emailed movies. It maintains terrific audio quality, but compresses the sound a great deal, producing files small enough to deliver over the Internet. Apple's favorite example: One minute of music from an audio CD requires 11 MB of disk space, but after compression by this codec, it consumes only 150 K and sounds almost as good.

- **Qualcomm PureVoice.** The good news is that this codec compresses the audio down to almost nothing, which makes it great for transmission over the Internet or playing on a cellphone. The bad news: The quality is just barely enough to produce intelligible recordings of human speech. In other words, it isn't quite as good as telephone quality. The very low quality makes it lousy for music or anything else besides speech. (And no wonder—Qualcomm, who developed this codec, makes cell phones.)

- **uLaw 2:1.** Like ALaw, uLaw is a common format for exchanging sound files with Unix computers.

Rate, Size

A computer captures and plays back sound by capturing thousands of individual slices, or snapshots, of sound per second. As though describing somebody at a wine tasting, computer nerds call this process *sampling* the sound.

The two controls here let you specify how *many samples* you want the Mac to take per second (the sampling Rate) and how *much data* it's allowed to use to describe each sample (the sampling Size).

Even if that technical explanation means nothing to you, the principle is easy enough to absorb: The higher the Rate and Size settings (see Figure 12-8), the better the quality of the audio and the larger the size of the resulting QuickTime file. Here are a few examples of the kind of file-size increase you can expect for each of several popular rate and size settings. (Note that the information here is *per channel*. If you're going for stereo, double the kilobyte ratings shown here.)

- **11 kHz, 8 bits.** Sounds like you're hearing the audio track over a bad telephone connection. Tinny. Use it only for speech. 662 K per minute.

- **11 kHz, 16 bits.** Sounds a lot better. Roughly the sound quality you get from the built-in Mac speaker. 1.3 MB per minute.

- **22 kHz, 16 bits.** Starting to sound very good. Suitable for playing on a computer equipped with external speakers. 2.6 MB per minute.

- **44.1 kHz, 16 bits.** This is the real thing, the ultimate audio experience. CD-quality audio. Suitable for listening to with headphones. The ultimate storage and transmission headache, too—this much data requires 5.3 MB per minute, mono. But of course, you'd never go this far without also including the stereo experience (make that 10.6 MB per minute in stereo).

Use: Mono/Stereo

These radio buttons let you specify whether or not your movie's soundtrack is in stereo.

As noted earlier in this chapter, exporting your QuickTime movie with a stereo format is often a waste of data. Most computers that might play back your movie, including tower Power Macs and iBooks, don't *have* stereo speakers.

Furthermore, even though most camcorders include a stereo microphone, there's virtually no separation between the right and left channels, thanks to the fact that the microphone is mounted directly on the tiny camcorder. Nor does iMovie let you edit the right and left audio channels independently. Even if people are listening to your movie with stereo speakers, they'll hear essentially the same thing out of each.

Therefore, consider using the Mono setting when you're trying to minimize the amount of data required to play back the soundtrack.

The Video Codecs: A Catalog

When you decide to export your iMovie production as a QuickTime movie, you can get a great deal of control out of how the Mac produces the resulting movie file by choosing Expert from the dialog box shown in Figure 12-1, then clicking Options (Figure 12-5), and then clicking Settings (Figure 12-6). You get access to a long list of codecs.

As you can read in this listing, few of these codecs are very useful for everyday use. Many of them are designed for saving still frames (not movies), for storing your movies (not playing them), or for compatibility with very old versions of the QuickTime software. Most of the time, the Sorenson Video 3 compressor (for CD or hard drive playback) or Apple H.263 (for Internet playback) are the ones that will make you and your audience the happiest.

Note: The list of codecs that pop up in your dialog boxes may not match what you see here. Your codecs reflect the version of QuickTime that you have installed, which may be older or newer than the 6.5.2 version described here.

- **Animation.** This codec is significant because, at its Best quality setting, it maintains *all* of the original DV picture quality, while still managing to convert files so that they're smaller than files with no compression at all. (As the name implies, this codec was originally designed to process video composed of large blocks of solid colors—that is, cartoons.) The resulting file is therefore huge when compared with the other codecs described here, but not as huge as it would be if you used the None choice in this pop-up menu.

  As a result, the Animation codec is a popular format for storing or transferring QuickTime footage from one piece of video-editing software to another. Because the files are so huge, however, it's not so great as a finished movie file format.

- **Apple H.263, Apple VC H.263, H.261.** These codecs were designed for video teleconferencing (VC), in which a tiny, jerky image of you is transmitted over a telephone line to somebody who's also equipped with a video telephone. Apple's version, however, does a very good job at maintaining a good picture, while keeping the file size very small. In fact, Apple H.263 should be one of your first choices if you plan to send your video by email or post it on a Web page.

Tip: These codecs work best in footage where very little is going on—like a person sitting in front of a video telephone. The more that the frame remains the same, the better the picture quality, which is yet another argument for using a tripod whenever you can.

- **Apple Pixlet Video.** Pixlet was designed for use by a professional film company— Pixar, to be exact. Film and TV editors want to be able to edit movies with perfect frame quality and perfect frame accuracy—without having to ship gargantuan, full-resolution, multi-gigabyte files across the network or across the country.

  Pixlet is the answer. It compresses the original, film-resolution movie down to about a twentieth of its original file size, without introducing any artifacts (specks or blockiness).

  Unlike other codecs, Pixlet doesn't compress video over time; that is, it doesn't memorize one key frame and then, for the following frames, store only the information for the pixels that have changed. Pixlet stores all of the color information for every single frame. (It achieves its compression solely by compressing the color information within each frame.) The point of all this is to permit editors to scrub back and forth through a scene, stepping frame by frame if they like, and viewing full, instantaneous, half-high-definition resolution at every step. The bottom line: It's not intended for compressing iMovie masterpieces.

- **Cinepak.** This compressor produces very tiny QuickTime files. Until the invention of the Sorenson codec described below, almost all CD-ROM-bound QuickTime movies were compressed using this codec. Unfortunately, the compromises are severe: The picture quality is often greatly degraded, and the compression and saving process takes a very long time.

- **BMP, PNG, Photo-JPEG, JPEG 2000, PNG, TIFF.** You may recognize these formats as popular *still image* file formats. Remember that QuickTime is designed to be a Grand Central Station for multimedia files of all kinds—not just movies, but sound files and graphics files as well. These graphics-format options are largely irrelevant to movies. (They appear in your Compressor list because they're among QuickTime's master list of codecs, *all* of which are made available to QuickTime-savvy software programs like iMovie.)

- **Component Video.** In the era before digital video, you could convert footage from your camcorder into a digital file only if you had a *digitizing card,* an expensive circuit board for this purpose. Component Video is the format these digitizing cards used, because it could store video extremely quickly on your hard drive during the digitizing (capturing) process. It was designed for real-time recording speed, not for compression. The files it creates require huge tracts of disk space.

- **DV-PAL, DVCPRO-PAL.** These options are here so that you can export your iMovie masterpiece in the European video format (PAL), while retaining full DV size and frame rate. (DVCPRO is a slight variant of the DV format, intended for use with super-expensive professional broadcast TV video gear.)

  Unfortunately, the quality of the video suffers when you make this kind of conversion, especially in action scenes.

- **DV/DVCPRO - NTSC.** Suppose you've just completed a masterful movie, and the thought of compressing it to some much smaller, image-degraded QuickTime movie breaks your heart. You can use this codec to turn your finished, effect-enhanced, fully edited iMovie production into a new, raw DV clip, exactly like the DV clips in the Media folder in your project folder. You might do so if, for example, you wanted to import your entire movie into another DV-editing program, such as Final Cut Express or Final Cut Pro, or if you wanted to turn it into a Video CD or DVD, as described at the end of this chapter. (*DV,* of course, means digital video; NTSC is the format used in the Western Hemisphere and Japan.)

- **Graphics.** Uses a maximum of 256 colors to depict each frame. The result is grainy and blotchy. Use it only if your movie contains nothing but solid-colored images, such as cartoons, pie charts, or other computer-generated simple images. Even then, this aging codec doesn't compress the video very much.

- **Motion JPEG A, Motion JPEG B.** These codecs don't perform any temporal (frame-to-frame) compression. Each movie frame is saved as an individual, full-sized color picture. The disadvantage is, of course, that the resulting files are extremely large. In fact, you need to buy a special circuit board for your computer just to play back this kind of movie. In other words, motion JPEG is occasionally useful when editing video, but never for distributing it.

So what good is it? Motion JPEG is the format used by many professional DV-editing machines (such as those from Avid, Accom, and Discreet). Because there's no key-frame business going on, editors can make cuts at any frame. (Doing so isn't always possible in a file created by a codec that stores only the *difference* between one frame and the next. A particular frame might contain data that describes only new information, as shown in Figure 12-4.)

Tip: Motion JPEG is *not* the same thing as MPEG, which is the format used to store movies on the DVD discs you can rent from Blockbuster. Despite the similarity of names, the differences are enormous. For example, MPEG uses temporal compression and requires special software to create.

- **None.** If quality is everything to you, and disk space and Internet-ability are nothing, you can use this option, which (like the DV codecs) doesn't compress the video at all. The resulting QuickTime file may contain so much data that your computer can't even play it back smoothly. You can, however, put it in a cryogenic tank in anticipation of the day when superfast computers come your way.

- **Planar RGB.** This format is another one that's designed for use with still images, not with video. This one preserves the *alpha channel* of the graphic (a transparency

Secrets of the Sorenson Codec

Because the Sorenson Video 3 codec offers such high quality at such small file sizes, getting the most out of it has become the subject of many a Web page and Internet discussion group. A few highlights:

- When you play back a Sorenson movie in QuickTime Player (Chapter 14), you can use the Movie→Double Size command to enlarge the "movie screen." Technically, all QuickTime Player does is double the size of each pixel of each frame—but the result looks very good when compared with movies prepared by other codecs.

- Don't create key frames any more often than one per second: They take up a lot of disk space and degrade the movie quality. If your movie plays at 12 frames per second, therefore, use a number that's twelve or higher in the Key Frames box shown in Figure 12-6.

- If you're a professional, or soon to become one, $300 buys you something called the Sorenson

Video Pro codec. It offers a number of extremely technical added options that, in the right hands, lead to even better quality QuickTime movies.

For example, the Pro version generates key frames automatically at the beginning of each new cut, and offers *variable bitrate encoding*—a compression scheme whereby frames filled with motion or transitions get the most "attention" by the data in the movie, and less active frames get correspondingly less. The result is more efficient use of the movie's data—and better visual quality.

(Note, though, that only high-powered software like Cleaner and Sorenson's own Squeeze software can apply the Sorenson Pro codec. iMovie and QuickTime Player alone cannot.)

If you've ever wondered why your iMovie films, when exported as QuickTime movies, don't look quite as good as the Hollywood movie ads on the Apple Web site, now you know part of the story.

feature), so that, if you owned a fancier editing program, you could superimpose a photo on top of the video.

- **Sorenson Video, Sorenson Video 3.** Here it is—the codec that gives you very high quality with very good compression, and files so small that you can play them from a CD-ROM or even over the Internet. Sorenson-compressed movies play back on either Macs or Windows computers, too. (Use Sorenson Video 3 if possible. Use the older Sorenson Video—without a number—only if your audience might still be using some ancient version of QuickTime to play back your opus.)

- **Video.** You might think of this, one of the original QuickTime codecs, as the "fat Sorenson." The quality is very high, and it doesn't take very long to compress and save the movie in this format—but the compression is light. The resulting files aren't suitable, therefore, for transmitting on the Internet.

Tip: The Video compressor doesn't take very long to save a QuickTime file. For that reason, it's a great choice of format when you want to *test* your finished iMovie. You can see how it will look as a QuickTime movie, see how your transitions and titles will look, experiment with different frame rates, and so on.

Burning QuickTime Movie CDs

As you may have read in the previous chapter, iMovie makes it easy to preserve your masterpiece on videotape, suitable for distribution to your admiring fans. As you'll read in Chapters 15 through 18, you can retain even more of your digital quality and still reach the masses by burning your opus onto a DVD.

There is, however, an in-between step. You can also preserve your QuickTime movie files (the ones you export from iMovie using the instructions in this chapter) on a CD.

Of course, in the world of video, what's meant by "CD" varies dramatically. There have been as many different incarnations of videodiscs as there have been of Madonna. These days, if you claim to have put video on a CD, you probably mean one of these two things:

- You took some ordinary QuickTime movies and burned them onto a CD (or a DVD, for that matter), which you can play only on the computer. You insert the disc, see the icon for the QuickTime movie file, and double-click it. You then watch it in the QuickTime Player program (see Chapter 14).

- You created a *Video CD,* a weird, low-budget cousin of the DVD. A Video CD is indeed a videodisc, and it can indeed be played by many DVD players. But the quality is no better than that of a VHS videocassette. (Technically speaking, this disc contains an *MPEG-1* movie file, as opposed to the *MPEG-2* files on DVDs.)

The following discussion offers a road map for creating both kinds of "video CDs."

Burning a CD or DVD for File Storage

Having exported a QuickTime movie as described in this chapter, it may be that you simply want to store it where it isn't eating up the space on your hard drive. Or maybe you want to distribute a few of these movies to friends, but because QuickTime movies are much too big to fit on floppies or Zip disks, a CD-ROM seems like a convenient and inexpensive way to go.

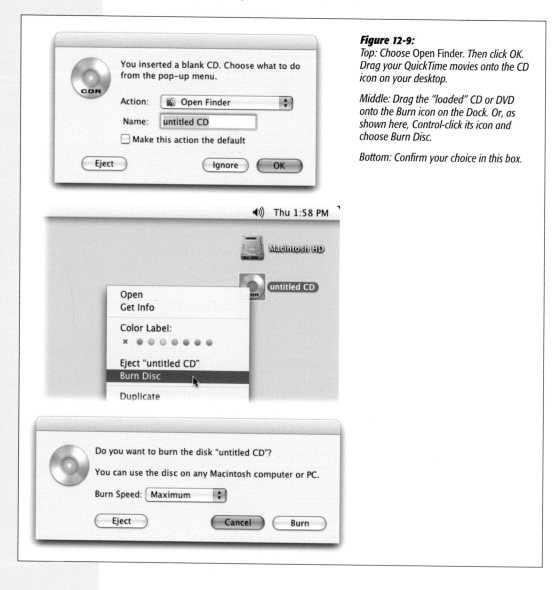

Figure 12-9:
Top: Choose Open Finder. Then click OK. Drag your QuickTime movies onto the CD icon on your desktop.

Middle: Drag the "loaded" CD or DVD onto the Burn icon on the Dock. Or, as shown here, Control-click its icon and choose Burn Disc.

Bottom: Confirm your choice in this box.

If your Mac, like all Macs made since about 2001, has a CD burner, you're good to go. This drive can accept either CD-R (recordable) discs, which can't be erased, or *CD-RW* (rewritable) discs, which are slightly more expensive than standard blank CD-R discs—but you can erase and rerecord them over and over.

In fact, if your Mac can burn DVDs (DVD-R or DVD-RW discs), you can use blank DVDs instead of CDs. Either way, the following steps show you how to use discs as data repositories for backing up your QuickTime movies and iMovie projects. The resulting disc will *not* play on a TV. (For that, see Chapter 15.)

You can buy blank CDs and DVDs very inexpensively in bulk via the Web. (To find the best prices, visit *www.shopper.com* or *www.buy.com* and search for the terms *blank CD-R* or *blank CD-RW.*)

Insert a blank disc into your Mac. After a moment, the Mac displays a dialog box asking, in effect, what you want to do with this blank CD (Figure 12-9, top).

Choose Open Finder and click OK. You'll see the disc's icon appear on the desktop after a moment (Figure 12-9, middle). At this point, you can begin dragging your QuickTime movie files or iMovie project files onto it, exactly as though it were a teeny, tiny hard drive. You can add, remove, reorganize, and rename the files on it just as you would in any standard Finder window. You can even rename the disc itself just as you would a file or folder.

When the disk contains the files you want to immortalize, do one of these things:

- Choose File→Burn Disc.

- Drag the disc's icon toward the Trash icon on the Dock. As soon as you begin to drag, the Trash icon turns into what looks like a bright yellow fallout-shelter logo. Drop the disc's icon onto it.

- Control-click the disc's icon on the Dock and choose Burn Disc from the contextual menu that appears (Figure 12-9, middle).

In any case, the dialog box shown at bottom in Figure 12-9 now appears. Click Burn. The Mac's laser proceeds to record the CD or DVD, which can take some time. Fortunately, you're free to switch into another program and continue using your Mac.

When the recording process is over, you'll have yourself a newly minted disc that you can insert into any other Mac (and most PCs, for that matter). It will show up on that computer complete with all the files and folders you put onto it.

Burning a Video CD

Now, storing your QuickTime movies on a recordable CD or DVD doesn't create a videodisc. When you do this, you're simply copying a QuickTime *file* onto another disk, exactly as though it were a Zip disk or external hard drive. You can't play the resulting disk on a DVD player attached to your TV.

A Video CD, on the other hand, is the cheap, less talented sibling of DVD. A Video CD plays back about 60 minutes of video with roughly VHS-tape quality, 352 x 240 pixels. (Some Video CD software can create *Super* Video CDs, which hold 30 minutes at higher quality.)

That's not nearly as good as the original DV video. But not everyone's Mac can burn DVDs—and all you need to burn a Video CD is a CD burner. Because Video CDs are so cheap to produce, they have a small cult following in North America—and a huge following in Asia.

Where you can play your Video CDs

Commercial Video CDs play back in most recent DVD players and some laserdisc players. (As a bonus, they also play back on any modern computer, including the Mac.) Unfortunately, only certain DVD players—those with a *dual-wavelength laser*—can play back Video CDs that *you've* created. Most recent DVD players work well with homemade Video CDs, but many older models don't recognize them.

You can, and should, check the compatibility list at *www.dvdrhelp.com/dvdplayers*. But there's no sure way to know in advance whether a particular DVD player will

Figure 12-10:
Top: If you own Toast, creating a video CD requires finding your reference movie, the .mov file shown here at bottom. Drag it into the Video panel of Toast.

Once you've loaded up Toast with movies, click the big red Record button. Toast then begins recording the video onto the CD. After about 20 minutes (depending on the speed of your burner), the deed is done. Your disc pops out of the burner like toast from a toaster. (Get it?) Now the CD is ready to play, either on your Mac or in a DVD player attached to your TV..

Reference movie, deep inside the iMovie HD project "package" play back your homemade Video CDs until you try it. Create a Video CD as described here, using the brand of blank discs that you intend to use, and then take the result to an electronics store to try it on the different DVD player models you're considering buying. (And if you already own a DVD player, insert your homemade CD and hope for the best.)

Making Video CDs with Toast

The easiest way to make a Video CD is to use Toast Titanium (*www.roxio.com*), the popular disc-burning software. (It's about $70 online.)

When your iMovie project is ready to go, save it and quit iMovie. Figure 12-10 provides all the instructions you need except for one tiny detail: finding the reference movie you're supposed to drag into the Toast window.

- If you've been editing a movie from an older version of iMovie (and it's therefore in a project *folder* as described on page 112), open that folder. The reference movie is the file whose name ends with .mov.

- If you've been editing a movie that began life in iMovie HD (or was "Save Project As"'ed out of iMovie HD), it's represented by a single icon on your hard drive. Control-click it. From the shortcut menu, choose Show Package Contents. Open the Shared→iDVD folder. Once again, the reference movie is the file whose name ends with .mov (see Figure 12-10). (For more on iMovie files vs. iMovie folders, see page 112.)

Then proceed as shown in Figure 12-10.

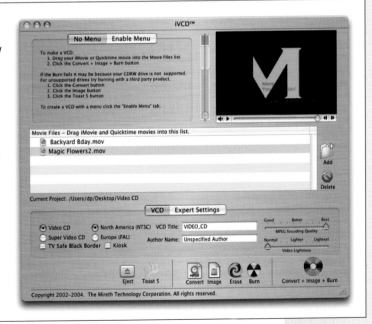

Figure 12-11:
Drag your QuickTime movies—for example, the reference .mov document in each iMovie project folder—into the iVCD list. Click Convert, Image, and Burn, as each stage finishes. iVCD does the rest.

The program costs $30, but it's free for tryout purposes. (Until you pay, a watermark appears on your finished movies when the disc plays back.)

Making Video CDs with Shareware programs

Toast is a popular commercial program, but it's not the only game in town when it comes to burning Video CDs. The shareware world has nicely filled in the gaps for people who don't regularly drop $70 on a piece of utility software.

Figure 12-11, for example, illustrates iVCD (*www.mireth.com*), an attractive Mac OS X utility ($30) for turning QuickTime movies into Video CDs.

Movies on the Web– and On the Phone

After editing your iMovie to perfection, you'll want to show it to the world. Sure, you can preserve your work on videotape (Chapter 11) or CDs (Chapter 12); that's fine if you want to make a handful of copies for a few friends.

But the big time is the Internet. This 200-million-seat megaplex is where the action is, where unknown independent filmmakers get noticed, and where it doesn't cost you a penny to distribute your work to a vast worldwide audience.

Make the Big Screen Tiny

All of the techniques described in this chapter assume that you've exported your iMovie production as a QuickTime movie (see Chapter 12).

Now, you *could* post your 24-frames-per-second, 640 x 480, stereo-CD-quality sound motion picture on your Web page. But you'd have to include instructions that say, "Please download my movie! It's only 2 GB—about five days of continuous downloading with a 56 K modem. But trust me, it's worth the wait!"

A vast audience still connects to the Internet using an ordinary telephone-line modem, such as a 28.8 K or 56 K model. These modems receive data very slowly, so they're not very well equipped for receiving video from the Internet.

If you expect anyone to actually watch your movies, therefore, you, like thousands of Internet moviemakers before you, will have to make your Web-based movies *tiny*. To make your movie watchable by people with telephone-line modems, use the Expert settings described on page 295 to specify:

- A frame size of 160 x 120

- The H.263 or Sorenson 3 codec

- A frame rate of no more than 12 frames per second

- A monaural soundtrack, not stereo

If the need to downsize your movie like this doesn't crush your artistic pride, the worst is over. Here, then, is how you can make your videos available to the universe.

Posting to Your .Mac Account

By far the easiest way to post your movies on the Internet is to use one of Apple's $100-per-year .Mac accounts (visit *www.mac.com* for details, or open System Preferences, click .Mac, and click Sign Up). A .Mac account gives you a whole raft of Internet-based services and conveniences: electronic greeting cards, synchronizing of calendars and Web bookmarks among the different Macs in your life, a backup program, an antivirus program, the ability to check your email online—and HomePage, which lets you generate your own Web page and occupy it with an iMovie movie.

In iMovie, you can post your finished masterpiece on a .Mac Web page with little more than a couple of clicks:

1. **In iMovie, choose File→Share; in the resulting dialog box, click HomePage.**

    The dialog box tells you how jerky your movie will be online (Figure 13-1).

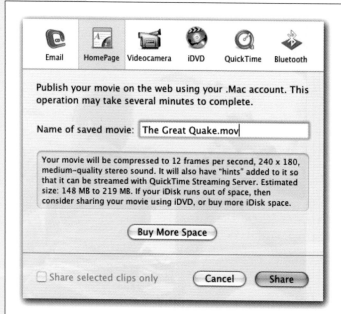

Figure 13-1:
The message here tells you just how small and jerky your movie will be on the Web—12 frames per second, 240 x 180 pixels—and how many megabytes it will occupy. (All of your Web-based movies together can't exceed your 125-megabyte iDisk account limit, unless you pay more money to Apple for more storage.)

Of course, you don't have to post the entire movie online. If you select only specific clips in iMovie before choosing the Share command, you're now offered the "Share selected clips only" checkbox, which posts only the selected stretch of your movie online.

2. **Type a name for your movie and then click Share.**

   iMovie springs into action, compressing your movie to Web proportions and up-loading it to the .Mac Web site. (This is not, ahem, a particularly quick process.)

   When the uploading is complete, your Web browser opens automatically and takes you to the .Mac sign-in page.

3. **Type your name and password. (Capitalization counts.) Click Enter.**

   The HomePage screen appears (Figure 13-2). A miniature version of the movie appears at center, and begins playing automatically for your approval and enjoyment. Farther down the page, you're offered about a dozen standard iMovie Web-page templates, such as Invite, Baby, and so on.

4. **Click the "theater" style you prefer.**

   Next you arrive at the "Edit your page" page (Figure 13-3, top).

5. **Fill in the movie title, description underneath the movie, and so on.**

   If you'd like to omit one of the proposed pieces of information (if you don't have any particular directorial notes, for example), edit it anyway, if only to delete the dummy text that appears there (see Figure 13-3).

Figure 13-2:
The "Publish your iMovie" page is a summary of the three page-preparation steps you're about to take. At this point, the most urgent task is step 3, choosing a "frame" for the movie as it will appear on the finished Web page.

Remember that your movie will occupy only a small rectangle in the center of your visitors' screens; the rest is graphic fluff to fill up the window.

6. **Click Preview to see how the Web page will look.**

   Click the triangular Play button, shown in Figure 13-3, to try playing your movie over the Internet.

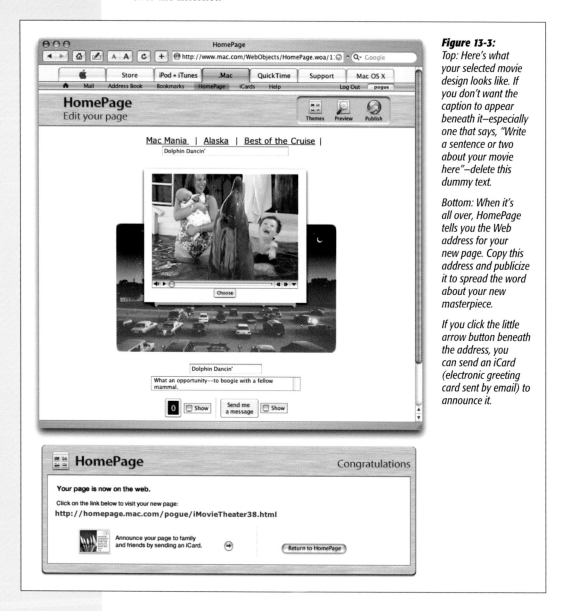

Figure 13-3:
Top: Here's what your selected movie design looks like. If you don't want the caption to appear beneath it—especially one that says, "Write a sentence or two about your movie here"—delete this dummy text.

Bottom: When it's all over, HomePage tells you the Web address for your new page. Copy this address and publicize it to spread the word about your new masterpiece.

If you click the little arrow button beneath the address, you can send an iCard (electronic greeting card sent by email) to announce it.

8. If everything looks good, click Publish.

When you click the Publish button at the top of the screen, the URL (Web address) for your Web page appears on your screen. You can copy and then email this link to anyone who'd be interested (Figure 13-3, bottom).

Tip: Unfortunately, the address is not particularly catchy; it's along the lines of *http://homepage.mac .com/YourMemberName/imovie.html.* If you'd prefer a URL that's shorter and catchier, investigate a free URL redirection service like *www.here.is.* These sites let you choose a more convenient Web address to distribute—and then they auto-forward your visitors to the longer address. (And if the *here.is* service isn't working as you read this, do your own shopping for free redirection services by searching Google for "free URL redirection.")

Finally, your Web page is now available for everyone on the Internet to see. Corporations and professional Web designers may sniff at the simplicity of the result, but it takes *them* a lot longer than ten minutes to do the same thing.

You can create as many Web pages as you want (within the space constraints of your iDisk). When you return to the HomePage screen, a list of your existing Web pages appears (complete with Edit and Delete buttons, described next). So does the Add button, which you can click to start the process of building another Web page.

Editing your Web page

To make changes to your Web site using the .Mac tools, proceed like this:

1. In your Web browser, go to *www.mac.com.* Click "Log In." Type your name and password and then click Enter.

Now you arrive at the main .Mac screen.

2. Click HomePage.

The HomePage screen appears. At the top left of the page is the list of Web pages you've created so far.

3. Click the name of the movie you want to edit, and then click the small Edit button beneath it.

You arrive at the main iMovie configuration page shown in Figure 13-3 at top, where you can change the movie you want to play (click the Choose button), the title you want to give it, and any notes you want to appear underneath it.

4. When everything looks good, click Publish.

You've just updated your Web page.

Behind the Screens

Behind the scenes, iMovie builds your movie Web site by placing new Web page (HTML) documents in the Sites folder of your iDisk (Figure 13-4). If you know how to use a Web-page creation program like Dreamweaver or even Microsoft Word, you can make changes to your Web page by editing these documents.

Other Internet "Film Festivals"

The .Mac system is very simple, and it's the ideal place to post home movies—flicks for whom the target audience is friends and family.

It's not, however, the only place to post your movies on the Web. Fueled by the recent success of independent, low-budget movies, Web sites have sprung up whose sole purpose is to accept and show independent, student, and amateur movies.

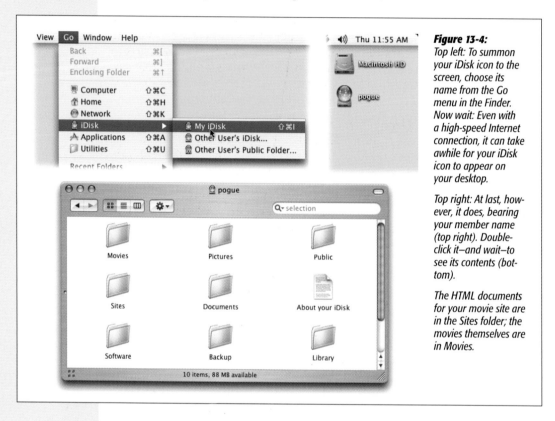

Figure 13-4:
Top left: To summon your iDisk icon to the screen, choose its name from the Go menu in the Finder. Now wait: Even with a high-speed Internet connection, it can take awhile for your iDisk icon to appear on your desktop.

Top right: At last, however, it does, bearing your member name (top right). Double-click it—and wait—to see its contents (bottom).

The HTML documents for your movie site are in the Sites folder; the movies themselves are in Movies.

A number of these sites went under during the Great Tech Industry Meltdown of 2000–2003. Those that remain have much more obvious links to commercial Hollywood studios (that is, they show ads and sell DVDs). But the independent gene is still alive within them.

Most of these sites don't accept porn or home movies. But if you've attempted anything more ambitious, you lose nothing by posting your work on the sites. There's no charge. You generally retain the rights to your movie. And if your work is great, it *will* be noticed.

Tip: Before posting your movies, watch a few of the featured movies already on these Web sites to get a feel for what people are doing and what kinds of movies each of these sites accepts. You may get more out of watching the movies that *other* people have posted than posting your own. The lessons you can learn from other amateurs and independents—both in the mistakes they make and in the clever techniques they adopt—make this book's teachings look like only Chapter 1.

For example, *www.atomfilms.com* is the big time—the most commercial and professional Web site of its kind. The site specializes in short films and animations, from 30 seconds to 30 minutes long. Your stuff has to be good to make the cut, however, as Atom posts fewer than 10 percent of the movies it receives. Its explicit purpose is to get them sold to TV producers and Hollywood studios. (Unfortunately, very few of the movies here are available in QuickTime format. Atom isn't one of the most Mac-friendly movie sites.)

www.iFilm.com is Atom's biggest rival. Since it's less fussy about what gets posted, several hundred movies are available. The odds are pretty good, then, that some of its contributors will get picked up. As made famous by *Time* magazine, two guys who made the short black comedy *Sunday's Game,* for example, were offered a TV development deal from Fox.

iFilm provides a special Web page for each movie, complete with your synopsis, credits, and feedback ratings. And the site is overflowing with special resources for filmmakers, such as news, reviews, lists of film festivals, and so on.

Tip: Want to get your movie posted—and popularized—on some of these Internet film festivals? Then make a *spoof* of a popular commercial movie. No matter how poor the quality, nor how inexpensively done, clever satires rise to the top on these sites and get thousands of viewings. *Saving Ryan's Privates, Pies Wide Shut,* and *The Sick Scents,* for example, constantly top the iFilm.com "Most Viewed" list.

Posting a Movie on Your Own Web Site

Posting movies on other people's Web pages is one thing. In many cases, however, you might prefer the control and the freedom of putting movies onto your *own* Web page, designed the way you like it.

You'll quickly discover that this process is more technical than the ones described so far in this chapter. For example, the following discussion assumes that you do, in fact, already have a Web site.

Playing the Movie in its Own Window

If you have a Web page, you're probably already familiar with the notion of *FTP* (file transfer protocol), the method you use to deposit new Web pages, graphics, and other elements onto your Web site. You do this using a program like Captain FTP or RBrowser, both of which are available for download from the "Missing CD" page at *www.missingmanuals.com.*

Setting up streaming playback

QuickTime provides a feature called Fast Start, which means that when a Web page visitor clicks your movie, he can begin to watch it before it's downloaded in its entirety. His copy of QuickTime estimates when enough movie data has been downloaded so that the whole movie can play without having to pause for additional data. The effect is a lot like the *streaming video* feature described earlier, except that there's a considerable pause as the first portion of the movie is downloaded. (On the other hand, you save thousands of dollars on the cost of specialized hardware and software that's required for a true streaming-video system.)

To take advantage of this feature, use the Expert Settings dialog box when you're creating your QuickTime movie from the iMovie project. As shown in Figure 12-5 (in the previous chapter), iMovie offers a checkbox called "Prepare for Internet Streaming." If you turn on this checkbox and choose Fast Start from the pop-up menu, iMovie automatically encodes some extra instructions into the resulting QuickTime file that permit your movie to do this "fast starting" when played back from your Web page.

Playing your movie

Once you've uploaded your iMovie, you—and everyone else on the Internet—can watch it just by typing in the correct address. If your Web site's usual address is *www.imovienut.com,* and the name of your movie file is *mymovie.mov,* then the URL (ad-

Figure 13-5
The easiest way to put a movie on your Web page is simply to upload it there. Then create a link to it. When clicked, the link makes the movie pop up in its own, separate window. Your viewers can use the Play, Stop, and scroll controls as they see fit.

dress) for your new movie is *www.imovienut.com/mymovie.mov*. (If you placed it into a folder within your Web site listing—called *flicks*, for example—then the address is *www.imovienut.com/flicks/mymovie.mov*.)

Tip: Mac and Windows computers consider capital and lowercase letters equivalent in Web addresses like these. The Unix machines that dish out Web pages by the millions, however, don't. Therefore, using only lowercase letters is a good precaution to avoid subjecting your visitors to "Web page not found" messages.

If one of your fans types this address into the Web browser or clicks a link that goes to this address, one of three things happens:

- If your visitor's computer has the *QuickTime plug-in* software installed (almost all modern Macs do), a new little movie window opens automatically. (See Figure 13-5.) A few seconds later, it begins to play automatically.

- If your visitor doesn't have this QuickTime plug-in installed, which is possible if she's using a Windows computer, a message appears onscreen. It offers three choices: Track down the necessary plug-in, download the QuickTime movie to the hard drive, or choose another program to play the movie.

Tip: To make it easier for your Windows friends to download the plug-in necessary to watch QuickTime movies, create a link on your Web page that says something like: "To watch this movie, please download the free QuickTime plug-in at *http://www.apple.com/quicktime.*"

- Some browsers have been configured to hand off all downloadable files whose names end with *.mov* to a *helper application*, such as QuickTime Player. In such cases, QuickTime Player now opens (independently from the browser), and the movie appears in its window.

UP TO SPEED

Getting a Web Site

If you want a Web site, you've got to get somebody to *host* it, somebody with a full-time, high-speed Internet connection who's willing to lend a few megs of hard drive space to hold your text, pictures, and movies. Fortunately, most Internet service providers—including America Online and EarthLink—offer a small amount of Web space at no charge. Check your ISP's Web page (or, on America Online, keyword: *MyPlace*) for rudimentary instructions on creating a Web page and posting it online. (For more detailed instructions, consider reading a book on the topic.)

If your ISP doesn't offer Web hosting, or if you need more room for your movies, you'll find hundreds or thousands of Web hosting companies only too eager to sign you up as a client. A search at *www.google.com* should unearth as many hosting services as you'd ever need.

And one more thing. If you want to share a movie with only a small circle of admirers, and you have a high-speed connection like cable modem or DSL, you can turn *your own Mac* into a Web site, thanks to the Web Sharing feature built into Mac OS X. It's very convenient, because you don't have to upload your movies to *anything*.

See *Mac OS X: The Missing Manual* for step-by-step instructions.

Creating alternate versions

If your Web hosting service makes enough hard drive space available, consider creating an alternate version of your movie for viewers who don't have the QuickTime plug-in.

For example, the Windows equivalent of QuickTime is called the *AVI* format. Using QuickTime Player Pro, described in the next chapter, you can convert your movie into an AVI file, which you can post on your Web page exactly the same way you posted the QuickTime movie. Then you can put two different links on your Web page: "Click here for the QuickTime version (Mac users)," and "Click here for the AVI version (Windows users)."

Of course, your Windows visitors won't enjoy the quicker gratification of the Fast Start feature provided by QuickTime. But you'll save them the trouble of having to download and install a special plug-in. (Creating a very tiny movie—no larger than 160 x 120 pixels, for example—is especially important when saving in AVI format. Thanks to the lack of the Fast Start feature, Windows users who don't use the QuickTime plug-in must wait for the entire movie to download before they can begin watching it.)

The HTML code

If you'd like to make the presentation of your movie a little bit more elegant, you can use the sample HTML code listed here as a template. Even if you've never programmed in the HTML language, you can simply type these codes anywhere fine Web pages are written—in Dreamweaver, BBEdit, or whatever program you use to make your Web pages.

In a pinch, you can type the following directly into TextEdit and then drag the resulting document into your Web space exactly as shown in Figure 13-4. (Of course, you should change the italicized text to match the actual address and name of your movie.)

```
<HTML>
<HEAD>
<TITLE> Watch my iMovie here!</TITLE>
</HEAD>
<BODY>
<P> Click <A HREF="http://www.myserver.com/foldername/mymovie.
mov">here</A> to watch my iMovie!</P>
<P>You'll need the free QuickTime plug-in to watch my movie in
your browser. You can also download it to your hard disk and
watch it with the free QuickTime Player.</P>
<P>You can get the QuickTime plug-in and QuickTime Player
for Mac and Windows at <A HREF="http://www.apple.com/quicktime">
http://www.apple.com/quicktime</A>. </P>
<P>Thanks for watching!</P>
</BODY>
</HTML>
```

Embedding the Movie in Your Web Page

In the previous section, you read about how to create a link that makes your movie pop up in a separate window. But the really smooth operators on the Internet scoff at such an amateur hack. It's far more elegant to create a movie that plays in place, directly on your Web page—no pop-up window necessary.

Doing so requires yet further immersion in the HTML programming language—but only up to your ankles. If you're not afraid, proceed:

The <embed> command

Creating this effect requires a few more lines of HTML code. One of them is the <embed> tag, which instructs your visitor's Web browser on how to handle media types it doesn't ordinarily know how to display (in this case, a QuickTime file). It can learn to understand QuickTime movies, however, either by relying on a helper application or a plug-in. Following the <embed> tag, you'll want to type in a variety of *embed tag attributes,* additional HTML commands that give the browser further instructions on formatting and displaying the file.

And that used to be all there was to it.

A couple of years ago, though, Microsoft pulled a switcheroo in the way it wrote its flagship Web browser, Internet Explorer. The result: millions of QuickTime movies on the Web didn't show up correctly in versions 5.5 or 6 of Internet Explorer for Windows. The following blob of code solves the problem. It embeds the movie on your page in such a way that the ugly "broken plug-in" icon will never appear, even for those long-suffering Windows users. (If they don't have a version of QuickTime that will work seamlessly, they'll see a message that offers to download and install the latest QuickTime software automatically, without having to close their browsers.)

```
<OBJECT CLASSID="clsid:02BF25D5-8C17-4B23-BC80-D3488ABDDC6B"
WIDTH="240"HEIGHT="196"

CODEBASE="http://www.apple.com/qtactivex/qtplugin.cab">

<PARAM name="SRC" VALUE="mymovie.mov">

<PARAM name="AUTOPLAY" VALUE="true">

<PARAM name="CONTROLLER" VALUE="false">

 <EMBED SRC="mymovie.mov" WIDTH="240" HEIGHT="196"
AUTOPLAY="true" CONTROLLER="false" PLUGINSPAGE="http://www.
apple.com/quicktime/download/">

 </EMBED>

</OBJECT>
```

Here's what each line means:

- **<OBJECT CLASSID=...** The OBJECT element is a giant wrapper (you'll notice that the code blob ends with another OBJECT statement) that's designed to handle the broken Windows plug-in situation described above. Don't change this long, ugly string of numbers.

- **CODEBASE=.** This line tells Windows browsers where to go to download the latest QuickTime software for Internet Explorer (called an ActiveX control) automatically, without making Internet Explorer quit and restart.

- **PARAM name=.** The next three lines tell the browser how to play the movie using ActiveX controls instead of the QuickTime plug-in, just in case the plug-in is absent or doesn't work for that browser.

- **<EMBED SRC="mymovie.mov">.** This command instructs the browser to play the QuickTime file you've uploaded to your Web site, called, in this example, *mymovie.mov.* Upon reading this instruction, the visitor's browser will check its preferences file to see how she's configured it (using the Edit→Preferences command) to handle this particular media type. If the QuickTime plug-in is installed, the browser will use it to play your movie. If not, the browser will check to see which helper application (if any) she's specified to display .mov files, and then attempt to open the file with *it.*

  If no plug-in *or* designated helper program exists, the browser simply announces that it's unable to process the mymovie.mov file. The error message lets your visitor either manually choose a helper application on her hard drive, download the QuickTime plug-in, or download the QuickTime movie file to the hard disk.

- **<WIDTH=240 HEIGHT=196>.** These attributes tell the browser the dimensions of your movie—in this case, 240 pixels wide and 196 pixels high. (If you decide not to make the QuickTime scroll bar appear, as described below, make the height 180 [the actual movie height]. The additional 16 pixels accommodate the scroll bar.)

- **<AUTOPLAY=true>.** You can set this action to either *true* or *false.* When you write *true,* the movie begins to play automatically once the browser has received enough data from the server. (This feature works only when QuickTime 4 or later is installed on your visitor's computer, and when you've turned on the Fast Start option for the movie you saved.) If it's *false,* your visitor must click the Play button.

- **<CONTROLLER>=false.** This true/false command specifies whether or not the QuickTime scroll bar (controller bar) appears at the bottom of the movie picture.

Tip: If <AUTOPLAY> is set to *false,* you should have <CONTROLLER> set to *true.* Otherwise, no one will be able to start your movie!

- <LOOP=false>. The <loop> attribute tells the plug-in to play the movie once (*false*), over and over continuously (*true*), or forwards to the end, then *backward* to the beginning, then forward to the end, and so on (*palindrome*). In most cases, you'll want to set this one to *false*. (Besides, if you've decided to make the Quick-Time controller scroll bar appear as described in the previous paragraphs, your viewers can replay the movie themselves by clicking the Play button, if they really think they missed something the first time.)

- <PLUGINSPAGE="http://www.apple.com/quicktime/download">. This handy attribute provides a hyperlink to the Web page where your visitors can download the necessary plug-in (in this case, QuickTime). It's by no means necessary to include this line of code, but it's a helpful thing to do, and can spare your viewers a lot of aggravation when they can't figure out why your movie doesn't show up on their screens.

More <embed> tag attributes

If you're kind of getting into this, here are a few more commands you can use to tweak the way your movie is presented:

- <BGCOLOR>. If you specified <width> and <height> attributes that are larger than the dimensions of the movie itself, you can specify the color of the extra background space with this attribute. You can use either the name of the color (such as *silver* or *blue*) or its *hexadecimal value* (such as *#C0C0C0* or *#0000FF*), if you know it.

- <STARTTIME> and <ENDTIME>. Using these commands, you can specify exactly which section of your movie should play, so that you don't have to subject your viewers to the entire thing. You can choose the exact start and end points for the movie, down to 1/30th of a second. Do so in the minutes:seconds:frames format that you know from using iMovie, like this:

```
<EMBED SRC="mymovie.mov" width="240" height="196" START-
TIME=1:01:01 ENDTIME="2:15:07">
```

If you don't include these commands, the movie plays from beginning to end.

- <HIDDEN>. Use this attribute if you want the *video* part of the movie to be invisible, so that only the sound plays. You don't need to modify this command with any particular number or modifier. Just include the word in the HTML line, like this:

```
<EMBED SRC="mymovie.mov" WIDTH="240" HEIGHT="196" HIDDEN>
```

- <HREF>. This attribute creates a link to another Web page that opens when your Web page visitor clicks the movie. The link can open another Web page, a picture, or even another movie, which, in turn, opens the door for the creation of elaborate, interactive, you-control-the-action-on-my-movie projects. The HTML might look like this:

```
<EMBED SRC="mymovie.mov" WIDTH="240" HREF="http://www.myserver.
com/foldername/anotherpage.html HEIGHT="196" HIDDEN>
```

- **<TARGET=QUICKTIMEPLAYER>.** This command makes the QuickTime plug-in launch the QuickTime Player program as a helper application, so that your movie will play within the QuickTime Player window instead of right there on your Web page. (If your movie opens in QuickTime Player, you give your viewers the option of enlarging the picture using the commands in the Movie menu, for example.)

This attribute works in conjunction with the <HREF> attribute, like this:

```
<HREF="mymovie.mov" TARGET=QUICKTIMEPLAYER>
```

Making a poster movie

Using the <embed> tag in conjunction with the QuickTime plug-in is great, because it lets you embed a movie directly into your Web page. Trouble is, the data for your entire movie starts downloading to your visitors' Web browsers the instant they arrive at your page. (This downloading takes place even if you turned off the Autoplay option. It's true that the movie won't start *playing* instantly, but the data will nonetheless begin transferring, so that the movie will be ready to play when your visitor *does* click the Play button.)

This automatic downloading could annoy your visitors, both because it slows their Web browsers down substantially, and because some people have wireless connections where they're charged by the *amount of data* transferred. If your movie file is

Figure 13-6:
Using poster movies is crucial if you're embedding more than one movie in a single Web page. Otherwise, your audience has no way to choose which movie they want to see. As a bonus, the poster movie scheme preloads the QuickTime plug-in software (if it's installed), which shortens the wait your visitors will experience when they finally decide to play the movie.

on the hefty side, or if you've got more than one movie on the Web page, this kind of unsolicited data-ramming could infuriate your visitors.

You can solve this problem easily enough by creating a *poster movie*, a separate movie file that contains only one single picture (see Figure 13-6). Rather than embedding the actual movie in your Web page, you can embed this poster movie, turning it into a button that downloads the real movie file when clicked.

This arrangement gives your viewers the ability to look over the Web page before deciding whether or not to download the movie in its entirety.

To make a poster movie, you can use a still image from the original iMovie file. (See Chapter 9 for instructions on exporting a single frame from your movie as a JPEG file.) Actually, any old graphic image will do, such as a JPEG or GIF file, as long as it's the right size (see page 249).

Note: In the following steps, you'll turn this still picture into a *one-frame movie*. The explanation is technical, but juicy: By turning a tiny QuickTime movie (instead of a plain JPEG or GIF file) into a poster frame, you'll force your visitors' QuickTime movie-playing plug-in to become activated as soon as they arrive at your Web page. When they then *click* your poster frame, the actual movie will begin playing promptly, having already loaded the QuickTime plug-in.

---

1. **Create a new iMovie document. Choose File→Import, then navigate to the still image, and then double-click it.**

   The image appears on your Clips pane or Movie Track, depending on your iMovie Preferences setting.

2. **Drag the graphic into your Movie Track, if it isn't already there. Set its timing to play for only one frame.**

   Instructions for specifying how long a still image should play in your movie are on page 246.

3. **Choose File→Share.**

   The Share dialog box appears.

4. **Click the QuickTime icon. From the pop-up menu, choose Expert Settings. Then click Share.**

   Now the Save dialog box appears.

5. **From the Expert pop-up menu, choose "Movie to QuickTime Movie." Then click Options.**

   The Movie Settings dialog box appears. (All of these dialog boxes and steps are described in greater depth in Chapter 12.)

6. **Click Size. Specify a height and width to match that of the actual movie.**

In other words, you want your poster frame to be exactly the same size as the movie itself.

7. **Click OK. Click Settings.**

Now the Compression Settings dialog box appears.

8. **From the top pop-up menu, choose Photo-JPEG. Specify one frame per second; click OK.**

In essence, you're creating a movie that's only one frame long. By specifying JPEG compression, you've ensured that this single frame will be as small (data-wise) as possible, for faster downloading.

9. **Click OK again. Name the movie, and then click Save.**

You might name the picture *MoviePoster.mov,* for example.

So far, so good—you've got a poster movie frame on your hard drive.

Now you need to embed this new poster movie into your Web page. The process resembles the one where you embedded the movie into the Web page, but this time, you'll need a couple of additional commands:

```
<EMBED SRC="movieposter.mov" WIDTH=240 HEIGHT=180 AUTOPLAY=TRUE
CONTROLLER=FALSE LOOP=false HREF="mymovie.mov" TARGET="myself"
PLUGINSPAGE="http://www.apple.com/quicktime/">
```

First, note that the <controller> attribute is set to *false.* Since the movie frame is just a single still picture, having a scroll bar underneath it would confuse the heck out of your visitors—and it wouldn't even work. Without the controller bar, the poster movie appears as a still image, as it should.

The attribute <HREF="mymovie.mov"> tells the browser that as soon as the visitor clicks the poster-movie image, the browser should load the mymovie.mov file.

POWER USERS' CLINIC

QuickTime Streaming Server

The Fast Start feature of QuickTime is a great feature. Without it, your movie wouldn't begin to play until its entire multimegabyte mass had been downloaded to your visitor's browser.

That's a good beginning. But in the professional world of Web video, the next step is *QuickTime streaming.* This relatively young technology lets many viewers simultaneously watch your movie in real time, live, as it's played from the host hard drive—without waiting for *anything* to download.

QuickTime streaming makes possible live *Webcasts,* such as the occasional Steve Jobs keynote speech and other historic events.

Serving up QuickTime streaming isn't something that the average Mac can do. It requires a Power Mac equipped with special streaming QuickTime software, a full-time, high-speed Internet connection, and a copy of the Mac OS X Server operating system. Apple's QuickTime Streaming Web site has the details at *www.apple.com/quicktime/servers.*

<TARGET="myself"> specifies that the new movie should load directly *in place of* the poster movie. Because the poster frame and the movie have the same <height> and <width> attributes, the movie will seamlessly appear where the poster frame used to be.

Tip: As with any graphic on any Web page, you or your Web design software should remember to *upload* the newly created poster-frame graphic. You can use Captain FTP for this purpose, for example.

Optimizing Online Movies

This chapter covers the fundamentals of putting your iMovie on the Web, but there's a lot more to online video. The next step is tweaking the movie files *themselves* to optimize them for online viewing.

When you put your movie on the Web, millions of people can see it, which is wonderful. Unfortunately, some of those people connect to the Internet using dial-up modems, some use high-speed broadband connections like cable modems and DSL, while the luckiest connect through such ultrafast pipes as T1 lines. If you had the time, hard drive space, and inclination, you could actually create *different versions* of your movie, one for each of these connection speeds. For instance, a cable modem owner would see a high-resolution, 320 x 240 movie playing at fifteen frames per second. His neighbor, dialing in on a 56 K modem, would see a 240 x 180 version (an *alternate* version) playing ten frames per second. Each person would see an appropriately sized rendition that would be as large and beautiful as that kind of Internet connection would permit.

(How does a Web page know which version of the movie to transmit? The answer lies in the QuickTime panel of System Preferences. If you click the Connection tab, you'll see the list of different connection methods—modem, DSL/Cable, and so on. You're supposed to choose the one that connects you to the Internet. When you click a movie on a Web page, the Web page computer actually asks your Mac what kind of connection speed you've got. Your Mac responds with whatever setting you've made in System Preferences.)

Performing this kind of optimization is an elaborate field of study that, as you can imagine, gets massively complicated. It requires, among other things, a program like Cleaner 6 (*www.discreet.com*). The company's Web site is worth visiting if you're interested in pursuing this degree of customization. It's absolutely teeming with information about producing online video.

Furthermore, Apple's own QuickTime Authoring Web site (*www.apple.com/ quicktime/authoring*) has some excellent tutorials on these more advanced strategies.

Movies on Your Phone

When most people hear the word movie, they think "big screen." But high-tech has marched on, small is beautiful, and suddenly we've entered an era when people are content to watch video on *very small* screens. Mind-blowing though it may seem, you can now send movies directly to the screens of certain cellphones, like the Nokia 6600, 3650, 6230, and 6630. No longer must you show people lame wallet photos of your family; you can play them *movies* of your family, right there on the street.

Unfortunately, you can't send your movies to any old cellphone—only those with *Bluetooth* that are *3GPPP-compliant.* Here's what that means:

- **Bluetooth** is a radio technology with a maximum range of 30 feet. The whole idea isn't so much networking as eliminating cables from our lives, which is an idea most people wholeheartedly support.

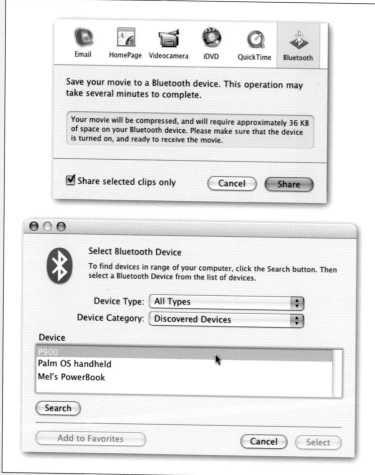

Figure 13-7:
If you're reading this, then congratulations on your very new, very cool phone—specifically, your Bluetooth-equipped, 3GPPP-compliant multimedia cellphone.

Top: On the Bluetooth pane of the Share sheet, the message tells you how much precious memory this movie will consume once transferred to your phone.

Bottom: Once you click Share, iMovie compresses the footage to within an inch of its life, and then uses your Mac's Bluetooth antenna to search for a nearby cellphone that's turned on, "discoverable," and ready to receive your masterwork. Click its name and then click Select to send the film on its merry way.

Already you can get Bluetooth—either built-in or as a plug-in USB device—for computers, printers, cellphones, cellphone headsets, Palm and PocketPC organizers, Sony camcorders, and so on. Apple's wireless keyboard and mouse both rely on Bluetooth.

All iMovie cares about, though, is whether or not your Mac has Bluetooth—many models do, including all PowerBooks—and whether your cellphone does. (Technically, iMovie can send movies to more than just phones and Macs; it can send to palmtops, too. At the moment, though, there aren't any 3GPP palmtops.)

- **3GPP** is a video standard for cellphones. (It stands for Third Generation Partnership Program, since you asked.) If your Bluetooth phone is fairly recent, it may be 3GPP-compliant, but check with your cell company.

The phone has to have a movie-playing program on board, too; all 3GPP videophones do.

If you're suitably equipped, here's how the transfer goes:

1. **When your movie is fully edited, save it. Choose File→Share.**

   The Share sheet appears, as shown at top in Figure 13-7.

2. **Click the Bluetooth icon on the toolbar.**

   As usual when you export a movie, you can turn on "Share selected clips only" if you want to send only a piece of your movie (and you highlighted the appropriate clips before choosing File→Share).

3. **Click Share.**

   iMovie takes quite awhile to compress your movie. Of course, ordinarily iMovie strives to maintain the best quality possible, with high resolution, full TV-screen size, CD-quality stereo sound, and so on. But for a phone, you want super-compressed, ultra-tiny, monophonic movies, and converting from the high-res format to the low-res one takes some time.

   When the compression is complete, the Select Bluetooth Device dialog box appears (Figure 3-7, bottom). Make sure your phone is turned on. Make sure, too, that in its Bluetooth settings, Bluetooth is turned on and *discoverable*, meaning that your Mac can "see" it.

4. **Click Search.**

   After a moment, your phone's name appears in the list.

5. **Click the phone's name, and then click Select.**

That's all there is to it. On the phone's screen, you'll probably see a message to the effect that it's receiving a file. After a while, the movie's transmission will be complete. Open the phone's media-playing program and play away.

Tip: iMovie stores a copy of the super-compressed movie in your project folder→Shared→Bluetooth folder. Its file name ends with .3gp.

If you're ever inclined to send that movie again—to one of your many other friends who have 3GPP-compliant, Bluetooth phones—you can shoot it right over without having to wait for iMovie to crunch the thing down to pocket size, thus eliminating step 3 above. Use the Bluetooth File Exchange program in your Applications →Utilities folder to do it.

QuickTime Player

I f iMovie is the program on your hard drive that's the master of *DV* files, its sibling software, the corresponding master of traditional *QuickTime* movies, is QuickTime Player, a small, free program that comes with every Macintosh. It usually comes filed in the Applications→QuickTime folder. It does three things very well: show pictures, play movies, and play sounds (Figure 14-1).

If you're willing to pay $30, you can upgrade your copy of QuickTime Player to the Pro version. Doing so grants you a long list of additional features, most notably the ability to *edit* your QuickTime movies, not just watch them.

There are two reasons QuickTime Player is worth knowing about. First, if you turn your iMovie projects into QuickTime movies (Chapter 12), QuickTime Player is the program you'll probably be using to play them on your screen. Second, the Pro version acts as an accessory toolkit for iMovie, offering you the chance to perform several tricky editing maneuvers you couldn't perform with iMovie alone.

This chapter covers both versions of the program, using QuickTime 6 for illustration purposes.

QuickTime Player (Free Version)

The free version of QuickTime Player is designed exclusively to *play* movies and sounds. You can open a movie file by double-clicking it, by dragging it onto the QuickTime Player icon, or by opening QuickTime Player and then choosing File→ Open. As shown in Figure 14-1, a number of controls help you govern the movie's playback:

- **Audio level meters.** This tiny graph dances to indicate the relative strength of various frequencies in the soundtrack, like the VU meters on a stereo. If you don't see any dancing going on, then you've opened a movie that doesn't have a soundtrack.

- **Q button.** Click this peculiar, spherical button to summon QuickTime TV—the icons of Web sites that provide video feeds, as described below.

- **Resize handle.** Drag diagonally to make the window bigger or smaller.

Tip: When you drag the resize handle, QuickTime Player strives to maintain the same *aspect ratio* (relative dimensions) of the original movie, so that you don't accidentally squish it. If you want to squish it, however (perhaps for the special effect of seeing your loved ones as they would look with different sets of horizontal and vertical genes), press Shift as you drag.

If you press Option while dragging, meanwhile, you'll discover that the movie frame grows or shrinks in sudden jumping factors of two—twice as big, four times as big, and so on. On slower Macs, keeping a movie at an even multiple of its original size ensures smoother playback.

- **Scroll bar.** Drag the diamond (or, in the Pro version, the black triangle) to jump to a different spot in the movie.

Tip: You can also press the right and left arrow keys to step through the movie one frame at a time. If you press *Option*-right or -left arrow, you jump to the beginning or end of the movie. In the Pro version, Option-arrow also jumps to the beginning or ending of a selected stretch of the movie.

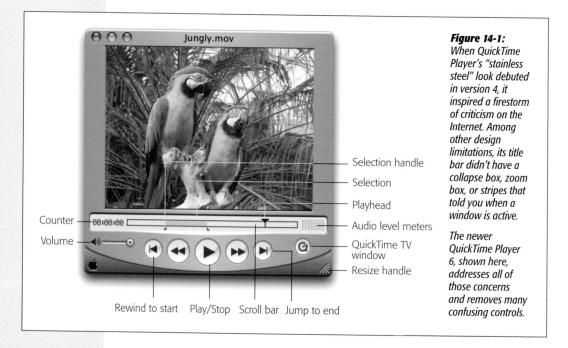

Figure 14-1:
When QuickTime Player's "stainless steel" look debuted in version 4, it inspired a firestorm of criticism on the Internet. Among other design limitations, its title bar didn't have a collapse box, zoom box, or stripes that told you when a window is active.

The newer QuickTime Player 6, shown here, addresses all of those concerns and removes many confusing controls.

- **Play/Stop button.** Click once to start, and again to stop. You can also press the Space bar, Return key, or ⌘-right arrow for this purpose. (Or avoid the buttons altogether and double-click the movie itself to start or stop playback.)

Tip: You can make any movie play automatically when opened, so that you avoid clicking the Play button. To do so, choose QuickTime Player→Preferences→Player Preferences, and turn on "Automatically play movies when opened."

- **Selection handles.** These tiny black triangles appear only in the $30 Pro version. You use them to select, or highlight, stretches of footage.

- **Volume.** If you like, you can make the soundtrack louder or softer by dragging this slider with your mouse or clicking in its "track." You may find it easier, however, to press the up or down arrow keys.

FREQUENTLY ASKED QUESTION

QuickTime Player vs. QuickTime Player Pro

Every time I launch QuickTime Player, I get this stupid ad about upgrading to QuickTime Pro. How can I get rid of it?

Easy one. Click Later, and then Quit QuickTime Player. Open System Preferences; click Date & Time. Reset your Mac to a date far beyond its obsolescence point—the year 2020, for example. (If necessary, turn off "Use a network time server" on the Network Time tab first.) Close the window.

The next time QuickTime Player shows its ad (which it does only once a day), click the Later button for the very last time. Quit the program, reset your clock to the correct date, and enjoy the fact that you've played a little trick on the program's calendar-watching feature. You'll never see the ad again—at least not until 2020.

All these shenanigans are only necessary, of course, if you've decided not to upgrade to QuickTime Player Pro, whose additional editing playback and exporting features are documented in this chapter.

For $30, Apple will sell you a password that turns your copy of QuickTime Player into QuickTime Player Pro. (To obtain this password, call 888-295-0648, or click the Upgrade Now button to go online to *www.apple.com/quicktime/buy*.)

To record your password, choose QuickTime Player→ Preferences→Registration. Your password gets stored in your Home folder→ Library→Preferences folder, in a file called QuickTime Preferences. (Remember that when you upgrade to a new Mac.)

Once you've upgraded, you gain several immediate benefits—not the least of which is the permanent disappearance of the "upgrade now" advertisement. Now QuickTime Player is QuickTime Player Pro, and it's capable of editing your movies, as described later in this chapter. It can also import many more sound and graphics formats, and—via the File→Export command—convert sounds, movies, and graphics into other formats.

QuickTime

Export in dozens of file formats.

Why Go Pro? | Get QuickTime Pro Now | Later

Tip: To mute the sound, click the little speaker icon, or press Option-down arrow. Press Option-up arrow to make the volume slider jump to full-blast position.

- **Counter.** In hours:minutes:seconds format, this display shows how far your diamond cursor has moved into the movie.

  If you have QuickTime Pro, the counter reveals the position of the selection handle you've most recently clicked (if any).

- **Rewind, Fast Forward.** By clicking one of these buttons and keeping the mouse button pressed, you get to speed through your movie backward or forward, complete with sound. This is a terrific way to navigate your movie quickly, regardless of whether you're using QuickTime Player or QuickTime Player Pro.

- **Jump to Start, Jump to End.** These buttons do exactly what they say: scroll to the beginning or end of your movie. In the Pro version, they can also jump to the beginning and ending of the selected portion of the movie (if any). All of this, in other words, is exactly the same as pressing the Option-left arrow or -right arrow keys.

Tip: Try minimizing a QuickTime Player window while a movie is playing. It shrinks to the Dock—and *keeps on playing.* Do this enough times, and you'll know what it's like to be Steve Jobs on stage.

Hidden controls

Don't miss the Movie→Show Video Controls and Movie→Show Sound Controls commands. As shown in Figure 14-2, they let you fine-tune the video and audio you're experiencing.

Tip: Clicking the tiny, grayed-out grid to the right of the scroll bar is a quicker alternative to choosing Movie→ Show Audio Controls.

Video controls

Sound controls

Figure 14-2:
Click the word Brightness to summon the Contrast or Tint sliders. Drag your mouse across the vertical bars to adjust the picture accordingly. (The Sound controls replace the scroll bar.) When you're finished adjusting the balance, bass, or treble, choose Movie→Hide Sound Controls to make the scroll bar return.

Fancy playback tricks

Nobody knows for sure what Apple was thinking when it created some of these additional features—exactly how often do you want your movie to play backward?—but here they are. Some of these features are available only in the unlocked Pro version of QuickTime Player, as indicated below.

- **Change the screen size.** Using the Movie menu commands, such as Double Size and Fill Screen, you can enlarge or reduce the actual "movie screen" window. Making the window larger also makes the movie coarser, because QuickTime Player simply doubles the size of every dot that was present in the original. Still, when you want to show a movie to a group of people more than a few feet away from the screen, these larger sizes are perfectly effective.

- **Play more than one movie.** You can open several movies at once and then run them simultaneously. (Of course, the more movies you try to play at once, the jerkier the playback gets.)

  As a sanity preserver, QuickTime Player plays only one soundtrack—that of the movie you most currently clicked. If you really want to hear the cacophony of all the soundtracks being played simultaneously, choose QuickTime Player→ Preferences, and turn off "Play sound in frontmost player only." (The related checkbox here, "Play sound when application is in background," controls what happens when you switch out of QuickTime Player and into another program.)

Tip: If you have Player Pro, you can use the Movie→Play All Movies command to begin playback of all open movies at the same instant. It's a handy way to compare the quality of two or more copies of the same exported movie, each prepared with a different codec.

- **Play the movie backward.** You can play the movie backward—but not always smoothly—by pressing ⌘-left arrow, or by Shift-double-clicking the movie itself. (You must keep the Shift button pressed to make the backward playback continue.) There's no better way to listen for secret subliminal messages.

- **Loop the movie.** When you choose Movie→Loop and then click Play, the movie plays endlessly from beginning to end, repeating until you make it stop. (Loop Back and Forth makes it loop backward again, from end to beginning.)

- **Play a selection (Pro only).** Movie→Play Selection Only, of course, plays only what you've highlighted on the scrubber bar.

- **Play every frame (Pro only).** If you try to play a very large movie that incorporates a high frame rate (many frames per second) on a slow Mac, QuickTime Player skips individual frames of the movie. In other words, it sacrifices smooth motion in order to maintain synchronization with the soundtrack.

  But if you choose Movie→Play All Frames and then play the movie, QuickTime Player says, "OK, forget the soundtrack—I'll show you every single frame of the movie, even if it isn't at full speed." You get no sound at all, but you do get to see each frame of the movie.

QuickTime Player Pro

If you've spent the $30 to upgrade to the Pro version of QuickTime Player, you've unlocked a number of additional features. Some of these are playback tricks described in the previous section; others are especially useful for iMovie work. Read on.

Presenting Your Movies

After going to the trouble of editing down your footage (as described in Part 2) and exporting it as a QuickTime movie (as described in Chapter 12), what you may want to do most of all is to *show* the movie to other people. Even the non-Pro version of QuickTime Player can play movies, of course, but the Pro version offers a much better showcase for your work: the Movie→Present Movie command.

"Presenting" your movie is the best possible way to view a QuickTime movie on your screen. When you use this command (Figure 14-3), QuickTime Player blacks out the screen, automatically magnifies your monitor image (by choosing a lower resolution) so that the movie fills more of the screen, and devotes all the Mac's power to playing the movie smoothly. (To interrupt the movie, press ⌘-period.)

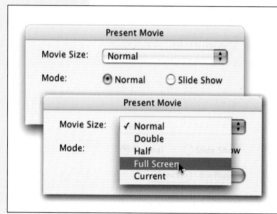

Figure 14-3:
The Present Movie command makes the movie fill your screen (although enlargement makes the movie grainier and coarser).

Editing Movies

The most powerful feature you gain in the Pro version is its ability to *edit* QuickTime movies. You can rearrange scenes, eliminate others, and save the result as a new movie with its own name.

All of this is perfectly possible within iMovie itself, of course, but sometimes you'll want to edit one of the QuickTime movies you've already exported from iMovie—to make it shorter for emailing, for example.

Tip: QuickTime Player can open and edit DV clips, which is iMovie's format. In fact, you can drag any clip directly out of iMovie (either the Movie Track or the Clips pane) directly onto the QuickTime Player icon on your Dock, if it's there. (If not, you can drag the clip out of iMovie's window and onto the desktop; double-clicking opens it up in QuickTime Player.) This trick may come in handy if you want to edit a clip you've already imported, using some feature that's available only in QuickTime Player but not in iMovie.

Selecting footage

Before you can cut, copy, or paste footage, QuickTime Player needs to provide a way for you to specify *what* footage you want to manipulate. Its solution: the two tiny gray triangles beneath the horizontal scroll bar, visible in Figure 14-4. These are the "in" and "out" points, exactly like the crop handles in iMovie. By dragging these triangles, you're supposed to enclose the scene you want to cut or copy.

Tip: You can gain more precise control over the selection procedure shown in Figure 14-4 by clicking one of the triangles and then pressing the right or left arrow key, exactly as when using the Scrubber bar under iMovie's Monitor window. Doing so expands or contracts the selected chunk of footage by one frame at a time.

You may also prefer to select a piece of footage by Shift-clicking the Play button. As long as you hold down the Shift key, you continue to select footage. When you release the Shift key, you stop the playback, and the selected passage appears in gray on the scroll bar.

Once you've highlighted a passage of footage, you can proceed as follows:

- Jump to the beginning or end of the selected footage by pressing Option-right or -left arrow key. (This doesn't work if one of the handles is highlighted.)

- Deselect the footage by dragging the two triangles together again.

- Play only the selected passage by choosing Movie→Play Selection Only. (The other Movie menu commands, such as Loop, apply only to the selection at this point.)

- Drag the movie picture out of the Player window and onto the desktop, where it becomes a *movie clipping* that you can double-click to view.

- Cut, copy, or clear the highlighted material using the commands in the Edit menu.

Tip: If you paste some copied text directly into QuickTime Player Pro, you get a 2-second title (such as an opening credit) at the current frame, professionally displayed as white type against a black background (Figure 14-4). QuickTime Player automatically uses the font, size, and style of the text that was in the text clipping. You can paste a graphic image, too; again, you get a 2-second "slide" of that still image.

If you find it easier, you can also drag a text or picture *clipping file* directly from the desktop into the QuickTime Player window; once again, you get a two-second insert. To make the text or picture appear longer than 2 seconds, drag or paste it several times in a row.

In either case, you specify the fonts, sizes, and styles of your low-budget titling feature by formatting the text that way *before* you copy it from your word processor. (This feature requires a word processor that preserves such formatting on the Clipboard. Stickies, TextEdit, Word, AppleWorks, and America Online are all examples.)

Pasting footage

After cutting or copying footage, you can move it elsewhere in the movie. Specify where you want the pasted material to go by first clicking or dragging in the horizontal scroll bar, so that the black Playhead marks the spot; then choose Edit→Paste. The

---

selection triangles (and their accompanying gray scroll bar section) show you where the new footage has appeared. (That makes it easy for you to promptly choose Edit→ Cut, for example, if you change your mind.)

By pressing secret keys, moreover, you gain three clever variations of the Paste command. They work like this:

- If you highlight some footage before pasting, and then press Shift, you'll find that the Edit→Paste command has changed to become Edit→Replace. Whatever footage is on your Clipboard now *replaces* the selected stretch of movie.

- If you press Option, the Edit→Clear command changes to read Trim. It's like the Crop command in iMovie, in that it eliminates the outer parts of the movie—the pieces that *aren't* selected. All that remains is the part you first selected.

- If you highlight some footage, and then press Option, the Edit→Paste command changes to read Add. This command adds whatever's on the Clipboard so that it plays *simultaneously* with the selected footage—a feature that's especially useful when you're adding a *different kind* of material to the movie (see Figure 14-4).

- If you highlight some footage and then choose Edit→Add Scaled, whatever you're pasting gets stretched or compressed in time so that it fits the highlighted region, speeding up or slowing down both audio and video. The effect can be powerful, comical, or just weird. (Can you say, "Alvin and the Chipmunks"?)

Tip: You can edit sounds exactly as you edit movies, using precisely the same commands and shortcuts. Use the File→Open command in QuickTime Player Pro to locate a sound file you want to open. It opens exactly like a QuickTime movie, except with only a scroll bar—no picture.

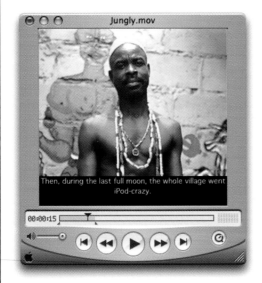

Figure 14-4:
QuickTime Player Pro has a little-known subtitling feature, complete with freedom of type style. Copy some formatted text from a word processor; highlight a slice of footage in QuickTime Player; and choose Edit→Add. The copied text appears as a subtitle on a black band, beneath the picture, as shown here.

Exporting Edited Movies

After you've finished working on a sound or movie, you can send it back out into the world in any of several ways.

The Save As command

If you choose Edit→Save As, you're offered only two options, both of which can be confusing:

- **Save normally.** The term "normally" is a red herring. You'll almost never want to use this setting, which produces a very tiny file that contains no footage at all. Instead, it's something like an alias of the movie you edited. An edited file that you "save normally" works only as long as the original, unedited movie remains on your hard drive. If you try to email the newly saved file, your unhappy recipient won't see anything at all.

- **Make movie self-contained.** This option produces a new QuickTime movie—the one you've just finished editing. Although it consumes more disk space, it has none of the drawbacks of a "save normally" file.

The Export command

Usually, your primary interest in using QuickTime Pro will be to export its edited clip, either for use in iMovie or to use in other programs (PowerPoint, Web pages, and so on).

When you find yourself in that situation, choose File→Export. The resulting dialog box should look familiar: It's the Expert Settings dialog box that appears when you save an iMovie project as a QuickTime movie (page 295). This is your opportunity to specify the size, frame rate, color depth, special effects, and many other aspects of the movie you're about to spin off.

This is also where you can convert the QuickTime movie into some other format: AVI (Windows movie) format, Image Sequence (which produces a very large collection of individual graphics files, one per frame), and so on—or convert only the soundtrack to AIFF, System 7, or WAV (Windows) formats, for example.

How to Use QuickTime Player with iMovie

But as an iMovie fan, what you'll probably want to do the most is open your iMovie clips in QuickTime Player Pro, make changes to them, and then save them for further use in iMovie.

In that case, you'll probably adopt a routine like this.

1. **Make sure QuickTime Player Pro is represented on your screen.**

   That is, make sure its icon is on your Dock, or else just open QuickTime Player so that it's running.

2. **In iMovie, drag the clip you want to edit directly onto QuickTime Player's Dock icon.**

You can drag the clip from either the Movie Track or the Clips pane, and you can also drag it into the QuickTime Player window, if it's visible. Either way, the movie clip opens before you. Edit it as described in this chapter. (The following pages walk you through some rather spectacular special-effect edits.)

When you're finished, go on:

3. **Choose File→Export. In the "Save exported file as" dialog box, use the Export pop-up menu to choose "Movie to DV Stream."**

   Technically, iMovie can import any kind of QuickTime movie. But you've just created a real, live DV clip, in its original quality, exactly the kind iMovie works with.

4. **Save the file to the desktop.**

   You're not allowed to save the file over the original iMovie clip, since QuickTime Player considers it still "in use." (That's a good thing, too. Imagine shortening a clip by a few seconds behind iMovie's back—and then reopening the project! Chaos would reign.)

5. **Switch back to iMovie. Choose File→Import, then navigate to the desktop and open the edited movie.**

   It becomes a new iMovie clip, which you can use to replace the original, if you like. After the import, you can delete the one you saved to the desktop in step 4.

Advanced QuickTime Pro: Track Tricks

As far as QuickTime Player is concerned, a piece of footage is nothing more than parallel *tracks* of information: audio and video. Most movies have only two tracks—one video and one soundtrack—but there's nothing to stop you from piling on multiple audio tracks, overlapping video tracks, and even specialized layers like a text track or an animation track.

The key to understanding the multiple simultaneous tracks in a QuickTime movie is the set of three commands in the Edit menu:

- **Extract Tracks.** This command brings up the dialog box like the one shown at the top in Figure 14-5, which shows you a list of all the tracks in your movie. "Extract" actually means *copy*; double-click the name of the track you want to copy into a new Player window. (If you double-click a soundtrack, it appears as nothing but a scroll bar with no picture.) At this point, you can copy some or all of the extracted track, in readiness to paste it into another movie.

- **Delete Tracks.** As the name implies, this command brings up a dialog box in which you can double-click the name of a track that you want to remove from the movie. For example, after experimenting to see which of several soundtracks you prefer (as described next), you'll want to delete the rejected versions before you save the final movie.

- **Enable Tracks.** This fascinating command highlights an intriguing feature of QuickTime Player Pro—its ability to embed more than one audio or video track into a single movie. If you really wanted to, you could create a movie with six different soundtracks, all playing simultaneously.

  The trick to inserting a new audio track is to press Option as you open the Edit menu. When you do so, the Paste command magically turns into the Add command. Choosing it inserts the new audio track into the selected portion of the movie. When you choose Edit→Enable Tracks, you'll see a list of all of the movie's tracks.

Tip: Suppose you've created two different versions of a movie—one with throbbing, insistent background music, and one with New Age noodling. By choosing Edit→Enable Tracks and then clicking the On/Off buttons beside the track names (Figure 14-5), you can quickly and easily try watching your movie first with one soundtrack, and then with the other.

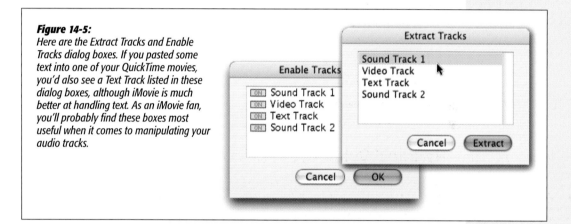

Figure 14-5:
Here are the Extract Tracks and Enable Tracks dialog boxes. If you pasted some text into one of your QuickTime movies, you'd also see a Text Track listed in these dialog boxes, although iMovie is much better at handling text. As an iMovie fan, you'll probably find these boxes most useful when it comes to manipulating your audio tracks.

Now that you know the general workflow, here are a few recipes that illustrate how iMovie + QuickTime Player Pro = Fun and Creativity.

Flip a Clip

So you caught some prize-winning footage of a twister ripping through your county—while lying prone under your pickup truck, with the camcorder upside-down on the ground? How will you ever sell that clip to the local news stations?

By fixing it first:

1. **Open the clip in QuickTime Player Pro.**

   See the steps on page 343.

2. **Choose Movie→Get Movie Properties (⌘-J).**

   The Properties dialog box appears—a tiny little box with a huge assortment of movie-editing powers (shown at top right in Figure 14-6). The first pop-up menu lists all of this movie's tracks, so that you can operate on each one independently.

CHAPTER 14: QUICKTIME PLAYER

3. **From the first pop-up menu, choose Video Track. From the second, choose Size.**

You can do a lot more than just resize the frame for this video track:

4. **Click the Flip Vertical button (the second button in the row of four that are visible in Figure 14-6).**

As you watch, your entire video picture flips upside-down—or, in this example, right-side up. The other buttons here would flip the entire picture horizontally or rotate it 90 degrees.

5. **Send the edited movie back to iMovie as described on page 344.**

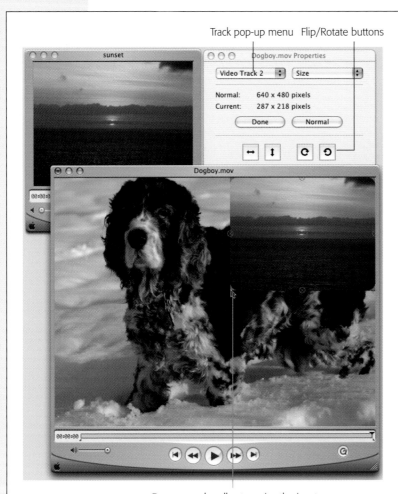

Track pop-up menu   Flip/Rotate buttons

Figure 14-6:
QuickTime Player can create very fancy picture-in-picture effects. After copying footage from a second movie (upper left), paste it over the first movie (bottom), and then use the Properties dialog box (top right) to shrink it enough to reveal what's underneath.

Drag corner handles to resize the inset

Now, this is a goofy example, of course, because you could have just used the Mirror effect in iMovie to flip a picture upside-down. But consider this a training exercise.

Picture-in-Picture

Ever wonder how news channels manage to show a video *inset*—a little TV picture floating in the corner of the bigger TV picture, just over the anchorperson's shoulder (Figure 14-6)?

It's a piece of cake in more advanced programs like Final Cut Express and Final Cut Pro, and it's even possible in iMovie with the help of some shareware add-ons (page 177). But the following steps show you how to simulate that effect for free:

1. **Open the newscaster clip in QuickTime Player Pro.**

   See the steps on page 343. (Of course, you can put *any* video on top of *any* video. This newscaster thing is just an example.)

2. **Choose File→Open Movie in New Player. Open the second clip, the one that will appear in the smaller, picture-in-picture frame.**

   It appears in its own window.

3. **Copy as much of it as you want.**

   If you want the whole thing, choose Edit→Select All, then Edit→Copy.

4. **Switch back to the newscaster window. Click in the scroll bar where you'll want the video insert to appear.**

   If you want it to occupy only a certain number of seconds, use the triangles beneath the scroll bar to highlight that stretch.

5. **While pressing Option, choose Edit→Add.**

   Or, if you chose a stretch of footage in step 4, choose Edit→Add Scaled instead. (Keep in mind that QuickTime Player will stretch or shorten the pasted material to fit the selected region.)

   Either way, the pasted video now appears on top of the newscaster, covering him up. (Your Playhead is at the end of it; press the left arrow a few times to back up so that you can see it.) In the next steps, you'll shrink this overlaid video track so that it's no longer obscuring the main character.

6. **Choose Movie→Get Movie Properties (⌘-J).**

   The Properties dialog box appears.

7. **From the first pop-up menu, choose Video Track 2. From the second, choose Size (top right in Figure 14-6). Click Adjust.**

   A red rectangle appears around the pasted video, which you can manipulate in fantastic ways. For example, **drag a red corner handle inward** to make the overlay smaller. **Option-drag** to make the inset snap to one-quarter size. **Shift-drag** a corner handle to constrain your drag horizontally or vertically. **Drag inside** the inset to move it around, **drag from the red center dot** to rotate it, or **drag one of the red edge circles** to slant the picture, distorting it.

Unfortunately, there's no key you can press to make the inset maintain its original proportions as you drag. You'll have to drag a corner freehand, watching the Size palette's pixel readout until the inset is a perfect fraction of its original size.

8. **When the inset looks the way you like it, click Done in the Properties palette.** Export your clip back to iMovie as described on page 344.

The Video Wall

QuickTime Player isn't fussy. It's perfectly happy to accept two, three, four, or more videos, all pasted into the same clip. You can move, scale, and shrink them independently, creating a video-wall effect like the one shown in Figure 14-7.

To create this effect, just repeat the preceding steps, over and over again. The trick, of course, is keeping track of which videos are on top, so that you can control the overlapping.

Actually, it's not terribly difficult if you have good concentration and an assistant with a notebook; see Figure 14-7.

Figure 14-7:
Each time you paste another layer of video, it becomes a new track, listed independently in the Properties palette. (You might want to rename each track to help you keep them straight. You can do that by choosing General from the upper-right pop-up menu, and then clicking Rename.)

To specify the front-to-back layering order of your video tiles, choose a layer's name, and then choose Layers from the upper-right pop-up menu. Use the Layer control arrows, shown here, to move this video track closer to the top than the one you want it to cover up. Just remember that higher-numbered tracks cover up lower-numbered ones.

Part Four:
iDVD 5

4

From iMovie to iDVD

i DVD is the software that lets you turn your iMovie movies and iPhoto slideshows into Hollywood-style DVDs that people can watch on their TVs. Visions of Block-buster may dance in your head, because as you'll see in the following chapters, iDVD 5 is loaded with enhancements that help you make your personal DVD look even more like a commercial Hollywood DVD than ever before.

iDVD lets you add menus, playback controls, and other navigation features to your iMovie movies, resulting in dynamic, interactive DVDs that look amazingly professional. iDVD handles the technology; you control the style.

The software requirement is iDVD. The hardware requirement is a DVD recording drive, preferably an Apple SuperDrive built into your Mac.

Note: The word is *preferably* a built-in SuperDrive, because you don't necessarily need one. For starters, you can do the design work on a Mac that doesn't have a DVD burner, and then burn the actual disc on another machine later. That's a great feature in, for example, school computer labs that have 12 Macs but only two that can burn DVDs. (For step-by-step instructions, see page 445.) Furthermore, now you can even use external, non-Apple DVD burners to create DVDs. See page 450.

Why iDVD?

You already know from Chapter 11 that you can export your finished iMovie project back to a good old VHS cassette, one of the world's most sure-fire distribution methods. Anyone who doesn't have a VCR in this day and age probably wouldn't appreciate your cinematic genius anyway.

But preserving your work on a DVD gives you a boatload of benefits:

- **DVD blanks are inexpensive.** In fact, blank DVDs nowadays are cheaper than VHS tapes.

- **DVDs are durable.** VHS tapes begin to deteriorate in 10 to 15 years. DVDs, though, are built to last—up to a century or more, if you believe the manufacturers. Store your recordable DVDs in a dark, cool, dry place, avoid flexing them, and they'll last a lifetime. (Your DVD player will stop working before the discs do!)

Tip: They'll last, that is, *if* you stick to buying brand-name blanks like Verbatim and Imation. Cheaper brands don't use the same amount of organic dyes and are more likely to suffer premature deaths.

- **DVDs are compact.** You can store your DVD collection in small, convenient DVD jewel boxes or in soft, protective loose-leaf sheaths—and you can cram hundreds of them into the space occupied by only 25 video tapes.

- **DVDs never need rewinding.** No one ever had to pay Blockbuster for not rewinding a DVD. In fact, you can skip around a DVD almost instantaneously using the navigation buttons on your DVD player's remote control.

- **DVDs are cheap to ship.** DVDs cost less to ship than a VHS tape, and no wonder. They take up less room. They weigh less. They're more rigid and have zero moving parts.

Still, there are reasons to pause before committing your work to DVD. For one thing, homemade DVDs don't work in as many DVD players as commercially pressed discs do. Stick an iDVD production into an older DVD player, and you may see the dreaded "No Disc" message on the TV screen. (In this regard, DVD-RW discs—the ones that you can erase and re-record over and over—are worse than DVD-Rs, which you can record on only once.)

DVD players sold since 2002 are generally a safe bet, but check the master player compatibility list at *www.videohelp.com* if you're ever in doubt. (Some players are fussy about which DVD-R brand discs they'll play, too. Here again, sticking with brand names like Verbatim is your best bet.)

Getting iDVD 5

If you have iMovie HD, that means you also have iDVD 5, because they both come on the same iLife DVD from Apple.

In addition to a DVD burner, iDVD requires a Mac with a 733 MHz G4 or faster processor, plus 256 MB of memory or more…preferably *a lot* more. Few programs rely on computing horsepower as much as iDVD, so faster computers work a lot better than slow ones.

iDVD 5 also requires Mac OS X 10.3.4 or later to run, and 10.3.6 or later to create widescreen DVDs.

What You're in For

In the following chapters, you can read about using iDVD *manually*, where you can integrate movies, still pictures, and sound in very flexible ways. But especially at first, most people take one of the two simplest approaches: (a) create the movie in iMovie, and then hand it off to iDVD, or (b) burn your DVD directly using the new OneStep DVD process (page 381).

This chapter guides you through the five broad steps of using iMovie and iDVD together:

1. **Prepare your audio, video, and pictures.**

   In addition to movies, iDVD can incorporate audio and graphics files into your shows. iDVD doesn't, however, offer any way to *create or edit* these files. You must prepare them in other programs first.

2. **Insert chapter markers.**

   In a commercial Hollywood DVD, you can jump around the movie without re-winding or fast-forwarding, thanks to the movie's *scene menu* or *chapter menu*. It's basically a screenful of bookmarks for certain scenes in the movie. (One way to create these useful scene breaks in iMovie HD is to position the Playhead and then choose Markers→Add Chapter Marker.)

3. **Hand off to iDVD.**

   The beauty of iMovie HD and iDVD 5 is that they're tied together behind the scenes. The former can hand off movies to the latter, automatically creating menu buttons in the process.

4. **Design the menu screen.**

   In iDVD terms, *menus* doesn't mean menus that drop down from the top of the screen. Instead, a DVD menu is a menu *screen,* usually containing buttons that you click with the remote control. One button, called Play, starts playing the movie. Another, called Scene Selection, might take you to a second menu screen full of individual "chapter" buttons, so your audience doesn't have to start watching from the beginning if they don't want to.

   DVD menu design is at the heart of iDVD. The program lets you specify where and how each button appears on the screen, and also lets you customize the overall look with backgrounds and titles.

5. **Burn your DVD.**

   To create a DVD, iDVD compresses your movie into the universal DVD file for-mat, called *MPEG-2,* and then copies the results to a blank recordable DVD disc. This process, called *burning,* lets you produce a DVD that plays back either in a computer or in most set-top DVD players.

Phase 1: Prepare Your Video

For the most professional results, prepare your video in iMovie HD (or some other video-editing program) before importing it into iDVD. Here are a couple of key issues you should address before you start to build your iDVD projects.

Safe Colors

Standard-definition American TV sets weren't designed to display extremely bright colors. Highly saturated colors, especially red, "bleed" on most TV sets, meaning that they seem to leak out beyond their natural boundaries on the screen.

To counter this problem, you can apply a *brightness limiter* to your iMovie footage before using it in iDVD. Brightness limiters cut out the top and bottom 5 percent of possible illumination levels, restricting video to the middle 90 percent of available colors, thereby ensuring you won't have bleeding colors.

Note: Although this color-bleed problem is specific to NTSC video (the standard in North America and Japan), you can also apply color limit technology to PAL projects (the standard in Europe and Australia). The problem doesn't affect HDTV sets.

The results are very subtle. In fact, you might not even notice the difference unless you examine spots of bright colors in solid white zones. The "after" clips will be slightly subdued, with grayer whites and less prominent colors.

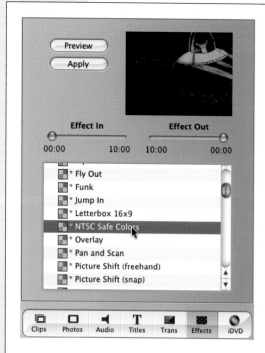

Figure 15-1:
You can find a brightness limiter for iMovie in the Practical Plugins Sampler pack at www.ericasadun.com/imovie. Download a copy, unstuff the file, and double-click the .dmg file to make the disk image appear onscreen. Drag the NTSC plug-in to your Home→Library→iMovie→Plug-ins folder. If iMovie is running, quit and reopen it. Use the Clip viewer or the Timeline to choose the clips that need adjustment. Open the Effects pane; choose the NTSC Safe Colors effect. Leave the Effect In and Effect Out sliders at the proposed 00:00 positions. Click Apply. Wait as iMovie applies the NTSC Safe Colors effect to your footage. You may want to take a break and grab some coffee as you wait.

Figure 15-1 shows how to use a safe color plug-in in iMovie.

Safe Zones

Most standard-definition tube televisions *overscan* to compensate for the way picture tubes age over time. Overscanning TVs display only the central portion of the video picture, while clipping (hiding) the rest behind the bezel (screen frame).

In particular, broadcasters refer to two danger margins of a video image: the *title-safe area* and the *action-safe area* (see Figures 15-2 and 15-3).

Tip: Flat-panel TV sets like plasmas and LCDs don't have picture tubes, and therefore don't overscan.

The Title-Safe Area

When a TV chops off parts of your title, making it difficult or impossible to read, your audience can't help but notice (see Figure 15-2). As noted on page 185, you can make sure that your iMovie titles will always be safe in the resulting DVD by turning *off* the QT Margins box as you add titles and credits. iMovie won't allow the title to expand into the outer 10 percent on either side.

Figure 15-2:
Poor planning may produce overly wide titles that extend beyond visible screen boundaries when played back on a TV. Use title-safe settings to avoid this overextended, snipped text.

The Action-Safe Area

Professional broadcasters also refer to the *action-safe* area of the screen. It's not quite as broad a margin as the title-safe area, because your audience can usually figure out what's going on even if the action is slightly clipped at the outer edges of the screen. Still, it's vital that your action remains mostly within the central portion of the screen.

Imagine, for example, a science-fiction video. A mysterious enemy teleports your hero and his sidekick to a moon of Jupiter. The sidekick throws something to the hero—something that can save the day. In Figure 15-3 at top, for example, what's in the hero's hand may be obvious to you, but most TV viewers would have a hard time guessing what it is because it's outside of the action-safe zone.

In Figure 15-3 at bottom, the sidekick's hand and the phone he throws appear completely within the action-safe zone. Even if the TV winds up chopping off the

Title-safe boundary   Action-safe boundary

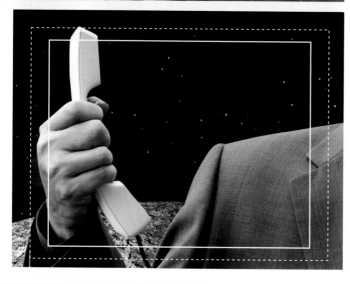

Figure 15-3:
Top: Avoid placing key visual action outside the action-safe zone of your video. Objects that appear outside the title-safe area may be cropped; objects outside the action-safe region almost certainly will be cropped by North American picture-tube TV sets.

Bottom: Although you should keep all key visual elements within the title-safe zone, you may allow non-vital portions of those elements (such as the knuckles and cord in this example) to stray into the action-safe zone.

outer edges of the picture, the visual story is preserved, and your hero can safely call home.

Note: Readers and their lawyers will please forgive the science of this example, in that (a) there is no such thing as teleportation, (b) there is no air to breathe on the moons of Jupiter, let alone to talk with, (c) the hero and his colleague would die almost instantly from catastrophic depressurization, and (d) even assuming the hero could make the call out, the speed of light ensures that it would take hours for his message to reach earth. When writing computer books, authors are limited by the royalty-free art collections they have on hand. The art used here appears courtesy of Ulead's Royalty Free Media collection (*www.ulead.com/pap*).

You can keep your action within the action-safe area in either of two ways:

- **Frame correctly to begin with.** Keeping important visual features and motion away from the edges of your video as you record it is by far the easiest solution.

- **Resize the footage.** You can also buy iMovie plug-ins (see the end of Chapter 6) that resize your video and center it within the frame. This approach, however, takes a lot of time and effort, and may degrade the video quality.

Phase 2: Insert Chapter Markers

If you've ever rented or bought a movie on DVD, you're already familiar with *chapters,* better known as scenes (Figure 15-4).

Figure 15-4:
Most DVDs offer something called a scene menu like this one (from the movie Ronin*), which lets viewers jump directly to their favorite scenes in the movie. Your DVD scene menus probably won't be quite this elaborate, but you get the idea.*

DVD chapters let viewers skip to predefined starting points within a movie, or pick up where they last left off watching, by either using the scene menu or pressing the Next Chapter or Previous Chapter buttons on the remote control. Thanks to the partnership of iMovie and iDVD, you can add markers to your own movies that perfectly replicate this feature.

iMovie HD offers two ways to go about adding chapter markers. The easiest way is to press Shift-⌘-M at each spot where you want a chapter marker, even while the movie is playing. (That's the shortcut for the Markers→Add Chapter Marker command.) Although that's quick and easy, you still have to open up the iDVD chapter-marker palette to *name* the markers (Figure 15-5).

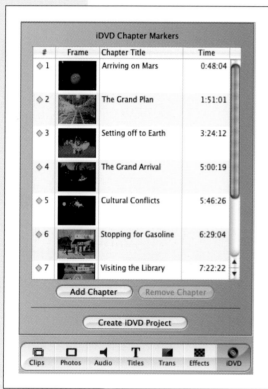

Figure 15-5:
The iDVD palette lets you add, remove, and name chapters—and then publish your iMovies to iDVD. New iMovie chapters are numbered sequentially, as they appear in your movie from left to right. Chapter references appear in your timeline as small yellow diamonds, just above the video track. Amazingly, iMovie can add up to 99 chapters per movie with the iDVD palette.

You can also create and manage chapter markers all in one tidy list, using the older iDVD panel in iMovie. Here's how that goes:

1. In iMovie, click the iDVD button.

You'll find it among the other palette buttons, just to the right of the Effects button, as shown in Figure 15-5. In any case, the iDVD palette now opens. If you've added any chapter markers using the Add Chapter Marker (Shift-⌘-M) method, you'll see them listed here bearing names like Clip 12, Clip 16, and so on.

2. **In the iMovie monitor, drag the Playhead along the scrubber bar to locate the position for your new chapter.**

   You may want to choose Edit→Select None (Shift-⌘-A) first, which ensures that no individual clip is selected. Now you can move the Playhead anywhere in your movie.

   Tip: *Use the arrow keys for precise Playhead positioning, or press Shift-arrow to jump 10 frames at a time.*

3. **Click Add Chapter.**

   You'll find this button near the bottom of the iDVD palette. iMovie adds the chapter to your list, as shown in Figure 15-5.

   Tip: *You can also use the keystroke Shift-⌘-M at this point, or even choose Markers→Add Chapter Marker.*

4. **Type a chapter title into the Chapter Title box.**

   Whatever you type here will wind up as the chapter name in the finished DVD menu. Select a short but meaningful name. (You don't have to delete the proposed name first; just type right over it.)

5. **Repeat steps 2–4.**

   Repeat until you've added all the chapters for your movie.

6. **Save your project.**

   Choose File→Save to save your iMovie project, including the chapter marks you just defined.

Removing Chapters

Suppose you change your mind about where a chapter should begin. Or, you may have added too many chapters to suit your taste, or even put a marker in the wrong place. In any case, you remove a marker by using one of these techniques:

- Click its name in iMovie's iDVD palette and then click the Remove Chapter button.

- Click the diamond-shaped marker in the Movie Track and then choose Markers→ Delete Chapter Marker (Option-⌘-M).

Tip: *You can also select a bunch of chapters in the iDVD panel at once, using the usual list-keyboard shortcuts—⌘-click individual markers to select them, or select a consecutive batch by clicking the first and Shift-clicking the last. Now clicking Remove Chapter nukes all of them at once.*

Changing Chapter Names

To change the name of any chapter that appears in the iDVD Chapter Markers list, just double-click it to open the editing box, and then edit away.

When you press Return or Enter, iMovie accepts the new chapter name and automatically moves to the next chapter. When you're at the last chapter of your project, iMovie cycles back to the first one. As a result, you can edit a bunch of chapter names in sequence with a minimum of mouse clicks. To finish editing chapter names, click the mouse outside the iDVD palette.

Chapter Marker Pointers

Here are a few key points to keep in mind about chapters:

- **Chapter markers appear in the Timeline Viewer.** They appear as small, yellow diamond shapes. (Chapter markers don't appear in the Clip Viewer.)

- **You can't move a chapter marker.** If you've used the wrong start frame when creating your chapter, you have no choice but to delete the chapter marker and create a new one with the correct starting point.

- **You can't drag chapter markers in the iDVD palettes.** Chapter order depends on the associated starting times, which appear chronologically in the palette.

- **When you move (and erase) clips, chapter markers go along for the ride.** iMovie associates chapters with individual clips. Therefore, if you reorder your clips, the

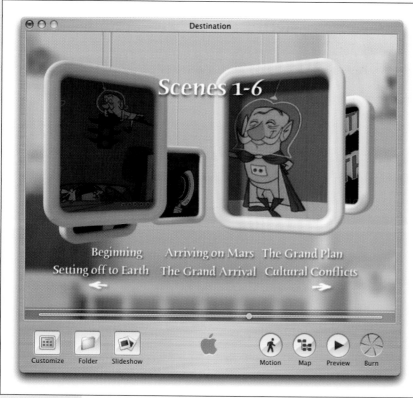

Figure 15-6:
Some iDVD menu themes can accommodate only six or seven buttons per screen. If you've got more than that, left and right arrows appear, so that your audience can navigate to additional screens full of buttons. iDVD automatically adds the scene numbers to your menu title for easier navigation.

chapter markers move with them. If you delete a clip, iMovie removes the included chapters.

- **When you** *copy* **a clip, you copy chapter markers.** When you duplicate a clip, iMovie copies all of its chapters at their original positions.

- **Frames matter, not timing.** When you slow down or speed up a clip, the included chapter marks slide accordingly, retaining their relative positions within the clip.

- **There's a "secret" unlisted chapter.** iMovie and iDVD always create one more chapter than you see on the iDVD Chapters list. This extra chapter corresponds to the very beginning of your movie (00:00:00), and starts out with the label "Beginning." (You won't see it until you arrive in iDVD.)

- **Your finished iDVD screens can fit up to 12 buttons per screen.** The actual number used depends on the *theme* you pick. (Themes are prebuilt designs with coordinating backgrounds, buttons, fonts, and, if you like, background audio.) When you include more chapters per screen than the theme allows (including "Beginning"), your scene-selection menus will extend to more than one screen, as shown in Figure 15-6.

Phase 3: Hand Off to iDVD

Once you've added your chapter markers in iMovie, you're ready to hand off the whole thing to iDVD, where you can do your menu design and DVD burning.

Start by saving your iMovie project—a necessary step before handing off to iDVD. Then click the Create iDVD Project button at the bottom of the chapter list. If your movie contains slow motion, fast motion, or reverse-motion clips, you'll be asked if you want them to be *rendered* for better quality. Say yes.

Your hard drive whirs, thunder rolls somewhere, and after a few moments, you wind up in iDVD itself. If this is your first time using iDVD, the factory-setting design is called Travel 1, in which empty postcards scroll slowly from right to left, confirming your arrival in iDVD land (Figure 15-7); if you've run iDVD before, you see whatever design theme you used last. (Those "postcards" are actually *drop zones*—areas of the design that you can fill with your own pictures or movies.)

Tip: To turn off the Apple logo that appears in the lower-right corner of every iDVD Project, choose iDVD→ Preferences and turn off "Show Apple logo watermark."

Phase 4: Design the Menu Screen

On the main menu screen now before you, you'll find two buttons:

- **Play.** On the finished DVD, this button means, "Play the movie from the beginning."

- **Scene Selection.** On the finished DVD, this button will take your audience to a second screen, which is filled with individual buttons for the chapters you created. (In fact, this second screen may well have arrows that lead to third and fourth screens, since iDVD menus vary in the number of buttons that fit per screen. Travel Cards holds six buttons per scene-selection menu.)

If you'd like to have a look at this scene-selection screen, double-click the words Scene Selection. To return to the main menu, click the left-pointing arrow on the scene-selection screen.

Tip: If iDVD seems sluggish when you change screens, it's because the program is busily processing video in the background. To make it work faster, choose iDVD→Preferences, click the General icon, and turn off "Enable background encoding." (Finally, close the General window.)

Creating your DVD at the end of the process will take longer now, because the video hasn't been preprocessed. But at least you'll be able to work in the program without feeling like you're walking through quicksand.

If things are still slow, your Mac may need more memory. iDVD consumes RAM like the ravenous triple-toed dire sloth of the Northern Antipodes consumes white-tailed wombats. (Dire sloths can be very, very ravenous indeed.)

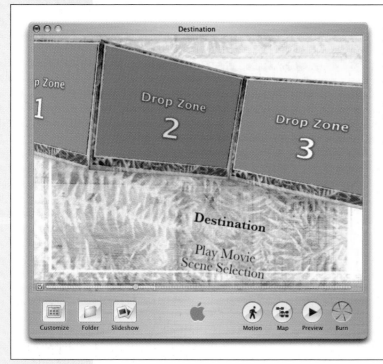

Figure 15-7:
iDVD provides a What-You-See-Is-Pretty-Much-What-You-Get layout of your final DVD. Here, you add, edit, and manipulate the buttons, pictures, movies, and titles that will make up the menus for your DVD. "Travel Cards" (shown here) is iDVD's factory-setting theme.

All about Themes

The moving drop zones, any music that's playing, and the font for your buttons are all part of a *theme*: a unified design scheme that governs how the menus look and behave, complete with attractive backgrounds, coordinated typography, and background music. iDVD 5 comes with 15 eye-catching new themes that include a host of visually stunning effects.

It takes a lot of individual design decisions to make a theme. For example:

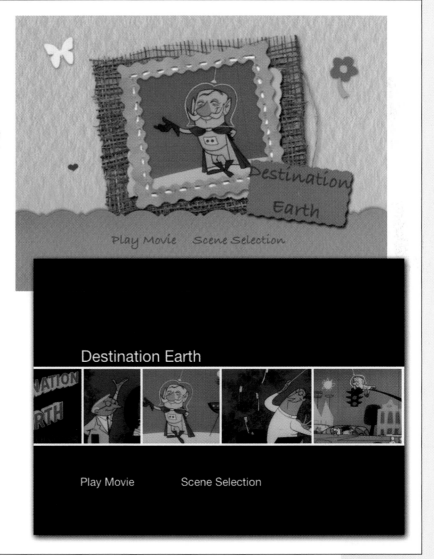

Figure 15-8:
iDVD Themes can create strikingly different menu screens for similar projects. Top: The Scrapbook theme uses a script font based on handwritten text and a series of drop zones that fly across an animated background video.

Bottom: The Lines theme features a row of drop zones (the series of pictures that, if this weren't a frozen picture on a book page, would be scrolling to the left), a plain black background, and text buttons in an informal font.

- **Background image or video.** Whatever art appears in the background, still images, or video clips, is part of the theme. The movement of the desert in the Anime Pop theme is one example of video in action.

Tip: If the repetitive looping of a theme's motion drives you crazy, click the round Motion button below the menu-design screen. The Motion button turns the looping motion on and off while you're working on a DVD. (It also affects the finished DVD, so check its status before you burn the disc.)

- **Button type.** The buttons in iDVD Project can be either little graphics or text phrases that your audience will "click" with the remote control.

- **Button look.** The look of your buttons can vary. Text buttons may have simple backgrounds; graphic buttons may have borders.

- **Button positions.** Each menu can accommodate up to 12 buttons, depending on the theme you've chosen. Themes are preset to place their buttons in certain favored positions.

- **Drop zones.** Drop zones are areas into which you can drag a favorite video clip (sometimes more than one) that plays continuously as a background for the main menu screen. If you've ever seen a commercial Hollywood DVD movie, you've seen this effect. One key scene from the movie plays over and over, looping until you choose one of the buttons on the menu screen—or go quietly insane.

  In iDVD 5, advanced *dynamic* drop zones can now move across the screen, even passing in front of each other, providing amazing visual effects.

- **Text boxes.** Text boxes let you freely add text blocks to your menu screens so you can provide, for example, instructions to your viewers, copyright notices, or details about what they're about to see.

- **Font selections.** Themes also specify the color, font size, and typeface for menu titles and buttons.

Figure 15-8 illustrates two very different looks for the same project. The difference lies only in the chosen theme.

Choosing a Theme

Goodness knows, you don't have to be satisfied with the tropically inspired Travel Cards theme. A wide range of canned themes awaits your inspection:

1. **Click Customize to open the Customize drawer, if it isn't already open.**

   The Customize button shows or hides the *drawer* shown in Figure 15-9. (You can also close the drawer by dragging its outside edge inward.)

2. **From the pop-up menu at the top of the drawer, choose a theme set.**

   iDVD offers three built-in theme sets: **5.0 Themes** (15 new themes in this version), **4.0 Themes** (20 designs from iDVD 4), and **Old Themes** (24 themes inherited from iDVD 3, including the excellent Book and Projector offerings). If you've bought additional themes online (Figure 15-10), this pop-up menu may offer other choices. In any case, you can use this pop-up menu to switch between them, or just choose All to see all installed themes in a single scrolling list.

You'll notice that some of the themes seem to appear twice: "Wedding Theme Bronze One" and "Wedding Theme Bronze Two," for example. That represents another iDVD feature: predesigned screens for *submenu* screens, like the Scene Selection screens you'd find on a commercial DVD. The "Two" designs are intended for these second-level screens full of buttons.

Scroll through the list of themes, clicking each one to see what it looks like in the main work area, or just rely on the little thumbnail icons to get a sense of the theme's overall flavor.

3. **Select a theme by clicking its thumbnail.**

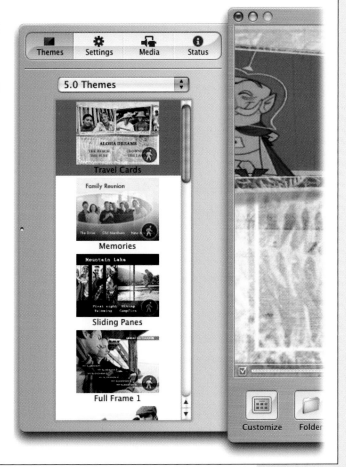

Figure 15-9:
The Customize button reveals iDVD's Customize drawer. You'll be spending a lot of your time here, so mastering its layout is important. For example, when you click one of the buttons at the top, the pane changes to show its contents. **Themes** lets you choose a design scheme. **Settings** lets you choose motion menu duration, background video and audio, title fonts, and the look and placement of buttons. The **Media** panes reveal the contents of your iTunes and iPhoto collections.

If your DVD menu system consists of only a single screen—the main menu you've been looking at the whole time—it takes on your chosen theme instantly.

A movie you've exported from iMovie, however, probably has chapter markers in it, and therefore your movie probably has at least one additional menu screen: your scene-selection screen.

It turns out that clicking a theme choice in the Customize drawer affects the *current* menu screen only. If you click, say, the Techno B&W theme on the main menu, your scene-selection screen remains unaffected; it still shows the yellow and brown Travel Cards theme. Therefore, follow up like this:

4. **Choose Advanced→Apply Theme to Project.**

   This command applies the same theme to every screen. Now all of your menu screens look alike.

Tip: If you want all of your menu screens to have the same look except for the main menu, first use the Apply Theme to Project command described here. Then return to the main menu screen and click the theme thumbnail you want for it only.

For example, you might apply Travel 2 to your entire project, and then choose Travel 1 for your main screen.

Figure 15-10:
You can buy additional themes, or download free samples, from other companies (such as iDVDThemePAK.com *or* iDVD-themetastic .com). *You install them by creating a folder called Favorites in your Library→iDVD folder (the Library folder in the main hard drive window, not in your Home folder), and then putting them inside.*

When you're happy with the way the new theme looks, you're ready to proceed with your iDVD design work. Fortunately, you don't have to commit to a theme at this moment; you can swap in a different theme at any time until you actually burn the DVD.

Editing Menus

If you like the way everything looks when you click a desired theme, terrific. You're good to go. Skip ahead to "Phase 5: Burn Your DVD."

Note, however, that a great deal of flexibility and control await in the meantime. You don't have to accept every element of the theme as it appears when you first select it. You can move your buttons around, change the labels on them, and so on.

Chapter 17 offers the full scoop on these procedures, but here are a few of the most common redesign tasks.

Editing Titles and Buttons

iDVD usually adds a title to your menu screens, often near the top of the page, and usually in a larger font than any other text. You can edit it just as you would a Finder icon name: Click inside it to open up an editing box, type your changes, and then press Enter or Return.

Editing button names works almost the same way, except that you single-click the button first, and then click the text itself to open the editing box.

Keep these points in mind when working with iDVD text:

- **Be succinct.** DVD screens are small, so there's not much room for long and involved text.

- **Be contained.** Don't let one text box overlap another.

- **Spell check.** Nothing speaks worse of your attention to detail than a lovingly crafted masterpiece called "For Mouther's Day."

Tip: If your buttons' text labels are crashing into each other, try making the text wrap into a narrow column, so that it's several lines long. Simply press Return to start a new line; unlike previous versions of iDVD, pressing Return doesn't close the editing box.

Moving Buttons Around

Each theme comes with predetermined locations for your buttons. In fact, internally, each theme stores separate layout maps: one that specifies the button positions if you have *three* buttons, another for *four* buttons, and so on.

iDVD lets you move your buttons around into new positions, but it's not as easy as just dragging them with your mouse. There's no grid to guide you, so the new button positions might not look especially professional. For example, when you play your iDVD disc on a standard DVD player, your menu buttons will sprout glowing rectangles to indicate which button is highlighted. If you've positioned the buttons too closely together, this highlighting might overlap other buttons—with ugly results.

If you're absolutely, positively sure that you want the freedom to drag buttons around into new positions, open the Customize drawer. Click the Settings button at the top, and then in the lower third of the pane, turn on Free Position. Now the buttons are liberated from their grid. (You may want to choose Advanced→Show TV Safe Area so that you don't wind up dragging the buttons off the TV screen.)

Apple disavows all responsibility for the cosmetic quality of the results.

Tip: At any time, you can make your buttons snap back to their original positions by choosing Snap to Grid from the Settings pane.

Reordering Buttons

Apple may not want you to drag buttons randomly around the screen, but reordering them is a different story. See Figure 15-11.

Figure 15-11:
Dragging one button on top of another generally swaps the two positions only if they're adjacent. More often, if you drag the first button into the fourth position, the sequence becomes #2, #3, #4, #1 (instead of just swapping #1 and #4). iDVD attempts to maintain as much of the original sequence as possible, so that when your audience uses the remote control's arrow button on the resulting DVDs, the highlighting won't jump around confusingly.

Removing Buttons

To remove a button from a menu screen, click it and then press the Delete key.

Tip: You can also click the first button, and then Shift-click another button, to highlight all of the buttons in between. Or ⌘-click individual buttons to highlight only those.

Of course, if your purpose in removing a button is to move it to a different menu screen, you can use the Cut and Paste commands in the Edit menu. (See page 393 for details on navigating screens.)

Setting Button Images

In some themes—including all of the iDVD 5 designs—the buttons on your menu screen are just bits of text.

In some older themes, though, the buttons can actually be icons, pictures, or tiny movie clips that preview what's in store if viewers click it. In those situations, here's how you specify what that image is.

Moving previews

Suppose you have a button that, when clicked, plays a movie you've created. Here's where you can make iDVD display up to 30 seconds of that movie right there on the button.

Tip: A button can display video only if that button actually links to a video—not to a folder or a slideshow, as described in the next chapter.

1. **Select the button.**

   When you click a button, a slider and a Movie checkbox appear above it, as shown in Figure 15-12.

Figure 15-12:
Turn on Movie to create a video button. Use the slider to specify where you want the tiny button movie to begin looping.

2. **Turn on Motion, if necessary.**

   If motion isn't already turned on, click the round Motion button at the bottom of the iDVD window. (The button turns green when it's on, gray when it's not.) All the little movie buttons come to life, all playing simultaneously.

Note: If your movie clips don't start playing, don't worry. Some menus, including Kids Theater Two, come with their button loop times set to zero.

To make your video buttons come alive, you have to adjust their timing manually, as described below.

---

3. **Make sure the Movie checkbox is turned on. Drag the slider to the spot where you want playback to begin.**

   The slider is a map of your entire movie, from start to end. Pinpoint where you want the button's video playback to begin. You've just set what Apple calls the *poster frame* for the linked movie.

   So how do you specify where you want the buttons' looping video to *end?*

4. **Make sure the Customize drawer is open. Click the Settings icon at the top, and then drag the Menu Duration slider to specify how many seconds of video you want your buttons to loop.**

   The maximum loop time varies by theme and project. For some themes, you can specify a loop of up to 30, which should be plenty of time for your audience member to make a selection from the menu screen. In other themes, the loops can last as long as your movies. That's a very long time, menu-wise.

   Note, however, that changing this duration affects the loop times of *all* the menu buttons, *and* the looping time of the background video (see "Drop Zones" on the facing page). Also keep in mind that all your motion menu times added together cannot exceed 15 minutes for your entire project.

5. **Click anywhere on the background to hide the slider and the Movie checkbox.**

   If Motion is turned on, you'll see the video begin playing on the button immediately.

Tip: If your video buttons don't seem to be moving, remember to set their loop lengths to more than 0 seconds, as described in step 4. Also confirm that you've turned on the Motion button at the bottom of the screen, so that it's green.

A still frame from the movie

Instead of a looping video, your button's face can display a still image that comes from a particular frame of the movie. This is a typical style in Hollywood DVD movies, where a still image represents the scene that lies behind each button.

The steps are exactly the same as described in the previous section—except that you turn *off* the Movie checkbox shown in Figure 15-12.

Drop a picture or movie

The picture on a button doesn't have to be a scene from the movie. It can be any graphic you want. Just drag any graphics file right onto the button itself; you'll see the button image change instantly.

This graphic can come from just about anywhere. For example:

- **The Finder.** Drag any graphics file out of a folder window or from the desktop.

- **iPhoto.** In the Customize drawer, click the Media button and choose Photos from the pop-up menu. You now see a list of all of the albums in your Mac's iPhoto collection. You can drag any photo onto a button to install it as the new button face.

Drop Zones

Drop zones let you use video, slideshows, and graphics as the backgrounds of your menu screens. Not every theme offers drop zones, but nearly all of the new 5.0 themes do: Travel Cards, Sliding Panes, Anime Pop, Baby Mobile, and so forth. As if you couldn't guess, the words "Drop Zone" (see Figure 15-13) indicate where the drop zones are.

GEM IN THE ROUGH

Secrets of the Theme Scrubber

iDVD 5's new scrubber bar (the thin white scroll bar beneath the menu screen) lets you preview an entire theme at once. Just drag the scroll bar handle to view how the theme and its drop zones change over time.

Many themes, including the one shown here, include a "play once" introduction—a preliminary animation that plays before your menu buttons even appear. It's represented in iDVD by a cross-hatched area of the scrubber bar, to the left of the main section (which represents the looping portion of your menu animation).

At times, you might want to turn off that introductory animation, especially when you're designing secondary menu screens (like the Scene Selection screen). If you turn off the checkbox to the left of the scrubber, you hide the crosshatched section of the scrubber bar. You also eliminate

the introductory portion, both as it plays in iDVD *and* on the final, burned DVD. Now only the main, looping portion of the menu-screen animation will play. (You can always restore the intro by turning the checkbox back on again.)

Speaking of scrubber-bar secrets: If you turn off the Motion button at the bottom of the iDVD screen, you bring the menu's animation to a halt. (The menu will be frozen on the finished DVD, too.)

But once Motion is turned off, you can drag the thumb on the scrubber bar to find the most attractive moment in the preprogrammed background animation. Whatever frame you bring into view this way remains the permanent still background for your menu screen. (Permanent, at least, until you adjust the scrubber bar again or turn Motion back on.)

Tip: If you don't see the telltale phrase "Drop Zone" followed by a number, choose iDVD→Preferences. Click the General icon, and then turn on Show Drop Zones. (This checkbox just hides the words "Drop Zone," not the drop zones themselves.)

Note, by the way, that not all drop zones are onscreen at once. The Scrapbook theme, for example, shows only one of its three drop zones at a time. Similarly, the drop zones in several iDVD 5 themes take their time in parading onto the screen, or rotating through it. To give yourself a quick tour of all the drop zones in your chosen theme,

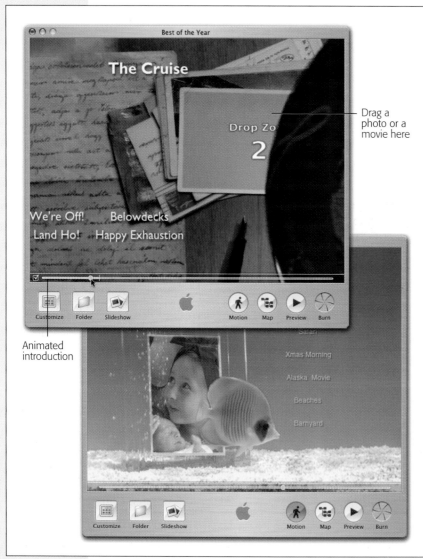

Drag a photo or a movie here

Animated introduction

Figure 15-13:
Top: The words "Drop Zone" show you where each drop zone is. In some themes, a preliminary animation appears before your main-menu buttons do; that interval is represented by the notched area on the scroll bar.

Bottom: Drop zones aren't always perfect rectangles or squares, so your video may get clipped around the edges. On the other hand, you can drag the picture or movie around within the drop zone outline so that the most important part shows up. In this theme, the animated fish actually swims around in front of whatever's in the drop zone!

drag the handle of the thin white scroll bar at the bottom of the menu window to cycle through the entire presentation; see the box on page 371 for details.

Here's how drop zones work:

- **Adding to a drop zone.** Drag any video, photo album, image, or collection of images right into a drop zone outline to install it there. You can drag icons out of the Finder, or directly out of the Media pane in the Customize drawer.

Tip: Albums in drop zones can display 30 images at most. What you'll get is a mini-slideshow, right there within the drop zone. (More on dragging out of the Photos pane in Chapter 16.)

- **Replacing items in a drop zone.** To replace what you've installed in a drop zone, just drag something new into it.

- **Removing items from a drop zone.** To delete an item in the drop zone, drag it away from the spot, just as you'd drag something off the Mac OS X Dock or the Sidebar. You get a cute little puff of smoke to indicate the movie or picture's disappearance. (If you drag it onto a menu button in the process of removing it from the drop zone, it becomes a video menu button.)

Figure 15-14:
Top: When you click the drop zone itself, a transparent control panel appears just above it. Use the slider to specify which photo appears on the button, or click the Edit Order button to open the Drop Zone editor.

Bottom: In the Drop Zone slideshow editor window, a thumbnail display lets you drag the photos around. (The two buttons in the lower-left corner of the editor switch between this column view and an icon-based view.) Reorder the slides until your aesthetic sensibilities are satisfied, and then click Return twice—once to return to the Drop Zone Editor screen (Figure 15-15), and again to go back to the menu editor screen.

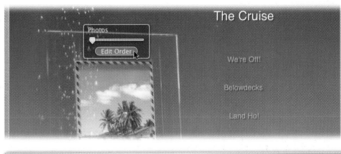

- **Editing a drop zone slideshow**. If you've decided to create a mini-slideshow within the drop zone, you may wonder how you're supposed to adjust the order of the photos. Figure 15-14 tells all.

Tip: Instead of clicking the drop zone and then clicking Edit Order, you can just double-click the drop zone. You go straight to the Drop Zone Editor window.

- **Add sounds**. Drop zones have no sound, although you can import audio into the menu screen that *contains* the drop zone. See page 425.

- **Turning on Motion.** If you've installed video into a drop zone and it doesn't seem to be playing, click the round Motion button at the bottom of the iDVD window. (When it's turned on, the button is green; when it's turned off, it's gray.) If it still doesn't seem to be playing, the menu duration may be set to 0 (page 370).

  Turning off Motion also turns off any background audio track and brings motion menus and motion buttons to a standstill. (Caution: The status of this button affects both your onscreen project and the final DVD.)

- **Locating a drop zone**. As noted above, drop zones in several iDVD 5 themes appear only one at a time. To see them all (so that you can fill them with pictures or movies), drag the thin white scroll bar at the bottom of the menu screen until the zone you want flies into view.

  Alternately, you can visit the Drop Zone Editor window, which appears when you either double-click a drop zone or choose Project→Edit Drop Zones. Figure 15-15 shows how to use this new iDVD 5 feature. (Click Return when you're done.)

Figure 15-15:
The Drop Zone Editor screen lets you view (and modify) all of a menu's drop zones at once. Drag and drop pictures, movies, or photo albums from the Customize drawer into the broad drop-zone rows, as shown here. To clear a drop zone, drag from the well clear out of the window. You can also double-click a thumbnail to open the corresponding editor (to rearrange a slideshow, for example).

- **Changing the duration.** Use the Settings pane in the Customize drawer to adjust the loop duration for your menus (how long a movie clip plays before starting over). Whatever time you specify here controls the loop length of movies in menu backgrounds, video buttons, *and* drop zones.

Note: If you drag a movie into a drop zone, you can't control where the movie begins as you can with button movies. In a drop zone, a movie always begins at the beginning. Startling, huh?

Redesigning the Theme

You can change every tiny aspect of your theme—the music, the background, the colors, the fonts, and so on—if you have the time and patience. If you're so inclined, turn to Chapter 17 for a full discussion of theme creation.

Phase 5: Burning Your DVD

Once your scene-selection screen is looking pretty good, you're almost ready to burn the DVD. Before you go using up a blank disc, however, you should test it to make sure that it works on the virtual DVD player known as the Macintosh screen.

Previewing Your Project

iDVD's Preview button lets you test your menu system to avoid unpleasant surprises. When you click it, iDVD enters Preview mode, which simulates how your DVD works on a standalone set-top DVD player. You even get a simulated remote control to help you navigate through your DVD's menus, movies, and so on, as shown in Figure 15-16.

To return to iDVD's edit mode, click Exit, Stop (the filled square), or reclick Preview.

Tip: Instead of using the arrow buttons on the remote to highlight and "click" screen buttons, you can just use your mouse. You'll find it's not only less clumsy, but also a decent indication of how your DVD will play back on computers that can play DVDs.

Previewing Widescreen Footage

iDVD can create widescreen DVDs, just like the ones you rent from Blockbuster—that is, movies that produce a wide, rectangular picture to fit today's wide, rectangular high-definition (and enhanced-definition) TV sets. The key is to make sure that your widescreen movie begins life as a widescreen *iMovie* project, and then hand it off to iDVD from there.

In fact, iDVD-created discs even add letterbox bars automatically when they're played on traditional, squarish sets. That's the effect, in fact, that you see in Preview mode (Figure 15-16). The words "Widescreen Preview" are telling you, in effect, "This is what I'll look like when played on a regular TV. When I'm played on a widescreen set, these gray letterbox bars won't appear."

Note: If you *don't* see the words "Widescreen Preview" during preview, on the other hand, something has gone wrong. iDVD won't treat the footage as widescreen, and will squeeze it horizontally when played on a standard TV. In that event, try reimporting it from iMovie.

Figure 15-16:
To "click" your onscreen buttons, use the arrows on the remote to highlight the one you want, and then click the Enter button in the middle of the remote. Click the |< or >| buttons to skip back or forward by one chapter, or hold them down to rewind or fast-forward.

Maximum DVD Playback Time

In iDVD 5, you don't have to make the Hobson's choice between 60 minutes of video at best quality and 90 minutes at lower quality, as you did with earlier versions. Apple has thoughtfully raided its own professional DVD creation software (DVD Studio Pro) to bless iDVD with one of its best features: Now any DVD you burn can contain up to 120 minutes of footage at best quality.

To see the on/off switch for this feature, choose iDVD→Preferences. On the General panel (Figure 15-17), you'll see two options under Encoding Settings. Both produce video quality that's superior to what you got from early versions of iDVD:

• **Best Quality.** This option gives you 120 minutes of video at best quality. The tradeoff: It takes a lot longer to burn your DVD, as the program performs quite a bit of analysis before burning.

- **Best Performance.** Your video will look fantastic, and your Mac will burn the disc relatively quickly. On the downside, the DVD you burn this way can contain a maximum of 60 minutes of video.

Figure 15-17:
iDVD 5 offers two ways to compress the video on your masterpiece. Choose Best Performance for up to 60 minutes of excellent-looking footage or Best Quality for up to 120 minutes of video.

When iDVD's work is over, the DVD that pops out of your Mac will come delightfully close to looking and working like a professionally mastered, commercial DVD from Blockbuster. There will, however, be one giveaway: It won't be over two hours long.

POWER USERS' CLINIC

Best Quality/Best Performance: How It Works

When a DVD-burning program goes to work, it faces an important decision. Given that a blank single-layer DVD contains a limited amount of space (4.7 GB or so), how much picture-quality data can it afford to devote to each frame of video?

The Best Performance option in iDVD 5 makes that decision like this: "I'll allot a fixed, predetermined amount of data to each frame of video—enough to make it look great—no matter how many minutes of video my human master has included. A lot of the DVD might wind up being empty if, for example, the project contains less than an hour of video. But at least the burning process will go quickly, and the video will look really great."

The Best Quality option takes a different approach. It says, "I'm going to use every micron of space on this blank DVD. I'm going to analyze the amount of video my human has included, and divide it into the amount of space available on the DVD. The amount of information used to describe an individual frame of video will vary from project to project, and it will take me a lot longer to burn the DVD because I'm going to have to do so much analysis. But at least my human will get two hours of great-looking video per disc."

Incidentally, if you'd like some insight into how iDVD is thinking of the project you're working on at the moment, open the Customize drawer and click the Status button. This panel shows you how close you are to filling up the DVD with your movies, menus, and other elements.

In fact, iDVD prefers to burn 60-minute DVDs, because they have the best quality. The instant you try to add the 61st minute of footage to your project, you see the message shown in Figure 15-18. You can change your settings as suggested, or delete some video from the project to make it fit within 60 minutes again.

Figure 15-18:
iDVD is telling you that you've put more than 60 minutes of footage onto this DVD. To fit all this video onto your disc, you'll need to use the General Preferences (c-comma) window to switch from Best Performance (60 minutes max) to Best Quality.

A disc that exceeds 60 minutes uses a lower bit rate—that is, it uses less data to describe the video, which allows iDVD to fit more information on the same size disc. (For example, 60-minute iDVD projects depict video using 8 megabits [Mbps] per second; 90-minute projects use 5 Mbps; 120-minute discs use 4 Mbps.)

FREQUENTLY ASKED QUESTION

Hollywood, DVD Length, and You

The Hollywood DVDs I rent from Blockbuster are sometimes much more than two hours long. How come I'm limited to 120 minutes in iDVD?

Most Hollywood DVDs use dual-layer technology—discs that are recorded in two layers of video data. The extra layer increases the DVD's capacity from 4.37 GB to nearly 8 GB.

When you watch one of these movies, you may even be able to spot the moment when the DVD player's laser jumps from one layer to the other. You'll see the movie pause for a moment during playback, always at the same place in the movie.

Unfortunately, iDVD can't burn dual-layer discs. It will take several years for the price of dual-layer burners and discs to come down and for Apple to update iDVD to handle the new discs.

Hollywood uses another trick, too: variable bit-rate (VBR) encoding. When creating a DVD movie for commercial dis-

tribution, professional DVD authors use advanced software to analyze each piece of the movie, using more or less data to describe each frame depending on how much action is visible. The disc stores the same amount of data as a constant bit-rate recording like the ones iDVD makes, but conserves data for when the video needs it the most.

The trouble is, VBR encoding takes a very long time. The software often requires several passes through the whole movie to analyze it and optimize the data. Apple figures that iDVD fans would just as soon not wait all night to see their finished productions.

If you feel that iDVD's 120-minute limitation is standing between you and a glorious career in filmmaking, you could always upgrade to a program like Apple's DVD Studio Pro. It can squeeze up to six hours of video onto a single 4.37 GB disc (at marginal quality, of course). It can also export files for those 8 GB DVDs that can be produced at a professional replication plant.

The tradeoff, of course, is video quality. Higher bit rates generally provide clearer and more accurate picture reproduction than lower bit rates do, especially in action scenes.

If the bit rate of a DVD is *very* low, you get blocky-looking, unclear video. But iDVD's "lowest-quality" mode—4 Mbps—is still above the minimum bit rate needed for clear video for home movies. Don't constrain yourself needlessly to the 60-minute format until you've given the Best Quality format a try.

Burning Your Project

When you've finished editing your disc and testing it thoroughly, it's time to proceed with your burn. This is the moment you've been working toward.

Note: The following steps walk you through the process for burning with an internal Apple SuperDrive (or equivalent). If you want to burn your discs to an external drive, see page 450.

---

1. **Make sure iDVD is ready to burn.**

   Part of iDVD's job is to *encode* (convert) your movies, music, and pictures into the MPEG-2 format required by standard DVDs.

   Therefore, it's a good idea to open the Customize Drawer, click the Status button at the top, and make sure that the word "Done" appears next to each *asset*. (Apple uses the term "asset" as shorthand for "picture, movie, soundtrack, or what have you.") See Figure 15-19.

Tip: If iDVD doesn't say "Done" for all assets in the list, and yet it doesn't seem to be processing them automatically, make sure you've turned on background compression. Choose iDVD→Preferences, click the General button, and turn on "Enable background encoding."

The only time you'd want to turn off background encoding is when you discover that it's slowing down your Mac as you work.

Figure 15-19:
Look for the word "Done" to the right of each asset. If a status bar appears instead, let iDVD 5 continue encoding until "Done" appears. There's no further action you must take. iDVD encodes in the background without any intervention.

2. **Check your Motion setting.**

Remember, the Motion button at the bottom of the window determines whether your finished DVD will have animated menus, buttons, and backgrounds, and whether music will play. If the Motion button is green, you'll get all this stuff. If you click it so that it turns gray, motion and audio features won't appear on the final disc.

(This button has no effect on regular movies and slideshows—only the ones on menu screens.)

3. **Choose File→Save Project.**

Or press ⌘-S.

4. **Check your disk space.**

As iDVD rolls along, it needs some extra working space on your hard drive. Be sure there's plenty of free space—at least the amount indicated by the "Project size" statistic on the Status pane of the Customize drawer. If your hard drive doesn't have enough space, do some cleanup.

5. **Click the Burn button twice.**

See Figure 15-20.

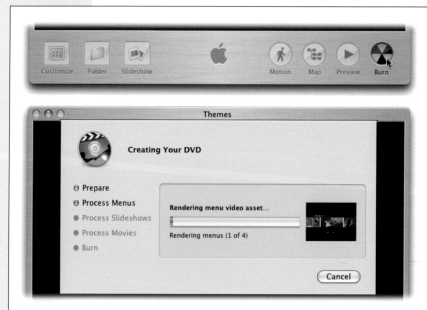

Figure 15-20:
Top: The first click on the gray, closed Burn button "opens" it, revealing a throbbing yellow-and-black button. The second click begins the burning process.

Bottom: During the burning process, iDVD keeps you posted on its progress.

6. **Insert a blank DVD when the Mac asks for it.**

Be sure you're using the correct kind of blank DVD for your DVD burner. For example, don't attempt to burn 1x or 2x blanks at 4x speed. Recent Macs can burn either DVD-R or DVD+R blanks (note the minus and the plus, denoting two incompatible blank DVD formats), as well as their re-recordable, more expensive –RW and +RW counterparts.

7. **Wait.**

It takes iDVD quite awhile to process all of your audio, video, and photos, encoding them into the proper format for a DVD. Your wait time depends on how complex your project is and how fast your Mac is.

Apple says that you should allow two or three minutes of processing per minute of video in your movie, but burning times vary significantly.

After a while, or a bit more than a while, a freshly burned DVD automatically ejects from your SuperDrive.

Note: After your new DVD pops out, a message says, "Your disc has been created. If you want to create another DVD, insert another disc now." Sure enough, if you want to spin out multiple copies of your project, you can insert another blank DVD right then, so that iDVD can record it while it's on a roll.

Otherwise, click Done.

OneStep DVDs

You know how iMovie offers the Magic iMovie—a very limited, one-click method of dumping a videotape into iMovie without any work on your part? In the same vein, iDVD offers a one-click method of dumping a tape onto a DVD. You just plug in a camera and record directly to a DVD, bypassing iMovie altogether.

You could argue that this feature is even more useful than Magic iMovie. Think of it: This feature turns any camcorder into one that churns out DVDs instead of tapes. It's also a handy way to offload footage from a bunch of tapes, either because blank DVDs are cheaper than tapes, or because tapes have a more limited shelf life.

You should note, though, that the OneStep DVD feature is just as limited as the Magic iMovie described in Chapter 4. For example:

- iDVD can record only from a prerecorded MiniDV tape in a camcorder. It can't record from the TV, a cable box, an analog-digital converter box, or your digital camcorder's video pass-through feature.

- You can't edit the video or choose which parts to include.

- Unless you intervene (details in a moment), iDVD will rewind the tape automatically and transfer the entire thing to the end of the recorded portion.

- You can't customize your project in any way; the resulting DVD won't have a theme, a menu screen, or buttons. Instead, it will be an Autoplay DVD—a disc that begins playing automatically when inserted into a DVD player.

Note: As with iMovie, OneStep DVD does not play well with 12-bit audio, which is the standard audio-recording setting for most new digital camcorders. Record your video using the 16-bit setting (which you change in the camcorder's menus), otherwise your audio and video may drift apart on the DVD.

Here's how you use OneStep to copy a tape onto a DVD:

1. **Insert a recorded DV tape into your camcorder, and connect the camcorder to your Mac using a FireWire cable.**

   As noted in Chapter 4, the camcorder's FireWire socket may be labeled FireWire, iLink, IEEE-1394, or even Digital.

2. **Turn on the camcorder and set it to VCR mode.**

   This mode may also be called Playback, VTR, or Play.

3. **In iDVD, choose File→OneStep DVD.**

   Alternatively, just close whatever iDVD project window is open. You arrive at the dialog box shown in Figure 15-21; click the OneStep DVD button.

   If your Mac's DVD drive has a slide-out tray, it now opens automatically.

Figure 15-21:
The Create Project dialog box in iDVD is a lot like the Create Project dialog box in iMovie. That is, it appears whenever you close your iDVD project window without quitting.

4. **Insert a blank recordable DVD.**

   Close the DVD tray, if necessary.

5. **Wait.**

   iDVD takes over your camera, automatically directing it to rewind, play back, and stop. After the capture process is complete, iDVD takes the normal amount of time to compress your video and burn it to disc, so schedule the whole thing for a time (a *long* time) when you won't be needing your Mac. Go get a coffee, found a new spiritual movement, or do something else that will occupy you as the tectonic plates move on inextricably and California continues its long, slow slide into Alaska.

Tip: For best results, make sure that no background programs are busy—rendering iMovie effects, downloading e-mail, playing iTunes music—while you're capturing directly to iDVD. A busy computer may introduce video glitches (like dropped frames) in the video capture.

Overriding OneStep

You don't have to live with OneStep's super-simple, super-limited way of doing things. If you're clever, you can work around some of its limitations.

Figure 15-22:
Top: If, at any time during the camcorder-capturing process, you think you've messed up, you've inserted the wrong tape, or you just don't want to continue recording to disc, click Stop in the OneStep dialog box. Middle: At that point, iDVD asks if you want to cancel the recording or continue creating the DVD using the already-captured video.

Bottom: As a matter of fact, OneStep doesn't actually begin recording the disc until after its video-encoding phase, which can take several minutes to several hours after the video-capturing process is complete. You can click the Cancel button at any time during this processing (encoding) stage to quit without burning, too.

- **You don't have to start from the beginning.** Although OneStep prefers to rewind every tape to the beginning, you can easily override this tendency. That is, *you* can specify where you want the transfer to begin, just by cueing up the tape in the camcorder before you begin the steps above.

  Then, after you insert your blank disc, iDVD displays a "Waiting for Device" message. At that moment, put your finger on the camcorder's Play button. Once iDVD recognizes the blank DVD, OneStep begins the rewinding—but you can interrupt it by pressing Play right away. You've just convinced OneStep that the tape has now been rewound completely. iDVD starts the capture at that point.

- **You don't have to wait till the end.** OneStep ordinarily tries to transfer the entire recorded portion of the tape to the DVD, but you can override this setup, too. Whenever you feel that you've transferred enough of the tape, press the Stop button on your camcorder to end the capture process. OneStep doesn't bat an eye; it moves right ahead to the compression and burning stages.

- **You can bail out at any time.** As shown in Figure 15-22, you can cancel out of the whole OneStep process at any time.

iDVD Projects by Hand

The previous chapter showed you how easy it is to convert a finished iMovie project into a bona fide DVD. But iDVD was around long before Apple combined iMovie and iDVD into the glorious package known as iLife. Then, as now, it's capable of much more than turning a single iMovie project into a single DVD.

For example, if all you ever do is click the Create iDVD Project in iMovie, you'll never be able to make a DVD that contains, for example, *six* of your greatest iMovie masterpieces all on one disc. You'll never be able to create a *slideshow* DVD, either, which happens to be one of the world's greatest methods for displaying digital photos. And you'll never know the joy of designing your own navigational menu system, complete with menus within menus.

This chapter has nothing to do with iMovie, and everything to do with iDVD. It shows you how, by doing a few more things manually, you can gain far more power and freedom.

Building iDVDs

Suppose that you've decided to create an iDVD project manually, rather than using the Create iDVD Project button in iMovie. While there's no one best way to put your project together, it helps to have a basic task list to work through. Here are steps for one convenient path through authoring a DVD.

1. **Create a new project.**

   In iDVD, a project file isn't really a single document on your hard drive. It's actually a *package*—a folder that Mac OS X disguises to look like a single icon. The package contains all of your project settings and materials. (As you know from Chapter 4, iMovie projects are package documents, too.)

2. **Choose a theme.**

Use any of iDVD 5's pre-designed, professional-looking design schemes for your project (or add-on themes you've bought on the Web), as described in the previous chapter.

3. **Add movies and slideshows by hand.**

If you've only created iDVD projects from within iMovie, this is the part that's new to you: adding iMovie movies to an iDVD project manually. In fact, you'll *have* to do it this way if you want your DVD to contain a selection of different movies.

You can also create fantastic slideshows this way, as you'll see in this chapter.

4. **Edit your menus.**

Customize the way your menus look. Edit your menu and button titles and add pictures or movies to your drop zones.

5. **Preview and burn the DVD.**

The process ends just as it did in the previous chapter: You look over your work and then feed your Mac a blank DVD to record for posterity.

Creating a New Project

When you're ready to start designing a new DVD, start by creating a project. These steps detail the process you need to follow.

Figure 16-1:
This dialog box pops up the very first time you run iDVD; whenever you close your iDVD project window without quitting the program; whenever you move or delete the iDVD preference file (in your Home→Library→Preferences folder, called com.apple.iDVD. plist); and whenever the most recent iDVD project file has been moved, renamed, or deleted.

Within the image:
iDVD 5

Create a New Project

Open an Existing Project

OneStep DVD

Quit

1. **Choose File→New (⌘-N). Or, if you're looking at the dialog box shown in Figure 16-1, click Create a New Project.**

   The new iDVD Create Project dialog box (Figure 16-1) is the twin of the one in iMovie. Once again, you'll probably see it fairly rarely.

   All other times, iDVD automatically opens whatever project you just exported from iMovie, or the most recent DVD project you worked on.

   In any case, choosing File→New makes the Save dialog box appear.

2. **Type a name for the project and specify where to save it on your hard drive.**

   If you don't type a more appropriate name, your DVD will be forever known as "My Great DVD."

3. **Click Create.**

   iDVD opens the main menu screen for your new DVD-to-be in the main iDVD window.

Your next step is to choose a visual theme for your DVD's menu screens. Full details appear beginning on page 364.

Adding Movies

When you get right down to it, all iDVD really does is add window dressing—menus, buttons, and so on—to movies, music, and photos created in *other* programs.

Take movies, for example. You already know that you can transfer an iMovie project into iDVD by clicking iMovie's Make iDVD Project button (that's what Chapter 15's all about). But that's just the beginning of the ways you can add movies to your iDVD projects. You can also:

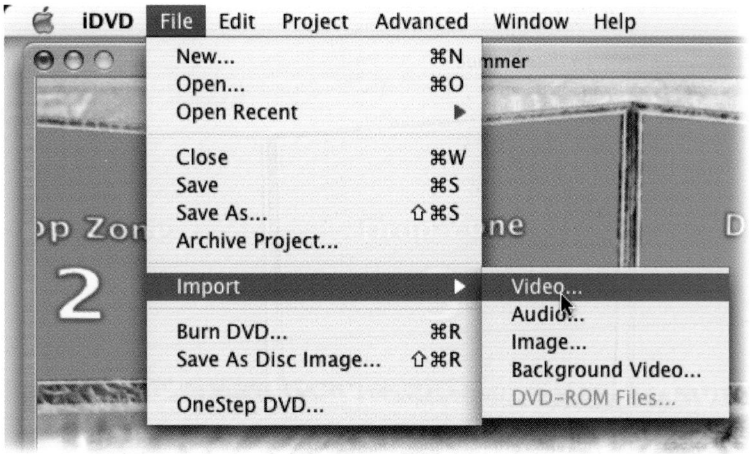

Figure 16-2:
To use the Import command, start on the menu screen you wish to update. When you choose File→Import→Video, the Open File dialog box appears, so that you can navigate to a movie and select it. (You can't select more than one movie to import at a time.) When you click Open, iDVD loads the movie and adds it to the current menu screen.

- Use the File→Import command.

- Drag movies into the iDVD window from the desktop.

- Choose movies from the Media pane of the Customize drawer.

- Drag clips or entire movies directly in from iMovie—a first in iLife history.

The following pages take you through these additional methods..

The Import Command

iDVD's File→Import command lets you install video, audio, pictures, and background movies into your project; see Figure 16-2.

The Finder

Another great way to install a movie into an iDVD menu screen is to drag it there, either right off the desktop or from an open folder window. Figure 16-3 tells all.

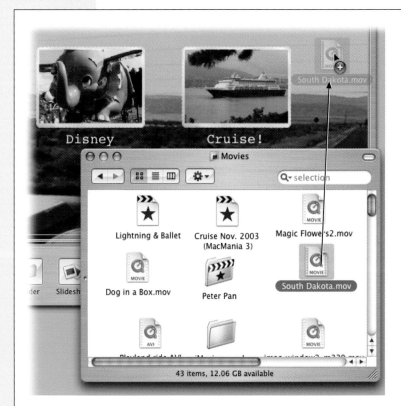

Figure 16-3:
Here's a very quick way to in-stall a movie into one of your menu screens: In the Finder, position the window that contains the movie so that you can see it and the iDVD menu screen at the same time. Then just drag the mov-ies onto the displayed menu and drop them there. (Note, however, that you can't drag iMovie project icons, like the ones with the star icons shown here—only finished QuickTime movies.)

The Movies Media Pane

Dragging files in from the Finder is great, but it assumes that you know where your movies are. Fortunately, if you're a little fuzzy on where you've stored all your movie files, iDVD can help.

Open the Customize drawer (click the Customize button at the bottom of the screen if it isn't already open). Then click the Media button at the top of the drawer and, from the pop-up menu, choose Movies (see Figure 16-4).

The Movies pane opens, showing a list of folders at the top of the pane. At the outset, this list contains only one folder, the Movies folder (which is actually in your Home folder). Click its name to see every digital movie and iMovie project that iDVD can find in that folder (although not in folders *in* that folder.) See the box on the next page for some tips on navigating it. (If you have movies somewhere else on your hard drive, see "Listing more movies," below).

Figure 16-4:
At the top of the pane, you see a list of all the QuickTime movies and iMovie HD project icons in your Home→ Movies folder, or other folders you've told iDVD to search. When you click one of these folders, you see its contents in the pane, exhibited as thumbnail images. Drag your selection into the menu screen to make it part of your DVD-in-waiting.

Listing more movie folders

iDVD starts out displaying only the contents of your Home→Movies folder. This arrangement spares you from looking at a list of the 50,000 individual clips that make up all of your various iMovie projects. The bad news is that it doesn't show you any other folders you have that might contain movies.

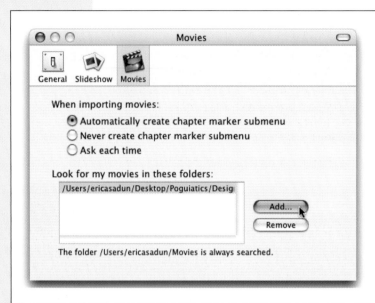

Figure 16-5:
On the Movies preferences panel, click the Add button. Navigate to the folder you need iDVD to search. Click it, and then click Open. iDVD adds the new folder to the list. To remove a file from the list, select it and click Remove. That's the only way you can remove folders from the list (short of trashing your iDVD preference file).

GEM IN THE ROUGH

Useful Pane Tricks

The following tricks and tips may help when using any of the panes (Movies, Audio, or Photos) in the Customize drawer.

Adjust your list panes. Drag the resize bar (the horizontal bar with the small dot that appears between the two panes) to reapportion vertical space between the upper and lower sections of the pane.

Play it. If you double-click a movie or sound, it plays. (You can also click it once and then click the triangular Play button at the bottom of the pane.) Click once anywhere to stop the playback. Use as needed to jog your memory.

Search. If you've got a seething mass of movies to root

through, click in the Search box below the list and type a few letters of the name of the movie, picture, or song you want. As you type, iDVD hides all entries except those whose names match. Capitalization doesn't matter, but you can search through only one folder, album, or playlist at a time. (Restore the entire list by clicking the little X at the right end of the Search box.)

Select more than one. You can highlight more than one movie, picture, or song at a time, and therefore save time by dragging them all onto the screen at once. Exactly as in the Finder, you can click the first entry, then Shift-click the last to select an entire group. Or you can ⌘-click random thumbnails to select a nonadjacent set.

Fortunately, you can teach iDVD to list the contents of additional movie folders. To do so, drag new folders from the Finder to the list in the Movies pane, or choose iDVD→Preferences (⌘-comma), click the Movies button, and follow the steps in Figure 16-5. Repeat for as many folders as you want to add.

Clips and Movies from iMovie

If you click the Create iDVD Project button in iMovie, as described in the previous chapter, iMovie creates a brand-new iDVD project. iMovie offers no obvious way to install a *second or third* movie into an existing iDVD project.

That's a shame, because most homemade DVDs are not, in fact, 90-minute opuses, complete with character development and a satisfying narrative arc. (In fact, an hour and a half of *anybody's* home movies is about 80 minutes too long.) Most of the time, people want to fill a DVD with *several* of their finished iMovie projects. They want each button on the DVD's main menu to represent a *complete movie*.

Figure 16-6:
After saving your iMovie project (right), you can drag the entire movie onto an iDVD menu screen (left) by using the project icon in the title bar as a handle. The trick is to hold down the mouse button on that icon momentarily until it darkens before you begin to drag.

Alternatively, you can drag individual clips from iMovie (either the Movie Track or the Clips pane) into iDVD, as shown here at bottom.

Fortunately, it's easy enough to create this effect. In iLife '05, you can drag either an iMovie *clip* or an entire iMovie *project* into iDVD—if you know what to drag. Figure 16-6 shows all.

Note: The drag-the-title-bar-icon trick illustrated in Figure 16-6 works only for iMovie projects that have been saved in the new, single-icon iMovie HD project format (page 112). If your project is still represented on your hard drive as a project folder, you can't drag its title-bar icon.

Whichever way you pick, whatever you just dragged turns into a new button on the menu page.

Movies with Chapters

You already know from the previous chapter that if you export a movie directly from iMovie, any chapter markers you've added automatically turn into buttons in iDVD.

But what happens if you drag an iMovie movie, itself containing chapter markers, into iDVD as described above?

Unless you've changed the iMovie settings, iDVD automatically turns those chapter markers into buttons, just as though you'd exported the movie from iMovie. They wind up on a menu screen of their own—a *submenu*.

Unfortunately, you've now created a fairly complex menu structure. To jump to a certain scene in your dragged-in iMovie, your audience has to navigate through three different pages of buttons.

For that reason, you might not always want iMovie to turn your chapter markers into buttons—at least not without asking your permission.

Choose iDVD→Preferences. On the General tab, you have three choices under "When importing movies":

- **"Automatically create chapter marker submenu."** This is the factory setting. When you drag an iMovie project into iDVD, it turns into a folder-icon button. Your audience must "click" that button with the remote control to get to a second screen, where they can either play the movie or access *its* scene-selection menu. (See the following section for more on navigating "folder" menus in iDVD.)

- **"Never create chapter marker submenu."** If you choose this option, dragging an iMovie movie into a menu screen creates a movie button, not a folder button. "Clicking" that button with the remote control makes the movie play immediately.

  Your audience no longer has the option of navigating your movie by viewing a page full of scene markers.

Tip: Even though your viewers won't see individual icons for these scenes, they can still jump to them using the Next Chapter or Previous Chapter buttons on their remote controls.

- **"Ask each time."** When you drag a chapter-filled movie onto a menu screen, iMovie says: "Do you want to add chapter markers for this movie?" Click Yes (if you want to create the nested-menus effect described three paragraphs ago), or No (if you want the invisible chapter-markers effect described two paragraphs ago).

Submenus ("Folders")

Depending on the theme you've chosen, iDVD may impose a limit of six or twelve buttons on a menu screen. Fortunately, that doesn't mean you're limited to twelve scenes in a movie, or twelve movies per DVD. You, or iDVD, can accommodate more movies by creating *submenus*—additional menu screens that branch off from the main menu—and even sub-submenus.

You may have seen this effect already, in fact, if you've tried to create an iMovie DVD containing more than a handful of chapter markers.

You can also create this effect manually. Whenever you click the Folder button at the bottom of the screen, iDVD adds a submenu button to the current menu screen. In some themes, especially those that began life in previous versions of iDVD, this button looks like an actual folder; in most, it's simply a new text button.

Behind the scenes, this button represents a second menu screen, a blank canvas with room for yet another six or twelve buttons.

Navigating Submenus

Navigating iDVD Folders while building your project is pretty easy, once you master these tips:

WORKAROUND WORKSHOP

Temporary Buttons

When you try to add more than twelve buttons to a menu screen, iDVD gracefully announces, "There are too many buttons in the current menu to add a new one."

As with previous versions of iDVD, you can click OK to dismiss the message and return to editing your project—without the new button you tried to add.

But iDVD 5 offers what's often a more convenient alternative: A Temporarily Allow button that lets you add those extra buttons to your menus for now,

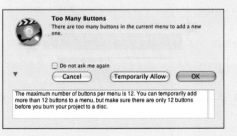

so that you have the convenience of (for example) cutting and pasting them to other menu screens.

But with great power comes great responsibility: iDVD wants you to understand that you can't actually burn a DVD with too many buttons on a menu screen. If you forget to dispose of the extra buttons before clicking the Burn button, another warning message appears (shown here at bottom), and your burning efforts come to a grinding halt.

• **Open by double-clicking.** Double-click any folder or submenu button to "open" it—that is, to bring up the menu screen it represents.

• **Return by clicking the arrow.** Each submenu screen contains a Back arrow. Click this arrow to return to the "parent" menu.

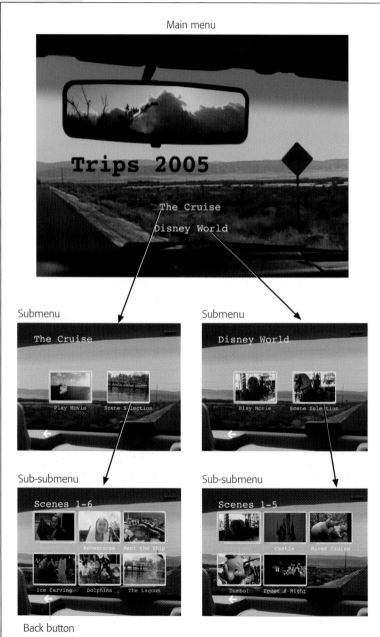

Main menu

Submenu

Submenu

Sub-submenu

Sub-submenu

Back button

Figure 16-7:
An iDVD menu screen can't hold more than twelve buttons. If you try to place any more, you'll have to branch off into submenu screens, or even sub-submenu screens. This DVD has two movies, each of which has chapters within. When your audience clicks a movie's name (with the remote control), they go to a submenu screen with a Play button (to play the whole movie) and a Scene Selection button (to open yet another menu screen, this one showing your chapter markers so that the audience can choose a point to begin playback). These submenus create extra room for navigation through your project. As your projects grow more complex, you must use folders to add enough space to showcase all your pictures and movies.

Tip: As you work with your menu and submenu screens, navigating folders may seem painfully slow unless you turn off iDVD's background encoding feature. (Its purpose is to quietly pre-process your video while you're working, so that burning the DVD will take less time.) To do that, choose iDVD→Preferences, click the General button, and then turn off "Enable background encoding."

- **Names may not match.** A folder/submenu button's label may bear no relationship to the title on the submenu screen. You have to edit the text individually in both places if you want to make a change.

- **Themes don't have to match.** Each menu screen can have its own theme. In fact, when you click a theme thumbnail in the Themes pane of the Customize drawer, iDVD changes *only* the menu screen you're looking at right now. If you want that theme to apply to all menu screens, you have to choose Advanced→Apply Theme to Folders.

- **Mind your minutes.** The more folders and more themes you add to your project, the closer you come to iDVD's limit of 15 minutes' worth of menu videos.

Reaching that limit isn't such a remote possibility, either; even one-minute video loops on 15 menu screens will take up all your available space, even if you use the same background video on every menu.

When you try to add a new menu that takes up too much space, you'll see the warning shown in Figure 16-8.

Figure 16-8:
When you try to add a new menu that would exceed iDVD's 15-minute background-video limit, this message appears. Click Cancel to eliminate the new menu. Click Ignore to add the menu despite the warning, with the understanding that you'll have to solve the space issue manually before you burn the DVD. Or click Fix to make iDVD shorten the menu's loop so that it fits within the remaining video menu space on your disc.

If, in that dialog box, you opt to ignore the warning, you're welcome to solve the too-much-background-video problem your own way—just as long as you solve the problem before you burn the DVD. If not, when you go to burn, you'll be prompted once again to lower the total menu minutes.

Tip: You can always peek at the current overall menu duration of your project by opening the Customize drawer and clicking the Status tab. The project size section lists the current total menu duration used by your project.

The DVD Map—and Autoplay

As you can see, menus and submenus can build up with alarming rapidity. At times your projects may grow out of control; pretty soon, you feel like Hansel and Gretel with not enough bread crumbs.

iDVD's Map pretty much eliminates these navigation problems. It's a living, interactive diagram whose icons represent your DVD's menus, videos, and slideshows and reveal

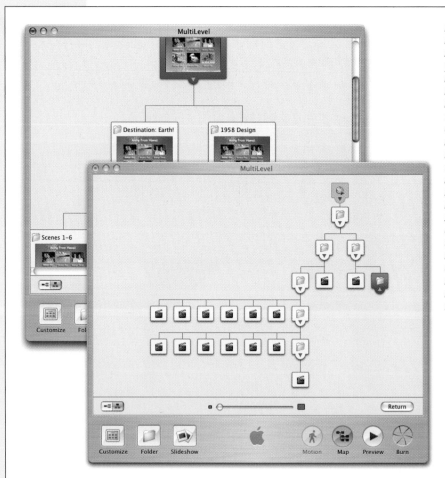

Figure 16-9:
In iDVD 5, the size slider lets you view the map either with large, slide-like icons (back) or with little tiny ones that reveal more of your DVD's structure without scrolling. Here, the right-most folder hides a series of submenus just as detailed as the ones shown in the left branch of the tree—but it's been hidden by collapsing the flippy triangle.

how they're connected. As your menu and button layouts grow more complex, you can use the map screen to help you keep track of your menu structure.

To view the map, click the Map button at the bottom of the main iDVD window. The element you were working on appears with colored highlighting (Figure 16-9).

- **Scroll it** by dragging in any blank space.

- Click one of the **view buttons** to flip the display between horizontal- and vertical-tree layouts.

- The **scale slider** lets you adjust the amount of map detail you can see at once. Working a big, complex project? Move the slider all the way to the left to view more elements at once. Working on a small project? The bigger the tiles, the more project details you'll see.

- Each menu tile now includes a **flippy triangle.** Click it to expand or collapse that limb of the menu tree (Figure 16-9, right).

- **Open a menu or slideshow** by double-clicking its icon in the Map.

- **Click the Map button again** or click Return to return to the menu screen you were working on.

Editing in the Map

Now, in previous versions of iDVD, the Map window provided a visual treat, but you couldn't really *do* anything there. But in iDVD 5, the map is interactive; you can actually do DVD design and editing work all on this single screen.

For example:

- It's easy to delete a bunch of menus or other elements all at once. Just Shift-click the ones you want to target for extermination (Shift-click a second time if you select an icon by mistake), and then press the Delete key.

- Similarly, you can quickly and conveniently apply new themes to the menu screens of your DVD without ever leaving the map. To do so, open the Customize drawer, click the Themes button, select the desired menu icons on the map, and then click the new theme's name.

- You can even add new menu screens and slideshows on the Map screen. Click the icon of the menu screen where you want to put the button that will link to the new menu or slideshow, and then choose Project→New Folder (for a submenu) or Project→New Slideshow. (At that point, you can then specify *which* movies or *which* photos you want on those new entities by dragging them in from the Customize drawer's Media panel.)

- Remember the transitions (cross-dissolve effects) that let you ease from one menu screen to another? You can apply or change these transition styles en masse using the Map, too. Just Shift-click to choose the menu icons you want to transition *out* of, open the Customize panel, click the Settings button, and then use the Transition pop-up menu to choose the style you want for all of them at once.

Autoplay

The DVDs described so far in this book behave like commercial Hollywood DVDs in almost every respect except one: they don't play a certain video clip automatically when the disc is inserted, *before* the menu screen appears. You know—a bright red FBI warning, previews of coming attractions, or maybe just a quick snippet of the movie on the DVD.

iDVD 5 makes creating this kind of "pre-movie" extremely easy. In Map view, the first tile (at the top or the left, depending on the view you've chosen) is technically called the Project tile (see Figure 16-10), but you can think of it as the Autoplay tile. Whatever you drag onto this tile will play automatically when the DVD is inserted, before your viewers even touch their remote controls.

These are the kinds of things you can put there:

- **A video clip.** In the Customize drawer, click the Media button, and then choose Movies from the pop-up menu. iDVD displays all the movies in your Home→ Movies folder (and any other folders you've listed here); drag the one you want directly onto the Project tile to install it there.

- **A still image.** In the Customize drawer, again, click the Media button, but this time choose Photos from the pop-up menu. iDVD shows your complete iPhoto collection, including all of your albums. To use one of these images as a startup screen for your DVD project, just drag it onto the Project tile. (You can add audio to it, too, just as you'd add audio to a slideshow—by dragging in an audio file from the Audio section of the Media pane.)

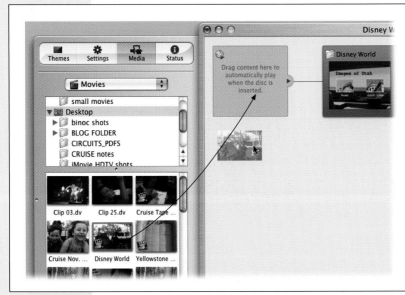

Figure 16-10:
If you decide to add or replace your Autoplay material, just drag new stuff right onto it. Or, to eliminate the Autoplay segment, drag it right off the Project tile. It disappears in a little puff of Mac OS X cartoon smoke.

Tip: If you tinker with the graphics tools in a program like Photoshop or AppleWorks, you could come up with a decent replica of the standard FBI warning that appears as the Autoplay of a commercial DVD. You could precisely duplicate the wording and typographical look—or you could take the opportunity to do a hilarious spoof of the usual warning.

- **A slideshow.** Once you've got the Photos list open in the Customize drawer as described above, you can also drag an entire iPhoto album onto the project icon. Alternatively, you can click and ⌘-click just the photos you want in the Customize panel, and then drag them en masse onto the project icon. In fact, you can even drag photos—as a group or in a folder—right out of the Finder and onto this icon.

To control how long your still image remains on the screen, or how quickly your Autoplay slideshow plays, double-click your Project tile. You arrive at the AutoPlay slideshow editor, a screen like the one shown in Figure 16-10, where you can adjust the timing, transition, and even the audio that plays behind the picture(s).

Tip: It's possible to create a DVD that never even gets to the menu screen—a DVD consisting only of Autoplay material. You could design a project that way for the benefit of, for example, technophobic DVD novices whose pupils dilate just contemplating using a remote control. They can just insert your Autoplay-only DVD and sit back on the couch as the movie plays automatically.

Looping

If you highlight the button for a movie, slideshow, or Autoplay tile—either in Map view or on a menu screen—and then choose Advanced→Loop Movie (or Loop Slide Show), you unleash another raft of possibilities. You can make a DVD that repeats the highlighted material (a slideshow or movie) over and over again and, in fact, *never* gets back to the menu screen.

Tip: In the Map, a small circle appears in the lower-right corner of any element you've set up for looping.

That would be a great way to create a DVD containing a self-running, self-repeating slideshow of digital photos that plays on a TV at a party or wedding reception. You could also use it to create a self-looping kiosk display at a trade show.

In any case, the DVD will loop endlessly—or at least until it occurs to someone in your audience to press the Menu or Title button on the remote, which displays your main menu. At this point, the Menu button redisplays the previous menu screen; the Title button causes a return to the main menu.

DVD Slideshows

The DVD may be the world's best delivery mechanism for digital photos. Your friends and family sit there on the couch—in the comfort of their own living room, as the saying goes. They click the remote control to walk through your photos (or, if you choose, they relax and let the slideshow advance automatically). Instead of passing around a tiny pile of fragile 4 x 6 prints, your audience gets to watch the photos at TV-screen size—accompanied by a musical soundtrack of your choice.

If you've installed movies into an iDVD menu screen, installing photos will seem like a piece of cake. Once again, you can do so using several different methods, each with its own advantages:

- **iPhoto albums.** When you open the Customize drawer, click the Media button, and choose Photos from the pop-up, iDVD presents your entire iPhoto picture collection, complete with the albums you've used to organize them.

  The great thing about this system is that iPhoto albums contain well-defined image progressions—that is, you presumably dragged the photos into an emotionally satisfying sequence. That's exactly how iDVD will present the pictures: as they appear in the album, from the first image to the last.

- **Folder drag and drop.** If the pictures you want to add aren't in iPhoto, you can also drag a folder full of them right off the desktop (or a Finder folder) and onto an iDVD menu screen. iDVD creates a slideshow from the images, all right, but puts them into an unpredictable sequence.

- **Slideshow editor.** iDVD comes with a special window called the Slideshow Editor, in which you can add individual photos to the slideshow and drag them into any order you like. This approach takes a little work, but it gives you the freedom to import images from many different sources without having to organize them beforehand.

Tip: A DVD slideshow (***any*** DVD, not just those produced by iDVD) can contain at most 99 slides, and one DVD can contain at most 99 slideshows. The designers of the DVD format obviously recognized that there's a limit to the patience of home slideshow audiences.

---

iPhoto Albums

You can use either of two approaches to create iDVD slideshows from your iPhoto album collection. One way begins in iPhoto; the other begins in iDVD.

Starting in iPhoto

As part of the much-heralded integration of iPhoto, iTunes, iMovie, and iDVD, iPhoto 5 offers a menu choice that exports albums and slideshows to iDVD. In the iPhoto Source list, click the album or slideshow you want to export, choose Share→Send to iDVD, and then wait as iPhoto transfers the data.

Tip: If you do a lot of this, you can add a Send to iDVD button to your iPhoto toolbar (at the bottom of the window). Just choose Share→Show in Toolbar→Send to iDVD.

Now, although the steps are the same for the iPhoto entities called *albums* and *slideshows,* the results in iDVD are different.

- If you export an iPhoto *slideshow* (a set of photos to which you've applied music, panning and zooming effects, specific crossfade styles, and even individual, per-slide timings), iDVD treats the result as a *movie.* Your audience will see a frozen slideshow when they press the Enter or Play buttons on their remote. They'll see the pictures in the sequence, and with the timings, *you* specified; they'll have no control over the show.

   You can work with this movie as you would any other movie you've imported from iMovie or the Finder.

- If you export an *album* (a "folder" full of photos, assembled and arranged by you), iDVD treats the result as a *slideshow*—a collection of pictures that your DVD audience can peruse, one at a time, using the arrow buttons on their remote controls.

   The rest of this discussion applies to these DVD slideshows.

In iDVD, a slideshow looks like a submenu button that bears the name of the album you exported. Double-click it to view the list of pictures inside, change their sequence, and make other adjustments, as described on page 405.

Tip: If you make changes to your iPhoto album—by adding photos or rearranging them, for example—click iPhoto's iDVD button again. Instead of adding a second copy to your DVD project, iDVD is smart enough to **update** the existing slideshow. Thanks to this smart feature, you can update your albums as often as you like without any adverse affects on your iDVD project.

Note, however, that you don't enjoy this luxury when you use the Photos pane within iDVD. Dragging an album out of the Photos pane onto a menu a second time gives you a second copy.

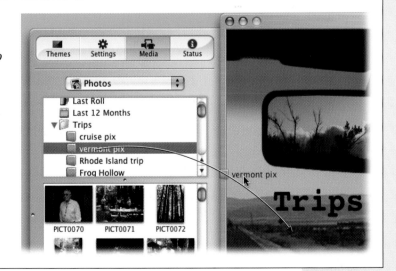

Figure 16-11:
To add a new slideshow, drag any album (from the top pane of the Media Photos pane) onto your iDVD workspace. You can also select more than one album and drag them en masse. (The usual multiple-selection tricks apply: ⌘-click several albums in turn to select all of them, for example.)

Starting in iDVD

If you haven't already been working in iPhoto, there's an even easier way to turn iPhoto albums into living slideshows. Just open the Customize drawer, click the Media tab, choose Photos from the pop-up menu, and voilà: You're presented with the tiny thumbnails of every digital photo in your collection. You even get to see the list of albums, exactly as they appear in iPhoto (Figure 16-11).

Drag Photo Folders from the Finder

Suppose you don't keep all of your pictures in iPhoto. (Hey, it could happen.)

In that case, you may prefer to drag a folder of photos out of the Finder and onto an iDVD menu screen. (Make sure that the folder contains nothing but pictures. If it contains any other kind of document, or even other folders, iDVD may complain that it can't handle the "Unsupported File Type: Unknown Format.")

In any case, the folder shows up on the menu screen as a new slideshow button. You're ready to edit your slideshow, as described below.

Add a Slideshow, Worry about the Pictures Later

If all of your photographic masterpieces aren't already together in iPhoto or even in a Finder folder, you can also bring them into iDVD individually.

To do that, start by creating a new slideshow folder: Click the Slideshow button near the bottom-left of the iDVD window (or choose Project→Add Slideshow). iDVD creates a new, empty slideshow. Double-click it to enter the Slideshow Editor described next.

Editing Slideshows

No matter how you got your slideshow folder button into iDVD, you edit it the same way: by double-clicking it to open iDVD's Slideshow Editor. See Figure 16-12 for a quick tour.

Adding or omitting slides

If you want to add new pictures to the slideshow, use any of the following techniques:

- **Drag from the Finder**. Drag an image, a selection of several images, or a folder of images directly into the slide list.

- **Use the Media Photos Pane**. Open the Customize drawer and click the Media button at the top; choose Photos from the pop-up menu. Drag a picture, a set of several shots, or an iPhoto album into the slide list.

- **Import an image**. Choose File→Import→Image. Navigate to any picture file, select it, and then click Open.

Tip: Before clicking Open, you can highlight several photos to bring them all in at once. If the ones you want appear consecutively in the list, click the first one, and then Shift-click the last one, to highlight all of them. If not, ⌘-click each photo file that you want to import.

Either way, click Open to bring them all into iDVD simultaneously.

To remove a picture from the list, just click it and then press the Delete key. You can also remove a whole bunch of pictures simultaneously by first Shift-clicking them or ⌘ -clicking them, exactly as described in the previous Tip, before pressing Delete.

Reordering Slides

Changing the sequence of slides involves little more than dragging them to their new position. Yet again, you can select multiple slides at once (see the preceding Tip) and then drag them en masse.

Slideshow Options

iDVD offers some useful options at the bottom of the Slideshow Editor window:

- **Loop slideshow.** If you turn on the "Loop slideshow" checkbox, the slideshow repeats endlessly, or until your viewer presses the Menu or Title button on the DVD remote control.

- **Display navigation.** When you turn on this option, you'll see navigation arrows on the screen as your slideshow plays. Your audience can click these buttons with their remote controls to move back and forth within your slideshow.

  Navigation gives your viewers a feeling of flexibility and control. On the other hand, remember that they can always use the < and > buttons on their remote controls to move through the slides, even if no arrows appear on the screen. (Furthermore, you may consider the majesty of your photography marred by the superimposed triangle buttons.)

- **Add files to DVD-ROM.** When iDVD creates a slideshow, it scales all of your photos to 640 x 480 pixels.

  That's ideal for a standard television screen, which, in fact, can't display any resolution higher than that.

  But if you intend to distribute your DVD to somebody who is computer savvy, you may want to give them the original, full-resolution photos. They won't see these photos when they insert the disc into a DVD player. But when they insert your DVD into their *computers,* they'll see a folder filled with the original, high-res photos, for purposes like printing, using as Desktop wallpaper, and so on. (In other words, you've created a dual-format disc that's both a DVD-video disc and a DVD-ROM.)

- **Slide Duration.** This pop-up list allows you to specify how much time each slide spends on the screen before the next one appears: 1, 3, 5, 10 seconds, or Manual.

Manual, of course, means that your audience will have to press the Next button on the remote control to change pictures.

Then there's the Fit to Audio option, which appears in the pop-up menu only after you've added a sound file or a playlist to your slideshow. In this case, iDVD will determine the timing of your slides automatically—by dividing the length of the soundtrack by the number of slides in your show. In other words, if the song is 60 seconds long, and you've got 20 slides in the show, each slide will sit on the screen for three seconds.

Tip: Fit to Audio offers a nifty way to create a simple, no-fuss DVD "mix tape" that you can play on your home theater system. Drop a song into the Audio well (page 406) but add only one photograph, which may be the album art for that song or a graphic showing the song's title. Make a series of "slideshows" this way.

Once you burn the whole thing to a DVD, you can choose a song to start playing in its entirety with the album cover on the screen. (If you add an album-in-a-playlist instead of just one song, you can choose an album to play in the same way.)

- **Transition.** You can specify any of several graceful transition effects—Dissolve, Cube, and so on—to govern how one slide morphs into the next. You can try each of these styles for yourself by selecting one and then watching your slideshow (click Preview to start the show; click it again to return to the editor). Viewing just a few slides will show you how the transitions work on real images.

Note: The transition you specify here affects all slides in the show.

In **Cube,** your slides rotate as though they're on the sides of a 3-D virtual picture cube. (If you're familiar with Apple's Keynote program, or if you've used Mac OS X's Fast User Switching feature, you've seen this animation before.) Use the arrows in the circle next to the pop-up menu to select the direction for the rotation.

Dissolve produces a standard (but gorgeous) crossfade effect, dissolving from one image to the next. In **Droplet,** a water-like wave allows each photo to progress to the next one. **Fade Through Black** brings back the look of an old carousel slide projector, as each slide fades in and out from black.

Each of the **Flip** options rotates an image from back to front to back again, updating to a new image each time it turns. Choose a direction for your flip. To use **Mosaic Flip Large** and **Mosaic Flip Small,** choose a direction as well. Segments of your slide flip over, as though on a mosaic with loose tiles, to reveal a new image.

Page Flip looks like an animated page turn. You choose the direction that each image is "paged" off the screen. **Wipe** is similar, except that here, one slide "wipes" across the previous one in the direction you specify.

When using **Push,** choose a direction. Your slides will "scroll" in that direction, with each new picture pushing the previous one out of the way. **Reveal** look like a stack of photos, as each picture sequentially slides away in the direction you pick.

If you're sure your audience will have a strong stomach, **Twirl** does exactly what the name suggests. It rotates away each picture before rotating in the next.

If you don't want any transition animation, choose **None.** iDVD will simply cut from one slide to the next.

Tip: iDVD can put crossfades and transitions between menus, too. That way, when your audience clicks a button on the main menu screen, the screen doesn't just *jump cut* to the selected move or slideshow; it crossfades, wipes, rotates on the face of a cube, or whatever.

To specify which transition you'd like, open the Customize drawer and click the Settings button at the top. Select one or more menu buttons and then use the Transition pop-up menu to specify the effect you want. (In iDVD 5, you can use a different transition for each button.)

Slideshow Audio

Music has a profound impact on the effect of a photo slideshow. You can't appreciate how dramatic the difference is until you watch the same slideshow with and without music playing.

iDVD starts out with whatever music you've selected in iPhoto, but if "Minuet in G" isn't your thing, fear not. You can use any music you like.

The easiest way to add music to your slideshow is to open the Customize drawer, click the Media button at the top, and select Audio from the pop-up. Conveniently enough,

Figure 16-12:
The iDVD Slideshow Editor lets you build and customize your slideshows. Each slide appears in order, with its number and a thumbnail; you can move them around by dragging, delete the ones you don't want, or add new ones by dragging graphics from the desktop or the Media pane of the Customize drawer. The buttons in the lower-left corner switch between a list view and an icon view (shown here). Click Return to go back to iDVD's menu-editing mode.

iDVD shows your entire iTunes music collection, complete with any playlists you've assembled (Figure 16-13).

Tip: This list also includes any music you've created yourself using GarageBand (and exported to iTunes). Such songs make great slideshow soundtracks, because you've tailored them to the mood and the length of the show.

When you find suitable musical accompaniment, drag its name out of the iTunes list and onto the rounded rectangle—the well, as Apple calls it—labeled Audio (also shown in Figure 16-13). You can even drag an entire playlist into the well; the DVD will play one song after another according to the playlist, so that the music won't die ignominiously in the middle of the slide show. You can also drag a sound file from any Finder window or the desktop—and directly onto this Audio well.

Tip: When it's empty, the Audio well looks like a small speaker. When it's occupied, its icon identifies the kind of audio file you've installed; the little icon will say, for example, AIFF, AU, or MP3. The icon used when you add a playlist rather than a single song varies, usually showing the first audio file type used in the playlist.

To try out a different piece of background music, drag a new song or audio file into the Audio well. And if you decide that you don't want music at all, drag the file icon directly out of the Audio well and onto any other part of the screen. You see an animated puff of smoke confirm your decision.

Tip: If you can play a sound file in iTunes, you can include it in an iDVD project. If not, use a converter program to bring it into a usable format. For example, iTunes can't import MIDI files, but GarageBand can—and GarageBand can export to AIFF, a format that iTunes understands.

Curiously enough, iTunes can play back soundtracks from iMovie projects. Just drag your iMovie HD project into iTunes and then import them into iDVD from your media pane. You can also drag a QuickTime movie directly onto the Audio well and drop it in. iDVD uses the first audio track.

Leaving the Slideshow Editor

To return to iDVD's menu editor, click the Return button at the bottom right of the Slideshow Editor.

Burning Your Slideshow

Once you've designed a slideshow DVD, previewing it and burning it onto a blank DVD works exactly as described beginning on page 375.

Since most people have never thrilled to the experience of viewing a digital-camera slideshow on their TV sets, a few notes are in order:

- Your viewers can use the remote control's Next and Previous buttons to move forward or backward through the presentation, no matter what timing you originally specified when you designed the show.

- They can also press the Pause button to freeze a certain picture on the screen for greater study (or while they go to the bathroom). Both the slide advancing and music stop until they click Pause or Play button, again.

- If the audio selection or playlist is shorter than the slideshow, the song starts over again.

- Your viewers can return to the main menu screen by clicking the Menu button on the remote.

- When the slideshow is over, the music stops and the main menu screen reappears.

CHAPTER
17

Designing iDVD Themes

S ome of Apple's iDVD themes offer great backgrounds but weak audio. Others provide terrific sounds but terrible text. Some create a nearly perfect package, while others seem broken beyond repair. Fortunately, in the end it doesn't matter, because iDVD lets you adapt themes to your taste and save them as new *Favorites*.

Favorites let you move beyond built-in themes and presets to create truly customized DVD menu systems. You can change font, adjust the length of the looping background video, move buttons around and change their styles, change the fonts and colors for button and menu titles, move text around the screen, substitute new background art or background patterns, replace or remove the audio loop that plays when the main menu is onscreen, and much more. Let this chapter be your guide.

iDVD's Built-in Themes

In iDVD 5, Apple added 15 new themes. Many of the new ones include fabulous motion backgrounds and moving drop zones, as described in the preceding chapters. Special events inspire some themes, like the wedding and new-baby themes. Others key into special interests, like sports and travel.

Themes also vary in complexity. Some offer completely realized presentations. Others provide little more than colors and fonts, leaving it up to you to mold them. Either way, the built-in themes, both old and new, provide an excellent jumping-off point for your DVDs.

The Themes Pane

All three collections—5.0 Themes, 4.0 Themes and Old Themes—appear in the Themes pane in the Customize drawer, as you can see in Figure 15-10 (page 366). (To view the Themes pane, click Customize to open the Customize drawer, then click the Themes button at the top of the pane.)

As you study the scrolling list of themes, you'll notice that:

- **Favorites appear together.** When you choose Favorites from the Theme Set pop-up menu at the top of the pane, all Favorites (themes that you've created) appear together in the same list. This list is empty when you start out using iDVD.

- **Most non-Apple themes appear separately.** Themes you've bought from other companies (like *www.idvdthemetastic.com* or *www.idvdthemepak.com*) are listed separately in the pane's pop-up menu.

- **View several sets at once.** iDVD 5 lets you view a single set of themes, or all themes at once. To view just one set, select its name from the Theme Set pop-up menu. To view all themes, choose All from that same menu.

- **The walking-man icon means sound or audio.** When you see a small, round, walking-man logo in the lower-right corner of the theme thumbnail, that's your signal that the theme uses a motion background or audio loop.

- **The ribbon means favorite.** A gray prize ribbon appears in the lower-left corner of certain themes. This icon lets you know that the theme is a Favorite—a theme that you created yourself. You'll find out how to create Favorites later in this chapter.

The Built-in Themes

In quality and usability, iDVD themes range from the elegant to the absurd. Here's a quick rundown of the themes built into iDVD 5.

Tip: You'll find an excellent interactive overview of iDVD's built-in themes, showing what they look like as completed DVD projects, at www.apple.com/ilife/idvd/theater/newthemes.html.

5.0 Themes

Name	Notes	
Travel Cards	This theme is the factory setting for new projects. It includes a series of six "postcards" (photo drop zones) that glide smoothly across the screen over a tropically inspired bamboo background. A vast improvement over the previous version's default theme.	

| Memories | Three water droplets fall into a placid pool, each creating ripples that widen into a drop zone. Unfortunately, the white lettering of the all-text buttons is hard to read unless you choose contrasting drop-zone contents. |  |

Sliding Panes

A silent theme, Sliding Panes features a series of drop zones that gradually get covered up with a seemingly random series of rectangular black blocks. Out of seven drop zones, only two appear in the main loop. Make sure to use short button names with this one—and don't even try to populate the seven drop zones directly. Instead, use the drop-zone editor (choose Project→Edit Drop Zones) so you won't have to play "catch the animated drop zone" with your cursor.

Full Frame 1 and 2

These all-text themes provide simple labeling on top of a single, full-frame photo or video clip background.

Anime Pop

This theme represents Japanese Anime-style animation at its most floral. Five drop zones fly around a desert background in happy, happy flowers. Plonky music plays and stars drift to the ground.

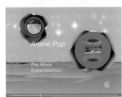

Wedding White

Elegant and easy on the eyes, this theme offers animated, semi-transparent white waves that roll by on the bottom half of the screen, as a slideshow of four photos fills the upper half of the screen. Triumphant music plays. Choose stills rather than slideshows or videos to create the best impact for this lovely theme.

Baby Mobile

Six drop zones, resembling photos hanging from a baby's crib mobile, rotate as sweet music plays. The lighting, shadow, and perspective effects are fabulous; it's almost worth having a baby just so you can use this theme. Keep the button names short.

Travel 1

A lively—very lively—travel-themed offering that never seems to stop. Eleven drop zones look like travel postcards shooting, nonstop, from right to left, obscured occasionally by animated globes and suitcases flying from left to right. You won't be able to catch a breath.

Travel 2

The sedate (and mercifully still) companion to Travel 1. Works out very handily as a submenu.

Techno B&W (and Color)

Three drop zones (either in B&W or color) recede, then shrink onto a white backdrop, while a "control bar" (purple in the B&W theme, gray in Color) offers text-button access. Keep the text short.

Lines

A strip of six drop zones scrolls slowly, silently, like frames of film, from right to left on a stark black backdrop. One of the better 5.0 themes.

Portfolio

Twelve drop zones jump up out of a mosaic layout to show themselves to you. Like a reverse of the Techno theme, except this version is attractive.

Scrapbook

Nice music highlights a scrapbook-inspired presentation with a rotation of three drop zones. Flowers, suns, and balloons dance around and change colors.

4.0 Themes

Wedding (Bronze and Silver)

A curtain billows silently in the background of this cool, elegant theme, offered in two colors and two styles: main page ("One") and submenu ("Two").

Drive-in

A retro-inspired Drive-in. Not the height of graphic design perfection, what with its busy design, huge drop zone, and somewhat grating audio loop. The submenu theme (Drive-in Two) is only slightly better.

Montage

Brash and stylish, Montage offers an exciting and usable screen design. With its flashing colors and loud rhythms, however, this theme isn't for the easily annoyed (or people trying to sleep).

Kids Theater

This theme is geared toward junior movie makers, although its "Good Old Summertime" calliope background loop may drive even children loopy. Parts of the design fall outside of the safe video zones. Kids Theater Two, the submenu version, is a tad better.

Road Trip

Good music and a clever drop zone. Your pictures or movies appear in the rear view mirror as your road-trip-mobile cruises through the desert. (Road Trip Two is a view out the back window of the car—cute, real cute.)

Pop-Art

Unfortunately, the thin, high-contrast text makes this theme almost unusable on standard television sets. It's pretty on your computer, not so pretty on disc.

Reveal

A basic, workable theme in which a column of drop zones slowly reveal their contents.

Fish

This stylish theme offers hints of Finding Nemo, as a realistic-looking fish swims back and forth in front of whatever photo or movie you've dropped into the drop zone. Clean and witty.

Blocks

Here's an awfully cutesy, baby-centered theme. At least it doesn't move.

Marquee

Looks like an old-style movie marquee, complete with old-style music.

Transparent (Blue, Green, Black)

The natural outgrowth of the iDVD team saying "Quick, we need three extra themes." Your drop zone fills most of the screen, with text buttons beneath.

Old Themes

Name	Notes	
Theater	Red drapes open and close to reveal a drop zone while soft music plays in the background. Text buttons. Bad fonts and a disappearing drop zone.	
Book	Overlapping books, one containing a drop zone. Folk guitar music. Text buttons. Very pleasant.	
Projector	A projector appears to play a movie (actually, a black-and-white drop zone with an overlay). Old-fashioned projector clicks and hisses provide an extra layer of realism. A fun theme, but its text buttons are small and hard to read.	
Gen Y	Cool funky music drives a stylish grunge presentation with a central drop zone. Well-designed text buttons. Well-built, balanced theme.	
Picture-in-Picture	Central drop zone. Text buttons. Overall, gray and uninspired. Some designer had a bad morning.	
Brush Strokes	Beige theme with black text buttons and a drop zone that appears to paint itself onto the screen. (This is what happens when designers get carried away with the video effect called *motion masking*.)	

Western

A wood background, an Old West text font, and a central drop zone. It's *Bonanza* all over again.

Sport

Text labels on a sports jersey–themed background. The large drop zone makes it very workable.

Passport

Caribbean music on a very busy passport-themed background. Text buttons and a small drop zone. May be hard for viewers to pick out the foreground details from the background.

Postcard

Large drop zone and text buttons on a postcard-style background. One of iDVD's best themes.

Fun

Retro music plays to a stylish retro foreground—it's right out of the *Bewitched* opening credits. Small drop zone. Multi-colored text buttons. Mediocre music, nice design.

Confetti

Confetti falls in the white motion background. Blue text buttons and a drop zone. Quasi–big band music. The font's small and hard to read, and the background is very busy. Take Dramamine before watching.

Rose Heart

White text buttons over a rose-petal bedecked background. Portions of a drop zone appear through the petals. The awkward heart shape covers rather than emphasizes drop zone material. Worse, it can be hard to read the

thin, white text on top of the overly textured background. Not one of Apple's masterpieces.

Blue, Pink, Orange

Jazzy clarinet music plays behind a static blue-on-blue menu (or pink-on-pink, or orange-on-orange) festooned with stars. Text buttons and a rectangular drop zone. Overall, inoffensive but dull.

Portfolio B&W, Portfolio Color

Black and white and color versions of the same thing: pictures on a pushpin corkboard. The cool part is that each button has a different shape—unusual for a theme.

Moving Bars

More masking madness. The drop zone picture plays behind the translucent buttons. Good design elements are overwhelmed by the overly busy, all-dancing, somewhat blurry drop zone. Not for the weak of stomach.

Brushed Metal One

Like the original iDVD 2 Brushed Metal theme, but with a drop zone. (Hint: Use Brushed Metal Two as the submenu theme.)

Brushed Metal Two

Like Brushed Metal with regular buttons and no drop zones. Missing the large, horizontal, rectangular box feature.

Green Linen One

An earth-tone green textured background with green text buttons and a drop zone.

Green Linen Two

Like Green Linen One but with regular buttons and no drop zone.

Lightbox

A bright background that looks like a light box…sort of. Two small drop zones and text buttons. A simple, easy-to-use theme.

Button Styles

When iDVD was first introduced, its flamboyant button thumbnails generated a lot of excitement. Each button could show a small video or photo, offering visual previews of the linked material.

Times have changed. These days, hyperactive drop zones zoom around the screen, and text buttons have quietly replaced the old button designs. In the 5.0 theme collection, not a single button can display videos or pictures.

If you choose one of the older themes for that reason, you don't have to be content with the proposed button style. To change the look of your buttons, do this:

1. **Open the Customize drawer, if it's not already open.**

   Click the Customize button if necessary.

2. **Click the Themes icon.**

   The Themes pane opens.

3. **From the pop-up menu, choose 4.0 Themes or Old Themes.**

   These are the only themes that contain buttons-with-previews.

4. **Click a theme to see what it looks like.**

   Choose one with non-text buttons, like Fish Two, Brushed Metal Two, or Green Linen Two.

5. **Click the Settings tab at the top of the Customize drawer.**

   The Settings pane appears.

6. **Near the bottom of the panel, click the From Theme pop-up button.**

   You get a pop-up menu of button shapes (Figure 17-1).

7. **Click the button style you want.**

Choices include gilded frames, file frames, hearts, ovals, and more. Choose T to use a text button (just words, no picture). To revert to whatever button style the theme originally came with, choose From Theme.

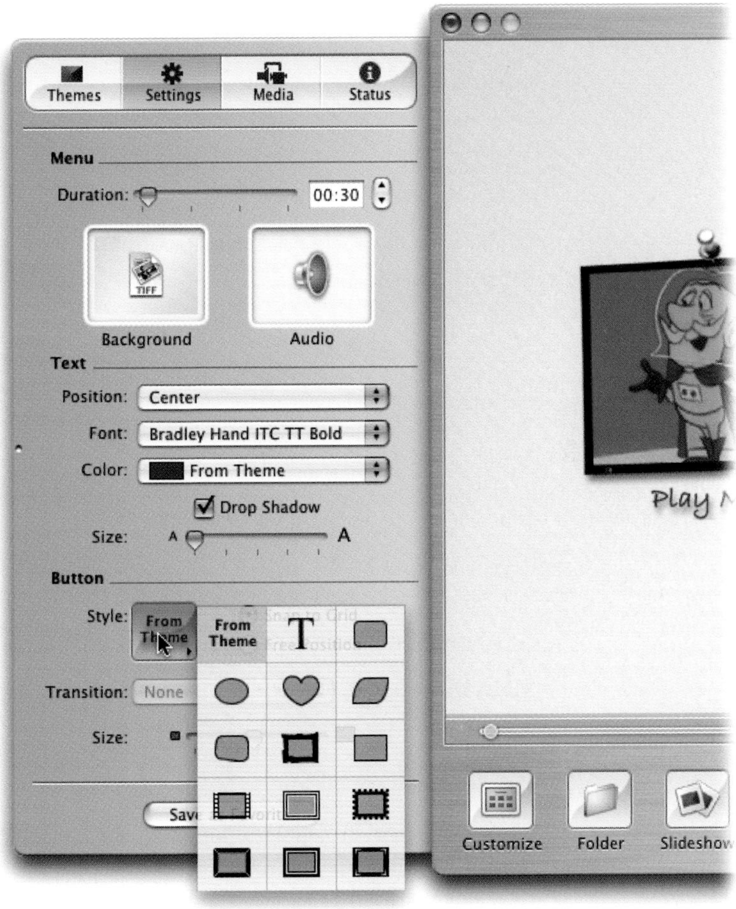

Figure 17-1:
iDVD offers 13 built-in button frames. Note, though, that some iDVD button shapes crop video inappropriately, producing odd-looking and less effective buttons, as shown here. Large subjects, particularly people's faces or still objects, may not appear properly under these conditions. (Unlike drop zones, you can't reposition button videos to produce a better composition.)

Editing and Positioning Text

Although most people focus primarily on iDVD's drop zones, video buttons, and so on, text also plays a critical role. It's a dependable, instantly recognizable part of a DVD menu system.

The text that you can fiddle with falls into three categories:

- **Menu titles** help viewers figure out where they are in the DVD menu system by providing clues to the current context: "Our Vacation," "Pictures (Week 1)," and

"Scene Selection Menu," for example. Title text usually appears at the top of the screen, although you can put it anywhere you like.

- **Button text** can appear all by itself, or as labels above, below, beside, or on top of graphic buttons.

- **Text boxes** can appear anywhere on your screen. Thanks to this feature, you can create text boxes on your menu screens and fill them with whatever explanatory text you think is appropriate—instructions, introductions, a description of the project, and so on.

Tip: In iDVD, as in life, don't be too talky. Brevity is the soul of DVD captions.

To add a text block, choose Project→Add Text (⌘-K). Double-click the placeholder text and type away. Use the Settings panel of the Customize drawer to specify the font, color, alignment, and size of the text.

It's a lot easier to edit text in iDVD 5 than in early versions, and a lot more consistent. Just select the text you want to modify and use the Text adjustments in the Settings pane.

Here, for example, is a boatload of techniques to help customize your text. Each method changes the selected text on only the *currently displayed* DVD menu screen.

Tip: Style changes (font, size, color) affect a title, text box, or the buttons on a screen, whichever is currently selected. That is, changes you make to one button apply to all buttons as a group (on the current menu screen).

- **Select the text box.** Click once on it. A brightly colored border appears. Now you can drag the box to move it, press Delete to remove it, Shift-click another text box to highlight both at once, use the Copy command so that you can paste them onto another menu screen, and so on.

- **Change the text.** To highlight a piece of text, double-click anywhere inside it. (If the text is the title of a picture or video button, you must first click the button and then single-click the associated text.)

  You'll note that iDVD automatically highlights the entire phrase, meaning that you can just begin to type, replacing the entire text blob, without first dragging across it. (Of course, if you want to edit only part of the existing text, drag with the mouse first.) Press Return or Enter when you're finished.

- **Choose a font.** To select a new typeface, choose from the Text→Font menu on the Settings pane. You're not allowed to mix and match fonts *within* a text box, but each *kind* of text (button labels, title, and text boxes) can have a different font.

- **Change the text color.** In the Settings pane, choose a new color from the Text→ Color pop-up menu). iDVD offers 18 colors and shades to choose from. Titles, buttons, and text boxes can each use different colors.

- **Add (or remove) a drop shadow.** Use the Drop Shadow checkbox to add a drop shadow—a faint shadow behind and below the text that creates an easier-to-read, almost 3-D effect.

- **Change the font size.** Adjust the Text→Size slider in the Settings pane to choose a new font size for your selected text. As with fonts, you can pick only one font size per text category.

- **Remove the title.** Highlight the text on the menu and then press the Delete key. The empty title text box remains, but it's invisible. Later, if you like, you can click inside the title box to reopen it and type new text.

- **Remove button text.** To remove the labels from your buttons, select any button and then choose No Text from the Text→Position pop-up menu (in the Settings pane). You've just removed labels from *all* the buttons, not just the selected one.

- **Reposition (icon) button text.** iDVD lets you place button text on any side of the button, or even directly in its center. Select a button and then locate the Text→Position pop-up menu in the Settings pane. Choose a button-label position relative to the button graphic: Top, Center, Bottom, Left, and Right.

- **Align text.** To change the alignment of text (titles, text boxes, or text buttons), select the text and then use the Text→Alignment pop-up menu. Choose from Left, Centered, and Right.

- **Position the title or text box.** You can drag titles and text boxes anywhere on the screen you like. (Be careful not to park one where the *overscanning* effect of older TVs [page 186] might chop off some of your letters. To avoid this problem, choose Advanced→Show TV Safe Area before you drag, taking care to keep the text inside the superimposed guideline rectangle that iDVD now puts onscreen.)

Changing Backgrounds

The menu-screen background sets the tone by providing the look and atmosphere that defines the entire screen. As a result, choosing a new background can add a unique twist to an existing theme.

Background Still Images

Using a graphics file as a backdrop is a lot easier than using a video as a backdrop. You don't have to think about timing and loops, and you don't have to worry about how the motion will interact with your buttons and drop zones.

Adding a background image 1: Preserving drop zones

It's incredibly easy to change the backdrop for a particular menu screen: Just drag any graphics file directly onto the existing background. (Your only challenge: To avoid dropping it onto a button or a drop zone.) You can drag a JPEG file, for example, right out of the Finder, out of iPhoto if it's open, or out of the Photos pane of the Customize drawer. iDVD instantly sets the image as your new menu background.

Adding a background image 2: Overwriting drop zones

If you'd rather cover up any existing drop zones, replacing the background with a single image, drag a graphics file into the Background *well*, identified in Figure 17-2.

Tip: Both of the preceding techniques change only the currently displayed menu screen. To apply the change to *all* menu screens, choose Advanced→Apply Theme To Project.

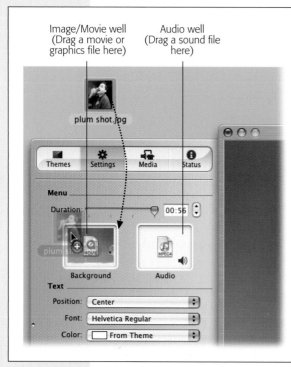

Image/Movie well
(Drag a movie or
graphics file here)

Audio well
(Drag a sound file
here)

Figure 17-2:
In the Customize drawer, click the Settings button. Drag a graphics file into the Background well (from the Finder or from iPhoto, for example). iDVD installs the graphic as the new background. In earlier versions of iDVD, this covered up drop zones but no longer. iDVD 5 fixed this annoying bug and everything now works the way you'd expect it to.

Replacing background images

If you want to try out a different picture in the background, just repeat the steps above. You can drop new graphics as many times as you want; iDVD displays only the most recent one.

Removing background images

If you decide that the original theme's background was superior to your own graphics after all, it's easy enough to restore the original image. On the Settings pane of the Customize drawer, just drag the graphic icon *out* of the Background well. iDVD deletes it, displaying the increasingly familiar puff-of-smoke animation. The original theme's background returns.

Background Video

Instead of a photo background, you can also create moving, animated, *video* back-grounds, just like the ones you find on many commercial Hollywood DVDs. It's far easier to customize your background video than, say, to administer anesthesia to yourself and then extract your own teeth.

Note: In all, iDVD provides three different places to install movies onto your menu screens. The following instructions pertain to only full-screen background videos. Don't confuse video backgrounds with drop zone videos or button videos.

Before you delve into this exciting new career, keep these points in mind:

- **Your video will loop.** Your background video file will play, then restart and play again as long as your audience leaves the menu on the TV screen. There's no way to make a video play just once.

- **iDVD adds both video and sound.** When your imported background video contains a soundtrack, that sound becomes the new soundtrack for the menu screen. It wipes out whatever music came with the theme.

- **iDVD handles timing.** iDVD automatically adjusts the Duration slider (at the top of the Settings pane) to match the length of your movie.

POWER USERS' CLINIC

Designing Video Loops in iMovie

Background videos don't have to jump between the end of one play-through and the beginning of the next. If you're willing to take a little time in iMovie, you can eliminate sudden visual changes that create unpleasant jumps. Consider these techniques:

Fade or Wash In and Out: Create a smooth fade out at the end of the movie clip, and a smooth fade in at the beginning, using the Fade In and Fade Out transition styles described in Chapter 6 (or, if you're partial to white, Wash In and Wash Out).

Use Cross Dissolve: If you prefer, you can design your movie so that the end cross-dissolves into the beginning each time it loops.

Move the playhead to 4:02 seconds before the end of your movie. Choose Edit→Split Video at Playhead to break off

that 4-second segment into a clip of its own.

Now drag this 4:02-second clip to the front of your movie, add a 4-second cross-dissolve between the transposed clip and the start of your movie, and save your work.

You can choose a different length for the crossfade; just make sure that the transposed clip lasts at least two frames longer than the desired transition time. This method works particularly well on stock footage, such as wind-swept grass, fish in an aquarium, and so forth.

You may discover a couple of drawbacks to this method. First, the start and end audio and video will overlap, and you may not like the results. Second, the background video will, unfortunately, start with the crossfade. There's no way yet to make it start playing from an un-crossfaded spot—iDVD 6, perhaps?

Tip: If you try to drag the Duration slider longer than the length of your movie, weird things happen. Suppose, for example, that you have a 15-second movie, a 20-second bit of audio, and you set the slider to 20 seconds. iDVD plays your movie once, plays 5 seconds more of the start of your movie, and then loops to start your movie again. It's an effect worth avoiding.

Background video selection

Choosing background video can be harder than selecting a still image, for two important reasons:

- **Video moves.** Make sure that the video doesn't hide or overwhelm your titles, buttons, and drop zones. "Audition" your videos and make sure they work with your menus before you burn. In particular, watch for moving objects and scenes that are too bright or too dark.

Tip: You can create a simple washed-out background video by applying iMovie HD's Fog effect. Leave the Wind slider at its factory setting. Drag the Fog slider to "more" and Color to "white," and then click Apply. This effect lightens your video, providing a more suitable backdrop for a DVD menu. Not light enough? Apply it a second time!

- **Motion menus loop.** Unless you take special care when creating your video, menu looping will create sudden, sharp, sometimes distracting transitions between the end and start of your video.

Adding background video 1: Preserving drop zones

iDVD offers two ways to add background video to a menu screen, as shown in Figure 17-2. (Once again, remember that each of them changes only the currently displayed menu screen. To apply the change to *all* menu screens, choose Advanced→Apply Theme To Project after following the steps here.)

This first method ensures that you won't wind up covering any drop zones that are part of your chosen theme.

1. **Bring up the menu screen you want to change.**

   Make sure that the Customize drawer is open.

2. **Switch to the Finder and locate the movie file you want to use as a background.**

   It can be a finished QuickTime movie, the *.mov* reference movie in one of your iMovie project folders (page 112), or a new iMovie HD movie project file.

3. **While pressing the Option key, drag the video file onto the menu screen.**

   Avoid all drop zones and buttons. Make sure that the entire menu screen is highlighted (a colored rectangle appears around the edges) before you drop the video.

Let go of the Option key when the new video appears in the menu background. (The Option key tells iDVD: "I'm installing this movie as a background, *not* as a movie of its own, represented by its own button on the menu.")

Adding background video 2: Covering up drop zones

To replace the background with a single, full-width video that *covers up* any drop zones, press the ⌘ key as you drag a movie file out of the Finder and into the Background well or the background of your iDVD menu. (As usual, avoid drop zones and buttons.) iDVD installs the video (and its audio) as the new background, hiding any drop zones in the process.

Removing background video

If you decide to restore the original background video and audio to your theme, drag the icons out of both the Background well and the Audio well. You'll get an animated puff of smoke with each drag, confirming that you've successfully removed both the audio and video that you had previously installed onto this menu screen.

Choosing Menu Audio

Some of Apple's canned themes come with a preinstalled musical soundtrack, and some don't. If you'd like some music to play during, for example, the Sliding Panes theme, you'll have to install it yourself.

You can also replace the music that comes with any of Apple's themes with a song you like better. In the case of musically challenged themes like Anime Pop, this ability is a true blessing, possibly saving lives and sanity.

- **iTunes method.** If you've got a decent music collection already in iTunes, adding background music is easy. In the Customize drawer, click the Audio button. You'll see a complete list of all your iTunes songs and playlists. Proceed as shown in Figure 17-3.

Tip: Keep in mind that some of the most satisfying and appropriate soundtracks of all are the ones that you create yourself, using GarageBand. Any finished compositions that you've exported from GarageBand show up in this iTunes list, too.

- **Drag-from-the-Finder method.** If you're not a big iTunes user, you can also drag in almost any kind of audio file straight from the desktop. Make sure that you've clicked the Settings button at the top of the Customize drawer, and then drag the audio file directly into the Audio well (identified in Figure 17-2) or onto the menu background.

Incidentally, iDVD doesn't do anything to compensate for background video and background audio that aren't the same length. If the music is too short, it repeats until the video is finished playing, cutting off the music if necessary to start in sync with the video track. If the music is too long, the video repeats until the music ends, cutting off the video mid-repeat. Use the Duration slider in the Settings pane to set the loop time, which applies to both sound and video.

Or, if you're really a perfectionist, you could always use a program like GarageBand to match the soundtrack length to the video. Create a nice fade-out at the end of the audio, and a fade-in at the beginning, so that the looping won't be quite so jarring.

Reminder: This technique affects the background music of only the currently displayed menu screen. To apply the change to *all* menu screens, wrap up by choosing Advanced→Apply Theme To Project. (And make sure you don't exceed your 15-minute total menu-length budget!)

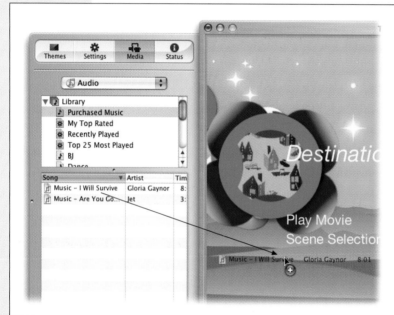

Figure 17-3:
Here's your mini-iTunes, right in the Customize drawer. Use the playlists list at the top, or the Search box at the bottom, to find an appropriate song for your menu screen. Use the Play button (or double-click a song name) to listen to a song before placing it. Finally, drag the song you want directly onto the menu screen to install it there.

Replacing Menu Audio

To replace a custom audio file with another, repeat the steps you used to install the music to begin with. iDVD replaces the current track with the new one.

Removing Menu Audio

To remove audio, drag it out of the Audio well, pictured in Figure 17-2. (When the audio well is empty, it shows a 3-D picture of a speaker.)

If you want to remove *all* audio from your menu screen, you may have to drag twice: Your first drag removes custom sounds, while the second removes the theme sound, if one exists.

Muting Menu Audio

To mute your audio, click the small speaker icon in the corner of the Audio well (Figure 17-3). iDVD disables menu sound and hides the two tiny soundwaves. Click the icon again to restore menu audio. Don't forget to check your audio before burning, as muting the audio in the Settings pane affects the final DVD!

Saving Favorites

After applying all the techniques described so far in this chapter, you may end up creating masterpieces of adapted iDVD themes. Fortunately, iDVD allows you to save and reuse these modified themes after you adjust them to your liking. Here's how to go about it:

1. **Open the Settings pane in the Customize drawer.**

   Click Customize first to open the drawer, if necessary.

2. **Click Save as Favorite (at the bottom of the pane).**

   The Save sheet (dialog box) appears at the top of the window.

3. **Type the name for your new theme. Turn on "Shared for all users," if you like.**

   If you're the only person who uses your Mac, then never mind. But if you share a Mac with other students, workers, or family members, each of whom has a Mac OS X *account*, the "Shared for all users" option makes your new theme available to other people who use the machine. (Otherwise, your masterpiece will appear in the list only when *you* use iDVD.)

POWER USERS' CLINIC

Secrets of the Theme Files

Whenever you save a new Favorite theme, iDVD does a fair amount of administrative work. Behind the scenes, iDVD creates a new theme file on your hard drive. If you decided to share your theme with other account holders, this file appears in the Library→iDVD→Favorites folder. If not, it winds up in your Home→Library→iDVD→Favorites folder. Unlike regular themes, whose names end with the suffix .theme, Favorites use a .favorite file name extension. (See Figure 17-4 at right.)

Why is this important to know? Because it tells you how to remove a saved favorite: Just drag the .favorite file out of the secret folder and into the Trash. The next time you open iDVD, that favorite will no longer appear in the Themes pane pop-up menu.

It's also worth noting that when you create a favorite, iDVD copies all relevant materials, including background audio and video, to the newly created theme. (Don't believe it? To view these materials, navigate to the saved .favorite file. Control-click its icon; from the contextual menu, choose Show Package Contents. Then open the Contents→Resources folder.)

Because iDVD has made copies of your movies, pictures, and soundtrack files, you no longer need to keep the originals, as far as iDVD is concerned. Feel free to discard, rename, or move these components from their original locations on your hard drive.

---

4. **Turn off "Replace existing" if you want to create a new entry in the theme list.**

   If you turn *on* "Replace existing," iDVD will treat your adapted theme as a replacement for the one you based it on, rather than creating a new entry in the list.

5. **Click OK.**

   iDVD saves your theme as a new Favorite. You'll be able to apply it to other DVDs in the future by choosing its name from the Themes pane. (Choose Favorites from the pop-up menu to see its listing.)

Tip: It could happen: You could tire of a saved Favorite. See the box on page 427 for the secret instructions on removing one from your iDVD theme list.

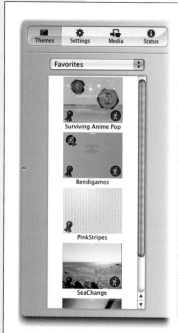 

Figure 17-4:
In general, you'll call up your stored Favorite themes by choosing Favorites from the pop-up menu of the Themes pane (left). Behind the scenes, your Favorites are actual icons hidden on your hard drive (right). That's good to know in case someday you want to throw one away.

Buying Sound and Vision

Let's face it. iDVD has a lot of nice themes—but they're not always the *right* themes. Life isn't limited to theaters, road trips, and weddings. There are other holidays, other life events, other styles. If you're celebrating Christmas or Valentine's, graduation day, or a new home, or if you're just looking for a *different* look, then you might want to think about going commercial. With some money to spend, you can expand the way your iDVD projects look and sound.

Third-Party Themes

If you want new themes that work the way built-in iDVD themes do, then buying prebuilt themes can be the way to go. Once installed, third-party themes appear in your iDVD themes list; just click to use. Theme prices start at about $6 for a single theme or about $30 for a pack of six or more. Price, quality, and availability vary. Figure 17-6 showcases several third-party offerings.

Figure 17-5:
You can buy new themes from, for example, www. idvdthemetastic.com or www.idvdthemepak.com. iDVD Themetastic (top) sells themes á la carte, specializing in holiday items. iDVD ThemePak (bottom) sells themes in groups, offering great-looking motion and still graphics. Check their Web sites for some free downloadable samples.

Motion Backgrounds

If you're looking for another way to kick up your DVD productions a notch, then consider buying some commercial video loops for your menu backgrounds. Dozens of companies sell royalty-free video clips for use in movies and television. The price varies from barely affordable to "they've got to be kidding." Page 424 describes how to add a commercial motion background to your iDVD project for a professional flair.

Among the least expensive are Ulead's Pick-a-Video and Pick-a-Video Pro lines (*www. ulead.com/pav_pro*), which, at $60 per disc, cost a fraction of what you'd pay through a normal royalty-free video clearinghouse like FotoSearch (*www.fotosearch.com*). A typical Ulead disc contains about eight motion backgrounds with coordinating still images (ideal for submenus) and video overlays (great for iMovie and Final Cut, not so great for iDVD). The CG Festivities disc (volume 20), for example, has ringing bells, floating balloons, flying stars, streaming ribbons, rotating hearts, and gift boxes, among others.

Stock Art

Don't overlook commercial graphics when customizing your themes. *Stock art* (professional photos and illustrations that you can buy) can add a professional look to your menus without costing a lot of money. As Figure 17-6 shows, the right stock image may look better than the snaps you took with your digital camera.

Figure 17-6:
Stock photos are available individually and as collections (at www.istockphoto. com, *for example), but you may already own more art than you think. Check out the software CDs in your library. Many, especially graphics programs, come with sample images that you're free to use in your projects. These "extras" don't always get installed along with the programs, so take time to review the discs themselves.*

Third-Party Buttons

In the crazy, blossoming world of homemade DVDs, there's now such a thing as commercially available *buttons*. They let you add stylish new buttons to your menu screens without having to buy full themes. Stylized buttons can give a personalized twist to even fairly plain backgrounds, as shown in Figure 17-7.

Figure 17-7:
Why buy an entire custom theme when button styles do so much to create an individual feel for your iDVD menus? Mix and match buttons with background art to create a unique look on a budget. These samples are from iDVDThemePak ($40 for 21 custom buttons, or $75 for 42).

Audio

When you buy songs at the iTunes Music Store, you also buy the right to use them in any iLife creations for your personal use. Why settle for the mayhem of the Kid's Theater audio track when you can throw a buck at Apple and pick the music you really want?

Tip: Stop by *www.freeplaymusic.com* for a vast collection of free, royalty-free music. (It's free for personal, noncommercial use.)

iDVD Secrets

Although iDVD appears simple, straightforward, and direct, there's more power lurking inside than you might expect. You can see, change, and control things you never knew you could—if you're willing to try new and unusual approaches. Some of these approaches require add-on software programs. Others demand nerves of steel and a willingness to dive into hidden iDVD files. And a few even require some familiarity with programming.

In this advanced chapter, you'll discover how some of these sideways (and backwards and upside down) methods can expand your iDVD repertoire.

iDVD—The DVD-ROM Maker

iDVD's ability to add data files to the DVD-ROM portion of your disc may be its least known feature. When it creates a DVD-ROM, iDVD sets aside a portion of your DVD for normal computer files. This area of the disc won't show up on a DVD player—only on a computer.

With iDVD, you can store any variety of data on your DVD. Here are just a few ways you can use this feature to enhance your disc:

- **Store documents that relate to your DVD contents.** The DVD-ROM area provides a perfect place to store copies of documents that concern the material presented in the DVD. This might include the script used to film a movie, the different versions that eventually led to a final event invitation, extended family narratives, copies of email and other correspondence, and so on. Remember: TV sets aren't much good for displaying text, but a DVD-ROM and a computer can come to the rescue.

Or store the full-resolution versions of the digital photos featured in your DVD slideshow (one of the most common uses for this feature).

- **Store Web pages.** Web pages are perfect additions to the DVD-ROM disc area. Create a Web site that relates to your DVD and add your source files to the disc. When distributed, your viewers can open these files with an ordinary Web browser. For example, a DVD with a training video can contain supplementary lessons in HTML (Web page) format.

- **Store "email quality" versions of your video.** Use the DVD-ROM area of your disc to store small, compressed versions of your video, or "wallet size" pictures from a slideshow, suitable for email. Now your audience can share your movie experience with other people.

Adding Files to DVD-ROM

iDVD's DVD-ROM file management couldn't be simpler. Just drag icons out of the Finder and into the DVD-ROM Contents list (Advanced→Edit DVD-ROM Contents), as shown in Figure 18-1.

Warning: The DVD-ROM editor in early versions of iDVD 5 (as shown in Figure 18-1) is still fairly buggy. Consequently, your edits may not work as expected. If the program starts acting strangely, stop. Quit from iDVD and relaunch the program before continuing with your DVD-ROM setup.

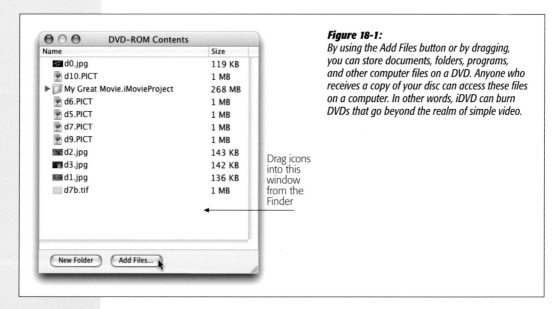

Figure 18-1:
By using the Add Files button or by dragging, you can store documents, folders, programs, and other computer files on a DVD. Anyone who receives a copy of your disc can access these files on a computer. In other words, iDVD can burn DVDs that go beyond the realm of simple video.

Organizing DVD-ROM Contents

The DVD-ROM Contents pane lets you organize your files in several ways:

- **Add folders.** Click New Folder to add a folder to your list.

- **Remove things.** Either drag files or folders right out of the list, or select them and then press the Delete key. (Dragging out of the list gives you the cool puff-of-smoke animation.)

- **Move items into or out of folders.** You can drag icons into one of the little folder icons to file them there—or drag them out again to remove them.

- **Reorder the list.** Drag icons up or down the list into new positions.

- **Create subfolders.** Drag one folder into another to create subfolders.

- **Rename a folder.** Double-click the name of a folder to select and edit it. Press Return or Enter when you're finished typing.

- **List/hide folder contents.** You can click a folder's "flippy triangle" to expand it and see what's inside, exactly as in Finder list views.

Project Info

iDVD 5 offers two particularly helpful tools that address project information: the Status pane and the Info window. They provide valuable feedback about your project, its resources, and its limits.

The Status Pane

The Status pane shows you how much of the DVD capacity you've used, the amount of time you have left to use for motion menus, and the number of tracks (that is, movies) and menus you've included. Figure 18-2 describes how to locate and open the pane.

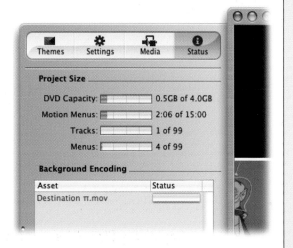

Figure 18-2:
To access the Status pane, start by opening the Customize drawer. Next, click the Status icon. This opens the pane and reveals information about your project contents.

The Status pane gives important feedback on several iDVD features, mostly because these features come with important limits. These limits include:

- **12 buttons per menu.** Each menu can't contain more than 12 buttons at the time you burn the disc. If you've gone a wee bit button-crazy (or just forgot to dispose of some temporary buttons) on a particular screen, iDVD will warn you at burning time, and won't proceed until you've reduced the button count.

- **99 images per slideshow.** You can't include any more than 99 pictures for any one slideshow, although you can add several slideshows to your disc.

- **99 movies and/or slideshows per disc.** Because it's a good soldier that endorses the official DVD specification, iDVD doesn't let you add more than that. Each movie and slideshow counts as a "track"—a single playback element—and 99 is the max.

- **99 chapter markers per movie.** Same deal. That's the maximum a DVD can have.

- **99 menus per disc.** If you need more menu screens than that, well, heaven help the audience who has to navigate your DVD.

- **4.0 GB per disc.** This is, more or less, the amount of data you can cram onto a standard recordable DVD after taking into account the required amounts of digital overhead.

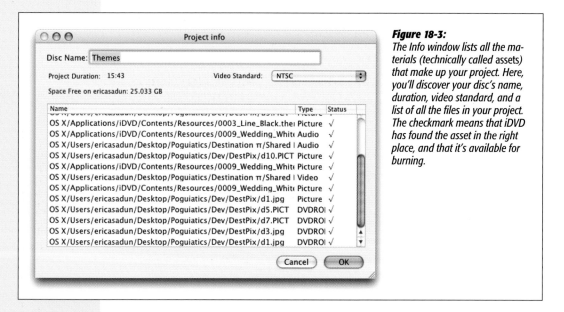

Figure 18-3:
The Info window lists all the materials (technically called assets*) that make up your project. Here, you'll discover your disc's name, duration, video standard, and a list of all the files in your project. The checkmark means that iDVD has found the asset in the right place, and that it's available for burning.*

The Info Window

Choose Project→Project Info (⌘-I) to open the Info window associated with your project, where you can see more details about the status and contents of your project (Figure 18-3).

Tip: You can change the name of your disc by editing the text field at the top of the window. As a rule, use the letters A–Z, the numbers 0–9, and the underscore (_). The resulting name will be case insensitive, with all lowercase letters converted to uppercase.

Uncover Your DVD Project File

Behind the scenes, iDVD stores all the pieces of your project inside the .dvdproj "file" that you created when you first saved your work. However, the .dvdproj file isn't really a file, even though it looks like a single icon on your desktop. It's actually a *package*—a disguised Mac OS X folder—that contains many subfolders and files. To peek inside, follow these steps:

1. **Quit iDVD.**

   Never mess with your project files when iDVD is running.

2. **Control-click the project file. From the shortcut menu, choose Show Package Contents.**

   If you have a two-button mouse, you can right-click instead. Either way, you've now opened that "file" into a folder window.

3. **Open the Contents→Resources folder.**

   You're in. Here are all the different files that make up your DVD. (See Figure 18-4 for an example.)

Figure 18-4:
Your .dvdproj file stores all the movies, sounds, graphics, and data associated with your iDVD project in a series of hidden subfolders and files. This column-view shot shows the progression of folders within folders.

So what is all this stuff?

- Your **ProjectData** file stores all the settings for your DVD project, in the form of a binary *property list*. It tells iDVD how to put together the menus, sound files, graphics, and other pieces that comprise your DVD.

Tip: For a really interesting afternoon of insight, drag the ProjectData icon onto the icon of, say, TextEdit. Turns out ProjectData is just a humble text file, and—as long as you're careful not to make or save any changes—you can pass an enlightening afternoon studying its contents to discover how it's structured.

- iDVD stores compressed video files—the ones that your audience will actually see on the DVD player—in the **MPEG** folder. If you really want to, you can play one of these files right on your Mac. To do so, copy it to the desktop, add an .m2v suffix to its file name, and watch it using a program that can play MPEG-2 files (like VLC, a free movie player from *www.videolan.org/vlc*).

- If you're using an older theme, one whose buttons are represented as little pictures or videos, then a **Thumbnails** folder stores the tiny QuickTime videos that play on the buttons. Double-click one of them to play it in QuickTime Player right on your Mac.

iDVD doesn't fill the remaining folders until it actually burns the DVD. At that point, iDVD uses these folders to store intermediate files as it works. For example:

- In the **Menu** folder, iDVD stores MPEG-2 (.m2v) files that represent the video loops used on your menu screens, complete with buttons, thumbnails, and so on.

- As you could probably guess, the **Slideshow** folder stores all the digital pictures you've chosen for use in your slideshows, and the **Audio** folder contains all the sound files. (You could double-click one of the sound files to play it in QuickTime Player, if you really wanted to.)

- The **Overlay** folder holds *menu overlays* (videos that animate buttons when your viewers highlight them) and *motion overlays* (animations that play on top of drop zones—the Theater theme curtains or the Brush Strokes paint effect, for example).

AppleScripting iDVD

As any power user can tell you, AppleScript is one of the best features of the Mac operating system. It's a built-in, relatively easy programming language that lets you control your programs by writing little software recipes known as *scripts*—and lets your programs control each other by issuing invisible commands. (Not all programs respond to AppleScript commands, but, happily, iDVD does.)

As it turns out, you don't have to compose your own AppleScript programs to capitalize on iDVD's AppleScript-friendliness. Apple has created a series of useful scripts that you can download and install right now, for free, and use without having to type up a single line of code.

You'll find them on Apple's iDVD scripting page. Visit *www.apple.com/applescript/idvd* to read about them and download them.

Tip: Once you've downloaded these AppleScripts, you'll want to drag them into your Home→Library→ Scripts folder, so that you can trigger them by choosing their names from the Script menu. (If there isn't already a tiny black scroll icon on your menu bar–the Script menu–here's how to put it there. In Mac OS X 10.3, open your Applications→AppleScript folder and double-click Install Script Menu. In Mac OS X 10.4, use the AppleScript Utility program to add the menulet instead.)

In any case, choosing an AppleScript's name from this menu is a very convenient and quick way to run it.

In the following list, only the items identified as droplets or applications don't belong in your Scripts menu.

Here are some of the canned Apple scripts for iDVD:

- **iDVD Companion.** This is an actual application (not a script) that endows iDVD with the floating palette shown in Figure 18-5. This palette offers a number of useful controls that aren't available in iDVD alone, like one that snaps your menu buttons into horizontal or vertical alignment (buttons that you've dragged freely, for example).

  iDVD Companion also offers a menu of all your menu screens, so that you can jump directly to any portion of your menu system; a list that lets you jump to any

Figure 18-5:
This free program from Apple isn't actually an AppleScript, but it uses AppleScript to add new features to iDVD–like the ability to align buttons that you've dragged by hand.

slideshow in a certain DVD project; a quick menu command that lets you turn the automatic button grid on or off; and more.

- **Create DVD From Folder.** This script is a *droplet*—a little application icon that does its work when you drag-and-drop something onto it. In this case, when you drag a folder of files onto this droplet, it opens iDVD and creates a new project automatically, based on the folder's contents and hierarchy. Complete instructions and examples come with the download.

- **Photoshop to iDVD.** This script automatically converts whatever document is currently open in Photoshop into a background image for the current menu screen in iDVD. It can be a real timesaver if you like to create your own DVD backgrounds.

- **iTunes to iDVD.** You know from Chapter 17 how to turn an iTunes song into the background music for a menu screen. But if you're already *in* iTunes, you can use this script to turn a selected track into the audio background for the current menu.

- **Sequential Movie.** This droplet creates a series of iDVD menu screens that guide your audience through a sequence of movies. It results in a well-structured and well-ordered movie sequence that's ideal for how-to projects (letting your viewers follow the steps in order), video treasure hunts (keeping your viewers from skipping ahead to clues before they're ready), educational videos (increasing the complexity of your instruction gradually as the lessons proceed), and so on.

Modifying iDVD Itself

As you've probably discovered, the iDVD program icon isn't really an application icon at all—it's a Mac OS X *package* (page 112). Because Mac OS X programs are often built as packages in this way, they give you a great opportunity to hack the program itself—to change its look, reassign its keystrokes, and so on.

POWER USERS' CLINIC

Developer Tools the Download Way

If you can't seem to find the Developer Tools disc, you can download it from the Web for free, although doing so requires you to sign up for Apple's developer program—also free. A high-speed Internet connection and lots of patience is recommended, since the files are over 300 MB.

In your Web browser, visit *http://connect.apple.com* and click Join Now. Follow the instructions to create an account. Next, log in at *http://connect.apple.com,* click Downloads, and click Mac OS X. You should wind up on a screen containing

recent XCode Tools releases.

Find the latest version, click Download, and then wait.

Once you've downloaded them, you install the XCode Tools the same way as many other Mac OS X programs. Just expand the archive, double-click the package installer, and then provide your administrative password when requested. Once the installation is done, you end up with a Developer folder on your hard drive containing all the goodies.

This is a rush, an illicit-feeling power trip, but it doesn't actually hurt anything. As long as you've got your original iLife DVD on hand, so that you can install a fresh, unmodified copy of iDVD if necessary, you can do whatever you want to a copy and still sleep peacefully at night.

Download the Developer Tools

The following instructions assume that you have a copy of Apple's XCode *Developer Tools.*

The Developer Tools are essential for anyone who writes software for Mac OS X. The programs that come with them help you create, debug, and compile programs. But the Developer Tools can be useful even if you're not a programmer. They include some useful utilities, including PropertyList Editor (which makes it easy to edit a program's preference files).

If you bought Mac OS X in the store, in a box, these programs are on a special CD called Developer. If Mac OS X came with your Mac, the Developer CD may be a disk image on one of your Software Restore discs. (Use Disk Utility to burn this image onto a real CD.)

If a Developer CD or disk image *didn't* come with your Mac or your copy of Mac OS X, or if you can't find it, you can also download it; see the box on the facing page.

Dive into iDVD

Follow these steps to open your copy of iDVD and begin your joyful hacking.

1. **Open the iDVD application package.**

   By now, you probably know the drill: Control-click the iDVD application icon; from the shortcut menu, choose Show Package Contents.

2. **Open the Contents→Resources folder. Open your language folder.**

   iDVD contains separate folders for each language. For this example, open the English.lproj folder.

3. **Double-click the icon called DVDDocument.nib.**

   This document opens in the program called Interface Builder, which is one of the developer tools programs.

   Interface Builder lets you both create and modify the interfaces of your programs. You can change window titles, move buttons around the screen, add or remove menu commands, and more.

   What you're now seeing is the behind-the-scenes layout of the iDVD program itself (see Figure 18-6).

In this example, you'll create a custom button that turns off the sound in iDVD without stopping the videos that play on your buttons, drop zones, and backgrounds. (Ordinarily, clicking the Motion button in iDVD simultaneously silences the music and stops all video playback.)

Tip: Remember to turn both sound and motion back on again before you burn a DVD—if, that is, you want these features to appear in the finished product.

Of course, your first worry is where you're going to put this button. The only space for buttons is the row of icons at the bottom edge of the iDVD window, and it's already pretty full.

Ah, but what about that Apple logo at the center of the bottom edge? (It appears here as a lowly broken-picture icon, but you can confirm that it's really the Apple logo by clicking it and then choosing Tools→Show Info.) It's using up prime real estate that might be better used by the button you're going to design.

4. **Move or remove the broken-picture Apple icon.**

Either drag the Apple icon's placeholder to the left, or click it and then press the Delete key to remove it entirely.

In the next step, you're going to need the Cocoa palette (Figure 18-6, top right). If it isn't already open (usually at the upper-right corner of your screen), choose Tools→Palettes→Show Palettes (⌘-/).

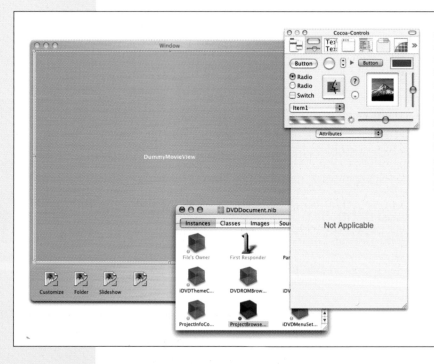

Figure 18-6:
Interface Builder shows you a map of the various buttons, checkboxes, and other elements that compose its screen. It doesn't look exactly like iDVD, because this is just its skeleton, but it's enough for the little experiment you're about to try.

5. **In the Cocoa palette, click the Buttons button (shown at top in Figure 18-6).**

The palette changes to show you a variety of button designs.

6. **Drag the round, clear button on the Buttons palette (the second button in the
top row of buttons) into the space you created by moving the Apple icon.**

You've just installed a new button in iDVD. Unfortunately, when you click it, it
won't do anything at all—yet.

7. **Choose Tools→Show Info (Shift-⌘-I).**

The Show Info dialog box appears. Make sure that the pop-up menu at the top
says Attributes.

8. **Click in the third line (Icon). Type *MiniAudio1N*.**

Type the phrase exactly as you see here, including spelling and capitalization.
(The second to last character is a 1, not an L.) You're directing Interface Builder's
attention to a certain graphic that's already in the Contents→Resources folder
of your iDVD Application. In short, you're giving your new button a face—an
icon of its own.

9. **Close the Info panel.**

A broken-picture icon now appears over your button. That's normal—and temporary.

In the next step, you're going to need the DVDDocument.nib window, which
should also be somewhere on your screen (Figure 18-7). Move the window until
you see both your new button *and* the iDVDThemeController cube at the same
time. (You can probably see only part of the cube's name: *iDVDThemeC*.)

Figure 18-7:
*The DVDDocument
window has five tabs:
Instances, Classes,
Images, Sounds,
and Nibs. Make sure
that the Instances
tab is selected. Set
your windows so you
can see both your
new button and the
iDVDThemeC cube at
the same time.*

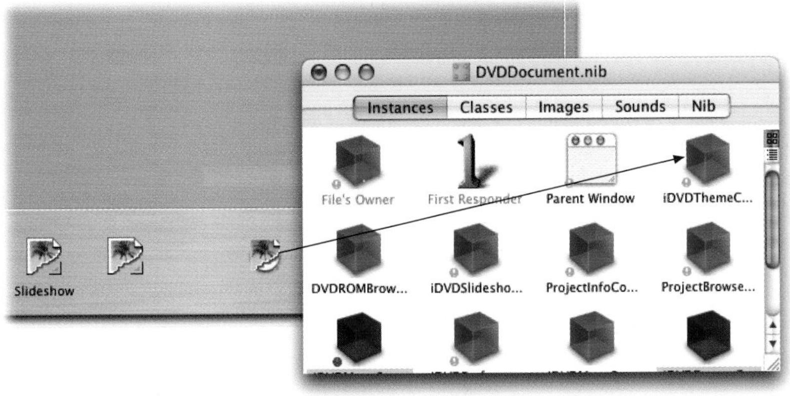

10. **While pressing the Control key, drag from your button to the iDVDThemeC
cube. Wait until a box appears around the cube before releasing the mouse.**

A strange little line connects your new button with the cube. When you let go, the Info panel reappears, with the Connections panel in view (Figure 18-8). You've just taught iDVD to make a connection between your newly placed button and some action, which you'll specify in the next step.

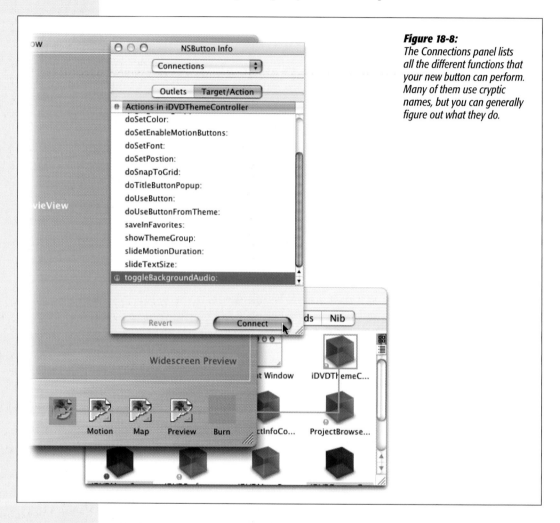

Figure 18-8:
The Connections panel lists all the different functions that your new button can perform. Many of them use cryptic names, but you can generally figure out what they do.

11. **At the very bottom of the scrolling list on the right side, double-click toggleBackgroundAudio: (or whatever portion of this term you can see in the list).**

An indented dot appears to the right of toggleBackgroundAudio:, as shown in Figure 18-7. You've just given your new button a purpose in life—something that will happen whenever somebody clicks it.

12. **Choose File→Save (⌘-S). Quit Interface Builder.**

If you open your modified copy of iDVD, you'll see that your new button appears at the bottom of the window (as shown in Figure 18-9). To test your new button, choose a theme that contains video and audio menu screens. Make sure that they're playing—and then click your new button. Marvel as the sound cuts out, but the video continues.

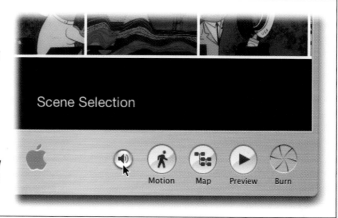

Figure 18-9:
After editing iDVD, your new button (the small speaker button) appears at the bottom of the window, ready to control sound playback for motion menus.

There's a lot more you can do with Interface Builder and iDVD; this was only one example. In step 11, for instance, you assigned your new button to the toggleBackgroundAudio function, but you probably noticed that there were dozens of other functions in that list that you could have assigned to. Explore other little cubes to find even more program features.

One small step for iDVD, perhaps, but a giant leap for your understanding of how Mac software is made.

Archiving Your Project

Ordinarily, iDVD doesn't store any videos, photos, or sounds in your iDVD project file. It remains a tiny, compact file that stores only *pointers* to those files elsewhere on your hard drive.

That's why, if you delete or move one of those media files, iDVD will mildly freak out. (See page 447 in that case.)

In previous versions of iDVD, you couldn't transfer a project from one Mac to another for this very reason. And that meant that you couldn't *design* a DVD on one Mac (one that lacked a DVD burner), and then *burn* it on another. You also couldn't back up your project file, content that you'd included all of its pieces.

Fortunately, Apple packed a solution into iDVD 5. The Archive Project command lets you completely "de-reference" your project, so that the project file *contains* every file that you've incorporated into your project: movies, photos, sounds, theme components, and DVD-ROM files. Your project file is now completely self-contained, ready for backup or transfer to another computer.

It's also now really, really huge.

Follow these steps to produce your archive.

1. **Save your project.**

   If you forget this step, iDVD will remind you.

2. **Choose File→Archive Project.**

   The Save As panel shown in Figure 18-10 appears.

Figure 18-10:
The Archive Project's Save As panel lets you specify whether you want to include themes and encoded files in your archived project. You can save quite a bit of disk space by leaving these options unchecked. The Size indicator to the right of "Include themes" tells you how much space your project will occupy.

3. **Turn the checkboxes on or off, if you like.**

   "Include themes" copies your theme files into the project—something that's unnecessary if you're using standard Apple themes. This checkbox is important only

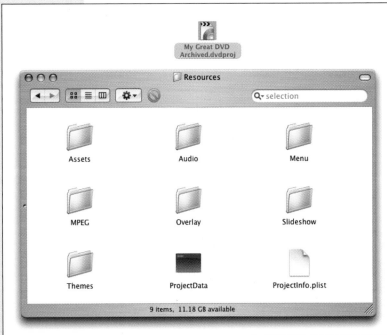

Figure 18-11:
When archiving a project, iDVD creates additional folders within the new project bundle. The Assets folder stores original copies of your audio and video files (in the "av" subfolder), DVD-ROM content (in "data") and images (in "stills"). If you've chosen to save themes, they show up in the Themes folder.

if the themes you've used come from other companies, were designed by you, or are modified versions of Apple's originals.

"Include encoded files" is the more important option, because it's very unlikely that all of your sounds, photos, and movies are also on the destination Mac.

Turn the boxes on and off to see how much space you'll recover.

4. **Name the archive file, choose a folder location for it, and then click Save.**

   Wait as iDVD builds the new archive. This can take a few minutes, so be patient. You may be working with *very* large files.

Archived projects look like any other projects, in that they use the same .dvdproj extension. But inside, they're very different. For proof, simply open it as a package (page 112). Inside its Contents→Resources folder, new folders called Assets and Themes store the extra archived elements (Figure 18-11).

Tip: In order to turn your photos and videos into DVD material, iDVD must encode (convert) them into a format called MPEG. Depending on your Preferences settings, iDVD may constantly be working on this time-consuming task, or it may do the job only when you burn the DVD.

Either way, an archived project also stores any MPEG files iDVD has created so far. They'll save you time when you burn the DVD, but they'll make the archive's file size balloon up like a blimp.

If you'd rather keep the file smaller, choose Advanced→Delete Encoded Assets before saving the archive. iDVD removes the remove encoded MPEG files—but you'll pay for this gesture in re-encoding time when you're ready to burn your discs.

Copying the archive to a different Mac

Suppose that you've designed a DVD using a Mac that lacks a DVD burner. Now, as Apple intended, you've used the Archive command to prepare it for transfer to a Mac that *does* have a burner.

Transfer the archive project using any convenient method: copy it across a network, burn it to a CD or a DVD-ROM, copy it onto an iPod, or whatever. (It's too big for email, of course, but you could instead post it on a Web site for downloading.)

The project opens normally on the other machine, with all of its pieces intact and ready to touch up and burn.

Relinking Missing Files

When you're working with regular projects (not archived ones), iDVD is pretty helpless if you move or rename any of the photo, movie, or sound files that it expects to use in your DVD (see Figure 18-12).

If you encounter the dialog box shown in Figure 18-10 at top, click Find File, navigate to a folder that contains at least one of the files, and click Open. iDVD dutifully inspects that folder for *any* missing files. Repeat until you've located all the missing files.

If you *can't* find a file—say, you deleted one by accident—then keep showing iDVD the files you *can* find. At the end of the process, click Cancel.

Your project will open just fine, but you'll see a big black space (Figure 18-12, bottom) where the missing file ought to be. At this point, you can replace it with a file that you do have.

Figure 18-12:
Top: If you open a project whose original movies, photos, or sounds have been moved or renamed, you see this message. Click Cancel to proceed without those files, or click Find File to show iDVD where the file is now.

Bottom: The broken link image indicates a file that iDVD can't find. Avoid this problem by keeping all your source files on the hard drive until after you've burned your project.

Disk Images and External DVD Burners

Thanks to a new iDVD 5 feature, you can now save your project as a computer file called a *disk image*. And from there, you can do something that many iDVD fans have always wanted to do: burn DVDs on an *external*, non-Apple DVD burner.

You may have run into the disk-image (.dmg or .img) format before; it's a popular storage format for software you download. It's so popular because you get a single, self-contained file that *contains* many other files, arrayed inside exactly as though they're on a disk. When you open a disk image file, in fact, it turns into a little hard-disk icon on your desktop, with all of its contents tucked inside.

Note: Don't confuse a disk image with a project archive; they're two very different beasts. A disk image is a virtual disk, a bit-for-bit copy of the data that would appear on an actual, physical DVD–it just happens to be stored on a hard drive rather than a DVD.

Project archives, in contrast, contain all the source project material used by iDVD. The only thing that can read or "play back" a project archive is iDVD itself.

To turn an iDVD project into a disk image, save it. Then, choose File→Save as Disc Image (Shift-⌘-R). Choose a file name (for example, *Summer Fun.img*) and a location, and then click Save. Now wait as iDVD compresses your movie data and saves it to disk. All of this takes just as long as an actual DVD burning, so now's your chance to catch up on some magazine reading.

When it's all over, you'll find a new .img icon—a disk image—on your desktop.

Disk images are amazingly high-octane, cool stuff for two reasons:

- **You don't have to burn a disc to watch your movies.** Mac OS X's DVD Player program can play back a disk image just as though it's a real DVD. You see all the menus, slideshows, and other iDVD features you've grown to love.

  As shown in Figure 18-13, the trick is to open the Video_TS folder. Never heard of it? Well, it's an important folder on *every DVD ever made*—it's where all the video files reside—and there's one on your disk image, too.

Figure 18-13:
Apple's DVD Player utility (in your Applications folder) can play back disk images as well as physical DVDs. In the Finder, double-click the disk image to make the virtual DVD appear on your desktop. In DVD Player, choose File→Open Video_TS Folder, as shown at top.

Bottom: In the dialog box, choose the Video_TS folder you want to play. Navigate into the disk image, choose the Video_TS folder, and click Choose. Press the Space bar to start playback.

Tip: This is a handy way to test a DVD before you use up a perfectly good blank.

- **You can burn your work to an external drive.** You can use Roxio Toast (a beloved, commercial burning program) or Mac OS X's own Disk Utility program to burn the disk image onto a real DVD. Figure 18-14 provides the amazingly simple instructions for this long-sought solution.

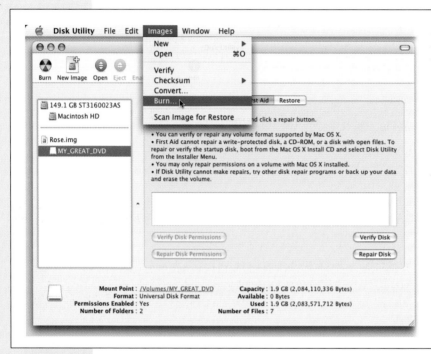

Figure 18-14:
Double-click your disk image in the Finder to make its virtual disk appear. Then open Disk Utility (in your Application→ Utilities folder), click the virtual disk, and choose Images→ Burn. Disk Utility prompts you to insert a blank DVD. Do so, and then click Burn.

- **You can burn copies of your DVD much faster.** The Mac already knows what's on the DVD, and has already encoded it into the proper format. Using Toast or Disk Utility as described above, you can whip out duplicates far faster than you would using iDVD itself.

Professional Duplicating

Maybe you've organized a school play, and you want to sell copies of the performance to parents as a fundraiser. Maybe you want to send out "new baby" videos to your family circle. Or maybe you've used iDVD to create a video brochure of your small business's products and services.

In each of these cases, burning the DVDs one at a time on your own Mac looks more and more like a time-consuming, expensive hassle. Accordingly, when you want to make more than a handful of copies of your DVD, you might want to consider enlisting the aid of a *DVD service bureau.* (DVD service bureaus are middlemen between you and the large replication plants, which don't deal directly with the public.)

Technically, these companies offer two different services:

- **Duplication.** Duplicated discs are copies of your original DVD. Service bureaus use banks of DVD burners, five or ten at a time, that churn out copy after copy on DVD-Rs (the same kinds of blanks as you used).

  You pay for materials and labor, usually by the hour. (Discs with less data burn quicker, producing more discs per hour.) This is the way to go if you need fewer than 100 copies of your disc. (On the other hand, remember that some DVD players don't play DVD-R discs.)

- **Replication.** Replication is designed for huge numbers of copies: 200 and up. In this process, the company actually presses the DVDs just the way Hollywood movie studios do it—and the results play back in virtually every DVD player.

  Replicated discs are produced in factories. When replicated, the data from your master DVD-R is placed on a pressed 4.7 GB "DVD-5" disc—a standard DVDs, not a DVD-R.

POWER USERS' CLINIC

DVD-R, DVD+R, and Drutil

Apple says that iDVD 5 can now record onto more kinds of blank DVDs than ever–not just DVD-R and DVD-RW, but also DVD+R and DVD+RW. (Both kinds of discs play on recent DVD players once they're burned. But most burners can record onto one format or the other–either "-" or "+." Thousands of people, not noticing the difference when they buy blanks at the store, inadvertently buy the wrong kind–and *they* wind up being burned.)

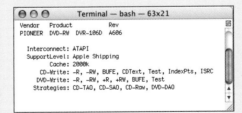

But not all Macs offer this new flexibility. You have to have the right kind of SuperDrive.

So how can you tell? One quick way is to use Terminal, the Unix command program that comes with Mac OS X. It's in your Applications→Utilities folder.

Once the program opens up, you see some Unix codes that end with a $ symbol. At this point, type *drutil info* and press Enter. You've just told Unix to run its *drutil* (disc recorder utility) program.

Instantly, the window fills with useful information about your Mac's disc-recording equipment, including who manufactured it (probably Pioneer).

Near the end of this block of info, you can see, quite clearly, which kinds of DVD it can write (that is, burn). For example, it might say, "DVD-Write: -R, -RW, +R, +RW, BUFE, Test."

If you see only "-R, -RW," then your Mac can't record on DVD+R and DVD+RW blanks. Shop accordingly.

(At this point, you can quit Terminal, unless of course you have other Unix work to do.)

Expect to pay about a dollar per disc for a run of 1,000 discs. Smaller runs will cost more per disc, larger runs less, but $1,000 is about the least you'll pay for a replication job.

Note: DVD service bureaus often call themselves replicators, even though they offer both duplication and replication.

Prepare to Copy

All DVD service bureaus accept DVD-R masters, of the sort that iDVD burns. Nevertheless, keep these tips in mind:

- **Submit two.** Always submit two copies of your master. It costs you almost nothing in materials and time, and can save your project if one of the discs fails.

- **Use name brands.** Burn your masters on the best-quality discs available. Brand-name blanks, like Verbatim, Maxell or TDK, are less likely to lead to duplication problems. (One replicator complains that if you hold those cheapie 30-cent discs up to the light, you can see light pass right through them!)

- **Use DVD-Rs.** Despite the format wars in DVD standards (DVD-R vs. DVD+R), the –R standard—the one used by more Macs—is better for replication. Many factories, in fact, don't accept +R discs, which leads to manufacturing problems.

- **You don't need a SuperDrive.** If your Mac doesn't have a DVD burner, most service bureaus can create the DVDs from a disk image (which you can now create directly from iDVD 5). You'll pay a little extra for the conversion.

- **Collect your copyright documentation.** Every replicator will ask you to sign a copyright release stating that you have permission to use the material on your disc. (If you're not asked about this, run away screaming. It's a red flag that you're dealing with an unsavory replicator.)

As a rule, anything you've videotaped is yours. You own it. If you use music from a friend, then a simple signed and dated letter will do: "Casey is my friend and has the right to use my music." If you're using royalty-free material, make a note of it.

And if you've using music you bought from the iTunes music store (or ripped from a commercial music CD), well, you may be on thin ice.

Choosing a Replicator

When choosing a service bureau or reseller, start by getting references—preferably on *recent* projects. Do your legwork and make the calls. You can also check with the Better Business Bureau to see if a service bureau has a history of customer complaints.

Tip: Choose a licensed replicator. Replicators and manufacturers must pay a small royalty on every DVD they produce, because DVDs are a copyrighted technology. Some factories, even in the US, operate with questionable practices—some pay all their fees, some pay part of their fees, some don't pay fees at all. Reputable service bureaus don't work with gray-market replicators.

Take cost into account when picking a service bureau, but keep in mind that you often get what you pay for. It may be worth paying extra to find a technically savvy reseller that will ask the right questions, hold your hand as needed, and make sure that your project turns out right.

Working with Replicators

When submitting a work order, be *very* specific. Unless you specify Amray cases (the Blockbuster-style cases, with a little plastic hub that holds the center of the DVD) and cigarette-stripped shrink wrap (standard clear plastic wrapping, so named because you pull a strip to open it, just as on a pack of cigarettes), you may end up with DVDs shoved into CD jewel cases. Sit down with your salesperson and go through all the options, from packaging to turnaround time.

Complex packaging takes more time and costs more. Consider ordering your discs in bulk paper sleeves or "slimline" cases (the most basic DVD delivery cases), without printing on them, to save on costs and time. To save even more money, you may be able to set up a deal where you pay to replicate 1,000 discs but package only 200 of them.

UP TO SPEED

Making DVDs Last

Your homemade DVDs (which are "burned" using dyes) probably won't last the 100 years expected of commercial DVDs (which are etched with lasers). But don't get too depressed by the occasional article about homemade DVDs "going bad" in a matter of months. Most cases of "DVD rot" come down to one of two things: problems created during manufacturing or poor handling by their owners.

There's not much you can do about manufacturing errors, apart from buying name-brand blank DVDs.

As for handling, these tips should ensure that your recordable DVDs will last for years:

Store your discs in a cool, dry place. DVD-Rs are sensitive to both temperature and humidity. In an ideal world, DVDs would love to live in a cupboard that's 68 degrees Fahrenheit with 30 to 50 percent humidity. In the real world, room temperature is fine as long as temperature *swings* aren't a fact of life. Recordable DVD's hate large changes in humidity, too.

Keep your discs out of the light. Prolonged exposure to ultraviolet light degrades the organic dyes in the recordable

layer, possibly making the data on your discs unreadable. Regular light may also hurt your discs, primarily through heat.

Don't flex your discs. With their laminated polycarbonate layers, recordable DVDs are very sensitive to of bending or flexing. In fact, the quickest way to destroy your disc is to bend it.

So don't. Store your discs in soft envelopes or in cases where you pinch a center hub to release the DVD. Don't store them in CD jewel boxes that have a snap-on hub.

Hold discs by the edges. Fingerprints, scratches, and dust on the disc surface interfere with a laser's ability to read data. DVDs are much more sensitive than CDs in this regard, because the data is crammed together so much more tightly.

Don't stick on labels. Adhesive labels throw off the disc's balance—and might even ruin your drive when the heat makes the glue melt. Instead, use a CD-safe marker to write on your DVD-Rs.

Fulfillment

If you're interested in *selling* your DVD masterpieces, you may want to hire yet another company to package, mail, and collect payment for them. *Fulfillment* companies, many run by DVD service bureaus, build a basic Web site, take orders, and mail out your discs. All you have to do is provide your iDVD masters, sign the contracts, pay the setup bills—and start working on your Oscar acceptance speech.

Part Five:
Appendixes

Appendix A: iMovie HD, Menu by Menu

Appendix B: Troubleshooting

Appendix C: Master Keyboard Shortcut List

5

iMovie HD, Menu by Menu

As you've certainly noticed by now, iMovie doesn't look like a standard Mac program. Part of its radical charm is that almost all of its functions are represented visually on screen. There simply aren't many menu commands. But don't get complacent: You'll miss some great features if you don't venture to the top of the screen much. Here's a rundown of the commands in iMovie's menus:

iMovie Menu

In Mac OS X, the first menu after the menu is named for the program you're using—in this case, iMovie.

About iMovie HD

This command opens the "About" box containing the requisite Apple legal information. There's really only one good reason to open the About iMovie window: It's the easiest way to find out exactly which version of iMovie you have.

iMovie HD Hot Tips

Each of the i-programs these days offers a Hot Tips command, which takes you online to Apple's Web page for a crash course in the latest new features. In iMovie's case, this page covers Playhead snapping, the Ken Burns effect, and so on.

Preferences

Opens the Preferences window (Figure A-1), which, in iMovie HD, has been split into three panels, each marked by an icon at the top. (*Keyboard shortcut:* ⌘-comma.) Here's a tour.

General

- **Beep when finished importing.** The idea here is that exporting (Chapter 12) can take a long time. Thanks to Mac OS X's multitasking abilities, you can switch into some other program to get some work done while iMovie chugs away. Trouble is, you won't know when the exporting process is done because you won't see the progress bar. This option solves the problem by playing a little *dink!* noise to alert you.

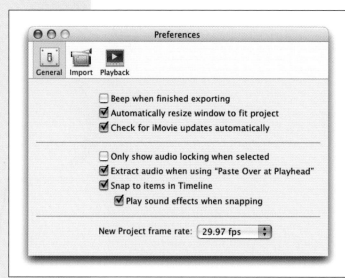

Figure A-1:
The Preferences dialog box is much less important in iMovie HD; some of the features once found here have been moved out to the menus, where they're easier to find.

It's worth noting that you can get to this box quickly by pressing ⌘-comma, which isn't so hard to learn considering it's also the keystroke that opens the Preferences box in iPhoto, iTunes, GarageBand, and so on.

- **Automatically resize window to fit project.** When you first create an iMovie project, you're asked to specify what kind of video you plan to edit: DV, high-definition, widescreen DV, or whatever. But if this option is turned on, you don't have to mess with that; iMovie automatically detects the incoming video type and adjusts its own window accordingly (so that the Monitor window is a wide rectangle for HDTV, for example).

- **Check for iMovie updates automatically.** As you may have discovered already, Apple often releases small, "double decimal-point" updates to the iLife programs. Each one patches bugs and makes features work more smoothly.

  If this option is turned on, then iMovie sends out an electronic feeler each time it's open and you're online, checking to see if a new update is available. If so, you'll be invited to download and install it.

- **Only show audio locking when selected.** "Audio locking" here means *pushpins,* of the sort illustrated in Figure A-2—the tiny thumbtack icons that help you spot audio clips that you've pinned to video clips. If you find these symbols distracting, turn on this checkbox; now the pushpins show up in the Timeline Viewer only when you've actually *highlighted* an audio clip.

- **Extract audio when using "Paste Over at Playhead."** In short, this option lets you paste video (without its audio) over existing audio tracks. See page 223 for details.

- **Snap to items in Timeline.** This checkbox makes the Playhead snap magnetically against important events in the Timeline viewer: the beginnings and ends of video clips, silence in audio tracks, bookmarks, chapter markers, and effects. And if you're dragging one of these items, it snaps against the playhead when you reach it (Figure A-2, bottom).

  This feature saves you a lot of fussing with the arrow keys, because very often, the edit you're trying to perform *is* right at one of these junctures.

Tip: When Timeline snapping is turned *on,* hold down the Shift key to turn it off temporarily. When Timeline snapping is turned *off,* press Shift to turn it on for the moment. In other words, Shift overrides the current Preferences setting.

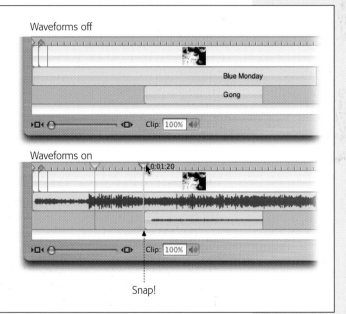

Figure A-2:
When audio waveforms are turned off (top), there's a lot less visual clutter, and you get to see the names of all your audio clips. When they're turned on (bottom), you have better luck lining up specific audio and video moments (not to mention identifying spoken expletives that you want deleted).

If you turn on "Timeline snapping," the Playhead jumps, as you drag it, to each important event in the Timeline—including the beginnings or endings of audio silence, as shown here at bottom. New in iMovie HD: at each snap, the vertical line extending from the Playhead turns yellow.

Waveforms off

Waveforms on

Snap!

- **Play sound effects when snapping.** Turn on this checkbox to add a zesty little *pop!* sound each time the Playhead snaps against something.

- **New Project frame rate.** This pop-up menu lets you tell iMovie whether you want the number of frames per second, in a newly created project, set to 29.97 (the North American/Japanese NTSC standard) or 25 (the European PAL standard). Apple added this option in iMovie HD in part to accommodate the new era of high-definition camcorders, some of which capture at 29.97 and some at 25 frames per second.

Import

- **Place clips in: Clips Pane/Movie Timeline.** When you first install iMovie, it stashes each captured clip from the camcorder in the Clips pane.

  If the scenes on your DV camcorder are roughly in the order you'll want them to be in the finished movie, however, you can save some dragging-from-the-Clips-pane steps by choosing to have iMovie stash them directly in the Movie Track as they're imported. (This option also affects imported graphics.)

- **Start a new clip at each scene break.** iMovie, when importing footage from your camcorder, can automatically create a new clip every time it detects that the camcorder was turned off and on again during filming. In other words, every shot becomes its own clip—a useful and sophisticated feature not found in even the pro editing programs. (If this option is turned off, then iMovie will import all footage in one big long clump.)

- **Filter audio from camera.** iMovie is supposed to screen out the beeps that indicate bad frames of audio recorded by the camera. But in some strange circumstances, this filtering can occasionally *introduce* audio glitches instead of fixing them. Don't turn off this box unless you're experiencing beeps in the imported audio, in which case turning this option off and reimporting the footage may help.

Playback

- **Quality: Standard/High/Highest.** Slower Macs may not be fast enough to display full-quality footage at full speed. When you view your movie in the Monitor window, therefore, you can choose between seeing slightly jerky video with a crisp picture ("High") or smooth video with a slightly blurry picture ("Standard"). On fast Macs, you probably won't see any difference at all between the two settings.

  You will, however, see the difference when you turn on "Highest." As Figure A-3 demonstrates, "Enhanced" eliminates most of the annoying, computerish "jaggies" and stairstepped diagonal lines.

- **Play DV project video through to DV camera.** This is the on/off switch for iMovie's remarkable ability to show your clips on your camcorder's LCD screen—or better still, a TV attached to the camcorder. (The new wording, "DV video" and "DV camera," is meant to remind you that this setup doesn't work with, for example, USB memory-card recorders.) See page 460 for details.

- **Keep Playhead centered during playback.** This feature is minor but helpful: It controls how the Movie Track scrolls when you're playing your movie. When this option is on, the entire Movie Track scrolls continuously, so that the Playhead can remain motionless in the center of the screen. The benefit here is that you can always see what audio or video events are about to scroll by.

  If you turn this option off, the Movie Track remains stationary until the moving Playhead reaches the right side of the window—and then the entire screenful changes. This system scan be frustrating, because you can never see what's just around the bend. You're often caught by surprise by events that were just offscreen to the right as they suddenly jump-scroll to the *left* side of the window.

Shop for iMovie HD Products

This isn't so much a command as it is a marketing ploy. It opens your Web browser to a page on Apple's Web site that offers to sell you camcorders, plug-ins, blank DVDs, and other accessories.

Provide iMovie HD Feedback

This command takes you to a Web form on Apple's site where you can register complaints, make suggestions, or gush enthusiastically about iMovie.

Register iMovie HD

This is a link to yet another Apple Web page. Registering iMovie simply means giving Apple your contact information so you can access Apple's online support documents, receive upgrade notices, get special offers, and so on. There's no penalty for not registering, by the way. Apple just wants to know more about who you are, so that it can offer you exciting new waves of junk mail.

Figure A-3:
On faster Macs—machines with the power to do the real-time processing—turning on the Highest quality setting (in iMovie's Preferences) makes a big difference in playback while you're working on your movie, as these before-and-after shots illustrate.

The difference is especially obvious when text appears in your movie.

Standard quality

Jaggies

Highest quality

Check For Updates

If iMovie isn't set to check for Apple patches and bug-fix updates automatically (page 458), you can make it check manually on your command, using this option.

Services

This submenu lists the standard Mac OS X *Services* (see *Mac OS X: The Missing Manual*), like Summarize and Reveal Finder. None of them work in iMovie.

Hide iMovie, Hide Others, Show All

These aren't iMovie's commands—they're Mac OS X's.

In any case, they determine which of the various programs running on your Mac are visible onscreen at any given moment. The Hide Others command is probably the most popular of these three. It zaps away the windows of all other programs—including the Finder—so that the iMovie window is the only one you see.

Tip: If you know this golden Mac OS X trick, you may never need to use the Hide Others command: To switch into iMovie from another program, hold down the Option and ⌘ keys when clicking the iMovie icon in the Dock. Doing so simultaneously brings iMovie to the front *and* hides all other programs you have running, producing an uncluttered, distraction-free view of iMovie.

Quit iMovie HD

This command (*keyboard shortcut:* ⌘-Q) closes iMovie after offering you the chance to save any changes you've made to your project file. The next time you open iMovie by double-clicking its icon, the program will reopen whatever project document you were working on.

File Menu

As in any Mac program, the File menu serves as the program's interface to the rest of the Macintosh world. It lets you open and close movie projects, import or export still frames, import QuickTime movies and audio files, and quit the program.

New Project, Open Project, Open Recent, Close Window

After you're finished working on a movie document (which iMovie calls a *Project*), you can take any of theses paths:

- Begin a new movie project by choosing File→New Project (⌘-N). (If you haven't saved the changes to the already open project, you'll be offered the opportunity to do so.)

- Open another existing project document. To do so, choose File→Open Recent (for quick access to a submenu of the movies you've most recently edited) or File→ Open Project (⌘-O). In the latter case, the standard Open File dialog box appears. Navigate to, and double-click, the project document you want to open (it's inside a *folder* bearing the same name).

- Choose Close Window (⌘-W) to close the project window without actually leaving iMovie. The result: The Create Project dialog box appears (see page 89).

Save Project

This command (⌘-S) preserves any changes you've made to your project, exactly as in a word processor or any other program.

iMovie saves such changes fairly quickly. It doesn't actually store any changes to the video clips you've captured; instead, it just makes a list of the changes you've made, which gets stored in the relatively tiny project document.

Note: The Save command also purges certain information that iMovie's been holding in memory—like your Undo trail. After a Save, you can no longer undo your recent actions using the Undo command.

Save Project As

For the first time, iMovie has a Save As command! It peels off a copy of your project in progress, creating a duplicate on your hard drive. The benefit, of course, is that you can "freeze" the first copy—a mid-editing backup—and travel down a different editing road with the copy, confident that you can always return to the first one if your editing inspiration turns out to be a bust.

The Save Project As command can take a long time and a lot of disk space, though, because it's duplicating all of your huge video files on the hard drive.

Revert to Saved

Here's another new one in iMovie HD. Revert to Saved undoes all the changes you've made to your files since the last time you saved it. It's a shortcut to using the Undo command over and over again, all the way back to the moment of your last Save—and a nice way to recover from a serious editing mess.

Import

You can use this command (or its keystroke, Shift-⌘-I) to bring all kinds of multimedia files into iMovie:

• **Still images** (photographs, scans, graphic "title cards," and so on), as described in Chapter 9. The program accepts JPEG, GIF, PICT, PNG, PDF, BMP, Photoshop, and other kinds of QuickTime-recognizable files. A graphics file you import in such a way behaves like a video clip, whose duration you specify using the slider in the Ken Burns panel.

• **Audio files** that have been saved in AIFF, MP3, WAV, or other QuickTime-compatible formats, as described in Chapter 8, for the benefit of your soundtrack. These files go automatically into your audio track.

• **Video files**, including any kind of QuickTime movie, AVI movie, DV clip from a camcorder, and so on. Among other things, this option lets you "borrow" a DV clip from another iMovie project (by importing from its Media folder).

Share

This essential command (Shift-⌘-E, because it was named Export in earlier versions) is, in a way, the entire point of iMovie. It lets you send your finished movie out into the world in search of an audience, the culmination of your video-editing adventure. You have several options:

- Export it to your email program at a highly condensed, reduced size.

- Export a tiny version to your .Mac account, if you have one, as a Web page for the entire global Internet village to enjoy.

- Export it back to the DV camcorder, and from there to a TV or VHS cassette.

- Export it to iDVD (Chapter 15), for making into a DVD.

- Export it into a QuickTime movie for viewing on a computer.

- Export a heavily compressed version to a Bluetooth cellphone to show off.

These options are described in gripping detail in Chapters 11 through 18.

Save Frame

A digital camcorder is also a digital *still* camera, thanks to this command. This command grabs whatever picture is visible in the Monitor window and opens the Save File dialog box, so that you can save the image to your hard drive as a graphics file. You can choose either PICT (better for reuse in your iMovie project) or JPEG format (better for exporting to other programs and people).

As Chapter 9 makes clear, the resulting images are nowhere near as sharp or as clear as the ones you get with an actual digital still camera. They're fairly low-resolution, for example, and the *interlacing* effect of the video signal makes it look like your image is composed of hundreds of thin horizontal lines—which it is.

Still, for creating images you plan to distribute electronically, the iMovie-exported pictures may suffice. You can improve the image quality by shrinking the frame size in a graphics program, thereby condensing the component dots and sharpening the image, before you distribute it. *Keyboard shortcut:* ⌘-F.

Burn Project to Disc

Once you've finished (or even half-finished) editing an iMovie project, what do you do with it? You can't leave it sitting on your hard drive forever, eating up multi-gigabytes of space. Sure, it's great that you can output the finished movie to a DVD or a tape, but what about the iMovie HD project itself? You'll need to hang onto it if you expect you'll ever want to return to it to make changes.

The purpose of the new Burn Project to Disc command is *not* to create a DVD that you can play on a TV. Instead, it's to create a data DVD, a DVD-ROM, containing a backup copy of your project file, so that you can get the original off your Mac.

Sure, you could accomplish the same thing by dragging the iMovie project's icon onto a blank DVD's icon, but this command is more convenient because it's right there in iMovie. Months or years later, you can insert the resulting DVD and open up the project for continued editing.

Show Info

Opens the Clip Info dialog box for whatever clip is highlighted in the Movie Track or Clips pane. (Unavailable if exactly one clip—audio, video, still, transition, or title—isn't highlighted.) The shortcut is simply double-clicking a clip. *Keyboard shortcut:* ⌘-I.

Show Trash

The Trash referred to by this command refers to the *project* Trash, the Trash can icon on the iMovie screen. Every time you delete or crop some footage, iMovie pretends to put it into this Trash can. Later, you can use this command to view its contents or selectively rescue items inside it. Page 126 has the details. (Single-clicking the Trash icon achieves the same purpose.) *Keyboard shortcut:* Shift-⌘-T.

Empty Trash

This command produces a message that asks: "Are you sure you want to permanently delete all items in iMovie's Trash?"

Never mind the split infinitive; what iMovie is saying is that you'll recover some hard-disk space, but you'll also lose your chance to use the Undo, Redo, Revert to Saved, Paste, or Revert Clip to Original commands. Now you know why many iMoviemakers avoid emptying the trash until the project is complete. *Keyboard shortcut:* Shift-⌘-Delete.

Edit Menu

The Edit menu contains all of the editing commands described in Chapter 5. In fact, along with the various drag-and-drop editing techniques described in this book, the commands in the Edit menu are the only tools you need to build your movies.

Undo

In iMovie, you can take back not only the last editing maneuver, not only the last ten (as in iMovie 4), but an infinite number of steps, all the way back to the last time you saved your document (or created it, depending on which came most recently). The ability to change your mind, or to recover from a particularly bad editing decision, is a considerable blessing.

The wording of this command changes to show you *which* editing step it's about to reverse. It might say Undo Import, Undo Move (after you've dragged a clip), Undo Split (after you've chopped a clip in half), and so on. *Keyboard shortcut:* ⌘-Z.

Tip: Remember, saving your project or emptying the project Trash command wipes out iMovie's memory of your last ten steps. You'll no longer be able to undo your previous editing actions.

Redo

We're only human, so it's entirely possible that sometimes you might want to *undo* your Undo.

For example, suppose that you've just used the Undo command a few times, retracing your steps back to a time when your movie was in better shape, and then decide that you've gone one step too far. That's when the Redo command is useful; it tells iMovie to undo your last Undo, so that you can step *forward* in time, redoing the steps that you just undid. (If you haven't yet used the Undo command, then Redo is dimmed.) *Keyboard shortcut:* Shift-⌘-Z.

Cut, Copy, Paste

You can use the Cut, Copy, and Paste commands in three different ways:

- **To move clips around** on the Clips pane, on the Movie Track, or between the Clips pane and the Movie Track. For example, you might click a clip in the Clips pane, choose Edit→Copy, and then choose Edit→Paste. Doing so creates a duplicate of the clip. Now you're free to edit, crop, or chop up the original, confident that you've got a duplicate as a backup. *Keyboard shortcuts:* ⌘-C for Copy, ⌘-X for Cut, ⌘-V for paste.

Tip: The beauty of copying clips in iMovie is that it doesn't really create new files on your hard drive and take up more disk space. Although it looks like iMovie's duplicated a physical clip, in fact, it's simply created a new *reference*—like an alias or pointer—to the original footage file.

- **To chop out some footage from a clip.** In other words, if you use the triangular handles under the Scrubber bar to highlight part of a clip (see Figure 5-3, for example), you can use the Cut command to delete that footage. The result is that you split the original clip into two clips—whatever was on either side of the part you excise. Now you can paste the cut material into the Clips pane or Movie Track, where it becomes a new clip of its own. (You can use the Copy command in the same way, except that it doesn't split the original clip or remove any footage from it.)

- **To transfer a clip to a different project.** In iMovie HD, you can copy and paste footage between documents (projects) exactly the way you might transfer text between two word-processing documents. All right, not exactly; iMovie can keep only one project at a time open, and pasting can take a very long time (because you're actually transferring huge video files on the hard drive). Still, this new feature is 100 times better than the old workarounds for re-using clips among different movies.

The Paste command produces different results, depending on what's highlighted:

- If a clip in the Clips pane is highlighted, iMovie puts the pasted clip there.

- If a clip in the Movie Track is highlighted, the Paste command always deposits the cut or copied material just *after* it.

- If no clip is selected anywhere, iMovie deposits the copied clip just after whatever clip contains the Playhead.

- If the Playhead is in the middle of a clip in the Movie Track, iMovie deposits the new material right there at the Playhead line, *chopping in half* the existing clip and shoving its end portion off to the right to make room.

Cut, Copy, Paste, and Clear also work when you're editing *text*, such as the names of your clips or the text for your credits and other titles.

Tip: To get an interesting "instant replay" effect, try this trick. Copy a short bit of interesting video, such as your friend tripping over his shoelace and hitting the ground. Paste the snippet twice, so that you wind up with three copies of the same short snippet all in a row. Now select the middle copy and apply iMovie's Reverse effect (page 170). Play through this sequence to see your friend fall down, bounce back up again, and then fall down again, for hours of family entertainment. (Of course, there are many other ways to use this technique that aren't quite so reminiscent of *America's Funniest Home Videos*.)

Clear

The Clear command is identical to Cut except that it doesn't keep the deleted material on the invisible Clipboard. Instead, it simply removes the highlighted clip or selection without affecting what was already on the Clipboard. *Keyboard shortcut:* the Delete key.

Select All

This command highlights all of the clips in the Clips pane, all of the footage in the Movie Track, or all of the text in a box, as described here:

- If any clip is highlighted, Select All highlights all of the clips in the same area (Movie Track or Clips pane). You might do this to select all the clips on the Clips pane, for example, in readiness to drag all of them into the Movie Track at once. If audio clips are highlighted, Select All selects all the audio clips.

- If no clip is highlighted anywhere, Select All highlights all the clips in the Movie Track.

- If you're editing text, such as a title or the name of a clip, this command highlights all the text in the box. Now you can copy it using Edit→Copy or replace it by typing over it.

Keyboard shortcut: ⌘-A.

Select Similar Clips

This intriguing new command highlights all of the clips that are the same kind as the one you've currently selected in the Clips pane or the Movie Track. For example, if you click a title clip and then choose this command, iMovie highlights all the other title clips, too. The same trick works to select all black clips, all photos, all transition effects, all clips that were chopped from the same original piece of footage, and so on.

This command can be a quick, efficient way to delete, move, consolidate, or modify a lot of similar material en masse. *Keyboard shortcut:* Option-⌘-A.

Select None

Memorizing this command (or better yet, its keyboard equivalent, Shift-⌘-A) is an excellent idea. It comes into play quite often; for example, every time you wrap up editing a particular clip and then want to watch your entire movie in progress. You can play back the entire movie only when no clip is selected.

Tip: You can also deselect all clips by clicking anywhere on the metallic-looking surface of the iMovie background.

You can also use Select None after you've been fiddling with the crop handles under the Scrubber bar. Select None makes them disappear, so that none of the footage is highlighted.

Crop

Use the Crop command to trim excess ends off a clip after you've isolated a portion of it using the triangular handles under the Scrubber bar. *Keyboard shortcut:* ⌘-K.

Split Video (Audio) Clip at Playhead

It's often convenient to chop a clip in half; this command does the trick. Drag the Playhead, or press the right and left arrow keys, to position it precisely at the location where you want the split to be made. After you choose Edit→Split Video Clip at Playhead, you wind up with two clips. If the original clip was called "Great shot," iMovie names the resulting clips "Great shot" and "Great shot/1," for example.

If an audio clip is selected in the Timeline viewer, and the Playhead is parked somewhere within it, the command says Split Audio Clip at Playhead instead, and it chops the audio clip in two. *Keyboard equivalent:* ⌘-T, just as it is in GarageBand.

Create Still Frame

This command adds, to your Clips pane or Movie Track, a new still-image clip created from the frame in the Monitor window. See page 256 for details. *Keyboard equivalent:* Shift-⌘-S.

View Menu

This menu is short but very sweet:

- **Switch to Clip Viewer/Timeline viewer** change the Movie track from its current view to the other one. The wording of the menu command may change, but the keyboard shortcut (⌘-E) remains the same.

- **Scroll to Playhead/Scroll to Selection** are ideal for situations when you scrolled off to a different part of the movie to check something out ("Have I already used that hilarious clip of the baby's spaghetti face?"), and then want to return to the spot where you stopped playback ("Scroll to Playhead") or to the clip you had selected a moment ago ("Scroll to Selection"). iMovie returns to the designated spot without losing your Playhead position or clip selection. *Keyboard shortcuts:* Option-⌘-P, Option-⌘-S.

- **Zoom to Selection** zooms the Timeline viewer precisely as much as necessary to fill the window width with whatever batch of clips you've selected. It even reveals just a tidbit of the preceding and following unselected clips, to help you gain your bearings. (Note that if you've highlighted only, say, a single 3-second clip, this command doesn't do much; it can't zoom beyond the limits of the Zoom slider.) *Keyboard shortcut:* Option-⌘-Z.

- **Show Clip Volume Levels** reveals the horizontal "rubber bands" that, in the Timeline Viewer, reveal the volume levels of your audio and video clips. (Page 228 has more detail.)

  Apple mercifully turned this function into a menu command—better yet, a keystroke (Shift-⌘-L)—so that you no longer have to trudge off to the Preferences dialog box every time you want to hide or show these volume levels, as in previous versions.

- **Show Audio Waveforms** makes those lie detector-style "sound waves" appear on your audio clips in the Timeline Viewer, so that you can identify louder and softer parts by eye. Details are on page 216. *Keyboard shortcut:* Shift-⌘-W.

Markers Menu

Most of these commands have to do with bookmarks, the little markers in your Movie Track that let you jump among important spots in your movie without any scrolling or hunting. Bookmarks are described in detail on page 140.

- **Add Bookmark** creates a little green diamond marker in your Movie Track at the position of the Playhead. *Keyboard shortcut:* ⌘-B.

- **Delete Bookmark** deletes whatever bookmark you've just clicked. *Keyboard shortcut:* Option-⌘-B.

- **Delete All Bookmarks** does just what it says.

- **Previous Bookmark/Next Bookmark** make your Playhead jump backward or forward to the next closest bookmark you've already created. Not nearly as useful as their keyboard equivalents, ⌘-[and ⌘-].

- **Add Chapter Marker** creates a different sort of marker: a tiny *yellow* diamond that denotes the beginning of a scene or chapter, as it will appear on a DVD's mainmenu screen once you export your movie to iDVD. You can place chapter markers only at the very beginnings of clips.

Remember that you can type names for your chapter markers—and access a second way to add and delete them—by clicking the iDVD button beneath the effects and sounds panel. See page 357 for more on chapter markers. *Keyboard shortcut:* Shift-⌘-M.

- **Delete Chapter Marker** deletes whatever chapter marker you've clicked in the Movie Track. *Keyboard shortcut:* Option-⌘-M.

Advanced Menu

This menu is a mishmash of miscellaneous iMovie features. For example:

- **Extract Audio** splits the audio from a highlighted video clip into an independent audio clip in the Timeline Viewer, as described on page 239. *Keyboard shortcut:* ⌘-J.

- **Paste Over at Playhead** performs a video overlay. It pastes your most recently cut or copied video *on top of* (replacing) whatever video is now at the Playhead. (Contrast with the Paste command, which shoves existing footage off to the right.) Depending on your settings in Preferences, a Paste Over preserves the original audio, so that the video appears to cut away while the narration or soundtrack continues uninterrupted. *Keyboard shortcut:* Shift-⌘-V.

Tip: If you highlighted some footage before opening the Advanced menu, this command fills the highlighted stretch of time with whatever you've got on your Clipboard.

- **Lock Audio Clip at Playhead** adds pushpins to the highlighted audio clip in the Timeline Viewer, as described on page 231, so that if the accompanying video clip shifts during editing, the audio moment will shift too, staying in sync with the moved video frame to which it was attached. *Keyboard shortcut:* ⌘-L.

- **Revert Clip to Original.** As long as you haven't emptied the Project Trash, this command offers you the luxury of restoring a highlighted clip to its original condition, the way it was when first imported from the camcorder, no matter how much you've sliced or diced it in the meantime. See page 125.

Window Menu

This window is fairly standard in Mac OS X programs. Its commands let you minimize iMovie (hide its window by collapsing into a Dock icon), or bring all iMovie windows out from under any window that's covering them up.

The one potentially puzzling command is Resize to Show Full DV. It's a reference to the fact that you can resize iMovie's window by dragging its lower-right corner. But as you do so, you make the Monitor window grow or shrink proportionally. As a result, the Mac has to work harder during playback (to compute the shrunken or enlarged playback image), and you may not be seeing all of the quality of your original digital video (DV) footage.

This command, then, makes the entire iMovie window snap to its preferred size, bigger or smaller than you've got it now, so that the Monitor window itself is 640 x 480 pixels, which is the "full DV" proportions referred to by the menu command. On a big screen, this usually means that the iMovie window gets much smaller than you'd like it; now you don't have nearly as much timeline to work with. But at least you're now seeing the video at its optimal size.

Figure A-4:
You can resize iMovie's window, sure—but because the Monitor window always occupies a fixed portion of the greater iMovie window, changing the window's size winds up shrinking or enlarging the original DV picture.

Want proof? Option-drag the lower-right corner to reveal the Monitor's current dimensions. If it ain't 640 x 480, it's not life size.

This command is dimmed if your monitor's resolution is set to 1024 x 768 pixels (the standard size for iBooks, among others)—iMovie needs a bigger playground for this particular feature—or if the window is already exactly the right size.

Tip: *If you press the Option (Alt) key as you drag to resize your iMovie HD window from the bottom right corner fo the window, your Monitor goes black and reveals its current size, in pixels (see Figure A-4). That can be a handy reality check if your playback isn't looking as good as it could be.*

Help Menu

iMovie doesn't come with a manual—if it did, you wouldn't need this book. Instead, you're expected to learn its functions from the online help.

iMovie HD Help

Choose this command to open the Macintosh Help window, where you'll see a list of iMovie help topics (Figure A-4).

You can use this Help program in either of two ways:

- Keep clicking blue underlined links, burrowing closer and closer to the help topic you want. You can backtrack by clicking the left arrow button at the top of the window, exactly as in a Web browser.

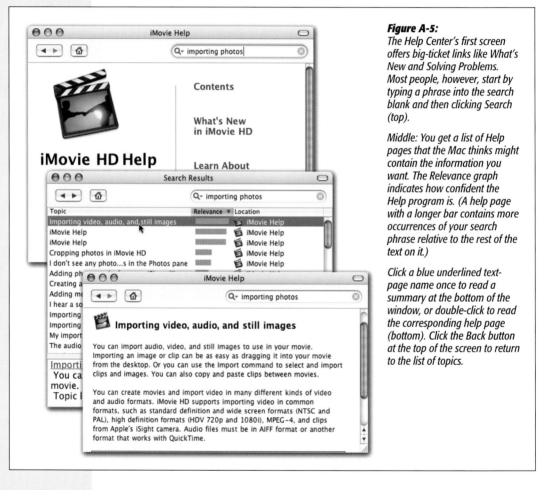

Figure A-5:
The Help Center's first screen offers big-ticket links like What's New and Solving Problems. Most people, however, start by typing a phrase into the search blank and then clicking Search (top).

Middle: You get a list of Help pages that the Mac thinks might contain the information you want. The Relevance graph indicates how confident the Help program is. (A help page with a longer bar contains more occurrences of your search phrase relative to the rest of the text on it.)

Click a blue underlined text-page name once to read a summary at the bottom of the window, or double-click to read the corresponding help page (bottom). Click the Back button at the top of the screen to return to the list of topics.

- Type a search phrase into the top window, such as *importing pictures,* and then click Search (or press Return), as shown in Figure A-4.

Either way, you'll probably find that the iMovie online help offers a helpful summary of the program's functions, but it's a little light on "what it's for" information, illustrations, tutorials, speed, and jokes.

iMovie HD Support

Opens your Web browser and takes you online to Apple's iMovie help Web site.

iMovie HD Keyboard Shortcuts

This is really just another link into the iMovie Help system, but a particularly valuable one. It takes you to a table showing about 50 keyboard shortcuts in iMovie. (They're among the listings in Appendix D of this book.)

Troubleshooting

Apple wasn't fooling around when it wrote iMovie HD. Big chunks of the program were *completely* rewritten in this version. Put another way, big chunks of this program are in their 1.0 version. And you know what that means, right? Right: bugs.

As of version 5.0.1, a number of peculiar glitches remain. Some offer easy workarounds; some remain baffling and have no simple solutions. Adding to the confusion is the fact that many of these bugs are *intermittent,* striking some people sometimes and other people not at all. Some of the best minds in the business are at a loss to explain the inconsistencies.

Here, though, is the world's most complete compendium of the problems that may occur—and the world's best attempts at solving them.

Two Golden Rules

If there's any common wisdom at all about iMovie, here it is: a pair of golden rules that will stave off a huge number of problems down the road.

- **Use the latest version.** Each ".01" or ".02" upgrade zaps a whole host of bugs and glitches. These updates are free, so when your Software Update program advises you that one is available, jump at the chance to install it.

- **Set your camcorder to 16-bit audio.** The typical digital camcorder can record its audio track using either 12-bit or 16-bit audio. The factory setting is 12-bit, which gives non–computer owners a chance to overlay a second audio track without erasing the original camera sound. Trouble is, 12-bit audio may slowly drift out of sync with the video when you burn the finished project to a DVD.

Use your camera's menu system to switch to 16-bit audio. You, an iMovie aficionado, can easily overlay additional audio using your computer, so you give up nothing—except a lot of frustration. (Make this change *now*, before you record anything important.)

General iMovie Troubleshooting

Let's start general, shall we?

Weird Inconsistent Problems

When a program's preferences file becomes scrambled, all kinds of peculiar behavior can result. Buttons and functions don't work. Visual anomalies appear. Things just don't work right.

If iMovie starts having a bad hair day, suspect its preferences file. Quit the program, open your Home→Library→Preferences folder, and throw away the file called *com. apple.iMovie.plist*.

The next time you run iMovie, it will automatically build a new preferences file. This file will have the original factory settings (for the options in, for example, the Preferences dialog box), but at least it will be healthy and whole.

Keeping Your Hard Disk Happy

Remember the old expression, "If Mama ain't happy, ain't nobody happy"? Well, if your hard disk isn't happy, iMovie won't be happy, either.

Here's a short list of maintenance suggestions. A little attention every week or so may help keep minor hard drive problems from becoming major problems.

- After installing or updating any software, use Disk Utility to Repair Permissions. (Disk Utility is in your Applications→Utilities folder. Click the First Aid tab, click your hard drive, and then click Repair Permissions.)

UP TO SPEED

Really Massive iMovie File Problems

The disk your iMovie HD project sits on must be prepared using the Mac OS Extended formatting scheme, also known as HFS+. All Apple drives come formatted that way, but some people have been known to buy an external FireWire hard drive from another company, plug it in, save an iMovie project onto it, and immediately run into massive problems. The fun may include dialog boxes that complain about file permissions, missing files, and "Icon" documents.

If you've just bought a new drive, check the disk format before using it. Do that by highlighting the disk icon in the Finder and choosing File→Get Info. Under the Format heading in the resulting dialog box, you'll see the formatting scheme identified.

If the format isn't correct, use Disk Utility to reformat the drive (which involves erasing the whole drive).

- Every couple of months, restart your Mac from the Mac OS X CD, choose File→ Disk Utility, click the First Aid tab, click your hard drive icon, and click Repair Disk.

- Mac OS X runs three behind-the-scenes Unix maintenance programs at regular intervals between 3 a.m. and 5 a.m. If your Mac is asleep or turned off every night, the maintenance probably isn't being done, because the Mac doesn't wake itself up to do the maintenance.

  If you don't regularly leave your Mac running overnight, take a minute, every month or so, to run MacJanitor—a free program that runs those same maintenance programs, but at your command. (You can get it from the "Missing CD" page at *www.missingmanuals.com,* among other places.)

Starting Up and Importing

Trouble getting going? Here's some advice.

"Some stray files were found" Message

This message is, fortunately, going the way of floppy disks; it occurs very rarely in iMovie HD projects. Even so, it may still pop up occasionally when you're opening older iMovie projects. Here's the explanation.

You're never supposed to move, delete, rename, or fiddle with any of the icons in your project folder's Media folder (page 113). iMovie itself is supposed to manage those clips, behind the scenes.

But if you put a clip into the Media folder *yourself*—a much more difficult proposition in iMovie HD—then the next time you open the project, you get the message shown in Figure B-1. iMovie doesn't recognize some of the clips it found there, and has moved them to the iMovie HD Trash. It invites you to (a) view the Trash contents, or (b) not.

That's the theory, anyway. In the real world, you'll probably get the "stray files" message from time to time, even when you haven't been anywhere near the Media folder. Sometimes iMovie just gets confused, as may be the case when the program bombs, or when you force quit it.

Figure B-1:
Movie has discovered clips that it doesn't remember being part of your project. Maybe you put them in the project folder (deliberately or not); maybe the clips were always part of the project, but iMovie somehow forgot.

Some stray files were found in the project, and were moved into iMovie's Trash.

Would you like to view the Trash contents?

[Don't View Trash]   [View Trash]

There's no real trouble to shoot here; click the option you prefer and get on with your life.

Nondestructive Editing: Pros and Cons

Two of the most dramatic changes to iMovie HD involve the Trash and something called nondestructive editing: the ability to restore a clip or adjust the way you've chopped it up, even years after making the movie.

But this overhaul has introduced both blessings and curses—and demands a good deal of new understanding.

The good news:

- You can revert an audio or video clip to its original state at any time, even after you've emptied the project Trash. And even when you shorten or split or crop a clip, iMovie never shortens the original, full-length video file.

- You can even restore or revert clips you've pasted into another project.

- You can pull a clip out of the Trash at any time until the Trash is emptied.

- When you empty the project Trash, you fling the associated video clip into the Mac's Trash (the one in the Finder). That gives you another safety net for recovering something you deleted by accident.

- You no longer have to worry about corrupting your project when you empty the iMovie Trash, as you did in previous versions.

The bad news:

- iMovie deletes a full clip only when you delete the last clip that references it. In other words, if you've used 2 seconds of a 45-minute clip in your movie, iMovie doesn't delete the 45-minute clip or give you back the disk space, even if you empty the project

Trash. As a result, large files always stay large.

- Copying and pasting clips between projects can cause projects to balloon in size. That's because, if you copy that 2-second clip from Project A into Project B, iMovie HD copies the entire, 45-minute underlying source file.

In fact, if you copy two clips ("Laughing" and "Laughing/1") that are both derived from the same original clip, iMovie copies the entire underlying 45-minute source file twice. (Unless you copy both at the same time, that is.)

- When you drag a clip out of iMovie (to the Finder, to iDVD, or anyplace else), iMovie HD copies the entire source file, not just the clip.

To export only the edited clip instead of the full-size original, export the clip instead of dragging it. That is, highlight the clip, choose File→Share, turn on "Share selected clips only," click the QuickTime button, and choose Full Quality from the pop-up menu. (If you're really squeezed for disk space, you can also use this trick to make iMovie "let go" of a full-length original file of which you're using only 2 seconds. Export the 2 seconds, then re-import it; use it to replace the one you exported. Now you can delete the original long one.)

- To recover disk space after emptying the iMovie Trash, you must also empty the Mac Trash.

- Because Trash-emptying rules are complicated, the Trash window sometimes conveys misleading information. For example, when you choose to delete a clip from the Trash window, you're never told whether or not other clips refer to the same original source file, and therefore, you never know whether or not you'll actually regain any disk space.

"Camera not connected"

If you get this message in the Monitor window when you click the Camera button, it probably means one of these things:

- Your camcorder isn't plugged into the Mac with a FireWire cable.

- The camcorder isn't turned on.

- You're using a camcorder whose FireWire circuitry isn't completely compatible with the Macintosh. (Some older JVC camcorders—circa 1999–2000—fall into this category.)

If you get the "Camera not connected" message the very first time you try to connect a new camcorder to your Mac, and you've checked to make sure that the cable is connected properly and the camera is turned on, then you probably need to replace either the camera or the FireWire cable. (The occasional iMovie owner has become frustrated that a new camcorder doesn't work, but upon exchanging it for another of the same model, finds that it works beautifully.)

Import from Camera Stops After 2–3 Seconds

FileVault, a feature of Mac OS X 10.3 and later, encrypts files in your Home folder so that ne'er-do-wells in the neighborhood can't break in when you're not at your desk. If you save an iMovie HD project into your Home folder, the Mac will try to encrypt the video you're importing from the camcorder in real time—and it can't be done.

Either turn off FileVault, or save your iMovie HD project someplace outside your Home folder.

Dropouts in the Video

A *dropout* is a glitch in the picture. DV dropouts are always square or rectangular. They may be a blotch of the wrong color, or may be multicolored. They may appear every time you play a particular scene, or may appear at random. In severe circumstances, you may get lots of them, such as when you try to capture video to an old FireWire hard drive that's too slow. Such a configuration may also cause tearing of the video picture.

Fortunately, dropouts are fairly rare in digital video. If you get one, it's probably in one of these three circumstances:

- You're using a very old cassette. Remember that even DV cassettes don't last forever. You may begin to see dropouts after rerecording the tape 50 times or so.

- You're playing back a cassette that was recorded in LP (long play) mode. If the cassette was recorded on a different camcorder, dropouts are especially likely.

- It's time to clean the heads on your camcorder—the electrical components that actually make contact with the tape and, over time, can become dirty. Your local electronics store sells head-cleaning kits for just this purpose.

If you spot the glitch at the same moment on the tape every time you play it, then the problem is on the tape itself. If it's there during one playback but gone during the next, the problem more likely lies with the heads in your camcorder.

Tip: Different DV tape manufacturers use different lubricants on their tapes. As a result, mixing tapes from different manufacturers on the same camcorder can increase the likelihood of head clogs. It's a good idea, therefore, to stick with tapes from one manufacturer (Sony, Panasonic, or Maxell, for example) when possible.

Banding

Banding in the video picture is a relative of dropouts, but is much less common. Once again, it may stem from dirt on either the tape itself or the heads in your camcorder. Most of the time, banding results when the tape was jammed or crinkled on an earlier journey through your camcorder. Now, as the tape plays, your camcorder heads encounter a creased portion of the tape, and then, until they can find clean information to display, fill the screen with whatever the last usable video information was.

If the problem is with the tape itself, the banding disappears as soon as clean, smooth tape comes into contact with the playback heads. If you get banding when playing different cassettes, however, it's time to clean the heads of your camcorder.

iSight Titles and Transitions Look Wrong

Sometimes iMovie HD imports video from an iSight camera with the wrong image size. The video looks fine in the iMovie window, but when titles and transitions are added to the video, they appear in the upper-left corner of the Monitor window.

Actually, the titles and transitions are OK; it's the iSight video that's the wrong size.

The trick is to choose Window→ Show Full Size Resolution before you import the video. Then the iSight video should arrive at the proper size.

Widescreen Video Gets Letterboxed

Some camcorders offer a special shooting mode called 16:9 video (that is, widescreen format). When you import this 16:9 video into a DV Widescreen project, iMovie HD sometimes wants to letterbox it, adding horizontal black bands above and below. (The letterboxing begins as soon as you switch from camera mode to edit mode and click a clip.) Since the video is *already* 16:9, that's probably not what you want iMovie HD to do.

You may be able to avoid this problem by *not* switching modes. That is, instead of switching to Edit mode, stay in Camera mode; save the project; quit iMovie; and turn off the camera. When you reopen the project, the video will stay 16:9.

Title Trouble

For some reason, titles and credits seem to have their own phalanx of problems and issues. For example:

Title Backgrounds Have Jaggies

The quality of the image behind a title in iMovie HD isn't as good as it once was, especially if you burn the movie to DVD. The title looks great, but the background behind acquires *jaggies,* the stair-step lines along hard edges (Figure B-2).

Figure B-2:
For some reason, as of version 5.0.1, iMovie HD intro-duces stairstepped, jagged lines in the video behind a title, as shown here before (top) and after. DV and DV Widescreen projects seem most vulnerable. The quantity of jaggies depends on the type of image and movement in the image. At its worst, the problem is distracting. At its best, it may not occur.

Some things to try to minimize the jaggies:

- Place your title over video that contains natural objects instead of man-made objects. Faces, landscapes, and flowers tend to be better than roof lines, deck railings, and fences. Avoid objects containing straight lines and hard edges.

- Place the title over video that doesn't move. A clip that zooms in on a building—or a Ken Burns clip that zooms in on a picture of the building—may look worse than a clip with no motion.

- When using a Ken Burns photo, import a large-dimension image, not small.

- Before importing the photo, soften the image a bit. Try iPhoto's Edit→Adjust→ Sharpness function, or Photoshop's Gaussian blur.

- Before adding the title, export the clip to a DVCPRO - NTSC QuickTime movie, then re-import that to iMovie HD. (If your video is in PAL format, use DVCPRO - PAL instead.)

- Create a title "Over black" instead of a video clip.

The Type Is Too Small

To make sure your title fits onscreen, iMovie limits the text size of the title to what fits within the movie frame. That's a nice feature that keeps all of your text on the screen, without the risk of chopping it off at the sides. Trouble is, even when you drag the type-size slider all the way to the right, the text may still be too small to read, especially when exported as a smallish QuickTime movie.

When making multiline titles, iMovie determines the maximum text size based on the longest line. If you're getting tiny text, then consider shortening the longest line or dividing it in two. You'll see the type size jump up accordingly.

Tip: You also gain another 10 percent size boost by turning on QT Margins. Do that only for movies you intend to save as QuickTime movies, however, not for projects you'll show on TV.

Chopped-off Type on Playback from Tape

The actual dimensions of a TV picture aren't what you'd expect. To avoid the risk that some oddball TV model might display a sliver of black empty space at a corner or edge of the glass, all NTSC television signals are *overscanned*—deliberately transmitted at a size *larger* than the TV screen. Sure, that means that the outer five percent of the picture at each edge doesn't even show up on your TV, because it's beyond the glass borders. But TV directors are aware of this phenomenon, and carefully avoid shooting anything that might get chopped off by the overscanning.

Unfortunately, iMovie has one foot in the world of video, and the other in the QuickTime world, where no overscanning is necessary. QuickTime movies always show *everything* in the picture, perfectly and precisely. Nothing is ever lost beyond the borders of a QuickTime window. That's why some footage that looks spectacular and perfect in iMovie (or in an exported QuickTime movie) gets chopped off around the edges when viewed on a TV.

(This phenomenon explains the "QT Margins" checkbox, described on page 185.)

Title Flows over Edge of Movie

There's a small bug in iMovie HD that sometimes allows a title to flow off the left and right edges of the movie. The solution is to drag iMovie's text-size slider to make the text smaller, and then try again.

Scrolling Block Title Scrolls Too Fast

Sometimes, scrolling block–style titles scroll by *way* too fast—much too fast to read (which is a definite downside). And iMovie HD doesn't seem to let you set the duration to a longer scroll.

To solve this problem, first note that iMovie HD lets you create scrolling block titles that are much longer than before: They can contain well over 4,000 characters.

The trouble is, as you add text to a long title, iMovie doesn't update the maximum title duration displayed next to the Speed slider. The slider limits you to the maximum duration for a *short* title, say, 20 seconds. So when you apply the settings, it scrolls way too fast.

Here's the trick: After typing your long text in the title, click again on the Scrolling Block style name in the title list. Voilà! Now the Speed slider offers a much longer duration. Set the Speed slider to the duration you want, then redo the title.

Photo Problems

iMovie HD's photo features are, in general, a delight—and they let you get mileage out of iMovie even if you don't own a camcorder. But you may encounter some rough edges.

Can't Change the Duration of a Still Photo

iMovie distinguishes between still *photos* and still *frames*, of the sort that you capture using the Edit→Create Still Frame command. Moreover, it differentiates between photos that exhibit the Ken Burns effect and those that don't.

It's so complicated, you practically need a cheat sheet—and here it is.

- To change the duration of a Ken Burnsized photo (imported from iPhoto or from the hard drive), click the clip and then use the Duration slider (or Duration box) in the Photos palette. Click Update.

- To change the duration of a still frame, double-click it. Change the duration in the Clip Info box.

- To change the duration of a *non*–Ken Burnsized photo, use either method: the Duration slider in the Photos palette, or the Clip Info box.

Ken Burns Accelerates Too Much

When the Ken Burns effect zooms in on an image, the clip sometimes appears to accelerate. There's a pause at the beginning of the clip, then the zooming goes faster and faster, all the way to the end. Most of the time, you probably want, if anything, a *deceleration*, so that the zoom comes to rest gently at the end of the magnification.

You can't eliminate this acceleration, but you can minimize it. These solutions rely on eliminating the pause at the start of the clip, which makes the zooming look smoother:

- Zoom less. A gentle zoom is usually better anyway.

- Add a Cross Dissolve transition before the Ken Burns clip; the transition covers the pause at the beginning. (The length of the pause depends on the duration of the clip and amount of zoom.)

- Set the Ken Burns duration a second or two longer than you actually need. Then, after the clip is finished rendering, crop out the first part of the clip by dragging its left edge to the right.

Ken Burns Zoom Always Shows 1.00

When the Ken Burns checkbox is turned off, it can look like the zoom is stuck on 1.00.

You'll see this situation when two conditions exist: First, the Ken Burns checkbox is turned off when you import a photo; second, the Ken Burns zoom setting is greater than 1.00. For this example, suppose it's 1.48.

When you click the Apply button, the zoom slider immediately jumps to 1.00, making you think that the image was imported with a 1.00 zoom instead of 1.48. That impression is only reinforced when you click the imported clip and see that the zoom slider still says 1.00. (Ordinarily, iMovie HD displays the zoom that was used to import the image when you click the resulting clip.)

In fact, though, the imported clip was imported correctly. These are all just cosmetic bugs. You can prove it by importing the image a second time using a 1.00 zoom, and comparing the two.

iPhoto Slideshow Fails to Import Video

Sometimes, a strange thing may happen when you try to drag a slideshow from iPhoto into iMovie HD: iMovie HD imports the song but skips the video.

In that situation, you've probably selected a copy-protected song, bought from the iTunes Music Store, as background music for the iPhoto slideshow.

If you have QuickTime Player Pro, open the iPhoto-exported movie, remove the audio track, Save, and try importing again. If you *don't* have QuickTime Player Pro, return to iPhoto, remove the song, export to a new movie, and try again.

Remember, you can always import the iTunes song directly into your iMovie HD project.

Problems Editing

All right: Your video is now in iMovie, and you're ready to get to work.

Direct Trimming Doesn't Work

One of iMovie's most delicious features is *edge dragging* or *direct trimming*, which means that you can drag the right or left end of a clip to change its length.

If direct trimming stops working—the cursor never changes to offer direct trimming—you have Show Clip Volume Levels turned on in the View menu. You can't drag edges when the little horizontal volume lines are displayed on your audio clips.

Effects Change a Clip's Color

How's this for weird? You apply an effect to one clip, and the background of the clip suddenly changes color to match the hue of the last *title* you created!

The workaround: delete the effect (select the clip and press the Delete key), save the project, close the project, and reopen it. Now the effects work correctly.

Split Clip Disappears from Clips Pane

Two clips should never occupy the same slot in the Clips pane, of course. But in iMovie HD, it's possible.

The problem can occur when you use the Scrubber bar to select the middle frames of a clip, and then you delete those frames. iMovie splits the clip, leaving behind the clips' ends. (If the original clip is named Clip 01, the new second clip is named Clip 01/1.)

The trouble is, sometimes the new clip gets hidden *underneath* some other clip in the Clips pane—especially when all the top slots in the Clips pane are full.

The workaround, if you call it one: look under the other clips in the Clips pane (by dragging them to other "cubbyholes").

Exporting Troubles

Now suppose that you're able to edit the video successfully, and even edit it into a masterful work of art. The big moment arrives: You're ready to play the movie back onto the tape, or export it as a QuickTime movie, so that you can then play it for friends and venture capitalists. Here are a few things that can go wrong.

You Live in Europe

If you bought your DV camcorder in Europe, it has probably been, as the Internet punsters say, "nEUtered." That is, it's been electronically rigged so that it *can't* record video from a FireWire cable.

Your PAL-format camcorder isn't broken. In fact, it's simply the victim of a European law, enacted under pressure from the motion picture industry, that any camcorder that can accept a video input signal is, technically speaking, a video *recorder,* not a camera. Video recorders are subject to a huge additional tax. Camcorder manufacturers, in an attempt to keep their consumer product line inexpensive, responded by taking out the digital-input feature from the built-in software of *inexpensive* DV and Digital8 camcorders. (More expensive DV camcorders don't have this problem.)

If you're clever with electronics, you can surf the Web in a quest for black market Web sites that explain how to *un*-disable FireWire recording—a simple procedure involving a technician's remote-control unit. Video repair shops in many European cities will perform this task for a small fee, too (but don't expect to see ads for this service). Otherwise, you have no choice but to limit your iMovie productions to QuickTime movies (instead of videotape), or to upgrade to a more expensive camcorder.

Export to Camera Fails to Stop Exporting Selected Clips

You don't have to export your entire movie once it's finished. If, in the File→Share dialog box, you turn on "Share selected clips only," iMovie is supposed to export only the clips that you first highlighted (as long as they're adjacent in the Movie Track).

As of version 5.0.1, however, iMovie HD sometimes fails to stop the export after the last clip. The export continues to the end of the project. The only way to halt the exporting is to click Stop. (Consider adding a 5-second black clip after the last selected clip to give you a clean stopping point.)

Warning: Clicking Stop can sometimes cause weird problems later. You should quit iMovie HD, then reopen the project.

Now, selected clips in the Clips pane (not the Movie Track) *do* stop exporting correctly, although the export order is unpredictable. If you need to export just one or two clips that are now in the Movie Track, Option-drag (to duplicate them) to the Clips pane, then export from there.

Export to HomePage Doesn't Have Fast Start

Fast Start is the QuickTime feature that allows your movie to start playing in your audience's Web browser before the download is complete. Unfortunately, Fast Start doesn't work when you export an iMovie HD movie to your HomePage.

For now, the solution is the shareware program called Lillipot. It lets you add Fast Start to your movie before you upload it to your HomePage. Lillipot is available from the "Missing CD" page of *www.missingmanuals.com.*

Exporting DV Widescreen Doesn't Make a Widescreen Movie

Sometimes, when you export your DV Widescreen project to QuickTime, the exported movie is not, in fact, widescreen.

Once again, the culprit is usually out-of-date iMovie HD plug-ins you've bought from other companies. Old versions can prevent iMovie HD from automatically exporting widescreen projects to widescreen movies.

Tip: Don't be confused by the dimensions shown in the Movie→Share dialog box. For widescreen projects, the text is wrong. It says the exported CD-ROM movie will be 320 x 240, for example, when in fact it will be 320 x 180.

DVD Problems

Exporting to iDVD Fails (Error -43)

As noted here and there throughout this book, you can extend iMovie's effects, transitions, and title styles by installing *plug-ins* from other companies. If you haven't updated your plug-ins to iMovie HD–specific versions, you've found the problem; they can prevent you from exporting to iDVD.

Video and Audio Aren't In Sync

On some longer movie projects (20 minutes or more), everything plays fine in iMovie, but when you turn your project into a QuickTime movie or burn it to a DVD, the audio and video grow slowly, horrifyingly out of sync. The longer the movie plays, the farther apart they drift.

The most important thing to check is the audio recording settings of your camcorder. As described at the beginning of this chapter, most camcorders come set to record *12-bit audio,* which lies at the heart of the video/audio drift problem. Change it to 16-bit audio, using the camcorder's own menus. (If you use a video converter like the Formac Studio or Dazzle Hollywood Bridge, make sure it, too, is set to import 16-bit audio, not 12-bit.)

If it's too late for that step, here are two possible fixes.

The back-to-camcorder solution

Set your camcorder to 16-bit audio. Once editing is complete, export the entire movie to your camcorder (see Chapter 11).

Then start a new iMovie project file and import the camcorder's footage right back into your Mac (Chapter 4). This time, you should be able to export the project without the drift.

The export-as-QuickTime solution

For this trick, you'll export the project as a high-quality QuickTime movie.

Chapter 12 offers details on exporting iMovie projects as QuickTime movies. For this particular task, though, these steps guide you through the proper settings:

1. Choose File→Share.

   The Share options sheet appears.

2. Click the QuickTime icon at the top of the window. From the "Compress movie for" pop-up menu, choose Expert. Then click Share.

   The Save Exported Movie dialog box appears.

3. From the Export pop-up menu, choose "Movie to QuickTime Movie." Click Options.

   The Movie Settings window opens.

4. Turn on Video and click the Settings button.

   Now the Compression Settings dialog box shows up.

5. From the pop-up menu, choose DV/DVCPRO - NTSC. (For PAL videos, choose DVCPRO - PAL.) Specify Best quality, 29.97 frames per second (for PAL, 25). Click OK.

   You return to the Movie Settings window.

6. Click Size.

   You meet the tiny Export Size Settings dialog box.

7. Click "Use custom size." For a standard DV project, set the Width to 720 and Height to 480; for a DV Widescreen project, set Width to 869 and Height to 480.

   The numbers are slightly different if you're working in the PAL format. For standard DV, set the width and height to 768 and 576; for widescreen, use 1040 and 576.

8. Click OK. Back in the Movie Settings window, turn on the Sound checkbox, and then click on the Settings button.

   The Movie Settings sound box opens.

9. **From the pop-up menu, choose None. Set the Rate to 48.00 kHz, Size to 16 Bit, and "Use" to Stereo.**

The resulting summary box should look like Figure B-3.

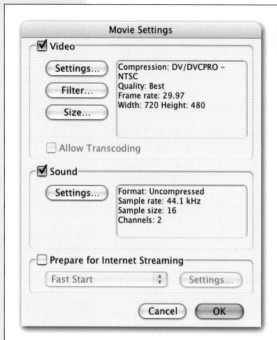

Figure B-3:
Here's how to properly set up for an export of a perfect QuickTime copy of your movie.

10. **Click OK, and OK again.**

You return to the Save dialog box.

11. **Name the movie, choose a folder location for saving it, and click Save.**

If all went well, you now have a very large, perfect-quality QuickTime movie on your hard drive.

If your project contains no DVD chapter markers, drag this exported movie into the iDVD window to place it there—with no audio-video sync problems, if the programming gods are smiling. If the project *does* require chapters, import the exported movie to a new iMovie HD project, add chapters, and *then* send it to iDVD as usual.

White Frames at Chapter Markers in Slideshows

You've created a gorgeous slideshow in iMovie. You've added chapter markers to help your audience navigate. And you've burned it to a DVD—and you've cringed at the blinks of white that appear at each chapter marker.

The workaround: *don't* put chapter markers in your main project file. Instead, once your movie is otherwise ready, export it as a Full Quality QuickTime movie. (Choose

File→Share, click the QuickTime button, choose Full Quality from the pop-up menu, click Share. Use any name and folder location.)

Import the exported movie into a new iMovie HD Project, and add chapter markers at *this* stage. Finally, export to iDVD and burn your disc as usual.

Photos Look Jaggy and Awful on DVD

All over the world, every single day, more Mac fans try to turn their digital photos into DVD slideshows using iMovie—and find out that the photos look *terrible.* What makes this syndrome so baffling is that the photos probably began life with super high resolution and look fantastic in Photoshop or iPhoto. But once they arrive on a DVD, the pictures look lousy.

It turns out that when you click the Create iDVD Project button in iMovie (the usual way to hand off the project to iDVD), iMovie offers to process any still photos—to *render* them, turning them into what amounts to motionless video. "Your movie contains still, slow motion, and/or reverse clips," it says. If you click "Render and Proceed," iMovie does a pretty poor job at converting them into video, resulting in jaggy blockiness. (This conversion is permanent in iMovie. Once it's done, your photos will always look bad in iMovie until you reinsert the originals.)

The solution is to bypass iMovie's low-quality photo-rendering cycle altogether. You can do that in either of two ways.

The Ken Burns Method

If you turn your photos into digital video clips, then iMovie doesn't consider them stills any more, and won't attempt to render them. Here's how to do that:

Turn on the Ken Burns Effect checkbox (page 251), configure the pan or zoom settings, then import the image.

After the bright red progress bar finishes its trip across your photo clip, you're left with a very high quality "still" video clip that iMovie won't attempt to process when you hand off to iDVD.

Repeat this process for any other still photos in your movie.

At this point, your still photos are no longer still photos. Clicking the "Create iDVD Project" button is now safe. iMovie will make no attempt to render your stills, because they've already been rendered by the far superior Ken Burns feature.

The Drag-into-iDVD Method

The second way to bypass iMovie's still-photo rendering feature is to avoid the "Create iDVD Project" button altogether. As you may remember from Chapter 16, there's another way to bring an iMovie movie into iDVD: drag its title-bar icon right into the iDVD window. See page 391 for the proper technique.

If you do that, iMovie's weak photo-rendering software doesn't touch your stills—and iDVD's own, much better rendering software processes them instead. You may find that the Ken Burns technique looks slightly better on some photos, but of course, it's much more work than the drag-into-iDVD method. Either way, though, you'll be delighted with the results.

At disc-burning time, iDVD will perform the photo processing itself, with much better results.

Project Corruption

Most of the time, iMovie stops people's hearts only with the beauty and magnificence of its creations. Unfortunately, every now and then, it can stop your heart in a much more terrifying way. At some random moment when you least expect it, some iMovie project that you've worked on for days or weeks refuses to open.

The odds of project corruption in iMovie HD are lower than in any previous version, but if it happens, that's little consolation.

FREQUENTLY ASKED QUESTIONS

How to Save Your Project for Future Generations

OK, I'm done editing my iMovie. How do I back up my project to reclaim the hard drive space?

That's an excellent question. Considering the hours you've probably spent building your masterpiece, preserving a full-quality copy, preferably in editable form, is probably extremely important.

(As you know, exporting the movie to QuickTime, cellphones, the Web, or VHS entails a huge deterioration in video and audio quality. Surprisingly, even burning to DVD involves losing some of the original quality, because the video is stored on the disc in a compressed form.)

In the end, there are only three ways to preserve a movie at its full original quality.

First, you can store it on a hard drive. This method is getting less expensive every day, and offers fast and convenient storage of your entire project. Because you can store your entire project package or folder, you'll be able to re-edit the project next year when iMovie 6 comes out with enhancements you can't resist.

Second, you can use a backup program like Retrospect to copy your project folder onto multiple DVDs (not video DVDs, but DVD-ROMs—like glorified blank CDs). It takes a

handful of these blanks to store one hour of video. But this solution is certainly cheap. And in a pinch, you'll be able to reconstruct your entire project folder, with full editing capability.

If the project is small enough to fit on a DVD, you can use the Burn Project to Disc command described on page 464.

Finally, you can send the movie back out to your DV camcorder, as described in Chapter 11. MiniDV tapes have about a 15-year life span, but they store the original video quality, even if you rescue the footage by copying it onto a fresh tape once every 10 years.

You lose the ability to edit your titles and substitute new background music, of course, but you don't lose all editing possibilities. If you ever re-import that movie back to iMovie, most of the clips will still appear as distinct, rearrangeable clips in your Movie Track (because clip boundaries are nothing more than breaks in the originally recorded time code).

(The exception: Clips that you create within iMovie, as opposed to those captured from a camcorder, don't have a time stamp, so they'll re-import as one conjoined clump of scenes.)

Using the Timeline Movie to Recover the Project

If the worst should happen, you may be able to rescue the project by importing its *timeline movie* to a new, fresh, iMovie project file. (More on the timeline movie in a moment.)

If you read page 112, you know that the modern iMovie "document" is, in fact, a tricky kind of folder. To open it, Control-click the project's Finder icon; from the shortcut menu, choose Show Package Contents. In the window that opens, double-click the Cache icon. Inside, you'll see an icon called Timeline Movie.mov.

The Timeline Movie is a *reference* movie. That is, it contains no video or audio of its own—just pointers to the video and audio files stored in the package's Media folder. If those files are intact, then the reference movie will play the project just as iMovie HD did.

Create a new iMovie project, and then drag the Timeline Movie.mov icon from the Finder window right into the Timeline Viewer of the new project.

Now, the resulting movie will contain all of the original movie project, but you should be aware that it will show up in the new project as a single, giant clip. You won't be able to edit the titles and transitions, but at least everything will play in the proper order.

Problems with Sound

Sound problems are especially frustrating when you're working with digital video, because they bear no resemblance to sound problems with more familiar equipment. In any other situation, if sound is too low or too loud, for example, you can adjust it with a knob. But what you do about random electronic beeps and buzzes that weren't there on the original tape?

Sound Is Too Soft

If one particular clip is too soft, see page 227.

If, however, the entire movie soundtrack plays back too quietly, it's probable that iMovie has nothing to do with the problem. Instead, your overall Mac volume is probably too low. Visit the Sound panel of System Preferences and adjust the output volume of your machine, or tap the Volume Up key on the top row of your keyboard. Make sure that iMovie's own volume slider (just above the Movie Track) is up all the way, too.

Random Electronic Beeps

It's hard to imagine anything more frustrating than finding a permanent—or, worse, intermittent—buzzing, crackling, or popping in the audio tracks of your project.

This problem has been on many minds, and its victims have come up with various solutions. Fortunately, most people manage to solve it by following one of these steps:

- Just as there are video dropouts, as described in the beginning of this appendix, cheap tapes may sometimes give you *audio* dropouts. The problem is exactly the same: a tiny bit of dirt or a nonmagnetized particle on the tape. But this time, it affects the audio, not the video. Try cleaning the heads of your camcorder, and then reimport the video.

- If cleaning the heads doesn't solve the problem, consider turning off the Audio Filtering feature. To do so, choose iMovie→Preferences. Turn off "Filter audio from camera." Click OK.

  Again, try reimporting the video to see whether the sound-buzzing problems have disappeared.

Of course, these workarounds assume that the audio glitch began life on the camera, rather than within iMovie itself.

If the pop is intermittent, there's not much you can do. But if you hear the pop in the same place every time you play your movie, you may be able to repair it using a sound-editing program, like this:

1. **Export the audio of the video clip as a sound-only AIFF file.**

   That is, turn on only the relevant audio-track checkboxes (at the right end of the Timeline Viewer). Then Choose File→Share. In the Share dialog box, choose the Expert Settings option, and then click Export. In the following dialog box, use the pop-up menu to choose Sound as AIFF.

   The result: You've just exported the soundtrack of your movie as a standalone audio file.

2. **Using GarageBand, cut out the beeps.**

   GarageBand lets you highlight the specific sound waves that represent the beeps and change their volume, or replace them with pieces of sound you've copied from neighboring moments in the soundtrack.

3. **Reimport the AIFF sound file into your iMovie project.**

   For example, choose File→Export to iTunes, and then, in iMovie, use the Audio panel to import that "track" from iTunes.

   Once it has appeared on an audio track, you can turn off the existing camcorder audio track.

Pops at Transition or Scene Breaks

Audio pops or snaps sometimes materialize where clips intersect—that is, at transitions and scene breaks. Fortunately, these audio defects don't survive to any DVDs you may burn.

If a DVD isn't the final destination for your project, the workaround is slightly more involved. First, remove the transition or title as described in Chapters 6 and 7.

Next, select the video clip that will be affected. Finally, choose Advanced→Extract Audio.

iMovie HD places the audio from that video clip into one of its two audio tracks. If you apply the title or transition now, iMovie HD will leave the audio—now an independent entity—alone.

Where to Get Help Online

You can get personal iMovie help by calling Apple's help line at (800) 500-7078 for 90 days after you bought the iLife DVD or a new Mac. (Technically, you can call within the first 90 days of ownership, but the clock really doesn't start until your first call.) After that, you can either buy an AppleCare contract for another year of tech-support calls ($170 to $350, depending on your Mac model), or pay $50 per individual call!

Beyond 90 days, however, consider consulting the Internet, which is filled with superb sources of fast, free technical help. Here are some of the best places to get your questions answered:

- **Apple's own iMovie HD discussion forum**. Here, you can read user comments, ask questions of knowledgeable users, or hang out and learn good stuff (*http://discussions. info.apple.com*).

  The iMovie FAQ link (Frequently Asked Questions) is at the top of the first forum page. Check it first—you'd be surprised at how likely it is that other people have had the same question or problem that you're having. Try using the Search box on the first page of the iMovie forum, too.

Tip: The Search box on the first forum page searches the entire forum. A Search box on an individual discussion page searches only that discussion thread.

- **MacDV List.** This outstanding resource is a *mailing list,* which is like a public bulletin board, except that each message is emailed to everybody who has signed up for the list. To post a message yourself, you just email it to a central address. It's attended by both iMovie fans and Final Cut Pro users (see Chapter 15), but the group tolerates both beginner and advanced questions.

  You sign up for this free feature at *www.themacintoshguy.com/lists*. Note that you can sign up either for the one-message-at-a-time membership, which sends about 20 messages a day to your email box, or for the Digest version, in which you get just one email each day containing all of the day's messages.

- **iMovie List.** Here's a mailing list—several, actually—dedicated to iMovie and only iMovie. In some of these lists, the level of technical discussion is much lower than the MacDV List—in other words, it's a perfect place to ask questions without embarrassing yourself. Sign up by visiting *www.egroups.com* and searching for *imovie.*

- **The Unofficial iMovie FAQ.** iMovie fan Dan Slagle stocks this site with useful accumulations of iMovie tips, workarounds, and information (*www.danslagle. com/mac/iMovie/iMovieFAQ.html*).

- **Official iMovie help pages.** Apple doesn't freely admit to bugs and problems, but there's a surprising amount of good information in its official iMovie answer pages (*www.info.apple.com/usen/imovie*).

- **Official iMovie HD tutorials.** Apple offers step-by-step instructions and movies at *www.apple.com/support/imovie/index.html*.

Master Keyboard Shortcut List

Here it is, by popular, frustrated demand: The master list of every secret (or not so secret) keystroke in iMovie HD, including all of the keys you can press while dragging things. Clip and post to your monitor (unless, of course, you got this book from the library).

Navigation

Action	Keystrokes
Play/Stop	Space bar
Rewind to start	Home
Jump to end	End
1 frame back/forward	Left arrow, right arrow
10 frames back/forward	Shift-left arrow, Shift-right arrow
Previous/next bookmark	⌘-[, ⌘-]
Add bookmark/Delete bookmark	⌘-B, Option-⌘-B
Add Chapter Marker	Shift-⌘-M
Delete Chapter Marker	Option-⌘-M

Timeline Viewer Editing

Select consecutive clips	Click first clip, Shift-click last one
Select nonconsecutive clips	Click first clip, ⌘-click each additional one
Nudge video clip	Click clip, then press right arrow (add Shift to move 10 frames at a time) to create black gap

Shorten clip (ripple edit)	Drag clip's edge inward (other clips slide left to close up the gap)
Shorten clip (creating gap)	⌘-drag clip's edge inward
Lengthen clip (ripple edit)	Drag clip's edge outward (other clips slide right to accommodate longer clip)
Lengthen clip (trim adjacent clips)	⌘-drag clip's edge outward (adjacent clip gets truncated by the overlap)
Switch to Clip Viewer	⌘-E (also switches back again)

Titles, Effects, Transitions

Delete title, effect, or transition	Select, then press Delete
Move between Title text boxes	Tab
Cancel rendering	⌘-period

Trash

Put selected clip(s) in Trash	Delete
Open Trash window	Shift-⌘-T (or click Trash icon)
Empty Trash	Shift-⌘-Delete

Project Files

New Project	⌘-N
Open Project	⌘-O
Close Window	⌘-W
Save Project	⌘-S
Import	Shift-⌘-I
Share	Shift-⌘-E

Clips Pane

Select multiple	Click first clip, ⌘-click each additional one
Show Info	⌘-I

Still Photos

Export still image	⌘-F
Create still clip from Playhead	Shift-⌘-S
Copy Ken Burns setting	Option-click the word Start or End (copies setting from the other button)

General Editing

Undo	⌘-Z
Redo	Shift-⌘-Z

Cut	⌘-X
Copy	⌘-C
Paste	⌘-V
Select All	⌘-A
Select similar clips	Option-⌘-A
Select None	Shift-⌘-A
Crop	⌘-K
Split Clip at Playhead	⌘-T
Scroll to Playhead	Option-⌘-P
Scroll to Selection	Option-⌘-S
Zoom to Selection	Option-⌘-Z

Audio Editing

Show/Hide Clip Volume Levels	Shift-⌘-L
Show Audio Waveforms	Shift-⌘-W
Nudge an audio clip horizontally	Click clip, then tap left or right arrow (add Shift to move 10 frames at a time)
Scrub audio	Press Option while dragging Playhead
Extract Audio	⌘-J
Paste Over at Playhead	Shift-⌘-V
Lock Audio Clip at Playhead	⌘-L

General iMovie Functions

Peferences	⌘-,
Hide iMovie window	⌘-H
Hide other programs	Option-⌘-H
Quit iMovie	⌘-Q
Accept dialog box	Return
Cancel dialog box	Esc

IMOVIE HD & IDVD 5: THE MISSING MANUAL

Index

Index

H

H.263 codec, 293, 306
hard drive space
  and emptying Trash, 3-4
  and iDVD, 380
  Copy and Paste, 478
  emptying Trash doesn't help, 128
  for each video format, 91
  iMovie HD quirks, 478
  when copying and pasting, 139
hard drives
  digital video files, 91
  exporting to save space, 277
  external, 95
  for long-term storage, 490
  free-space graph, 101
  keeping healthy for video, 476-477
  maintenance, 477
  watching DVDs from hard drive, 449-451
HDTV *see* **high-definition video**
HDTV sets, 104
HDV camcorders, 3
  defined, 104
  hard drive space, 91
  importing from, 103-105
  video screen dimensions, 249-251
Help menu, 88, 471-473
help online, 493-494
Hi-8 format, 15
high-definition video, 2-3 *see also* **HDV camcorders**
  1080i format, 92
  720p format, 92
  defined, 104
  hard drive space, 91
  importing, 103-105
Highest (field blending), 97
Home button, 94, 144
home movies, 1, 18, 264
HomePage, 316-320
  Fast Start feature, 486
  folder, 104
HTML, 321-331

I

i.Link *see* **FireWire**
icons (of iMovie projects), 109-115
iDisk, 316-320
iDVD, 335-454 *see also* **themes**
  adding movies, 387-392
  adjusting panels, 390
  and AppleScript, 438-440
  archiving, 445-448
  audio sync problems, 475-476, 486-488
  AutoPlay, 398-399
  basics of, 353

building manually, 385-415
burning the disc, 375-381
buying motion backgrounds, 429
buying new themes, 428-429
buying stock art for, 430
can't export to, 486
chapter markers, 358-361
copying DVDs, 445-451
creating a new project, 386-387
creating DVD-ROMs, 433-435
designing themes, 409-424, 427-428
drop zones, 371-375
DVD map, 396-399
DVD-ROM options, 403
editing and formatting text, 419-421
editing menu screens, 367
editing the program itself, 440-445
editing titles and buttons, 367
external DVD burners, 450
folders (submenus), 393-396
getting it, 352
iDVD folder, 104
kiosk mode (DVDs), 398-399
long-term storage, 490
looping, 399
Map view, 396-399
maximum playback time, 376
maximum video minutes, 395
Media pane, 383
menu backgrounds, 421-425
menu screens, 362
missing-link icon, 447-448
Motion button, 379
Movies pane, 389-393
movies with chapters, 393-396
music for menu screens, 425-426
one step DVDs, 381-384
package, 440-445
photos look jaggy on DVD, 489-490
previewing, 375-376
project files, 427, 437-439
Project Info window, 436-437
quality/burning time trade-off, 378
secret folders of, 438
slideshows, 399-407
Status pane, 435-437
status screen, 379
submenus, 393-396
text boxes, 419-421
Themes pane, 410
third-party buttons, 431
transferring from iMovie, 349-384
turning off Apple logo, 361
using with non-Apple burners, 450
watched movie folders, 392
what's new, 5

Colophon

This book was written and edited in Microsoft Word X on various Macs.

The screenshots were captured with Ambrosia Software's Snapz Pro X *(www. ambrosiasw.com)* for the Mac. Adobe Photoshop CS *(www.adobe.com)* and Macromedia Freehand MX *(www.macromedia.com)* were called in as required for touching them up.

The full-page photos that introduce each part of this book came from iStockPhoto. com.

The book was designed and laid out in Adobe InDesign 3.0 on a PowerBook G4, PowerMac G5. The fonts used include Formata (as the sans-serif family) and Minion (as the serif body face). To provide the and ⌘ symbols, custom fonts were created using Macromedia Fontographer.

The book was then generated as an Adobe Acrobat PDF file for proofreading, indexing, and final transmission to the printing plant.